Oracle9*i* for Windows® Handbook

Anand Adkoli
Rama Velpuri

McGraw-Hill/Osborne

New York   Chicago   San Francisco
Lisbon   London   Madrid   Mexico City
Milan   New Delhi   San Juan
Seoul   Singapore   Sydney   Toronto

McGraw-Hill/Osborne
2600 Tenth Street
Berkeley, California 94710
U.S.A.

To arrange bulk purchase discounts for sales promotions, premiums, or fund-raisers, please contact **McGraw-Hill/Osborne** at the above address. For information on translations or book distributors outside the U.S.A., please see the International Contact Information page immediately following the index of this book.

Oracle9*i* for Windows® Handbook

1234567890 CUS CUS 0198765432
ISBN 0-07-219092-2

Publisher
Brandon A. Nordin

Vice President & Associate Publisher
Scott Rogers

Acquisitions Editor
Jeremy Judson

Senior Project Editor
Pamela Woolf

Acquisitions Coordinator
Athena Honore

Technical Editor
Ramesh mani

Copy Editor
Laura Ryan

Indexer
Karin Arrigoni

Computer Designers
Carie Abrew, Lucie Ericksen

Illustrators
Michael Mueller, Lyssa Wald

Series Design
Jani Beckwith

Cover Series Design
Damore Johann Design, Inc.

This book was composed with Corel VENTURA™ Publisher.

Several million children worldwide are
forced to work for a living or go hungry to bed.
This book is dedicated to these special children.

About the Authors

Anand Adkoli is the founder and CTO of Liqwid Krystal Inc., a technology company that develops next-generation products to enhance IT learning. Prior to that he was a senior development manager in Oracle's Industrial Applications Division. During the course of his long career, he has delivered projects for Oracle Corporation in the United States, Australia, and India. He has published more than 50 technical papers and has made several presentations at international conferences on performance tuning, backup and recovery, and application development. He is also the founder and CEO of India Childcare Foundation (www.indiachildcare.org), a virtual organization that provides education and healthcare to underprivileged children in India. For more information, visit www.adkoli.net or e-mail him at anand@liqwidkrystal.com.

    Rama Velpuri is the founder and CEO of OraMasters Inc. OraMasters specializes in providing online support services for Oracle users worldwide. Before founding OraMasters, he worked with Oracle Corporation for more than 10 years. At Oracle, he was an executive director of the Oracle Application Development Center. He has built two offshore development centers for Oracle in India. Before that, he was a senior manager of the Mission Critical Support Center. Mr. Velpuri has presented numerous technical papers at various International Oracle Conferences and Oracle user conferences on disaster recovery, and he has trained Oracle support personnel in 22 different countries in problem-solving techniques. You can reach him via e-mail at rvelpuri@oramasters.com.

    Other Oracle Press books from Mr. Adkoli and Mr. Velpuri are:
Oracle8i Backup & Recovery Handbook
(ISBN: 0-07-212717-1; 2001),
OCP Oracle9i Database: Fundamentals II Exam Guide
(ISBN: 0-07-219543-6),
Oracle8 Troubleshooting (ISBN: 0-07-882580-6; 1999),
Oracle NT Handbook (ISBN: 0-07-211917-9; 1998).

Contents

Acknowledgments

Numerous people have helped in making this book a reality. First of all, we would like to thank Athena Honore, Pamela Woolf, Paulina Pobocha, Lisa McClain, Jeremy Judson and the entire team at Osborne/McGraw-Hill for their assistance and patience over the last many months.

We would like to thank Ramesh Mani for his incisive comments, which have helped us look view this book from the point of view of a typical reader. Sathyagith Lakshmana, D.G.K. Murthy and R.G. Srinivas have helped us in many ways from day one. We also have to thank our colleagues at Liqwid Krystal and OraMasters for their support and comments.

Finally, it would be impossible for us to even dream of embarking on a project of this nature without the support of our families. We want to especially thank our wives Sushma Veerappa and Anuradha Velpuri who have endured our long workdays and mood swings. We would also like to express our gratitude to Narayan Adkoli, Leela Adkoli, Akhil Velpuri, and Manasa Velpuri for helping us in their own little ways.

Introduction

ver the last decade, we have had the opportunity to interact with an incredible number of Oracle DBAs and application developers worldwide. Thousands of queries (not the database kind!) have been addressed to us. Many have wondered how they can become DBAs quickly, or asked how they can acquire the minimum subset of information necessary to become good DBAs—quickly. We have attempted to address these two needs in this book within the boundaries of the Windows operating system,

If you have been daunted by the extensive documentation provided by Oracle, *Oracle9i for Windows Handbook* should make a great starting point for you. We intend this to provide you with a jumpstart on Oracle database administration on Windows NT, 2000, and XP. Use this book to complete a routine task quickly without having to spend too much time searching for an answer!

Many suggestions and much work have gone into this book. We would love to get your feedback to help us make this book more useful in future editions. We hope you will find this book as useful as we enjoyed bringing it to you.

Audience and Scope

Any Oracle user or database administrator (DBA) who is charged with the installation and management of Oracle software on Windows will find this book useful. The book focuses on administrative topics related to Oracle9i Server and Oracle9i Application Server and will help you regardless of whether you are deploying a traditional client/server architecture or a three-tier architecture. It does not enter the realm of application development.

Basic Windows administration skills are assumed. You should be familiar with basic Windows administration and networking concepts and have some experience with software installation on Windows NT, 2000, or XP. While this book does not assume any experience with Oracle Server, you will find it useful to understand some Oracle-related concepts. If this is your first look at a book on Oracle-related technology, you will find it beneficial to browse *Oracle9i Database Concepts* in Oracle documentation before reading this book.

How to Use This Book

This book begins with the simple installation of Oracle9i database and ends with security-related topics. If you are a first-time DBA on Windows, you will find it beneficial to start with Chapter 1 and then move ahead to Chapter 5. At this point you should get familiar with Oracle Enterprise Manager in Chapters 7 and 8. Once you are comfortable with performing minimal DBA tasks, you can read Chapters 2 and 4 to help you perform advanced installations and Chapter 6 to configure Oracle software for a networked environment.

If you are migrating an Oracle database from another operating system such as UNIX or upgrading from an earlier version, read Chapter 3 after browsing Chapters 1 and 2. If you are planning to employ a middle-tier with Oracle9i Application Server, read Chapters 9 and 10 after you are comfortable with Oracle database administration on Windows.

Read Chapter 11 to understand security-related issues and enforce better security on your site. The case studies in Chapter 12 will help you to quickly address some typical situations on your site. The case studies are designed to show you how flexible and extensible Oracle9i can be.

This book is divided into 12 chapters and two appendices.

- Chapter 1 begins by tracking the evolution of Oracle and Microsoft. An introduction to Oracle9i software is followed by tasks that will help you perform a successful installation of Oracle9i on Windows.

- Chapter 2 covers advanced installation topics. You will learn how to perform non-interactive and remote installations with Oracle Universal Installer (OUI).

- Chapter 3 is useful if you want to migrate a database from another operating system to Windows or if you want to upgrade to Oracle9i. You can also get information on the new Oracle9i downgrade feature.

- You can use one of the templates provided with OUI to create a starter database during installation. However, if you want to design your own database, you can use one of the methods described in Chapter 4.

- Chapter 5 provides an overview of database theory and the Oracle architecture. Information on daily administration tasks such as user management, backup and recovery and space management is provided in this chapter.

■ If you are deploying Oracle9i in a network, Chapter 6 will help you configure Oracle Net Services—software that will help you access Oracle databases from remote clients.

■ Chapter 7 introduces Oracle Enterprise Manager (OEM), a GUI utility that will help you administer Oracle databases, application servers, and web servers.

■ In Chapter 8, you will learn how to perform common administration tasks with OEM. You also will learn how to perform administration tasks from a central console and how OEM can help you obtain information on the overall health of Oracle databases and how you can tune databases using this information.

■ Chapter 9 introduces Oracle9i Application Server (9iAS). A simple discussion on the 9iAS architecture is included. You will learn how to install 9iAS on Windows. Several workarounds for known issues are described.

■ Chapter 10 is useful for large sites that will deploy 9iAS with hundreds and thousands of users. Oracle Database Cache and Web Cache will help you design scalable sites. A discussion on Oracle Internet File System is also included in this chapter.

■ Chapter 11 provides an overview of security issues with Oracle software. The security features available in the database, middle-tier, and networking software are summarized. This chapter will help you design a sound strategy for security.

■ Chapter 12 has six case studies that are designed to help you extend the concepts in this book. You will learn how to extend the capabilities of Oracle HTTP Server and how to migrate non-Oracle databases to Oracle9i and design a sound backup strategy for your site. Enterprise security is also illustrated with a case study involving Oracle Internet Directory.

■ Appendix A provides a listing of additional resources on the web.

■ Finally, Appendix B summarizes new Oracle9i features on Windows.

CHAPTER
1

Oracle9i Installation

ecause this book is about a marriage of Oracle9i and Windows, we begin with a quick look at the evolutions of Oracle Corporation and Microsoft Corporation. When Larry Ellison, Bob Miner, and Ed Oates started Software Development Laboratories in 1977, they had no idea that the database product they built would evolve into Oracle9i in less than a quarter of a century. Software Development Laboratories was renamed Oracle Corporation in 1982. Within five years, Oracle positioned itself as the largest vendor of database management software in the world. The new economy brought with it a slew of e-business applications, including ERP and CRM, which firmly placed Oracle as the second-largest software company. Since the launch of Oracle Version 6 in 1992, Oracle has launched a new version of their industry-leading database software every two to three years. While Oracle8i was the world's first object relational database management system (ORDBMS), Oracle9i can rightfully claim to be the first RDBMS that delivers a development and deployment platform for the Internet.

It is interesting to note the almost parallel growth of Microsoft Corporation into the world's largest software company. Microsoft first became a household name in the early 1990s with its productivity software such as Word, Excel, and PowerPoint. Microsoft Windows NT 3.51 was first released in 1995. When Windows 95 was released with its groundbreaking look and feel, it became the operating system of choice on desktops throughout the world. Microsoft took advantage of the Windows 95 wave to release Windows NT 4.0, a server operating system with the same look and feel as Windows 95. Even though the earlier releases of Windows NT had significant issues, Microsoft quickly took over a significant chunk of the mid-size business server market with Windows NT 4.0. Competition in the form of Novell's NetWare Server and IBM's OS/2 was overwhelmed in the span of three years. Through all this, UNIX-based operating systems continued to hold their own in the enterprise market. With Windows NT 5.0, Microsoft planned to enter the enterprise market and compete with heavyweights such as Sun Microsystems, IBM, and HP. After long delays, Microsoft released Windows NT 5.0 as Windows 2000 in the summer of 2000. Within a few months, those who had criticized Microsoft's operating systems stood up and took notice of Windows 2000. In performance, reliability, and scalability, Windows 2000 outclassed its Windows predecessors within the first year. In fact, it is now estimated that there are more Windows 2000 servers than Windows NT servers.

Since its recent launch, Windows XP is fast becoming the operating system of choice on PCs; however, it is targeted toward home and small-business users and is not positioned in the server market.

While the big debate between UNIX and Windows communities continues, we believe that a majority of sites running Windows NT Server today will deploy Oracle on Windows 2000 Server by year-end. It is for this reason that this book focuses on Oracle9i on the Windows 2000 Server. Unless mentioned otherwise, all topics and discussions in this book apply equally well to Windows NT 4.0, Windows XP

Professional, and Windows 2000. We begin with topics related to a standard installation of Oracle9i on Windows.

NOTE
We have been successfully running Oracle9i Enterprise Edition on Windows XP Professional on one of our test machines for over three months. As this book goes to the press, Oracle has certified Oracle9i on Windows XP Professional. However, Microsoft has not positioned Windows XP as an operating system for servers and recommends that you use Windows 2000 on your servers.

Introducing Oracle9i for Windows NT/2000

Oracle9i for Windows 2000 is the latest release from Oracle Corporation. In contrast to Oracle8i Server, which was termed an object ORDBMS, Oracle9i claims to be a development and deployment platform for the Internet. This is because a wide range of development and management tools are available to support Internet data warehouses and applications. Visit http://www.oracle.com/ip for more information ⟶ *site* on the features that make Oracle9i a powerful platform for the Internet. Before going into the installation details, it is useful to review the features of Oracle9i.

Many of the enhancements in Oracle9i were seen in bits and pieces in later releases of Oracle8i, either as patches or separately licensed features. Oracle9i has combined these add-ons into one product. Some of the features of Oracle9i for Windows NT/2000 are described here:

- Oracle9i Enterprise Manager has been enhanced to include guided expert diagnostics and problem resolution. All essential management functions can now be managed from a standard Web browser.

- Oracle9i's public key infrastructure and single sign-on capabilities have been integrated with Windows 2000, Active Directory, and Microsoft Certificate Store. Integration with Microsoft Transaction Server, Microsoft Message Queuing, and Internet Information Server is much improved.

- Oracle9i offers a variety of features for Windows developers including enhanced native object linking and embedding database (OLEDB) support. Oracle9i also includes support for XML, COM+, and extensions through Oracle Data Objects for Windows (formerly Oracle Objects for OLE).

- Oracle9i includes a built-in Java Virtual Machine (JVM), which allows you to store and run Java code within the database itself. Developers familiar with Java can now write application logic using Java instead of Oracle's native PL/SQL.

- Oracle9i includes a product named iSQL*Plus, a Java-based implementation of the popular SQL*Plus utility that runs in a browser. You can use iSQL*Plus to connect to an Oracle database through the Internet and execute SQL commands. iSQL*Plus depends on the Oracle HTTP Server and the iSQL*Plus Server.

- Oracle9i also supports Common Object Request Broker Architecture (CORBA), the Internet Inter-ORB Protocol (IIOP), and Enterprise JavaBeans.

- Oracle9i includes support for SQLJ, a programming syntax that lets you embed SQL statements in Java programs.

- Oracle9i provides improved memory management for very large memory (VLM) Windows boxes having more than 4GB of RAM.

Now that you have looked at some of the new features of Oracle9i, you're ready to look at topics related to installation.

The Environment Used in This Book

Scores of illustrations and sample scripts are included in this book to help experiential learning. The configuration of the test installation is summarized in Table 1-1.

Category	Product/Component	Version/Specification	Comments
Hardware 1	PC	*256MB RAM *8GB disk, one primary partition and one extended partition with two logical drives named C: and D: Pentium III, 733Mhz *17" SVGA monitor *4MB VRAM	All device drivers for the HP machine were available on the Windows 2000 media.

TABLE 1-1. *Hardware Environment Used in Test Installation*

Category	Product/Component	Version/Specification	Comments
Hardware 2	Laptop	*256MB RAM *10GB disk, single partition, one logical drive named C: *Pentium III, 1GHz *15" SVGA monitor *4MB VRAM	Dell Inspiron Series.
Operating system for Hardware 1	Windows 2000 Server	With SP2	
Operating system for Hardware 2	Windows XP	Professional Edition	
Oracle software	Enterprise Edition	Version 9.0.1.0	Downloaded from technet.oracle.com.

TABLE 1-1. *Hardware Environment Used in Test Installation* (continued)

The Oracle9i Enterprise Edition was installed in the default folder named c:\oracle\ora90 under the Oracle Home ORAHOME90. Multiplexed data files, control files, and redo log files were stored in the folder d:\oracle\ora90. All folder names, filenames, and paths used in this book reflect the test environment. You must replace the names as appropriate for your installation before using the examples. Finally, Windows is installed in the c:\windows folder in the test installation.

Preinstallation Checks and Tasks

Sufficient planning is required to complete an Oracle9i installation on the first attempt. In this phase, you must decide how to organize the software and the database files, determine the hardware configuration for your server, and make choices on the operating system and file system types. This section covers the system requirements, provides tips, and describes some terms that will help you in your installation.

Oracle9i System Requirements

Oracle9i Server on Windows 2000 is available in three editions: Enterprise, Standard, and Personal. The system requirements vary based on the edition you choose to install. The requirements for Oracle9i Enterprise Server are summarized here.

Supported Windows Server Operating Systems

Oracle9i Server is supported on any computer with Windows 2000 (Professional, Server, Advanced Server, or Datacenter). Service Pack 2 is recommended. In addition, Windows NT 4.0 (Workstation, Server, Server Enterprise Edition, or Terminal Server) with service pack 6.0a is also supported.

Recommended Hardware

Choose the hardware for your Oracle9i installation carefully. Oracle recommends a system with Pentium 233MHz or better CPU and RAM of 256MB (128MB minimum). For better performance, we recommend that you use a system with a minimum of 512MB RAM in production. In our tests, we have noted that about 4.6GB of disk space is used on file allocation table (FAT) file systems for a typical Oracle9i (Enterprise Edition) installation; however, 3.1GB of disk space is sufficient on an NT file system (NTFS). We also observed that a page file of approximately 400MB was used during our test installation on a machine with 256MB RAM. If you have 256MB RAM, we recommend that you set your virtual memory settings to 400MB. A machine with video support for 256 colors is also recommended.

Oracle9i Client Software

Oracle9i client software can run on any computer with Windows 95, 98, Me, NT 4.0, XP, or 2000. Service Pack 6.0a is required for Windows NT clients, and Service Pack 2 is required for Windows 2000 clients.

We recommend that you use computers with Pentium 166 or better CPUs having at least 64MB of RAM (128MB recommended). In our tests, Oracle client software required about 1.05GB of disk space on a FAT file system and about 580MB on an NTFS.

If you are planning to administer Oracle9i Server over the Web, you will need Netscape Navigator 4.7 or Internet Explorer 5.0, or later. Information on Web Installation is included in Chapter 2.

File Organization

Oracle recommends using the Oracle Flexible Architecture (OFA). OFA has several advantages, including

- Better file system organization and easy administration.

- Improves scalability, as database files can be added easily.

- Better performance can be obtained by distributing the input/output (I/O) across disk drives.

- Data can be protected better by distributing it on multiple disk drives.

Understanding Oracle Home

If you have multiple installations of Oracle products (typically, different versions), then each installation is performed in a different base folder. Each installation is labeled as a separate Oracle Home by Oracle Universal Installer (OUI). Most Oracle components can be installed repeatedly in different locations. If an Oracle component is installed for a second time on the same computer, OUI detects the previous installation and takes appropriate action. Suitable logs are written in the c:\program files\oracle\inventory\logs folder. The following components, however, can be installed in only one location (single Oracle Home):

- Oracle Performance Monitor for NT
- Oracle Objects for OLE
- Oracle Open Database Connectivity (ODBC) Driver
- Oracle SNMP agent

FAT Versus NT File System

A great strength of Windows NT and 2000 is their ability to support multiple file systems. While both support FAT and NTFS, there are some inherent characteristics of these file systems that you must note before choosing your file system. A full discussion on this subject is beyond the scope of this book. Several good resources are available on the Web for this purpose. Refer to Appendix A for information on these resources. Some important considerations are summarized here.

Hardware

System partitions on Intel x86-based computers can be formatted either FAT or NTFS. RISC-based computers, however, support only FAT for their system partitions. The boot partition on both Intel x86 and RISC systems can be either FAT or NTFS.

On RISC systems, you can install Oracle software only on Windows NT. This is because Microsoft has dropped support for Windows 2000 Server on RISC-based systems. Microsoft has also dropped support for machines using extended industry standard architecture (EISA) and microchannel architecture (MCA).

Performance

By and large, NTFS provides better performance than FAT. A FAT file system maintains a FAT to track files and directories at the beginning of the FAT volume. To prevent corruption, the system maintains two copies of the FAT on the disk and can access this copy if the primary copy gets corrupted. Since these tables require constant updating, the hard disk heads have to return frequently to the beginning of the volume, which results in a degradation of performance. FAT can also result in fragmented files quite quickly. Disk defragmentation utilities are available with the operating system to resolve this problem temporarily. Executive Software's Diskeeper and Raxco Software's PerfectDisk2000 are two good tools to defragment NTFS partitions. Finally, since the directory structure on FAT has no formal organization, locating a file on a large FAT volume is time consuming.

Security

NTFS is far more secure than FAT simply because it is tightly integrated with the operating system security. NTFS also allows users to set file-level security and permissions on folders. Local or domain accounts can be used to provide different levels of access to files and folders. Windows 2000 also supports encryption on NTFS partitions, making them more secure.

Access

In some situations it is useful to access your volumes from other operating systems such as MS-DOS. In such a situation, FAT is recommended. Of course, MS-DOS can recognize only FAT volumes smaller than 2GB. Even today, some hardware devices and peripherals require MS-DOS for their configurations. In such situations, you must keep a FAT partition.

For a production environment, you are strongly encouraged to use NTFS partitions. A FAT partition of 2GB is simply not big enough or secure enough.

Reliability

In general, NTFS is considered to be a more reliable file system than FAT. NTFS is considered to be the finest journaling file system available by many in the industry. This is because it maintains a special transaction log to track file I/O events. This log is used automatically to recover from system crashes.

Disk Space

In general, NTFS uses less space than FAT32 for storing the same amount of data. In our tests, Oracle9i installation on NTFS needed much less space. Table 1-2 summarizes our findings.

Product	FAT32	NTFS
Oracle9i Server	4.6GB	3.1GB
Oracle9i Client	1.05GB	580MB

TABLE 1-2. *Disk Requirements for Oracle9i*

Understanding OUI

For a first-time user, OUI can be quite daunting, so this section begins with the basics. OUI is a Java-based application used by Oracle Corporation to install Oracle products on all platforms. Its features allow users to complete a variety of installations. These features include

1. Component and suite installations

2. Web-based installations

3. National language and globalization support

4. Distributed installation support

5. Unattended "silent" installations using response files

6. Deinstallation of components

7. Support for multiple Oracle homes

You should be aware of the restrictions imposed by OUI before you begin your installation. These restrictions are

■ Do not use Oracle9i OUI to install components into the same directories as those used by previous versions (7.x or 8.x). OUI will warn you if you attempt to do so.

■ OUI automatically installs Oracle's version of the Java Runtime Environment (JRE). This version is required to run OUI and other Oracle assistants. Do not modify the JRE without explicit instructions from Oracle support personnel.

■ OUI can perform noninteractive installation in *silent* mode. In this situation, it runs as a background process and does not display on the screen. This is normal behavior.

■ OUI is capable of performing a web-based installation. Refer to *Oracle Universal Installer Concepts Guide* in Oracle documentation for more information before attempting a web-based installation.

If you have not seen OUI before, we recommend that you first read the "Step-by-Step Guide to Installing Oracle Components" section to get a feel for OUI before continuing.

Understanding Product Options

Oracle9*i* is available in many different forms, each providing several components. Understand each package before you begin an installation, and understand the need for a component before installing it. Oracle9*i* Server is available in three *avatars*:

■ Enterprise Edition

■ Standard Edition

■ Personal Edition

Oracle9*i* Database Options

The following components require a separate license even if they are a part of your installation media:

■ Oracle Advanced Security

■ Oracle Data Mining

■ Oracle Diagnostics Pack

■ Oracle Label Security

■ Oracle Management Pack for SAP R/3

■ Oracle Management Pack for Oracle Applications

■ Oracle OLAP

■ Oracle Partitioning

■ Oracle Real Application Clusters (ORAC)

■ Oracle Spatial

■ Oracle Tuning Pack

Oracle Components in Enterprise Edition

The Enterprise Edition of Oracle9*i* Server is a good choice for sites that plan to deploy Oracle applications in a web or client/server environment. The components available on this edition are listed here:

■ Advanced queueing

■ Advanced replication

■ Character-set scanner

- Common schema demos

- Object-type translator

- Oracle INTYPE File Assistant

- Oracle OLAP services

- Oracle Net Services, including Oracle Net Configuration Assistant, Oracle Net Manager, Oracle Net Listener, Oracle Protocol Support (automatically installed for detected networking protocols during installation)

- Oracle Administration Assistant for Windows NT

- Oracle Advanced Security, including encryption and integrity support

Oracle Components in Standard Edition
The Standard Edition *does not* include the following components that are available with Enterprise Edition:

- Oracle OLAP Services

- Oracle Advanced Security

Oracle Components in Personal Edition
The Personal Edition includes a full-featured Oracle9i database; however, it is a single-user system that can be used in development or learning or for small applications. Oracle Net Services are not included on this edition.

Shared (Multithreaded) Server
If you are planning to use the Shared Server (called Multithreaded Server in earlier versions) option, you should not install the default (starter) database that is provided by OUI. This is because the starter database is configured for dedicated servers. Complete the installation without the starter database and then use the Database Creation Assistant to create a custom database. Shared Servers can be configured at this time.

Step-by-Step Guide to Installing Oracle Components

Log in to Windows as a user who has Administrator privileges. Place the Oracle distribution CD in the CD-ROM drive of your system. It should automatically start the installation process. If it doesn't start automatically, execute **setup.exe** from the base folder of the distribution CD. You should see the Java-based installer start with a screen similar to the one shown here:

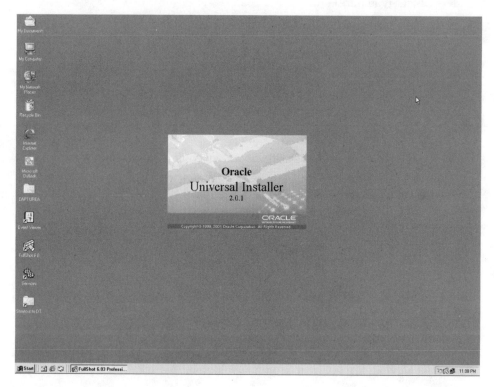

If you have used OUI in earlier releases, you will notice that the number of dialog boxes has been reduced in Oracle9*i*. OUI takes a few seconds to load. After this you should see a Welcome screen similar to the one shown in Figure 1-1.

You can proceed with the installation by clicking the Next button. You can also view previously installed products and deinstall Oracle components by clicking the appropriate buttons in the Welcome screen. For now, proceed with the installation by clicking the Next button. The File Locations dialog box, shown in Figure 1-2, should appear with the Source Path field pointing to your CD-ROM drive.

If you have downloaded Oracle software from Oracle's site, you should have three folders named disk1, disk2, and disk3. In this case, you must point the Source Path to the disk1\stage folder in your download location. The Destination area of the dialog box has two items. The Oracle Home, which defaults to OraHome90, is a label used to identify this installation. You can rename the Oracle Home if you wish; however, if you have a previous version of Oracle Server installed, use a different Oracle Home for this installation. OUI will generate an error later in the

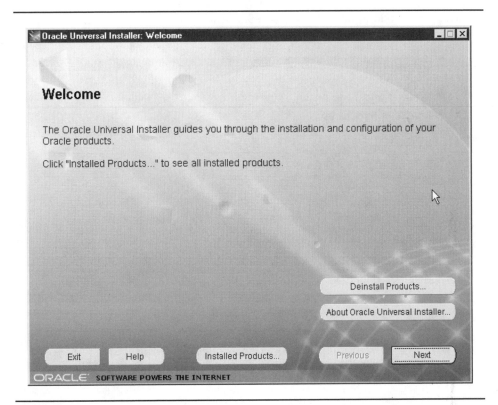

FIGURE 1-1.   *OUI Welcome screen*

installation if it was unable to use the Oracle Home specified by you. The second item is the complete path for the location. OUI defaults the location to the drive that has the maximum free space on your system. The path is constructed by appending the Oracle Base (Ora90) to the string *Oracle*. For example, a target location could be c:\Oracle\Ora90\. If you choose to install another Oracle product, for example, Oracle9i Application Server, you can install this in the same root directory, but it must be in a separate Oracle Base. For example, if you have installed Oracle9i in a folder named c:\Oracle\Ora90, you can install Application Server in c:\Oracle\isuites. OUI will warn you if you attempt to install Application Server in the folder c:\Oracle\Ora90. When you have these settings correct, click the Next button.

In this part of the installation, you choose the products that you want to install on your system. You can choose to install the Oracle9i Database (Server) or install an Oracle client. Optionally, you could install management and integration tools, which allow you to administer Oracle9i Server from a client. A sample screen is shown here:

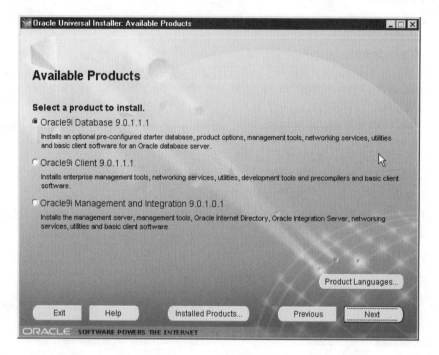

In the next step, you can specify the language support that you require for your Oracle9i installation. Choose one or more languages as appropriate and continue by clicking the Next button. A sample screen is shown here:

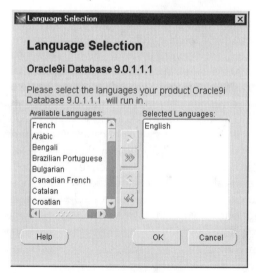

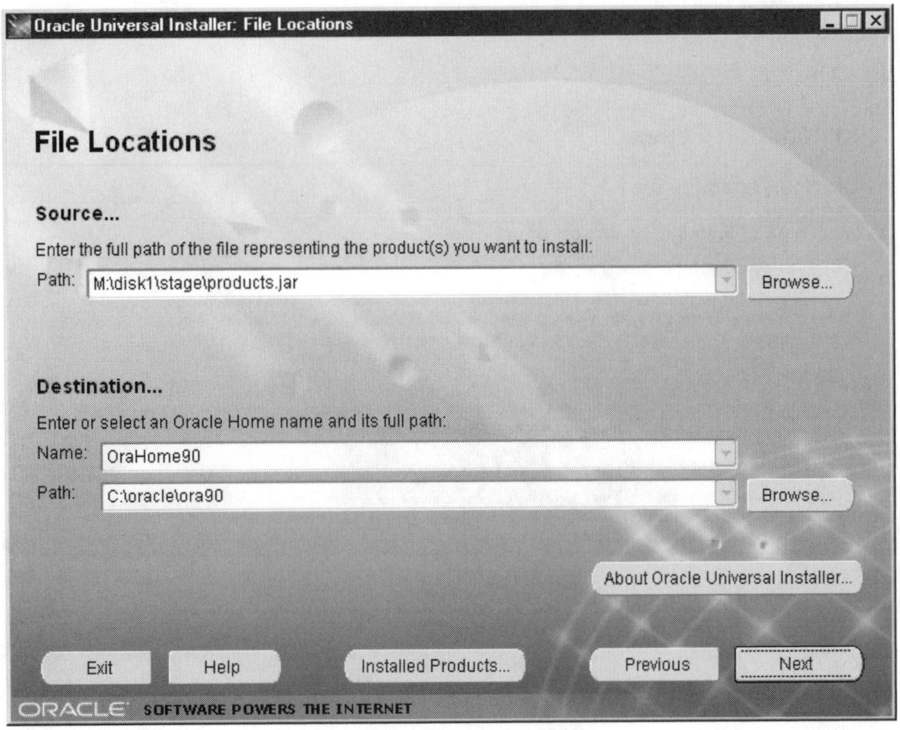

FIGURE 1-2. *File Locations dialog box*

In the next part of the installation, you can pick the Oracle edition that you want to install. The sample screen shown in Figure 1-3 appears only if you have chosen to install the Oracle9i database. Please review your license before you select this option. If you have installed Oracle products before, you could choose the Custom option and install only the components that you require. We recommend that you select one of the other options and go through with a mock installation. When you are sure of the components that you need for your site, you can selectively deinstall components that you do not need. The Enterprise Edition is being installed here.

The next screen (see Figure 1-4) lists the components you have chosen to install. If this is a fresh (first-time) installation, you should see New Install under the Install Status column. If you want to avoid installing a component, you can discard it from the list by clearing the appropriate check box.

Pay special attention to the list of components presented to you in this dialog box. Oracle products are shipped in a variety of packages. Even though the lists appear similar, there are small differences in components available on different packages. This dialog box also provides information on whether a component is required or

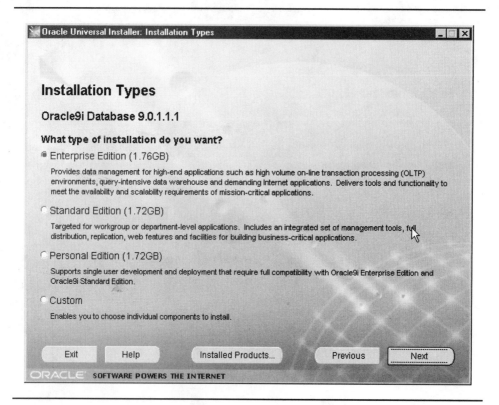

FIGURE 1-3. *Installation Types dialog box*

not. If a component is marked Optional, you can choose not to install it. Pay special attention to any components marked No. If you choose to install a component marked No, you might corrupt a previous installation.

You can confirm your choice of components by clicking the Next button to begin the installation. A typical Oracle9i installation takes 20–30 minutes depending on your system. View the installation log provided at the end of the installation to determine if the installation was successful. If any components failed to install, you can try to install them later by using a custom installation. Exit OUI when the installation is completed.

Post-Installation Tasks

By now, you should have a working Oracle9i installation. A few additional post-installation tasks are recommended to keep your site running smoothly. You might want to take a few minutes to read this section so that you can avoid some common pitfalls.

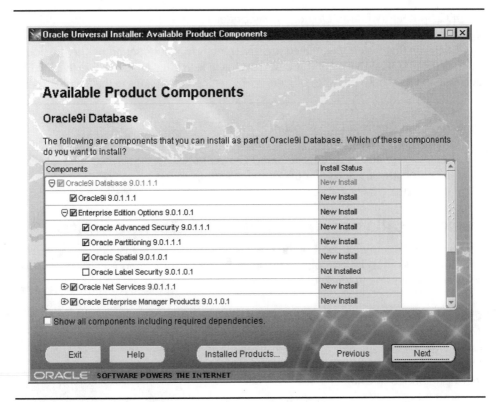

FIGURE 1-4. *Available Product Components dialog box*

A typical Oracle9i installation creates several files in several folders on your computer. The built-in Windows security account SYSTEM must have full permissions to these folders. However, these files are protected from user accounts on the system. You can use Windows Explorer to set appropriate permissions. Select the Oracle installation folder (c:\oracle), right-click, and choose Properties from the context menu. Set file and directory permissions such that the SYSTEM account has full permissions on the Oracle directory structure. Assign read permissions to *everyone* on the c:\oracle\bin folder since it contains executables such as SQL*Plus and Import/Export. Better yet, assign permissions to specific executables in the c:\oracle\bin folder.

Windows Registry

Oracle9i on Windows 2000 uses the Windows registry extensively. All environment settings required by Oracle components are in the registry. The HKEY_CLASSES_ROOT, HKEY_LOCAL_MACHINE, and HKEY_CURRENT_USER keys are used by Oracle components. You can locate these entries easily by searching for the strings Oracle or ORCL in Registry Editor. *Do not* modify or delete these entries manually as this can corrupt your installation!

To ensure that the Oracle-related registry entries are secure, set proper permissions on the HKEY_LOCAL_MACHINE\Software\Oracle key. Give full control to the SYSTEM account and read-only access to other users by setting Permissions in the Security menu.

NOTE
On UNIX systems, a DBA account is used for the installation. Suitable environment variables for Oracle Server are set for this account. On Windows, OUI automatically adds all environment settings to the registry.

Post-Installation for Individual Components

Although OUI completes most of the configuration during the installation, a few additional tasks must be completed for some of the Oracle components. This section provides an overview of these tasks.

Oracle Management Pack for Applications

After the installation of the management pack for Oracle applications, you need to configure Oracle Intelligent Agent on the managed nodes. You then need to configure Oracle Management Server and Oracle Enterprise Manager. More information on these is included in Chapter 7.

Shared Server Support

If you have installed the default database during installation, Shared Server support (called Multithreaded Server support in earlier releases) is not available for that database; however, you can configure Shared Servers if you use Database Creation Assistant to create a custom database.

If you have installed the default database, you can also manually configure Shared Servers later. A section on Shared Servers is included in Chapter 6.

Oracle Java Virtual Machine (JVM)

If you want to install Oracle JVM features such as servlets, Java Server Pages, EJB applications, or CORBA applications then unlock the following Oracle users and change their passwords:

- AURORAJISUTILITY$

- OSE$HTTP$ADMIN

- AURORAORBUNAUTHENTICATED

You can unlock a user account using Oracle Enterprise Manager or with the ALTER USER command as shown here:

```
SQL> ALTER USER aurora$jis$utility$ ACCOUNT UNLOCK;
User altered.
```

Oracle OLAP Services

Oracle OLAP services use two database users, OLAPSVR and OLAPDBA. These accounts are automatically created during installation; however, they are initially locked. You have to unlock them on Oracle Server before using OLAP services. Be sure to change the passwords for these users. More information is available in *OLAP Services Concept and Administration Guide* in Oracle documentation.

Oracle Administration Assistant for Windows

This tool requires Microsoft Management Console (preferably the latest version available) and HTML Help 1.2 to run. Microsoft Management Console is included in Microsoft Windows 2000, but it has to be installed manually in Windows NT from the Option Pack CD-ROM. You can also download the Option Pack from http://download.microsoft.com.

Oracle Advanced Security

Oracle Advanced Security (ASO) is available with the Enterprise Edition only. It provides additional security features for data encryption, integrity, and authentication. Industry-standard algorithms for encryption such as DES and RC4 are supported. The Single Sign-On (SSO) feature provides a user access to multiple databases with a single password. SSL support is also included. These components require you to complete post-installation tasks manually.

Oracle Enterprise Manager

You need to perform additional tasks to manage and monitor services with Oracle Enterprise Manager (OEM). OEM needs a database to house its repository. If you do not have an existing database, you must create one before starting OEM. OEM automatically creates a repository when you start it the first time.

OEM uses Management Server service on Windows NT/2000. If this service is not available on your server, it is created during the installation of OEM. We recommend that you set this service to start automatically. If you don't, be sure to start this service before starting OEM.

Oracle Management Server Repository

Oracle Management Server (OMS) requires a repository to be created before it can be used. If you have an older version (1.x or 2.x) of OMS repository, you can migrate it to the current version using OEM Migration Assistant after OMS installation is complete.

Oracle Internet Directory

If you are planning to run Oracle Internet Directory, you need to get third-party UNIX-emulation software to run the required shell scripts such as bulkload.sh, bulkdelete.sh, bulkmodify.sh, catalog.sh, and ldaprepl.sh. You can get these from either of the two approved vendors:

- **Cygnus**   http://sources.redhat.com/

- **MKS Toolkit**   http://www.datafocus.com/products/

Oracle Real Application Cluster

The Oracle Real Application Cluster configuration (previously called Oracle Parallel Server) allows multiple instances to share a single Oracle database. This configuration is useful for 24 x 7 sites since it provides high-availability and load-balancing. Post-installation configuration procedures must be performed for high availability and integration with OEM.

Oracle Services for Microsoft Transaction Server

If you are using Windows NT, install the Microsoft Management Console (MMC) before you install Oracle9i. If you have already installed Oracle9i, create an NT account for Microsoft Transaction Server with administrator privileges. Set the Transaction Server service to start automatically. Schedule a database server-level transaction recovery job in MMC.

Oracle Workflow

Workflow requires the following post-installation tasks:

- Additional settings in parameter file (init.ora)

- Installation and configuration of Web Server

- Verification of base URL for Workflow

- Setting up Workflow and HTML Help

Deinstallation of Oracle Products

In some situations, you might want to deinstall Oracle products because you no longer need them on the system. Even if you want to reinstall Oracle products, we recommend that you deinstall existing components before reinstallation.

Deinstallation Using OUI

Of course, the easiest way to deinstall Oracle components is to use OUI. Start OUI from the Oracle Shortcut folder. When you reach the Welcome screen, click the Deinstall Products button to see a screen similar to the one shown here:

Select the product(s) that you want to remove and click the Next button. Follow the wizard until you are finished with the deinstallation.

Manual Deinstallation

Sometimes, OUI leaves certain registry settings, files, and folders on your system after deinstallation. If you want to purge an Oracle installation from your system, you can manually deinstall Oracle components. The Enterprise Edition can be deinstalled as follows:

1. Log on to the Windows 2000 system as an Administrator. Stop all Oracle services by choosing the Services applet. Oracle services are typically named with a prefix oracle or ora. Once you have stopped all Oracle services, we recommend that you set them to manual start mode.

2. Take a backup of Windows Registry. Start Registry Editor and choose File | Export from the menu.

CAUTION
Microsoft recommends that you do not modify
Windows Registry manually. Modifying the
Windows Registry could result in other applications
or Windows not working properly.

3. Start Registry Editor by using the command **regedt32**. Navigate to the HKEY_CLASSES_ROOT node and delete all keys that begin with the string Oracle, ORA, or ORCL.

4. Navigate to the HKEY_LOCAL_MACHINE/SOFTWARE key and delete the Oracle and Apache Group keys.

5. Delete the Oracle ODBC Driver key under HKEY_LOCAL_MACHINE\ SOFTWARE\ODBC\odbcinst.ini.

6. Remove all keys beginning with the string ORACLE under the keys HKEY_LOCAL_MACHINE\SYSTEM\CurrentControlSet\Services and HKEY_LOCAL_MACHINE\SYSTEM\CurrentControlSet\Services\EventLog\ Application.

7. Delete all keys beginning with the string Oracle or ORCL under the key HKEY_CURRENT_USER\SOFTWARE\ORACLE.

8. Delete keys with the string Oracle in HKEY_CURRENT_USER\SOFTWARE\ ODBC\odbcinst.ini.

9. Search the registry for keys containing the strings Oracle and ORCL and delete them.

10. Close Registry Editor.

11. Edit your environment settings (System applet in Control Panel) and modify the PATH variable to remove all Oracle entries from the PATH.

12. Delete shortcuts for Oracle Home and Oracle Installation Products from the ALL USERS profile. This is available in the Path winnt | Profiles | All Users | Start | Programs menu on Windows NT and Documents and Settings | All Users | Start Menu | Programs on Windows 2000 and XP systems.

13. Delete the Oracle folder under Program Files. You might not succeed in deleting the folder as Windows might have locked some files (DLLs). In this case, reboot the system and delete the folder.

14. Delete the Oracle Base folder (named ORACLE, by default).

NOTE
When you attempt to delete the c:\oracle folder,
you might get the error "Access is denied." If you get
this error, rename the c:\oracle\ora90\bin\oci.dll
file to c:\oracle\ora90\bin\ocibak, reboot the
machine, and delete the c:\oracle folder.

Note that Oracle9i Enterprise Edition also installs third-party software such as Apache HTTP Server (the Oracle HTTP Server is a modified Apache Web Server).

In Chapter 1, you have learned how to perform a basic Oracle installation with OUI. The concepts that have been introduced in this chapter will be extended to advanced installation techniques in Chapter 2.

CHAPTER
2

Oracle9i Advanced Installation

hapter 1 covered the basic installation of Oracle9i Server. The wizard-based installation provided by OUI is sufficient for most sites. In some situations, the interactive nature of OUI is inconvenient, for example, when a noninteractive installation is required. Sometimes, it is even necessary to install Oracle9i Server over the Web. This chapter outlines advanced installation procedures that allow you to perform automated and unattended installations.

Today's business demands that many sites run 24×7. To ensure high-availability and load-balancing, Oracle Server supports a configuration known as Oracle Real Application Cluster (RAC). Additional requirements for RAC are described in this chapter.

Noninteractive Installation

Assume that you need to install Oracle9i Server on 50 separate machines that are going to be used for DBA training or that you want to install Oracle9i Server on a remote machine. It is quite painful to use OUI in such situations. A noninteractive installation or *silent installation* would be better suited.

A noninteractive installation takes its input from a response file instead of mouse clicks from the user. Response files are text files that contain variables and other values that act as inputs for OUI during the installation. Net Configuration Assistant, Database Configuration Assistant, and Enterprise Manager Configuration Assistant also support response files.

NOTE:
Noninteractive deinstallation is not supported at press time; however, you can write batch files using the steps defined in Chapter 1 for mass deinstallation.

A variety of response files are available in the Response folder of the installation media. This folder is usually available at the root directory level of the media. These files are listed in Table 2-1.

Oracle Software Packager (OSP) can also be used to create response files. You can download OSP from http://technet.oracle.com. OSP can also be used to create install procedures for your own applications. These applications can then be installed from OUI.

Editing Response Files

You must modify response files provided on the distribution media to suit your installation needs. Identify a suitable response file from the Response folder on the media, create your own copy of the file, and edit the file using any text editor.

Response file templates provided by Oracle include comments within the file that help you customize the template for your needs.

Name of Response File	Component for Installation
Enterprise.rsp	Oracle9i Server Enterprise Edition
Standard.rsp	Oracle9i Server Standard Edition
Custom.rsp	Oracle9i Server Custom Installation
Clientadmin.rsp	Oracle9i Client (Administrator)
Clientruntime.rsp	Oracle9i Client Runtime Installation
Clientcustom.rsp	Oracle9i Custom Client Installation
Oms.rsp	Oracle Management Server Installation
Oid.rsp	Oracle Internet Directory Installation
Ois.rsp	Oracle Integration Server Installation
Infrastructure.rsp	Oracle Management Infrastructure Installation
Dbca.rsp	Database Configuration Assistant
Netca.rsp	Net Configuration Assistant
Emca.rsp	Oracle Enterprise Manager Configuration Assistant and Repository

TABLE 2-1.   *Response Files for Noninteractive Installation*

Structure of a Response File

Every response file has a specific structure. This section overviews the structure of a response file. This will help you customize the response file for your installation.

Sections of a Response File

A response file has multiple sections. Each section has a specific purpose and includes certain settings. A list of sections and their purposes is provided in Table 2-2.

The General, Include, and Components sections are required for a silent installation to be successful. Each section includes one or more variable definitions. The general format for a variable definition is

```
<variable> = <value>
```

Section	Function
General	Includes the version number of the response file. This is the first section of the response file.
Include	Includes a list of response files to be included. This section is optional and is present only if other response files are being included.
Session	Lists the dialogs of OUI. This section follows the General and the Include section (if one exists).
Components	Public variables and installer variables are defined here. This is the last section of the response file.

TABLE 2-2. *Sections in Response Files*

Values for some variables are mandatory. Many others have default values. The format of each section of the response file and the variables that it contains are covered next.

General Section of a Response File   Each response file has exactly one version number that is defined in the General section. The format for the *responsefile_version* variable is shown here, along with an example:

```
[GENERAL]
RESPONSEFILE_VERSION = <version_number>
```

Example:

```
[General]
RESPONSEFILE_VERSION=1.0.0.0.0
```

Include Section of a Response File   Sometimes, it is helpful to include other (smaller) response files in a main response file. You can use the Include section for this purpose. An example is shown here:

```
[INCLUDE]
FILE1="C:/Oracle/oracle/dba.rsp"
```

If the same variable is specified in both the main file and the included response file, the value defined in the main response file takes precedence. Session sections must be defined in the main response file; otherwise, they are ignored.

Session Section of a Response File   In most cases, you will want a completely noninteractive installation; however, in some situations some user feedback through dialogs can be helpful. For example, you might want to follow the progress of an installation. The Session section includes predefined dialogs. If you set the value of a dialog variable to *true*, it is displayed during the installation. For example, to display the progress of an installation, you could use the following setting in the Session section:

```
[SESSION]
SHOW_INSTALL_PROGRESS_PAGE=true
```

The Session section also includes definitions for global variables. Global variables define settings that are used in one installation session (beginning of the installation to the end). A variety of variables is available. You can use these to define top-level components, languages, and so on. Some of these variables are listed here.

- FROM_LOCATION   This variable defines the location of the source from which the products are to be installed. The sources can be on a CD-ROM drive, a hard disk, or an addressable network drive.

- FROM_LOCATION_CD_LABEL   This variable is useful in installations that span CD-ROMs. The variable defines the label of the CD that contains the Products.jar file. The label can be found in a file named Disk.label in the same folder (the folder is usually named Stage).

- LOCATION_FOR_DISKn   You can use this variable to define the paths for continuing media (disks). The *n* defines the disk sequence. An example is shown here:

  ```
  LOCATION_FOR_DISK2="F:\teststage\cd\Disk2"
  LOCATION_FOR_DISK3="F:\teststage\cd\Disk3"
  ```

  If OUI is unable to locate files in the location specified by the LOCATION_FOR_DISK variable, then it automatically looks for them under the relative path ..\..*Disk{Disk Number}**stage*. For example, if you download the Oracle9i media from www.oracle.com in the folder c:\tmp, you get the following directory structure:

  ```
  c:\tmp\disk1\stage
  c:\tmp\disk2\stage
  c:\tmp\disk3\stage
  ```

  Now if you execute **setup.exe** from the location c:\tmp\disk1\, OUI will automatically look for disks 2 and 3 by using the relative paths ..\disk2\stage and ..\disk3\stage.

- NEXT_SESSION   If you want to proceed with another installation, set this variable to *true*. The installer will then proceed to the next File Locations page. The next installation starts after the current installation has completed successfully. If you want to start a second installation process regardless of whether the current installation completed successfully, use the NEXT_SESSION_ON_FAIL parameter described next.

- NEXT_SESSION_ON_FAIL   If you want to start another installation session even if the current session fails, set this variable to *true*.

- NEXT_SESSION_RESPONSE   If you want to begin another installation automatically after the current one has completed, you can use this to set the complete path of the next session's response file. You can use this parameter in conjunction with both the NEXT_SESSION and the NEXT_SESSION_RESPONSE parameters.

- ORACLE_HOME   The target (the "To" in OUI) for the installation.

- ORACLE_HOME_NAME   If you want to add components, or a new ORACLE_HOME for a new installation, use this as the name of an existing ORACLE_HOME.

- SHOW_COMPONENT_LOCATIONS_PAGE   If you set this variable to *false*, the user will not be allowed to override the entries in the Location page. Set this to *false* if you want to prevent the user from specifying alternative directories; otherwise, set it to *true*.

- SHOW_CUSTOM_TREE_PAGE   A setting of *true* displays the Custom Tree page that allows a user to select or unselect dependencies. This setting applies only to custom installations.

- SHOW_END_SESSION_PAGE   If you set this to *false*, the summary at the end of the installation, which shows whether the installation completed successfully or not, is suppressed.

- SHOW_EXIT_CONFIRMATION   A setting of *false* suppresses the dialog that confirms the exit from the installer.

- SHOW_INSTALL_PROGRESS_PAGE   If you want the user to view the progress of the installation, set this to *true*; otherwise, set it to *false*.

- SHOW_OPTIONAL_CONFIG_TOOL_PAGE   If you set this to *true*, the Optional Configuration Tools page is shown. This page is useful if you want the user to see the status of each tool (for example, Net Configuration Assistant).

■ SHOW_REQUIRED_CONFIG_TOOL_PAGE   This setting is similar to the Optional Configuration Tools page, except that it pertains to the required configuration tools.

■ SHOW_SPLASH_SCREEN   A setting of *true* displays the initial splash screen of OUI.

■ SHOW_SUMMARY_PAGE   The Summary page can be suppressed by setting this value to *false*.

■ SHOW_WELCOME_PAGE   Set to *true* if the Welcome page in the installer needs to be shown.

■ TOPLEVEL_COMPONENT   This variable defines the name of the component (products) that you want to install along with the version number of the component. This is a mandatory setting. The components are usually represented with a pair of strings; the first one representing the internal name, and the second representing the version. For example, Oracle Server 9.0.1 is represented as

```
{"oracle.rdbms","9.0.1.0.0}.
```

Component Section of a Response File   The Component section provides information on the components and the corresponding version numbers. An entry for the Oracle Server is shown here.

```
[oracle.server_9.0.1.0.0]
```

A component definition can include the additional variables. These are discussed next.

■ DEPENDENCY_LIST   This variable defines a list of dependencies for a given component. Components (dependents) listed here are automatically selected when the main component is selected. An example is shown here:

```
DEPENDENCY_LIST={"oracle.netclt","9.0.1.0.0",
"oracle.netmgr","9.0.1.0.0"}
```

Most Oracle components are aware of their dependencies. Therefore, when you install the main component, the dependencies are resolved in most cases automatically.

■ PROD_HOME   This variable defines the target location for the product. Typically, this is a folder under the ORACLE_HOME structure. Note that many components must be installed under the ORACLE_HOME. This variable applies only to components that are allowed to be installed outside ORACLE_HOME. Oracle9i Application Server is an example of a component that can be installed under a separate ORACLE_HOME.

■ OPTIONAL_CONFIG_TOOLS   You can launch optional configuration tools by defining this variable. Required configuration tools for a component are automatically launched by OUI. An example is shown here.

```
[oracle.server_9100]
OPTIONAL_CONFIG_TOOLS={"tool1"}
```

■ INSTALL_TYPE   This is a required setting that specifies the top-level component being installed by the response file. The following settings can be used to install Oracle9i Standard Edition and Oracle Management Server.

```
INSTALL_TYPE="SE"
INSTALL_TYPE="OMS"
```

■ COMPONENT_LANGUAGES   You can provide the language settings for the component being installed using internal names. Some common settings are listed in Table 2-3. An example is shown here:

```
COMPONENT_LANGUAGES = {"en"}
```

Setting Values for Variables

A typical response file includes many variables that need to be defined for your installation. Variables requiring values have placeholders within the response file. The placeholder is typically a string similar to *<values required>*. You must provide suitable values for all required variables.

Internal Name	Language
En	English
Fr	French
De	German
Ja	Japanese

TABLE 2-3.   *Common Language Settings for Oracle Components*

The typical structure of a variable definition is

```
<name> = <recommendation> : <value>
```

If a parameter is recommended, you can designate it as *forced* or *default*. If you designate the variable as *forced*, you will not be given an option to change the setting. If you designate the variable as *default*, you will get a dialog in which you can modify the setting for the variable. For example, to designate a default installation of type *minimum*, you could define a setting as shown here:

```
InstallType = Default : "Minimum"
```

You can also set default values for a variable. The structure of such a definition is shown here.

```
<name> =  <default> : <value>
```

Comments

Comments in a response file are marked by a hash (#) symbol. Information such as the type of variable, whether it appears in a dialog, and the variable's function is included in comments. An example is shown here:

```
#TopLevelComponent;StringList;Used in Dialog
TopLevelComponent={"Demo", "1.0"}
```

Headers

Separate comments are also included in headers. Headers describe formats and other conventions. An example is shown here:

```
#FROM_LOCATION;String;Used in Dialog
#Full path for the products.jar file.
#Replace the X: with the drive letter of your CD-ROM device.
FROM_LOCATION="X:\stage\products.jar"
```

Noninteractive Installation Using OUI

Once you have created a response file for your installation, you can use this as input to OUI. You can launch OUI by executing **setup.exe** from the command line as shown here:

```
C:\Program files\Oracle\Oui\install>setup.exe -responsefile
<PATH>\FILENAME {-SILENT} {-NOWELCOME}
```

The NoWelcome option suppresses the Welcome screen. The Silent option automatically suppresses the Welcome screen and Exit screen. If you choose to use the Silent option, the installer will abort the installation if a value for a required variable is invalid or missing. You can view the file **silentInstall.log** created in the folder c:\program files\Oracle\Inventory folder.

Case Study: Silent Installation of Oracle Net Client

This case study uses a silent installation of Oracle Net Client to illustrate a noninteractive installation. The assumptions, directory names, and filenames used in the installation are summarized in Table 2-4.

Follow these steps to install Oracle Net client on a machine:

1. Create Response file. Create your own copy of the response file template.

   ```
   C:\tmp\disk1> copy d:\response\clientadmin.rsp ourclient.rsp
   ```

2. Customize Response file. Edit the Ourclient.rsp file and customize it for your needs. The response file created for the installation is listed here:

   ```
   #We have deleted all comments in the file
   [General]
   RESPONSEFILE_VERSION=1.7.0
   [SESSION]
   FROM_LOCATION="c:\tmp\disk1\stage\products.jar"
   FROM_LOCATION_CD_LABEL=<Value Unspecified>
   NEXT_SESSION_RESPONSE=<Value Unspecified>
   ORACLE_HOME="c:\oracle\ora90"
   ORACLE_HOME_NAME="OraHome90"
   TOPLEVEL_COMPONENT={"oracle.client","9.0.1.1.1"}
   SHOW_SPLASH_SCREEN=false
   SHOW_WELCOME_PAGE=false
   SHOW_COMPONENT_LOCATIONS_PAGE=false
   SHOW_CUSTOM_TREE_PAGE=false
   SHOW_SUMMARY_PAGE=true
   SHOW_INSTALL_PROGRESS_PAGE=true
   SHOW_REQUIRED_CONFIG_TOOL_PAGE=true
   SHOW_OPTIONAL_CONFIG_TOOL_PAGE=false
   SHOW_RELEASE_NOTES=false
   SHOW_ROOTSH_CONFIRMATION=true
   SHOW_END_SESSION_PAGE=false
   SHOW_EXIT_CONFIRMATION=false
   NEXT_SESSION=false
   NEXT_SESSION_ON_FAIL=false
   ```

```
LOCATION_FOR_DISK2="c:\tmp\disk2"
LOCATION_FOR_DISK3="c:\tmp\disk3"
INSTALL_TYPE="Runtime"
[oracle.networking.netca_9.0.1.1.1]
OPTIONAL_CONFIG_TOOLS={"netca"}
s_responseFileName=<Value Unspecified>
b_launchNETCA=<Value Unspecified>
```

3. Perform Silent installation. Run OUI with Ourclient.rsp as the input response file.

```
C:\tmp\disk1> setup -responsefile c:\tmp\disk1\clientruntime.rsp -silent
```

4. Verify installation. Confirm that the installation is complete by reading the install log files. The file OraInstall.out should show you entries similar to the following:

```
In File Locations Page
In Available Products Page
In Installation Types Page
In Component Locations Page
In Summary Page
In End of Installation Page
The installation of Oracle9i Client was successful.
Please check C:\Program Files\Oracle\Inventory/logs\silentInstall.log
for more details.
```

If your installation has failed, fix the problem(s) listed in the file SilentInstall.log and try again.

Filename/Folder Name/Setting	Description
Destination for Installation	c:\oracle\ora90
Oracle Home	OraHome90
Response File Template Used	\response\clientruntime.rsp (from distribution media)
Name of Response File	ourclient.rsp
Log File Folder	C:\Program Files\Oracle\Inventory\Logs (all log files are created here)

TABLE 2-4.   *Assumptions for Silent-Installation Case Study*

Using OEM Configuration Assistant for Silent Installation

The OEM Configuration Assistant can also be run in silent mode to perform certain tasks. Unfortunately, advanced features such as repository management are not supported in silent mode. To run OEM Configuration Assistant as a standalone component, use the following steps:

1. Make sure OEM is installed.

2. Copy the response file Emca.rsp from the *response* folder of the Oracle media.

3. Modify Emca.rsp as required. You must provide a unique owner for the repository in the Emca.rsp file. More information on the repository is included in Chapter 7. You should also review additional instructions included in the Emca.rsp file itself.

4. Launch OEM Configuration Assistant from the command prompt:

```
C:\oracle\ora90\bin> emca -responsefile emca.rsp -SILENT
```

NOTE
OMS, which must be installed with the parent silent installation, is available for installation in one of these files: Enterprise.rsp, Custom.rsp, oms.rsp, or Infrastructure.rsp.

Error-Handling in Silent Installations

In the silent installation mode, any variables that have the wrong format or values are ignored. Variables defined outside any section are also ignored. Results of the installation are written to a log file. The installation will fail if an invalid response file is provided.

CAUTION
During the Oracle9i Enterprise Edition installation in silent mode, Oracle Net Configuration Assistant fails to configure the system at the end of the installation. After the installation is completed, you have to configure the system manually, using Oracle Net Configuration Assistant. Alternatively, you can copy the Net configuration files from another client across the network. These files typically reside in the c:\oracle\ora90\network\admin folder.

Installation Log Files

OUI generates log files that provide you complete information on the outcome of a silent installation. The following log files are created in the Program Files\Oracle\ Inventory\logs folder on your machine:

- InstallActions.log
- OraInstall.err
- OraInstall.out
- SilentInstall.log

The SilentInstall.log gives you an overview of the installation while the InstallActions.log gives you a step-by-step progress report on the installation.

Web-Based Installations

Since OUI is a Java-based installer, you can also install Oracle9i from a web server. The steps necessary to accomplish this are outlined here.

NOTE
OUI uses Java Native Interface (JNI) to create native executables that are run by the Oracle JVM bundled with the Installer.

1. Configure your web server to serve files from the Oracle media by defining appropriate virtual directories. The process for configuring virtual directories varies with the web server that you are using. For example, on the Apache HTTP Server, you can use the Alias directive to create a virtual mapping of a URL to the file system. The following example maps the URL *install* to the physical directory c:\tmp\oracle\disk1\stage.

```
Alias /install/ "c:\tmp\oracle\disk1\stage/"
```

2. Copy necessary files to local client. OUI requires certain files on the local client for a web-based installation. Copy the following folders to any temporary folder on the client from which you will initiate the installation. Ensure that these files are placed in a folder that can be read by *everyone*.

```
\disk1\stage\Components\oracle.swd.jre
\disk1\stage\Components\oracle.swd.jre
disk1\install
```

3. Initiate web installation. Execute the **setup.exe** from the install\win32\ folder to launch OUI. In the file locations dialog, use the URL to the Products.jar file as the path to the products area, as shown in Figure 2-1.

Note that the PATH for installation is given a URL instead of a physical path. There is one issue that you have to be aware of for web-based installations. Oracle Administration Assistant for Windows NT and Oracle Intelligent Agent do not install on a clean machine during web installation. You will see the following error messages:

```
Error Occurred.
There was an error during loading library: NtServicesQueries.
```

If you encounter this error, continue the installation of the remaining components. Restart OUI and perform a custom installation for these two components.

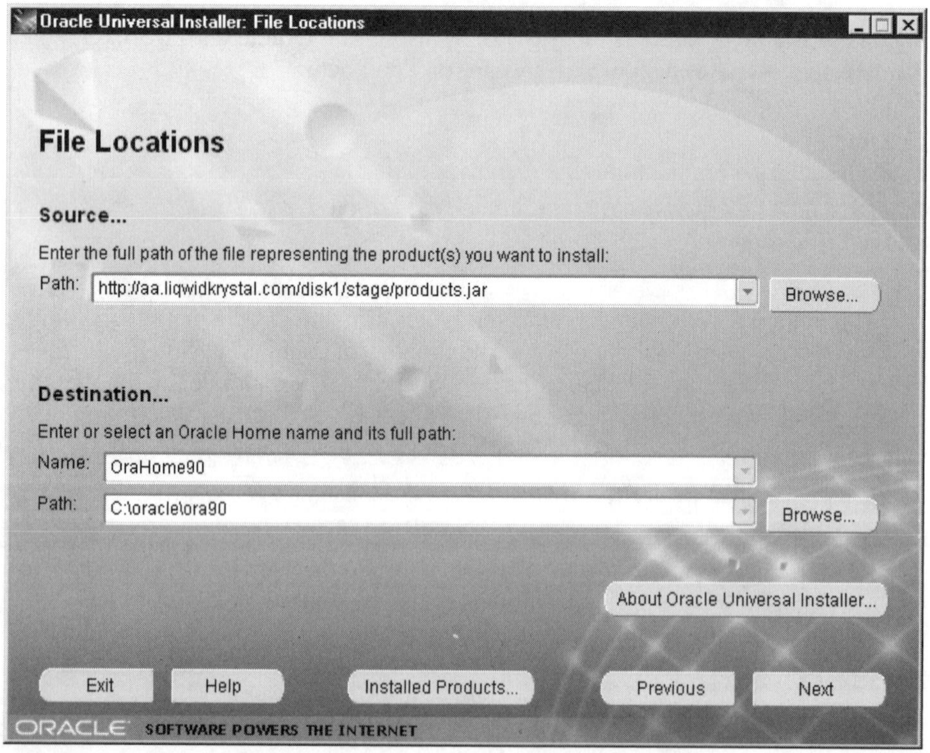

FIGURE 2-1. *File Locations dialog box*

Oracle RAC Installation Tasks

Since it supports automatic fail-over as well as load-balancing, RAC configuration can be used to achieve high availability. RAC is a configuration in which multiple instances of Oracle run on separate physical machines. These instances use a single database that is stored on an external storage device that is shared by all instances. The biggest challenge in such a configuration is to manage the database transactional locks. Oracle Server includes distributed locking features that automatically manage the locks between primary and secondary database instances. Status information and cache information between the instances are managed through inter-process communication (IPC) and controlled by Cluster Manager.

NOTE
In earlier versions of Oracle Server, Real Application Cluster was known as Oracle Parallel Server.

Since multiple machines (nodes) share a database in a RAC configuration, scalability and availability are much improved. Scalability in this case simply refers to the fact that the overall performance is improved by adding more machines to the cluster. Moreover, the failure of any one machine does not affect the use of data since other nodes can continue providing access to the database. In RAC configuration, clients are automatically switched to another instance in case the current instance fails. This is termed *fail-over*. Finally, available nodes are capable of distributing the sessions among themselves so that the load is shared among instances.

A complete discussion and detailed installation of RAC is beyond the scope of this book. The following Oracle documentation provides information on RAC:

- *Real Application Clusters Concepts*
- *Real Application Clusters Deployment and Performance*
- *Real Application Clusters Documentation Online Roadmap*
- *Real Application Clusters Guard Administration and Reference Guide*
- *Real Application Clusters Installation and Configuration*

System Requirements for RAC

To run RAC, there are software and hardware requirements in addition to those listed in Chapter 1. These additional requirements are

- External shared hard disks.

- 256MB of additional RAM for each instance.

- Certified, vendor-supplied, operating system–dependent clusterware.

- An Oracle-supplied layer clusterware.

- Public network names (hostname or TCP/IP names) for each node.

- For high-speed private interconnect, you need the private network names of each node.

- For virtual interface architecture (VIA), you also need the names of the network interface cards (NICs).

New RAC Terminology

Table 2-5 compares the features in Oracle 8/8i with new RAC features in Oracle9i. This table will help DBAs who have configured Oracle Parallel Server (OPS) in earlier versions to understand RAC.

In this chapter, you have seen how OUI can be used for unattended as well as remote installations over the Web.

Feature in Oracle Parallel Server (Oracle 8/8i)	Feature in Real Application Clusters (Oracle9i)	Comment/Description
OPS FailSafe	RAC Guard	Provides fail-over support
Distributed Lock Manager	Replaced by Global Cache Service and Global Enqueue Service	Supports the *cache fusion* feature, which is responsible for making database blocks available across instances
OPS Control Utility (OPSCTL)	Replaced by SRVCTL utility	Service control utility to manage instances
Lock Mastering	Resource Mastering	For concurrency control on data blocks
Lock Database	Global Resource Directory	Data structures in memory that are shared by all instances

TABLE 2-5. *Comparison of OPS with RAC*

CHAPTER
3

Upgrades, Migration, and Downgrades

ike other major software vendors, Oracle releases new versions of its database software with new features and bug fixes from time to time. Oracle recommends that you keep up-to-date with the latest Oracle Server software to derive the benefits from new features. This also enables you to obtain the latest bug fixes (patches), thus improving stability and performance, and sometimes even security. This chapter provides information that will enable you to maintain the latest version of Oracle software to keep your site running smoothly. In rare circumstances, you might need to downgrade from Oracle9*i* to an earlier version. Information on downgrading is also included in this chapter.

Migration versus Upgrades

In the Oracle world, the terms migration and upgrade are often used interchangeably; however, the Oracle documentation mostly uses the term *upgrade* to refer to the process of moving from one version of the software to a higher version. The term *migration* usually refers to the process of moving a database from one machine and/or platform (operating system) to another. This usage remains consistent in this book. Examples of an upgrade are

- Change from Version 8.1.5 to 9.0.1

- Change from Version 9.0.1 to 9.1.0

NOTE
Version 9.1.0 in the preceding example is used only for illustration. Oracle Corporation has not announced this release as this book goes to print.

Examples of a migration are

- Moving an Oracle9*i* database from one machine to another machine running the same operating system

- Moving an Oracle9*i* database from Linux platform to Windows 2000

Oracle recommends that you use documented migration procedures to move an Oracle database from Windows NT to 2000 and vice versa. Interestingly, it is also possible to *downgrade* from Oracle9*i* to a lower version. Oracle did not support downgrades in earlier versions.

Understand Version Numbers

A version number of the form *a.b.c.d* identifies all Oracle software. The first portion (*a*) identifies the major version, and the remaining portion (*b*, *c*, and *d*) identifies the minor versions. In addition to the version number, Oracle Corporation is also branding their software for the Internet platform in recent years. In this context, *Oracle9i* refers to Oracle Server, Version 9 for the Internet platform. It is important to note that there could be several versions of Oracle9i, for example, 9.0.0.0 and 9.0.1.1. The minor version numbers typically include small feature enhancements and bug fixes. Typically, the second portion of the version (the *b* portion) is changed every two to three months and includes all the feature enhancements and bug fixes of interim releases. Oracle Corporation usually rolls out a version *a.b* on all platforms; however, the last portion of the version (the *c* and *d* portion) is usually operating system (OS) specific and includes a specific set of bug fixes. Table 3-1 illustrates a hypothetical release cycle of Oracle9i Server that should help you understand Oracle version numbers.

Major and Minor Upgrades

A major upgrade refers to an upward change in major version (the *a* portion of the version number). Upgrades involving a change in the *b*, *c*, or *d* portion of the version number are referred to as minor upgrades. Minor upgrades are sometimes also referred to as *patches*.

   Another way to look at upgrades is to assume that the version numbers from left to right *(a* to *b* to *c* to *d)* reflect the degree of change in the product. So a change in the *a* portion reflects a major upgrade, and a change in the *d* portion reflects a very minor change.

When to Upgrade?

Most DBAs often are faced with this dilemma. When should you upgrade? In general, a site should perform a major upgrade when the second version of a major version becomes available. Like much other software, it is likely that the first version of a major release has some pending features or some unknown issues. The second release of the major version occurs within a few weeks of the first release and is usually more stable. For example, if Version 9.0.1 is the first release of Oracle9i on your platform and Version 9.1.0 is the second release, you should plan on performing a major upgrade from Oracle8 when Version 9.1.0 is available. Of course, as a DBA you should obtain a new release as soon as it is available and get familiar with it on a test installation.

   The recommended practice is to schedule a minor upgrade whenever the second portion (the *b* portion) changes. This will ensure that your site remains

Version	Status	Time	Operating System	Comments
9.0.0.0	Beta	February 2001	First tier platforms such as Windows NT/2000 and Sun Solaris	First Beta
9.0.0.1	Beta	April 2001	First tier platforms	Second Beta
9.0.1.1	Production	August 2001	First tier platforms + IBM AIX + Linux	Second release on Windows NT/2000; first release on AIX and Linux
9.0.1.4	Production	August 2001	Patch release on Windows NT/2000	Includes a high-priority bug fix for Windows NT/2000
9.0.2.0	Production	October 2001	Release for UNIX platforms	Takes advantage of a special UNIX feature to manage Oracle processes
9.1.0.0	Production	November 2001	All platforms	Release on all platforms; Version 9.1 indicates feature enhancements and includes all features and bug fixes added between version 9.0 and 9.0.1.4

TABLE 3-1. *Hypothetical Release Cycle of Oracle9i Server*

current. Of course, if your site experiences a critical bug and Oracle provides a patch release to fix the bug, you must upgrade to the patch release in the interim.

NOTE
The term upgrade *can refer to a major or a minor version change.*

Detect Version Numbers

Sometimes a DBA needs to determine the version number of Oracle Server currently being used or the version number of a patch being applied. The version information of an existing Oracle Server can be determined by querying the V$VERSION view.

Connect to the database using an account that has DBA privileges and query the V$VERSION view as shown here:

```
SQL> select banner from v$version;
BANNER
-------------------------------------------------------------
Oracle9i Enterprise Edition Release 9.0.1.1.1 - Production
PL/SQL Release 9.0.1.1.1 - Production
CORE    9.0.1.1.1        Production
TNS for 32-bit Windows: Version 9.0.1.1.0 - Production
NLSRTL Version 9.0.1.1.1 - Production
```

As shown in the following, the Oracle Server version is also displayed in the banner information when you connect to an Oracle database from a SQL utility such as SQL*Plus.

```
Connected to:
Oracle9i Enterprise Edition Release 9.0.1.1.1 - Production
With the Partitioning option
JServer Release 9.0.1.1.1 - Production
```

The version information of Oracle software is also marked on the distribution media. Look on the back cover of the CD-ROM case or on the CD-ROM insert. Most distributions also include a README file (or a file named welcome.html) that contains version information. This README also provides information on the bug fixes (or patches) available on that release.

Finally, if you have downloaded the software (or patch) from an Oracle web site, the filename itself will indicate the version number. For example, the file named 9011NTSrv_Disk1 downloaded from Oracle's download area contains files in Disk 1 for the Windows NT/2000 platform for Oracle9 Version 9.0.1.1.

Tools and Methods for Migration and Upgrades

Oracle Corporation provides tools and methods that can be used for database migration and upgrades. It is important to note that there is some overlap in the functionality provided by these tools; however, each tool provides benefits in a given situation. Your level of knowledge and experience should also largely influence your choice. These tools and methods will be introduced before any discussion of how to perform database upgrades and migrations on the Windows NT/2000 platform.

Oracle Data Migration Assistant

Oracle Data Migration Assistant (DMA) is a Java-based utility provided with the standard Oracle installation. It has a graphical user interface (GUI) that allows a user to quickly perform an upgrade. DMA supports upgrades from Oracle Version 7.3 or higher to Oracle9i. DMA is fast in comparison to Export and Import utilities as it modifies datafile headers directly without modifying or moving data.

Oracle Migration Utility

Oracle Migration Utility (OMU) is a command-line tool that is available with Oracle9i. It can be used to migrate or upgrade from Oracle Version 7.3 and above to Oracle9i. OMU is similar to DMA except for the fact that it has a command-line interface (CLI) instead of a GUI.

Export and Import Utilities

Like earlier versions of Oracle Server, Oracle9i includes the Export and Import utilities. The Export utility *exports* or *extracts* data from an Oracle database and creates an operating system file, called a *dump*. The dump is in turn *imported* using the Import utility into another database. Together, these two utilities can be used to upgrade and/or migrate a database.

Export physically copies data to an operating system file. Similarly, Import reads the operating system file and re-creates the data in an Oracle database. Export and Import also use the SQL layer and are, therefore, time and resource intensive. If you are upgrading a database on the same operating system (platform), you should use DMA or OMU; however, if you are migrating the database to another operating system, you must use the Export and Import utilities.

Backup and Recovery Methods

If you are attempting to move a database from one machine to another using the same operating system, you can also use the backup and recovery methods described in Chapter 5. The steps are described here:

1. Perform a full backup (a *cold* backup) of your database.

2. Perform a custom installation of Oracle9i on the new machine; do not create a starter database.

3. Move the files from the backup to the new machine over the network or other media.

4. Recover the database from the backup.

If you use this method to move a database, it is easier to retain the same directory and file structures as the old machine. If you cannot do so, you will need to recover the database and use the ALTER DATABASE..RENAME command in SQL to move the datafiles and logfiles to the new paths.

SQL Commands

In some situations, it is possible to use the COPY and CREATE TABLE AS commands in SQL to upgrade or migrate data from one database to another. Of course, the source and target databases must be available and also be addressable on the network to use this method. You can use this method to upgrade or migrate specific portions of an existing database to a new (precreated) database.

Choose a Tool

By now, you should have some understanding of the available tools for migration and upgrades. This section includes some quick guidelines that will help you decide on the tool to use in a specific upgrade or migration.

If you want to perform a major upgrade of an existing database to a new version (for example, Oracle8i to Oracle9i) on the same machine, you should use DMA. In fact, you can perform the upgrade during the installation of Oracle9i itself.

If you want to perform a major upgrade of an existing database on the same platform (operating system), and you want to have complete control of the process, you should use Migration Utility. Of course, this requires a lot more care and a deeper understanding of the process.

If you want to migrate (and/or upgrade) from one platform to another, you should use the Export and Import utilities. If you want to simply move a database from one machine to another using the same operating system while retaining the same Oracle version, you can use the backup and recovery methods documented in Chapter 5.

Finally, if you want to move a relatively small portion of a database into another existing database on the network, you can use the COPY or CREATE TABLE command.

DMA versus OMU

DMA and OMU are very similar in the manner in which they perform an upgrade; however, there are some benefits of using one over the other depending on the situation.

Since DMA has a GUI with a wizard, it is much easier to use for the inexperienced user. Extensive help is available during the process of upgrading. Some tasks are automatically performed by DMA during the upgrade. For example, obsolete parameters in the parameter file (INIT.ORA) are automatically removed during the migration. In some situations, you might want more control during the migration. For example, you might want to set specific INIT.ORA parameters during the upgrade. In such a situation, you should use OMU.

In addition to the differences in the previous paragraph, there are two important considerations. DMA performs the tasks specified during the upgrade at every step. If you want to abort the upgrade process in the middle of the process, you must recover the (old) database before starting the process again. In contrast, since an upgrade performed with OMU is manual, you have closer control of the upgrade process. You can simply continue to the next step quite readily without needing to recover a database.

Finally, if you use raw devices for storage or use OPS, you must use OMU since DMA does not support these.

Tasks Before an Upgrade or Migration

Before you jump into an upgrade or a migration, you must clearly understand the process that you will use along with the tools that you will use during the process. In addition, there are other considerations, which are discussed in this section.

Understand Available Features

Every new version of Oracle Server includes feature enhancements. Some of these enhancements could impact your existing database or applications. Sometimes an existing feature is obsoleted. In other cases, a new feature allows you to perform a previously complex task more easily. Spend sufficient time understanding the new features of Oracle9i. If you are an experienced DBA, you can refer to *Oracle9i Database New Features Guide* in Oracle documentation.

Here is a list of services and configurations that were available in earlier releases but are no longer supported in Oracle9i:

- Identix and SecureID methods

- NDS External Naming and NDS Authentication

- PROTOCOL.ORA file

- Prespawned Dedicated Servers

- SPX Protocol for Net8

Choose Your Tools and Methodology

Pick the tool(s) that you want to use for the upgrade or migration. Select a methodology that is best suited for your level of experience and situation. If you are unsure which method will give you the most benefits, use DMA. The wizard will guide you through the process and alert you if there are any issues.

Estimate Resources

You must properly estimate the resources required for the upgrade or migration. For example, if you have an existing Oracle8i installation, and you want to upgrade to Oracle9i, you must calculate the incremental disk space and memory required to run both versions of the database during the upgrade. In some situations, the disk space required for the same amount of data can also change because of the upgrade. You might need more disk space to store the same amount of data because of the manner in which the new version manages the data, or, you might need lesser disk space because free space will be recovered during the upgrade. In addition, the Oracle software itself requires incremental space. In fact, on average, a complete installation of Oracle9i Server requires more than three times the space required by Oracle8i Server!

NOTE
You should always ensure that the disk containing the folder for temporary files has sufficient space.

System Tablespace

The System tablespace on Oracle9i requires more space. Ensure that the System tablespace has at least 200MB of free space before you begin the upgrade. Query the DBA_TABLESPACES view to obtain this information, as shown here:

```
SQL> select sum(bytes) from sys.dba_free_space where
tablespace_name='SYSTEM';
SUM(BYTES)
----------
 230961152
```

You can also use OEM to obtain this information. More information on this is included in Chapter 7.

Select an Oracle Home

Major versions of Oracle need to reside in separate Oracle Homes (see the section "Understanding Oracle Home" in Chapter 1). If you have an existing Oracle8/8i installation, you must install Oracle9i into a separate Oracle Home. This will also allow you to keep the old installation in use while testing the new installation. Once you are convinced that the upgrade is successful, you can migrate your users to the new installation and remove the old installation.

Use the Oracle Home Selector utility to switch between coexisting Oracle Homes. This utility ensures that the appropriate environment is created for you. The PATH that is set in the environment is especially critical to JRE. Since most of the utilities provided by Oracle are Java-based, you want to ensure that the right version of JRE is used by the utility. The Oracle Home Selector utility places the proper JRE version in the PATH.

Prepare and Confirm Backup Strategy

Before you begin an upgrade or migration, you must take a full backup of the database. We recommend that you perform a mock recovery to ensure that the backup you have taken allows you to recover your site completely in case your upgrade fails. Analyze the downtime and time for recovery during this mock test. In fact, you should make it a habit to take at least two backups. Too often, DBAs find out that the only backup that they have is corrupted or invalid for some reason. Chapter 5 provides more information on database backups on the Windows NT/2000 platforms.

Prepare Test Plan

Prepare a test plan that you can use to determine if the upgrade or migration was successful. You must ensure that all your data and applications are running smoothly before you switch users to the new installation. The test plan should include load tests, functionality tests, and performance tests. We recommend that you conduct a mock upgrade and test the test plan itself before attempting to migrate a database in use (a production database).

Check Dependencies

An upgrade or migration could impact existing users and applications. Your test plan should include tests for checking such dependencies. Some common dependencies are listed here:

- **Net connections** The client software required for connecting Oracle clients to Oracle servers might need to be upgraded or changed. For example, if the Oracle clients were using the TCP/IP protocol to connect to an Oracle database on a UNIX server, they can now use the Named Pipes protocol to connect to Oracle Server on Windows NT/2000 Server. This requires different software and connection identifiers.

NOTE
Oracle9i does not support Novell's IPX/SPX protocol. In fact, the Internet has made TCP/IP an automatic choice for networking. It is for this reason that you should use TCP/IP for networking. Most software is likely to be well-tested on TCP/IP.

- **Initialization parameters** Some initialization parameters might be obsolete or have new settings. Review the initialization parameters available in the new version and understand the impact of new parameters. One parameter that is of particular interest is the DB_DOMAIN parameter. This parameter had a default value of *WORLD* in earlier releases. In Oracle9i, this is set to *NULL* by default. Set this to *WORLD* to ensure that existing clients do not have to be reconfigured.

- ROWID Some applications use Oracle's internal ROWID (row identifier). The ROWID format could be different in the new version. In this case, the existing applications using ROWID will fail. You can use the built-in package DBMS_ROWID to convert ROWIDs, if necessary.

NOTE
The ROWID format was drastically changed in Oracle8/8i. Make it a habit to refer to the New Features *document in Oracle documentation, and pay special attention to ROWID changes.*

- **Character set** Character sets must be taken into consideration before performing an upgrade. In Oracle9i the NCHAR, NCLOB, and NVARCHAR2 datatypes are encoded only in Unicode (UTF8 or AL16UTF16 character set). If your old database used UTF8 encoding, it will be retained; however, other character sets are changed to AL16UTF16.

■ **Special users** Sometimes, an upgrade can result in a clash of Oracle user (names). For example, Oracle9i creates a special user named OUTLN during the installation. If you already have a user by this name in your database, you must re-create this user and move all database objects to a new schema.

Downtime and User Notifications

Conduct a mock run of the upgrade or migration to estimate the downtime and the impact on users. Users must be provided suitable notice of any downtime and changes that will affect them because of the upgrade. You can take advantage of the unattended installation feature, described in Chapter 2, to perform the upgrade overnight.

Upgrade Path

Determine a suitable upgrade path. There are two upgrade paths available: *direct* and *indirect*. A direct upgrade path allows you to upgrade to the target version directly without an intermediate version. An indirect path requires you to upgrade to an intermediate version and then take the direct path. Table 3-2 lists some common upgrade paths to Oracle9i.

Old Version	Upgrade Path	Summary
8.0.3, 8.0.4 or 8.0.5	Indirect	Upgrade to 8.0.6 using instructions in READMEMIG.DOC file and then use direct upgrade.
8.0.6 or 8.1.x	Direct	Use DMA or Migration Utility.

TABLE 3-2. *Common Upgrade Paths to Oracle9i*

Perform a Database Upgrade

Now that you have sufficient information on the tools and prerequisites for performing an upgrade, you are ready to look at the upgrade process itself. There are three separate methods that can be used for upgrade:

■ Upgrade with DMA

■ Upgrade with Migration Utility

■ Upgrade with Export and Import

More information on each of these methods is provided in the sections that follow.

Upgrade with DMA

DMA is the recommended tool for DBAs. If you have an existing database on an earlier version of Oracle Server, you can upgrade to Oracle9i during the installation using Oracle Universal Installer (OUI).

NOTE
If you have already installed Oracle9i software, you can upgrade an existing database using DMA separately. You can launch DMA from the Start menu by selecting Programs | Oracle – OraHome90 | Configuration and Migration Tools | Data Migration Assistant.

To help you understand the process of upgrade, here is an illustration of a typical upgrade from Oracle Version 8.1.7 to Oracle9i.

1. Launch OUI from the Oracle9i distribution media. When you reach the Welcome screen, click the Installed Products button to view your existing (Oracle8i) installation.

2. Perform a custom installation. Be sure to provide proper target PATH and ORACLE_HOME information. The ORACLE_HOME that you choose must be different from your existing installation (since it is an older version).

NOTE
A custom installation is required since other installation methods precreate a database, which is unnecessary.

3. Choose a database configuration. Select a database configuration that is appropriate for your site. The following illustration shows the General Purpose database selected.

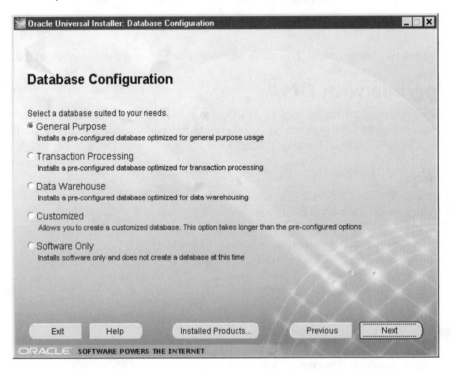

4. Select database for upgrade. OUI automatically detects existing databases on your machine. Choose the database that you want to upgrade. In the example, a database named ORCL8I has been chosen. Be sure to select the check box labeled Upgrade or Migrate an Existing Database, as shown here:

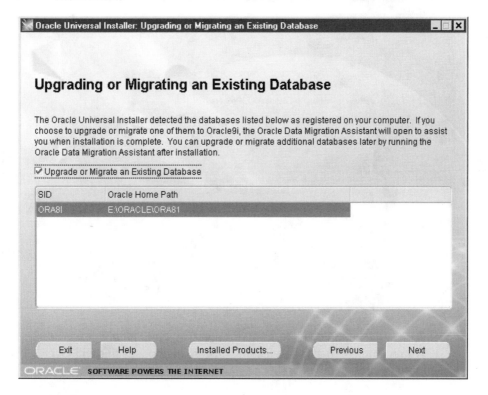

5. Confirm installation options. OUI provides you a summary screen of your installation options. Review the summary screen and click the OK button to begin the installation.

6. Authentication and parameter file. OUI automatically launches DMA after the Oracle9i software installation. You are prompted for the password for the SYS user and the location of the parameter file, as shown here:

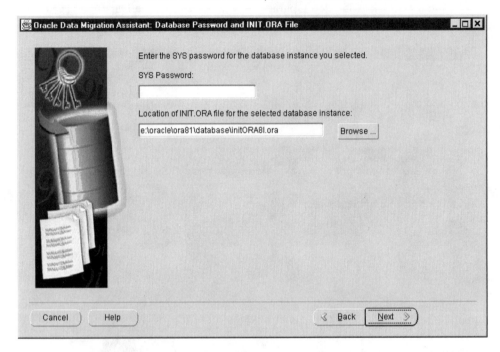

7. Select upgrade method. You are prompted to select an upgrade method. We recommend that you select the custom method, as this will give you more control on the upgrade.

8. Location of database files. You need to specify the location for the new database files. We recommend that you move the database files to a new location under the new ORACLE_HOME. A sample screen is shown here:

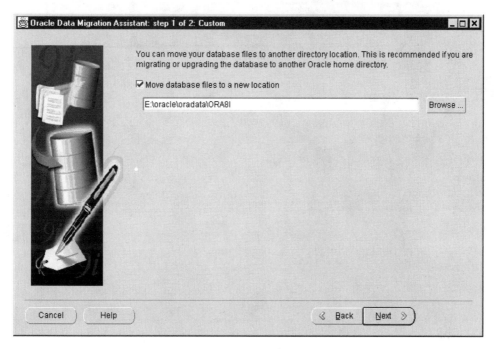

9. Recompile PL/SQL modules. You are prompted to recompile all PL/SQL modules. We recommend that you take this option.

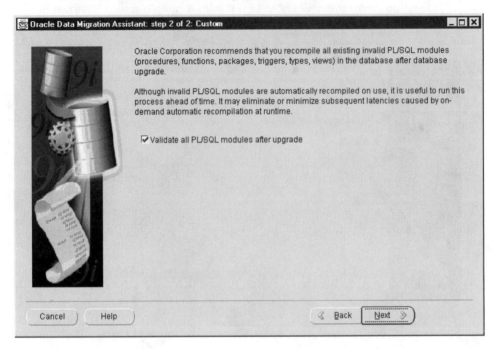

10. Back up the database. You must have a valid backup of the database before you attempt an upgrade. OUI provides you with the option to take a backup. If you already have a valid backup, you can skip the backup. The following illustration provides a sample screen.

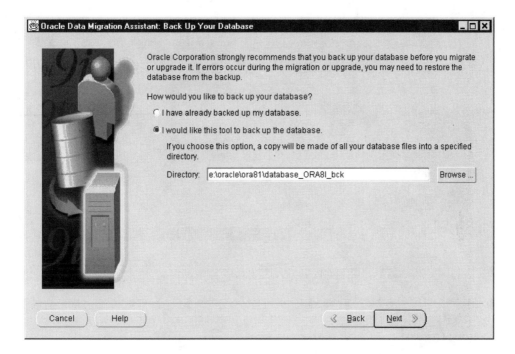

11. Confirm the upgrade options and perform the upgrade. OUI provides a summary screen with your selected options. Review the information and begin the upgrade. You must ensure that there are no users on the database before starting the upgrade. Because DMA automatically shuts down the database using the IMMEDIATE option before beginning the upgrade, existing sessions will be terminated.

12. Complete the upgrade. You see a screen that provides you information on the progress of the upgrade. Once the upgrade is completed, you see a screen that provides you with a log of the upgrade.

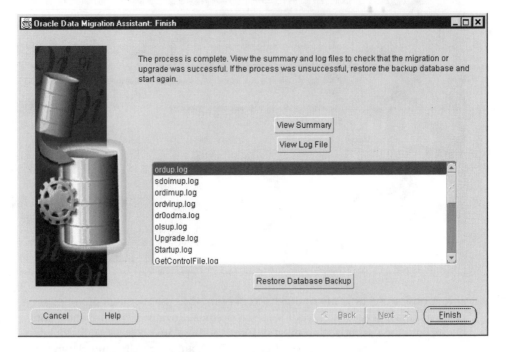

13. Review the log information. If you are satisfied with the installation and upgrade, click the Finish button. Otherwise, you can roll back your upgrade by clicking the Restore Database Backup button. You must correct the problems reported by DMA before repeating the process. DMA reports the problems onscreen.

14. Test the upgrade. Run appropriate tests against the upgraded database to ensure that existing data and applications are intact.

Upgrade Using Migration Utility

You have seen how you can use DMA to perform an automatic upgrade to Oracle9i. In some situations, DMA is unable to complete the upgrade successfully, so you must perform a manual upgrade. Experienced DBAs might also choose to perform a manual upgrade to exercise more control on the upgrade. This section looks at the steps required for a manual upgrade.

1. Perform the Oracle9i installation. You must install Oracle9i Server in a separate ORACLE_HOME using the process documented in Chapter 1. Choose a custom installation and set the appropriate options to complete the installation. In the Database Configuration screen, choose to install the software without any database. Also select the appropriate components for your installation. If you are using OPS, be sure to install the Oracle9i Real Application Cluster component in Oracle9i. If you are using Windows NT, reboot the machine so that the registry settings can take effect. This is not required on Windows 2000 or Windows XP.

2. Shut down the Oracle database. Shut down the database that you are attempting to upgrade. Stop the associated Oracle services from the command prompt, as shown here:

```
C:\>Net Stop OracleServiceORCL (for Windows NT)
C:\>Net Stop Oracle8iORCLAgent (for Windows 2000)
```

You can also use the Services applet to stop these services.

3. Delete Oracle Services. Next, delete the Oracle services for the old version from the command prompt.

```
C:\>ORADIM80-DELETE -SID (for Oracle8)
C:\>ORADIM -DELETE -SID sid (for Oracle8i and Oracle9i)
```

The site identifier for your database is *sid*. The default value for the site identifier is *OracleServiceORCL*.

4. Create the Oracle9i Service. Create a new Oracle service for the Oracle9i database. You will need to use the ORADIM command to do this. An example is shown here.

```
C:\> ORADIM -NEW -SID orcl -INTPWD S3je#0) -MAXUSERS 10 -STARTMODE
auto -PFILE c:\ora90\database\initorcl.ora
```

In this example, *orcl* is the identifier for the new database and *S3je#0)* is the password for an account with SYSDBA privileges. A maximum of 10 users with SYSDBA or SYSOPER privileges is planned. We have also chosen to start this service automatically. The PFILE parameter points to the parameter file.

5. Set the initialization parameters. Edit the parameter file initorcl.ora and provide appropriate settings for database parameters. We recommend that you provide the following settings before you begin the upgrade:

```
JOB_QUEUE_PROCESSES=0
AQ_TM_PROCESSES=0 (only for Advanced Queing option)
```

```
OPTIMIZER_MODE=choose
REMOTE_LOGIN_PASSWORDFILE=none
BACKGROUND_DUMP_DEST= target directory
USER_DUMP_DEST= target directory
COMPATIBLE=8.1.0
```

You can revert to the old values for the previous parameters after completing the upgrade.

6. Start the database in restricted mode. We recommend that you create a spool file to view a log of the scripts.

```
SQL> connect sys as sysdba;
Password: change_on_install
SQL> startup restrict;
SQL> SPOOL upgrade.log
```

If you have any invalid parameters in the parameter file, you will get an error while starting the database. Fix those errors and start the database in restricted mode.

7. Run the upgrade scripts. Oracle provides upgrade scripts that you must run at this time. The upgrade script is typically named using the convention uxxxxxxx.sql, where *xxxxxx* is the existing version number. Table 3-3 lists the upgrade scripts for common Oracle Server versions.

   You must run only one of the scripts even if your upgrade spans multiple versions. Pay attention to the feedback from the execution of the scripts. If you get any errors, fix them and run the upgrade scripts again.

NOTE
Ignore errors with text similar to "error occurred at recursive SQL level 1."

Database Version	Name of Script
8.0.6	u0800060.sql
8.1.5	u0801050.sql
8.1.6	u0801060.sql
8.1.7	u0801070.sql

TABLE 3-3. *Database Upgrade Scripts*

8. Restart the database. Shut down the database using the NORMAL or IMMEDIATE options and restart it. Do not use the ABORT option.

9. Test the upgrade. Run appropriate tests to ensure that the upgrade was successful.

Upgrade Using Export and Import Utilities

You can upgrade to Oracle9i using the traditional Export and Import utilities. This method works for upgrades from Oracle Version 6.0 through Oracle8. While this method can be used to upgrade portions of a database (for example, a specific schema), it is not recommended for full database upgrades, as it can be time-consuming. This section provides an overview of the steps necessary to perform an upgrade using the Export and Import utilities.

1. Take a dump using Export. A consistent dump of the database is required for the upgrade. The following sequence of commands can be used to ensure that the database is consistent and that no users are writing to the database while the export is taken.

```
SQL> shutdown immediate
Database closed.
Database dismounted.
ORACLE instance shut down.
SQL> startup restrict
ORACLE instance started.
Total System Global Area    118255568 bytes
Fixed Size                      282576 bytes
Variable Size                 83886080 bytes
Database Buffers              33554432 bytes
Redo Buffers                    532480 bytes
Database mounted.
Database opened.
SQL> shutdown
Database closed.
Database dismounted.
ORACLE instance shut down.
SQL> startup restrict
ORACLE instance started.
Total System Global Area    118255568 bytes
Fixed Size                      282576 bytes
Variable Size                 83886080 bytes
Database Buffers              33554432 bytes
Redo Buffers                    532480 bytes
```

```
Database mounted.
Database opened.
```

Now export the database using the Export utility. You can export the entire database or only the required portions of the database. To export the entire database, use the FULL=YES option.

```
C:\> exp userid=system/manager file=c:\tmp\expdat.dmp
compress=y full=y log=c:\tmp\exp.log
```

2. Install Oracle9i software. Install Oracle9i software as documented earlier in this chapter by performing a custom installation. Do not create a database during the installation.

3. Import the database. Use the Import utility to import the database from the dump file created in Step 1. If you want to alter the structure of the newly created database, you must precreate the tablespaces and users. You can use the FROM and TO options to change the owner of the database objects.

```
C:\> imp userid=system/manager file=c:\tmp\expdat.dmp full=y
```

Post-Upgrade Tasks

You must complete a few tasks post database upgrade. Some of these tasks are required for all installations. For example, you must take a full backup of the database soon after completing the upgrade. Some others are specific to certain components. For example, Java components require that you run special SQL scripts after completing the upgrade. This section summarizes such tasks.

Back Up Database

Take a full (offline or cold) backup of the database as soon as the upgrade is completed. Shut down the database before taking the backup. The procedure for a cold backup is outlined in Chapter 5. Having a valid backup will allow you to start over from this point in case a problem arises after upgrade.

Change Passwords

Change the passwords of privileged accounts such as SYS and SYSTEM. You can use the ALTER USER command in SQL to accomplish this task.

```
SQL> ALTER USER SYS IDENTIFIED BY xx;
User altered.
SQL> ALTER USER SYSTEM IDENTIFIED BY xx;
User altered.
```

Upgrade NCHAR Columns

Oracle9i uses a different format for columns using the NCHAR datatype available in Oracle8. If you attempt to use existing NCHAR data, you will get an error similar to the one shown here:

```
ORA -12714 Invalid national character set specified
```

To upgrade NCHAR columns (including NCHAR, NVARCHAR2, and NCLOB), you must run the **utlnchar.sql** script, as shown here.

```
SQL> shutdown immediate
SQL> startup restrict
SQL> @c:\oracle\ora90\rdbms\admin\utlnchar.sql
Warning:
The script is to migrate NCHAR data, including nchar
nvarcha2 and nclob, from 8i to 9i.
Once it runs, it cannot undo what has been done.
To run it, 1) use SQLPLUS  and 2) connect AS SYSDBA
Press ctrl-C, then Return to quit or any other key to continue:
SQL> shutdown
SQL> startup
```

NOTE
The output of the UTLNCHAR script is not shown in this sample session as it is too voluminous.

Install Java Component Classes

If you had not installed Java classes in the earlier version, you must do so with Oracle9i. You can do so by running the initjvm.sql script.

```
SQL> shutdown immediate
SQL> startup restrict
SQL> @c:\oracle\ora90\javavm\install\initjvm.sql
SQL> shutdown
SQL> startup
```

Additionally, if you plan to use SQLJ, you must run initsjty.sql. Finally, rebuild any function-based indexes that have become unusable. You can identify such indexes by running the following query:

```
SQL> SELECT owner, index_name from dba_indexes where
funcidx_status = 'DISABLED';
```

Considerations for Replication and OPS

If you are using the Replication or OPS option, you can use DMA, OMU, or Export/ Import to upgrade your database. All *materialized views* (called *snapshots* in Oracle Version 7 and Oracle8) must be refreshed after the upgrade.

To use the replication features of Oracle9i, you must also ensure that all your sites are using at least Oracle8. In particular, primary key materialized views require that both the view site and the master site use at least Oracle8. Additionally, the following restrictions exist:

- Oracle9i materialized view sites can interact only with Version 7.3.3 or higher.

- Oracle9i master sites can interact only with Version 7.3.4 or higher materialized view sites.

- Oracle9i master sites can interact only with Version 7.3.3 or higher master sites.

Upgrade Components

Some Oracle components require other upgrade tasks. This section includes information that will help you upgrade these components.

TIP
Unless mentioned otherwise, all SQL scripts documented in this section must be run using an account with SYSDBA privileges. Also assume that Oracle9i is installed in the c:\oracle\ora90 folder in all examples.

JServer
The JServer component requires a special upgrade script that is located in the c:\oracle\ ora90\javavm\install folder. The script has a name of the format jvmunnn.sql. The *nnn* indicates the version. So, if you are upgrading from Oracle Version 8.1.7 to Oracle9i, run **jvmu817.sql**.

XML Developer's Kit for Java
If you are using the XML Developer's Kit (XDK) component for Java, first upgrade the JServer component. Then, run the appropriate upgrade script from c:\oracle\ ora90\xdk\admin folder. Again, your database must be in restricted mode. The name of the script is version dependent. If you are upgrading from Oracle Version 8.1.7, run **xmlu817.sql**.

Session Namespace, Common Object Request Broker Architecture (CORBA), and Oracle Servlet Engine (OSE)

Upgrade JServer and XDK components before upgrading these components. Also ensure that you have at least 100MB of space for rollback segments to extend. Start the listener and run the upgrade script. Again, the name of the upgrade script is version dependent. Run **jisu817.sql** to upgrade from 8.1.7 to Oracle9i.

Enterprise Java Beans

If you have deployed Enterprise Java Beans (EJB), these cannot be upgraded. EJBs must be deployed again after the upgrade.

Java Server Pages

Upgrade JServer, XDK, Session Namespace, CORBA, and OSE components before upgrading the Java Server Pages component. Run an appropriate upgrade script from c:\oracle\ora90\javavm\install folder. The name of the script is again version dependent. To upgrade from 8.1.7 to Oracle9i, execute **jspu817.sql**.

Oracle Spatial Option

To upgrade from Oracle Version 8.1.x to Oracle9i, you must grant certain privileges to the MDSYS user. Then, connect as the user MDSYS and execute **c81Xu900.sql**.

```
SQL> @c:\oracle\ora90\md\admin\mdprivs.sql
SQL> connect mdsys/mdsys
SQL> @c:\oracle\ora90\md\admin\c81Xu900.sql
```

Oracle Text

To upgrade Oracle Text, you must run two scripts. The first script must be run as a user with SYSDBA privilege, and the second as the user CTXSYS. The names of the script are version dependent. In the following example, the upgrade scripts for Version 8.1.7 are run.

```
SQL> @c:\oracle\ora90\ctx\admin\s080170.sql
SQL> connect ctxsys/ctxsys
SQL> @c:\oracle\ora90\ctx\admin\s090010.sql
```

LRS Data Migration

If you have linear referencing system (LRS) data, you must upgrade the data to Spatial Version 9.0.1 by performing the following steps:

1. Drop any spatial indexes on tables with the linear referencing data.

2. Determine the dimension of the object that has the linear referencing information. For example, if your data has three dimensions (X, Y, and height), the LRS geometry object is 4D, and the LRS dimension in this case is four.

3. Ensure that the data has four-digit SDO_GTYPE values (release 8.1.6 or higher).

4. Update the LRS geometry objects by setting the LRS dimension in the SDO_GTYPE field. Two examples are shown here:

   ■ **Example 1** The LRS dimension is three for the geometries in a column named GEOMETRY in the LRS_DATA table. Update the SDO_GTYPE using the following SQL:

   ```
   UPDATE LRS_DATA a SET a.geometry.sdo_gtype =
   a.geometry.sdo_gtype + 300;
   ```

   ■ **Example 2** The LRS dimension is four for the geometries in a column named GEOMETRY of the LRS_DATA table. Update the SDO_GTYPE as follows:

   ```
   UPDATE LRS_DATA a SET a.geometry.sdo_gtype =
   a.geometry.sdo_gtype + 400;
   ```

Oracle interMedia

Data Migration Assistant automatically detects and upgrades the Oracle interMedia component. If the upgrade has failed, you can manually upgrade Oracle interMedia using the information provided in the file c:\oracle\ora90\ord\im\admin\readme.txt.

Oracle Label Security

Oracle Label Security (a component of Trusted Oracle) needs one upgrade script to be run from the c:\oracle\ora90\rdbms\admin folder. This script has a name of the format olsunnn.sql, where *nnn* is the version number. For example, run the script **olsu817.sql** to upgrade Label Security from Version 8.1.7 to Oracle9i.

RAC

If you are upgrading to an Oracle9i database configured for RAC, you must set the CLUSTER_DATABASE parameter to *FALSE* before running the upgrade script.

```
CLUSTER_DATABASE=FALSE
```

Now run the script **catclust.sql** from the c:\oracle\ora90\rdbms\admin folder to add required schema objects for RACs. Earlier releases of Oracle Server did not have this feature.

Materialized Views

Materialized views were called snapshots in Oracle8. To upgrade from Oracle8, you must grant privileges, as shown here:

```
GRANT QUERY REWRITE TO owner
```

Alternatively, you can grant the QUERY REWRITE privilege globally using the GRANT GLOBAL QUERY REWRITE command. Next, issue the ALTER MATERIALIZED VIEW command for each materialized view being upgraded. For example, the following statement upgrades a materialized view named SORDERS.

```
ALTER MATERIALIZED VIEW sorders ENABLE QUERY REWRITE;
```

If you have many materialized views in your database, you can construct a SQL script by querying the dictionary and run this script to accomplish this task. The following sample session illustrates this little trick:

```
SQL> set head off
SQL> spool test.sql
SQL> select 'alter materialized view '||owner || '.'|| mview_name || '
enable query rewrite;' from all_mviews;
alter materialized view PORTAL30_DEMO.EMP_SNAPSHOT enable query rewrite;
alter materialized view SCOTT.EMP_SNAPSHOT enable query rewrite;
SQL> spool off
```

Edit the **test.sql** file in a text editor and strip the unnecessary lines before running the script.

Advanced Queuing Option

You need to upgrade Advanced Queuing (AQ) tables to use the following new (AQ) features in Oracle9i:

■ Addition of the original message ID column for propagated messages

■ Addition of a sender's ID column

■ Queue- and system-level privileges

■ Rule-based subscriptions

■ Separate storage of history

To upgrade an existing queue table, use the MIGRATE_QUEUE_TABLE procedure. For example, to upgrade a queue table named *tb.queue*, execute the procedure as shown here:

```
EXECUTE dbms_aqadm.migrate_queue_table (queue_table =>
'scott.tb_queue', compatible => '8.1');
```

To create a new queue table that is compatible with release 8.1 and higher, connect as the owner of the queue table and run the DBMS_AQADM.CREATE_QUEUE_TABLE procedure, specifying 8.1 for the COMPATIBLE option, as in the following example:

```
EXECUTE dbms_aqadm.create_queue_table(
    queue_table => 'scott.tkaqqtpeqt',
    queue_payload_type =>'message',
    sort_list => 'priority,enq_time',
    multiple_consumers => true,
    comment => 'Creating queue with priority and enq_time sort order',
compatible => '8.1');
```

You must have the AQ_ADMINISTRATOR_ROLE to upgrade AQ tables.

Compatibility Between Releases

Sometimes, features available in the newer version of the database after an upgrade can break an existing application. In such a situation it is necessary to get the behavior of an older version of Oracle Server. You can achieve this behavior by setting the COMPATIBLE parameter in the parameter file. By default, this parameter is set to the lowest possible setting for that release. So, the COMPATIBLE parameter has a default value of 8.0 for Oracle8i and 8.1.0 for Oracle9i. These are the lowest possible settings for Oracle8i and Oracle9i. You can use the features available in the new release only if you set this parameter to a higher value.

To check the current setting for this parameter, query the V$PARAMETER view as shown here:

```
SQL> SELECT name, value, description FROM v$parameter where
name = 'compatible';
NAME       VALUE      DESCRIPTION
----       -----      -----------
compatible  8.1.0      Database will be completely compatible
                       with this software version
```

You can also check the compatibility level of specific features of the database by querying the V$COMPATIBILITY view. For example, on our sample database, the queue tables feature behaves like Oracle8 Version 8.1.0 as shown in the following query:

```
SQL> select * from v$compatibility where description like
'Advanced Queueing queue%';
QUETABLE 8.1.0.0.0
Advanced Queueing queue tables
```

Before changing the COMPATIBLE parameter, take a full database backup. This allows you to revert back to the earlier version in case your database gets corrupted. You must issue the ALTER DATABASE command if you change compatibility, as shown here:

```
SQL> ALTER DATABASE RESET COMPATIBILITY;
```

This command instructs the database that you want to change the compatibility to a lower release. Oracle Server checks the compatibility level of each feature. If a feature has a compatibility level higher than the compatibility level specified by the COMPATIBLE parameter in the initialization parameter then Oracle fails to open and displays an ORA-402 error message, as illustrated here:

```
ORA-00402: database changes by release 8.1.0.0.0 cannot be used
by release 8.0.0.0.0
ORA-00405: compatibility type "New Image Format"
```

Compatibility Settings for Oracle Features

Many features have been added since Oracle8 Server, Version 8.1. Table 3-4 lists the Oracle Server features that require a compatibility setting of 9.0 or higher.

Functional Area	Feature
Tablespaces	Automatic segment-space managed Tablespaces default temporary tablespaces Automatic undo managed tablespaces
Tables	External tables

TABLE 3-4. *Features Requiring Compatibility Level of 9.0 or Higher*

Functional Area	Feature
Index-organized tables	Hash-partitioned index-organized tables Index-organized tables with mapping tables Large Objects (LOBs) in range-partitioned index-organized tables
Indexes	B-tree indexes on UROWID datatypes for heap- and index-organized tables Bitmap indexes for index-organized tables Domain indexes on index-organized tables Indexes with large keys
Hash clusters	Single-table hash clusters
Length semantics	Semantics for the sizing of CHAR and VARCHAR2 datatypes
LOBs	API for LOBs
Aggregate functions	User-defined aggregate functions
Object types	Type evolution
Type inheritance	Columns of nonfinal types
VARRAYs	Support in range-partitioned index-organized tables
Security	External initialized context
Oracle replication	Adding master sites to a master group without quiescing the master group Adding columns to a master table without quiescing its master group Replication of user-defined types and objects based on user-defined types in both multimaster and materialized view replication environments Row-level dependency tracking for improved parallel propagation (the ROWDEPENDENCIES clause in a CREATE TABLE statement) Fast refresh of materialized views with one-to-many or many-to-many subqueries Fast refresh of materialized views with a UNION operator Multi-tier materialized views

TABLE 3-4. *Features Requiring Compatibility Level of 9.0 or Higher* (continued)

Functional Area	Feature
SQL and PL/SQL	Nested transactions Pipelined table functions Parallel table functions
Constraints	View constraints
Summary management using materialized views	Support in index-organized tables

TABLE 3-4. *Features Requiring Compatibility Level of 9.0 or Higher* (continued)

Parameter File Considerations

Initialization parameters vary slightly on each version of Oracle Server. New parameters might be added, and some might get dropped. In some cases, the default setting for a parameter might have changed. It is important to consider the impact of changes in parameter settings when you perform an upgrade. This section highlights some changes in initialization parameters of Oracle9i.

DB_BLOCK_CHECKSUM

Oracle Server can detect corruption at the database block level. To enable this feature, set the DB_BLOCK_CHECKSUM parameter to *TRUE*. If you do so, a checksum is calculated from the number of bytes stored in the block and written to the database block header. The checksum is used to determine if a block is corrupted. The default setting for this parameter is *TRUE* in Oracle9i. This is because this feature adds only 1%–2% overhead on performance. The default value was *FALSE* in earlier versions. A checksum is maintained for database blocks belonging to the SYSTEM tablespace regardless of the setting for this parameter.

JOB_QUEUE_PROCESS

This setting defines the maximum number of job queue processes that an Oracle instance can spawn. While the default setting in earlier versions was 36, the setting in Oracle9i is 1,000. The replication and advanced queuing features are implemented using jobs. User jobs can be defined with the DBMS_JOB utility.

LOG_CHECKPOINT_TIMEOUT

Use this parameter to control the maximum amount of time a dirty buffer will be maintained in the database block buffer cache. The default value in Oracle9i is 1,800 seconds, while earlier releases defaulted to 0.

07_DICTIONARY_ACCESSIBILITY

This parameter controls Oracle Server's data dictionary behavior. On earlier versions, this parameter was set to *TRUE,* meaning that the data dictionary behaved like Oracle Version 7.0. In Oracle9i, the default value is *FALSE.*

DB_DOMAIN

The default value of this parameter was *WORLD* in earlier versions. In Oracle9i, this parameter is set to *NULL.* Existing Oracle clients will have to be reconfigured after upgrade. To avoid reconfiguring Oracle clients, you can add this parameter to the parameter file and retain the old setting of *WORLD.*

Parallel Execution

If the parameter PARALLEL_AUTOMATIC_TUNING is set to *TRUE* then the parallel execution message buffers are allocated from the large pool. In the previous releases (before Oracle Version 8.1), this was allocated from the shared pool. So, instead of increasing the size of the shared pool (defined by the SHARED_POOL_SIZE parameter), you should increase the size of the large pool (using the LARGE_POOL_SIZE parameter) in Oracle9i.

NOTE
The size of the large pool is determined by the settings for the following parameters:

- *PARALLEL_MAX_SERVERS*
- *PARALLEL_THREADS_PER_CPU*
- *PARALLEL_SERVER_INSTANCES*
- *MTS_DISPATCHERS*
- *DBWR_IO_SLAVES*

If PARALLEL_AUTOMATIC_TUNING is unset or set to *FALSE,* and you do not provide a setting for the LARGE_POOL_SIZE parameter, the large pool defaults to 0.

Archive Log Destination

These initialization parameters can be used to define destination folders for archive log groups. The parameters LOG_ARCHIVE_DEST_*n* and LOG_ARCHIVE_DEST_STATE_*n* have replaced LOG_ARCHIVE_DEST and LOG_ARCHIVE_DUPLEX_DEST in earlier releases.

Coexistence of Oracle8/8i and 9i

You can install Oracle8/8i and Oracle9i on the same machine; however, each version must be installed in a separate Oracle Home. This is especially beneficial during the process of upgrading itself. You can leave the Oracle8/8i installation running while you upgrade to Oracle9i. Once you confirm that the upgrade is completed, you can move your users to Oracle9i.

Database Migration

Sometimes, you will face a situation where you need to move a database to another machine. A database can be re-created (by moving or copying) on another machine. This process is called *migration*. The migration can also occur across operating systems.

Migration to Another Machine Using the Same Operating System

You can migrate a database to another machine using the same operating system in two ways: using export and import, and restoring a backup.

In the first method, use the Export utility to create a full dump of the database. Copy the file to the target machine and use the Import utility to re-create the database from the dump file. The procedure is similar to the one outlined in the section "Upgrading Using Export and Import Utilities" earlier in this chapter. The advantage of using this method is that you can restructure the database (define different structure for tablespaces and datafiles). You can also change ownership of objects using this method.

You can also upgrade the database from one version to another during the migration using Export and Import. For example, you can export an Oracle8i database and migrate it to Oracle9i on another machine.

In the second method, you can use an available (full) backup of the database and restore it on a new machine. You cannot modify the structure (tablespace and datafile definitions) of the database; however, the physical locations of the datafiles can be changed with some manual intervention. The ALTER DATABASE RENAME DATAFILE command must be used to accomplish this. Chapter 5 provides more information on this topic. This method does not allow you to change your database version during migration.

NOTE
You must use Export and Import if you want to modify the file system on Windows NT/2000 (FAT to NTFS or vice versa). This is because the file formats for FAT and NTFS are different.

Migration to Windows NT/2000 from Another Operating System

Many medium-sized sites have chosen Windows NT/2000 as their platform in the last couple of years. Companies that had invested significantly in RISC-based systems have moved to the Windows NT/2000 platform in an attempt to minimize increasing costs for hardware and management.

If you need to migrate (and/or upgrade) an Oracle Server to Windows NT/2000, you must use the Export and Import utilities. Other methods cannot be used because of differences in operating system file formats. The major steps for the migration are listed here:

1. Back up the old (existing) database.

2. Start up your database in restricted mode.

3. Export the database. Use the FULL=Y option to export the entire database; otherwise, export specific users.

4. Install Oracle9i on the (new) Windows NT/2000 Server.

5. Transfer the dump file from step 2 to the Windows Server using a network utility such as FTP. Be sure to transfer the file in *binary* mode. You will get an invalid dump file (with CTRL-M's) if you do not transfer the file in binary mode.

6. Import the database into Oracle9i on NT/2000.

NOTE
If you want to upgrade the database while migrating from another operating system to Windows, you must use native Export and Import utilities. For example, if you have an existing Oracle8 database on Linux and you want to migrate and upgrade it to Oracle9i on Windows 2000, use Linux Export Version 8 to create the dump file and use Oracle9i Import on Windows 2000 to import the database. In general, Import can be used to import dump files created from the same or lower version of Export.

CAUTION
There is a feature named transportable tablespace
*in Oracle Server. This feature can be used only
between two databases of the same version on the
same operating system. Transportable tablespaces
are discussed in Chapter 5.*

Downgrading to Oracle8i

Oracle9i also allows you to downgrade to Oracle8i. Why would you want to
downgrade? Some rare situations in which you might want to downgrade an
Oracle9i database to Oracle8i are listed here:

■ You were unable to successfully complete the end-to-end upgrade of
Oracle Server on your site in the given timeframe, and you have to roll
back to an earlier version.

■ You have encountered a bug in Oracle9i that forces you to go back to
Oracle8i until Oracle can provide a fix.

■ An existing application(s) has stopped working in Oracle9i.

■ Your site cannot provide the increased resources required for Oracle9i,
and you are not using any of the new features available in Oracle9i.

■ You are using a third-party software or application that does not work
with Oracle9i.

■ You are facing an interoperability issue in a replicated environment
between an Oracle9i database and an older version.

You can avoid a downgrade situation by performing thorough tests before you
upgrade to Oracle9i. In any case, if you are downgrading from Oracle9i, there is a
fairly compelling reason to do so!
The broad steps that you will need to perform to downgrade from Oracle9i to
Oracle8i are

1. Back up the database.

2. Remove incompatibilities.

3. Reset the compatibility level.

4. Downgrade the database.

We will provide information on performing a downgrade next.

Back Up the Database

Before you attempt to downgrade, take a full (cold or offline) backup using the procedures defined in Chapter 5. Of course, if you have a valid backup of your data and applications from Oracle8*i* days, you are probably better off restoring this instead of downgrading from Oracle9*i*.

Remove Incompatibilities

Check the compatibility level of your database. If it is lower or equal to the existing setting for the COMPATIBLE initialization parameter, you can ignore this step. Otherwise, follow these steps to remove incompatibilities before downgrading:

1. Check the current setting for the COMPATIBLE parameter. To check the COMPATIBLE level of your database, issue the following SQL statement:

```
SQL> SELECT name, value, description FROM v$parameter
WHERE name= 'compatible';
NAME      VALUE      DESCRIPTION
-------   ---------  ----------------------
compatible   8.1.7    Database will be completely
                       compatible with this software version
```

2. Identify incompatibilities. To identify any incompatibilities that might exist with the release to which you are downgrading, query the V$COMPATIBILTY view as shown here:

```
SQL> SELECT * FROM v$compatibility WHERE release
!= '0.0.0.0.0';
```

For your reference, a fragment of the output from the SQL statement is included here:

```
DROPCOL  8.1.0.0.0
Drop Column
QUETABLE 8.1.0.0.0
Advanced Queueing queue tables
SUMMARY  8.1.0.0.0
Summary
```

Note the values reported in the column named RELEASE. Any feature that has a value that is higher than your planned downgrade will result in incompatibility.

3. Removing the identified incompatibilities. The tasks that you perform to remove a specific incompatibility depend on the feature. The tasks for some common features are summarized here. To save space, the sample outputs from all scripts have been left out.

   Discontinue the use of automatic segment-space managed tablespaces. Query the DBA_TABLESPACES view to get information on such tablespaces.

```
SQL> SELECT tablespace_name FROM dba_tablespaces WHERE
segment_space_management = 'AUTO';
```

4. Next, discontinue the use of automatic undo managed tablespaces. You can identify such tablespaces using the following query:

```
SQL> SELECT tablespace_name FROM dba_tablespaces WHERE
contents = 'UNDO';
```

5. Drop all external tables before the downgrade. The following query can be used to identify external tables:

```
SQL> SELECT o.name AS TABLE_NAME, u.name AS TABLE_OWNER
FROM  sys.user$ u, sys.obj$ o, sys.tab$ t WHERE t.obj# = o.obj#
AND o.owner# = u.user# AND BITAND(t.property, 2147483648) != 0;
```

6. Next, drop all bitmap secondary indexes on index-organized tables. Such indexes can be identified using the following query:

```
SQL> SELECT index_name, i.owner, t.table_name FROM dba_indexes i,
dba_tables t WHERE i.index_type = 'BITMAP' AND i.table_name =
t.table_name AND t.owner = i.table_owner AND t.iot_type = 'IOT';
```

7. Rebuild index-organized tables without mapping after dropping all bitmap secondary indexes on nonpartitioned and partitioned index-organized tables. To identify the index-organized tables with mapping, use the following SQL query:

```
SQL> SELECT owner, iot_name FROM dba_tables WHERE
iot_type = 'IOT_MAPPING';
```

8. Use the ALTER TABLE command to rebuild these tables. Here is an example for a table named *iot:*

```
SQL> ALTER TABLE iot MOVE NOMAPPING;
```

9. You must drop all B-tree indexes on heap and index-organized tables in your database. In order to identify the B-tree indexes issue the following query:

```
SQL> SELECT index_owner, index_name FROM dba_ind_columns ic,
dba_tab_columns tc WHERE tc.data_type = 'UROWID' AND
tc.table_name = ic.table_name AND tc.column_name = ic.column_name;
```

10. You must drop indexes with large keys in your database before you downgrade. To identify such indexes, issue the following query:

```
SQL> SELECT u.name, o.name, i.flags FROM sys.obj$ o, sys.user$ u,
sys.ind$ i where u.user# = o.owner# AND o.obj# = i.obj# AND
BITAND(i.flags, 16384) !=0;
```

11. Discontinue the use of all hash-partitioned index-organized tables in your database. The following query will provide you with a list of such tables:

```
SQL> SELECT t.owner, t.table_name FROM dba_tables t, dba_part_tables
p WHERE t.table_name = p.table_name AND t.owner = p.owner AND
t.iot_type = 'IOT' AND t.partitioned = 'YES' AND
p.partitioning_type = 'HASH';
```

Discontinue the use of the following data types before you downgrade:

- TIMESTAMP
- TIMESTAMP WITH TIME ZONE
- TIMESTAMP WITH LOCAL TIME ZONE
- INTERVAL YEAR TO MONTH
- INTERVAL DAY TO SECOND

Use the ALTER TABLE command to modify columns using these data types.

12. If you are using LOB columns in partitioned index-organized tables, you must modify these columns. The following query can be used to identify such columns:

```
SQL> SELECT column_name, t.owner, t.table_name FROM dba_lobs l,
dba_tables t WHERE l.table_name = t.table_name AND l.owner =
t.owner AND t.iot_type = 'IOT' AND t.partitioned = 'YES';
```

13. Drop all user-defined aggregate functions before you downgrade to release 8.1.7 or lower. To identify the user-defined aggregate functions, issue the following SQL statement:

```
SQL> SELECT procedure_name FROM dba_procedures WHERE
aggregate = 'YES';
```

14. Drop all evolved types and their dependent types and tables. You can identify such types using the following SQL statement:

```
SQL> SELECT UNIQUE owner, type_name FROM dba_types
WHERE version_name != '$8.0';
```

15. Discontinue the use of subtypes and nonfinal types in tables. Use the following query to identify such types:

```
SQL> SELECT c.name AS COLUMN_NAME, o.name AS TABLE_NAME, u.name
AS TABLE_OWNER FROM user$ u, sys.obj$ o, sys.col$ c,
sys.coltype$ ct, sys.type$ t WHERE u.user# = o.owner# AND
o.obj# = c.obj# AND c.obj# = ct.obj# AND c.intcol# = ct.intcol#
 and ct.toid = t.toid AND o.type# = 2
AND BITAND(t.properties,  3153928) > 0;
```

Additionally, there are some SQL and PL/SQL downgrading issues. For example, pipelined table functions and parallel table functions cannot be used in Oracle8i. You must also drop all view-related primary keys and foreign key constraints.

Reset the Compatibility Level

Reset the compatibility level of the database using the following steps:

1. Connect as a user with SYSDBA privilege.

2. Remove any initialization parameters that are specific to Oracle9i.

3. Start the database in restricted session mode.

4. Run the c:\oracle\ora90\rdbms\admin\utlpitl.sql script.

5. Issue the ALTER DATABASER RESET COMPATIBILITY command.

6. Shut down the database using NORMAL or IMMEDIATE options.

7. Set the COMPATIBLE initialization parameter to match the release to which you are downgrading.

8. Open the database.

NOTE
If there are any remaining incompatibilities, the database will fail to open. You will need to fix the error reported onscreen when you attempt to open the database and try again.

Downgrade the Database

After verifying the compatibility of your database with the downgraded release, perform the following steps:

1. Connect as the user SYS or any other user who has SYSDBA privileges.

2. Copy the following files from the c:\oracle\ora90\rdbms\admin folder of the release from which you are downgrading to another location:

   ■ utlip.sql

   ■ utlrp.sql

3. Copy one or more of the following files from the c:\oracle\ora90\ javavm\install folder of the release from which you are downgrading to another directory:

   ■ jvmd815.sql (if you are downgrading to release 8.1.5)

   ■ jvmd816.sql (if you are downgrading to release 8.1.6)

   ■ jvmd817.sql, jisd817.sql, jspd817.sql (if you are downgrading to release 8.1.7)

4. Start the database in restricted session mode.

5. Run the appropriate downgrade script from the c:\oracle\ora90\rdbms\ admin folder. The name of the downgrade script is version dependent. For example, the downgrade script to downgrade from Oracle9i to Oracle8 Version 8.1.7 is named d0801070.sql.

6. Shut down the instance normally.

7. Stop all the Oracle services, including the Oracle Service SID of the database you are downgrading, and delete them, as shown below:

```
C:\> NET STOP OracleServiceORCL
C:\> ORADIM -DELETE -SID ORCL
```

8. Install the release to which you are downgrading using the media for that release in a separate Oracle Home.

9. Using the ORADIM utility, create the new Oracle database services.

```
C :\> ORADIM -NEW -SID SID -INTPWD PASSWORD -MAXUSERS USERS
-STARTMODE AUTO -PFILE ORACLE_HOME\DATABASE\INITSID.ORA
```

10. Export the server parameter file to create a traditional initialization parameter file.

```
CREATE PFILE [=pfile -name] [FROM spfile -name]
```

11. Start up the database in restricted mode and run the **utlip.sql** SQL script saved in step 2.

12. Run the **catalog.sql, catproc.sql,** and **catrep.sql** scripts.

13. Run the **catparr.sql** script if you have Oracle Parallel Server installed.

14. Run the appropriate downgrade for JVM.

```
SQL> @ORACLE_HOME/javavm/install/jvmd816.sql
```

15. Run the **utlrp.sql** script saved in step 2. This step is optional but recommended.

16. Shut down the database normally and restart.

This chapter touched on topics related to upgrades, migration, and downgrades. You should perform several mock tests to ensure that all the issues are understood and resolved for your site before moving a production database.

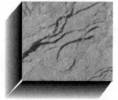

CHAPTER
4

Creating Oracle9i
Databases

I n the first three chapters of this book, you have learned how to perform standard installations and upgrades to Oracle9i. While such installations are sufficient for many sites, many others require customized databases to meet specific needs within the organization. Being highly customizable, Oracle9i allows an experienced DBA to tweak the database for special needs. This chapter provides information to help you create customized databases.

Planning a Database

Much research and planning is necessary before creating a custom-built database. You must collect data to help you determine the size and growth rate of your database to ensure that sufficient hardware resources are allocated. You must decide how the database will be logically organized (tablespaces, schemas, and so on). To determine the amount of disk space necessary for the database, consider all the space requirements for data, rollback segments, redo log groups, archived log files, temporary tablespaces, and so on. The number of users and sessions, the length and size of transactions, and so on will help you size the *system global area* (SGA). A well-thought-out plan will make the database creation process easier and avoid a situation in which you have to rebuild a database to cope with changing business needs. Following are some important tasks to complete before creating a database:

Create a list of database objects you need such as tables, indexes, synonyms, clusters, and sequences, along with their sizes. Organize them by the schema that owns them, and group them into tablespaces. Compute the amount of space required by these objects. For example, for a table, you need to determine or estimate the following:

- Number of rows
- List of columns, their data types, and column width
- Average size of a row in bytes
- How many rows will be added/modified in a day/week/month
- Associated indexes

You can get an approximate starting size for the table by multiplying the estimated number of rows by the average row size. Create the table with storage parameters to suit the size and growth rate. Ensure that fewer extents are allocated for the table to avoid fragmentation.

Determine how many indexes will be created for the table and the space required for these. For better performance, plan on creating the indexes in a separate tablespace and store the data files for this tablespace on a separate physical disk.

■ Estimate the size and rate at which you expect the database to grow.

■ Obtain a list of users and transactions for each table and estimate how many rows will be added to the table. Determine the growth rate of the associated indexes.

■ Plan the physical structure of the database. Distribute data files and log files across available disks to improve performance. If there are other databases on the same machine, ensure that the files belonging to these other databases are not overwritten. Use the Optimal Flexible Architecture (OFA) model, since it is designed to avoid such issues.

■ Create a list of databases required, the machines where these databases will reside, and the unique identifiers for these databases on the network. Assign a unique global database name by fixing values for the DB_NAME and DB_DOMAIN parameters. Remember that every database must have a unique name on the network.

■ Choose a suitable database character set. If your site has clients that use different character sets, choose a character superset that includes all the character sets that you anticipate your client machines will use.

■ Choose the block size for your database. The database block size is set using the DB_BLOCK_SIZE parameter. The specified block size is used by default for all tablespaces including the SYSTEM tablespace that is formed during database creation; however, you can override the database block size when you create other tablespaces. Once a tablespace is created, it is impossible to modify the block size without rebuilding the tablespace. Of course, you will have to re-create the database if you want to modify the block size for the SYSTEM tablespace.

■ Instead of using conventional rollback segments, consider using an undo tablespace to manage undo records. Rollback segments are much harder to manage since it is difficult to predict their size requirements. Additionally, database recovery is more complex if active rollback segments are involved. Undo tablespaces are designed for undo records and are managed by Oracle Server without necessitating DBA intervention.

■ Design strategies for backup and recovery of your database. Suitable choices for archiving and multiplexing (for control files and redo logfiles) must be made. Decide whether or not you want to run the database in ARCHIVELOG mode. Additional storage planning is required for archive log files.

■ Ensure that sufficient system resources are available on the machine prior to creating the database. In addition to the disk space required for your database, we recommend a minimum of 256MB of RAM for each Oracle instance on Windows NT/2000 Servers. To ensure redundancy, use multiple disks to maintain redo log groups and control files. Data files must be striped across disks to improve performance. A RAID configuration is highly recommended.

Before going into the process of creating an Oracle9i database, the next two sections introduce Oracle Server's initialization parameters and the OFA.

Initialization Parameters

Several settings are used by Oracle9i Server to determine the run-time resources for the database. These settings are provided by *initialization parameters* and are stored in the *parameter file*. This file is also commonly referred to as the INIT.ORA file in Oracle documentation.

NOTE
The name of the initialization parameter file is of the form init<SID>.ora. *So if your database is named PROD, the default name for the parameter file would be* initprod.ora.

Every database must have a unique parameter file associated with it. Prior to creating the database, create a suitable parameter file. Oracle9i Server provides a sample parameter file with the installation (a file named initsmpl.ora in the c:\oracle\ora90\admin\sample\pfile\ folder). It is best to begin by making your own copy of the sample parameter file, and make appropriate changes. The sample file provides typical settings for small, medium, and large databases. You can pick a set of recommended settings for initialization parameters based on the size of your database; however, you need to make a few changes before you create a database using the newly created parameter file. Information on important parameters is provided next.

Static versus Dynamic Parameters

Parameters in the INIT.ORA file are classified as *static* or *dynamic*. Static parameters are those that require the database to be restarted if the parameter setting is altered. In contrast, dynamic parameters do not require a restart of the database. You can change settings for static parameters by modifying the parameter file in a text editor. Dynamic parameters can be altered with the ALTER SYSTEM command.

NOTE
In earlier releases of Oracle Server, the parameter file was always in a text-only file; however, Oracle9i also supports a binary parameter file referred to as the Server Parameter File. If you are using a binary parameter file, settings modified with the ALTER SYSTEM command are written to the parameter file automatically. This ensures that the setting is preserved when the database is restarted. If you are using a textual parameter file, you must ensure that the change made with the ALTER SYSTEM command is also made in the parameter file. If you fail to do this, the changed settings are lost when the database is restarted because Oracle Server reads the INIT.ORA for settings at startup. Table 4-1 (later in this chapter) summarizes the behavior of the ALTER SYSTEM command.

Server Parameter File

Oracle Server has traditionally used a text file to read initialization parameters at startup. The new Server Parameter File (SPFILE) feature in Oracle9i is a binary form of the parameter file.

A SPFILE can be thought of as a repository for initialization parameters that is maintained on the same machine that is running Oracle Server (textual INIT.ORA files can also reside on the client machine if you are starting the database remotely). Initialization parameters stored in an SPFILE are persistent. Any changes made to the parameters while an instance is running will persist across instance shutdown and startup. This eliminates the need to manually update initialization parameters whenever the ALTER SYSTEM command is issued to change an initialization parameter. It also provides a basis for self-tuning.

An SPFILE is automatically created when you use Database Configuration Assistant (DCA) to create a database. If an SPFILE is not available, you can use the CREATE SPFILE command to build a SPFILE from the INIT.ORA for your database. Oracle Server provides means to view and modify parameter settings.

CAUTION
Although the SPFILE appears readable in a text editor, do not edit it manually. This will corrupt the file and you will not be able to start the instance.

At instance startup, Oracle Server attempts to read the SPFILE from an operating system–specific location (c:\oracle\ora90\database folder). You can also explicitly provide this location by setting the SPFILE parameter. If you prefer to use the traditional textual form of the parameter file, you can use the PFILE clause while starting up the instance. More information on database startup is included in Chapter 5.

Create an SPFILE

The SPFILE must be created from a traditional text initialization parameter file prior to issuing the database startup command. It can be created using the CREATE SPFILE command. You must have SYSDBA or SYSOPER system privilege to execute this command.

The following sample session creates an SPFILE from the (text) initialization parameter file named init.ora.

```
SQL> connect sys/change_on_install as sysdba;
Connected to an idle instance.
SQL> create spfile from pfile='c:\oracle\admin\aa\pfile\init.ora';
File created.
SQL> startup
ORACLE instance started.
Total System Global Area  218918824 bytes
Fixed Size                   282536 bytes
Variable Size             184549376 bytes
Database Buffers           33554432 bytes
Redo Buffers                 532480 bytes
Database mounted.
Database opened.
```

If you do not provide an explicit name for the SPFILE, a file with the name spfile$ORACLE_SID is automatically created in the c:\oracle\ora90\database folder. You can also explicitly set the name for the SPFILE, as shown in this example:

```
SQL> CREATE SPFILE='c:\oracle\ora90\database\test_spfile.ora'
  FROM PFILE='c:\oracle\ora91\database\init.ora';
```

Note that the SPFILE is always created on the machine running Oracle Server. If an SPFILE of the same name already exists, it is overwritten with the new information. When the SPFILE is created from the initialization parameter file, comments included on the same lines as a parameter setting are preserved. All other comments are ignored.

The CREATE SPFILE command can be executed before or after instance startup; however, if the instance has been started using an SPFILE, and you attempt to re-create the same SPFILE that is currently being used by the instance, an error is reported. The Oracle executable (**oracle.exe**) holds a file lock on the SPFILE when the database is open.

SPFILE Initialization Parameter

The initialization parameter SPFILE is used by Oracle Server to locate the SPFILE. You can override the default setting by explicitly setting this parameter. You can use the SQL command SHOW PARAMETERS SPFILE to determine the current setting for this parameter.

NOTE
The default SPFILE is created in the c:\oracle\oradata\ folder.

CAUTION
The SPFILE parameter can be thought of as equivalent to the IFILE parameter. While the IFILE parameter points to other textual files to be included in the parameter file, the SPFILE is exclusively for the binary SPFILE. Do not use IFILE for the SPFILE.

Migrating to an SPFILE

If you are currently using a traditional textual initialization parameter file, use the following steps to migrate to an SPFILE:

1. If the initialization parameter file is located on a client machine, transfer the file to the server using appropriate copy or file transfer commands from the command prompt or Windows Explorer.

2. Create an SPFILE using the CREATE SPFILE command and a utility such as SQL*Plus. The database does not have to be running to issue a CREATE SPFILE command.

3. Start up the instance using the newly created SPFILE.

Changing Initialization Parameter Values

The ALTER SYSTEM command allows you to set, change, or delete (restore to default value) initialization parameter values. The SCOPE clause can be used to specify the scope of the change when the ALTER SYSTEM command is issued. Table 4-1 summarizes the behavior of the SCOPE clause.

You can also choose to modify parameters so that the change is effective only for future sessions using the DEFERRED keyword. The currently active sessions use the existing setting. The COMMENT clause allows you to add comments while modifying the parameter setting.

Setting for the SCOPE Clause	Behavior
SCOPE = SPFILE	The change is applied only to the SPFILE. The change is effective only after the database is restarted and is persistent.
SCOPE = MEMORY	The change is applied only in memory and, therefore, applies to the current instance. Since the SPFILE is not modified, the effect is not persistent.
SCOPE = BOTH	The change is applied in both the SPFILE and memory. The effect is immediate and applies to the currently open instance. The change is also persistent across database startups since the SPFILE is modified.

TABLE 4-1.   *Scope of Modified Initialization Parameters*

The following example modifies the maximum number of job queue processes allowed for the instance:

```
SQL> ALTER SYSTEM SET JOB_QUEUE_PROCESSES=50 SCOPE=MEMORY;
```

The modification applies only to the current instance since the scope is set to *memory*. The next example illustrates a change that is effective after the next database startup.

```
SQL> ALTER SYSTEM SET LOG_ARCHIVE_DEST_4=
'LOCATION=c:\oracle\ora90\database\',
MANDATORY,'REOPEN=2' COMMENT='Add new destination on Nov 29'
SCOPE=SPFILE;
```

To restore an initialization parameter to its default setting, use the following syntax:

```
SQL> ALTER SYSTEM SET <initialization parameter> = '';
```

This syntax does not apply for parameters that take Boolean values. If the parameter takes a Boolean value, you must explicitly set the value.

Exporting the SPFILE

Consider a situation wherein you have to modify several settings in the parameter file. It can be laborious to issue the ALTER SYSTEM command for each of these settings. It is faster to create a text version of the parameter file, modify it, and re-create the

SPFILE. It is possible to export the SPFILE using the CREATE PFILE command, as shown in this example:

```
SQL> CREATE PFILE='c:\oracle\ora90\database\test_init.ora'
FROM SPFILE=' c:\oracle\ora90\database\test_spfile.ora';
```

Again, you must have SYSDBA or SYSOPER privileges to execute this command. The exported parameter file is created on the machine running Oracle9i Server. Ensure that you have the necessary write privileges on the target directory.

Handling SPFILE Errors

If an error occurs while performing an operation (for example, while exporting the SPFILE) on the SPFILE, the operation terminates. The error is reported to the user. If an error occurs while reading or writing the SPFILE during a parameter update, the error is reported in the alert file, and all subsequent parameter updates to the SPFILE are ignored.

Viewing Initialization Parameter Settings

A textual parameter file can be viewed in any text editor. To view settings in an SPFILE, you can use one of the methods listed in Table 4-2.

Method	Description
SHOW PARAMETERS	This command is available in SQL*Plus and lists all the initialization parameters along with their current settings.
CREATE PFILE	Create a textual form of the parameter file using this command, and view the resulting text file in an editor.
V$PARAMETER	Query this view to display the current settings for parameters.
V$PARAMETER2	Query this view to obtain the current settings for parameters. While this is similar to V$PARAMETER, it is easier to read the resulting output since each parameter is listed as a separate row.
V$SPPARAMETER	This view displays the current contents of the SPFILE. The view returns NULL values if an SPFILE is not being used by the instance.

TABLE 4-2. *Viewing Initialization Parameter Settings*

You can also explicitly query Oracle9i Server for a specific initialization parameter setting by using the SHOW PARAMETER command, as shown here:

```
SQL> show parameter shared_pool_size
shared_pool_size                    big integer 46137344
```

Initialization Parameters to Consider Prior to Database Creation

Many settings for initialization parameters must be decided prior to creating a database. This section discusses some important parameters to help you make choices for these parameters.

Global Database Name

A combination of the local database name and the database domain name determines the global database name. While the database name is a unique name for the database within the local network, the database domain is a logical name determined by the local network structure (similar to the concept of domain names in TCP/IP). The DB_NAME and DB_DOMAIN parameters are used to set the database name and domain, respectively, as shown in the example here:

```
DB_NAME = projectdb
DB_DOMAIN = adkoli.com
```

The global name of the database can be modified using the ALTER DATABASE RENAME command. The database must be restarted after changing the DB_NAME and DB_DOMAIN parameters. Control files are updated with information on the new global database name.

The DB_NAME is a string and should not exceed eight characters. When the database is created, the DB_NAME is recorded in all the control files, redo log files, and data files. The database name in the parameter file is matched against the name in the control file prior to database startup. The DB_DOMAIN is a text string that identifies the network domain where the database is located. It is typically set to the same value as the company's TCP/IP domain. This setting is especially important in a distributed database environment.

Control Files

Control files hold all the meta information about an Oracle database. The initialization parameter CONTROL_FILES is used to specify the location of the control files. If this parameter is not set, Oracle looks for the control files in a subfolder named after the Oracle SID in the c:\oracle\oradata\ folder. Oracle Server also allows for multiplexing of control files. In fact, Oracle recommends that you have at least two images of the control file on separate hard disks. To multiplex control files, specify multiple names for control files, with a comma separating the filenames in the CONTROL_FILES parameter, as shown here:

```
control_files=("C:\oracle\oradata\projectdb\CONTROL01.CTL",
"D:\oracle\oradata\projectdb\CONTROL02.CTL")
```

Database Block Size

The database block size specifies the unit of input/output (I/O) for Oracle Server. The database block size is set using the DB_BLOCK_SIZE parameter. The default block size on Windows NT/2000 is 2K (2,048 bytes). The SYSTEM tablespace is automatically created using the setting for this parameter since it is created when the CREATE DATABASE command is issued. Oracle9i Server also allows you to override this setting when you create other tablespaces using the CREATE TABLESPACE command. In any case, you must always set the database block size to be a multiple of the operating-system block size.

Nonstandard Block Sizes

Nonsystem tablespaces in Oracle9i can also be created with nonstandard block sizes up to 16K. The BLOCKSIZE clause of the CREATE TABLESPACE command is used for this purpose.

Buffer Cache

The buffer cache component of the SGA can be set using the DB_CACHE_SIZE and DB_nK_CACHE_SIZE parameters. The DB_nK_CACHE_SIZE parameter is necessary if you intend to use multiple block sizes. By default, these are set to _0,_ meaning that only standard database block sizes are used.

The buffer cache requires careful consideration since it directly affects database performance. Large buffer caches reduce the number of disk reads and writes; however, if set too high, they can cause paging or swapping.

The DB_CACHE_SIZE initialization parameter replaces the DB_BLOCK_BUFFERS initialization parameter from previous Oracle releases. The DB_CACHE_SIZE parameter specifies the size of the cache (with standard block-size buffers), where the standard block size is specified by DB_BLOCK_SIZE. The DB_BLOCK_BUFFERS parameter is still supported for backward compatibility, but it cannot be combined with other dynamic sizing parameters.

Oracle9i Server also supports the simultaneous use of nonstandard block sizes. These are specified using the DB_nK_CACHE_SIZE parameters. An example is shown here:

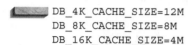

```
DB_4K_CACHE_SIZE=12M
DB_8K_CACHE_SIZE=8M
DB_16K_CACHE_SIZE=4M
```

Each parameter specifies the size of the buffer cache for the corresponding block size. In the preceding example, the size of 4K, 8K, and 16K buffers is set to 12MB, 8MB, and 4MB, respectively, DB_BLOCK_SIZE is set to 2K, and DB_CACHE_SIZE is set to 4MB.

NOTE
The DB_nK_CACHE_SIZE parameters cannot be used to size the cache for the standard block size. For example, if the value of DB_BLOCK_SIZE is 2K, it is illegal to set DB_2K_CACHE_SIZE. The size of the cache for the standard block size is always determined from the value of DB_CACHE_SIZE.

Shared Pool and Large Pool

The size of the shared pool in the SGA is defined by the SHARED_POOL_SIZE parameter. While this parameter was static in previous releases, it is dynamic in Oracle9i Server. The default setting for this parameter is approximately 46MB.

Similarly, the dynamic parameter LARGE_POOL_SIZE is used to set the size of the large pool component.

Limiting the SGA Size

The size of the SGA is determined largely by the size of the buffer cache, shared pool, and large pool. The SGA_MAX_SIZE parameter can be used to limit the size of the SGA. The default setting is approximately 118MB on Windows NT/2000. This is because the sum of all default SGA components on Windows NT/2000 is about 118MB.

Number of Processes

You can restrict the maximum number of operating system processes that can connect to Oracle9i Server by setting the PROCESSES parameter. This number includes the five background processes and (at least) one user process, so you must take these into account while setting this parameter.

Undo Space Management

Oracle9i Server automatically manages undo (rollback) changes to the database. Undo information includes a record of all actions to be performed up to that point and is stored in rollback segments or an undo tablespace. The UNDO_MANAGEMENT parameter is used to specify the undo behavior of Oracle Server. Setting this parameter to MANUAL forces Oracle Server to use rollback segments for undo. A setting of AUTO specifies that Oracle use an undo tablespace for undo. In this situation, you can use the UNDO_TABLESPACE parameter to specify the undo tablespace.

The default Oracle9i database uses a tablespace named UNDOTBS for undo. The CONTENT column of the DBA_TABLESPACES view contains the value UNDO for undo tablespaces. If you specify multiple tablespaces for the UNDO_TABLESPACE parameter, the first tablespace is used at instance startup. If you set the UNDO_MANAGEMENT parameter to AUTO and do not specify an UNDO_TABLESPACE, the SYSTEM tablespace is used for undo. Avoid using the SYSTEM tablespace for undo, as it can lead to fragmentation. The SYSTEM tablespace might also run out of space if a large amount of undo is written to it.

Oracle recommends that you use undo tablespaces to manage undo. Rollback segments are still supported for backward compatibility. The ROLLBACK_SEGMENTS parameter is used to specify a list of nonsystem rollback segments that Oracle Server can acquire at database startup. If this parameter is not set and the UNDO_MANAGEMENT parameter is set to MANUAL, system rollback segments are used automatically.

License Management

As a DBA, one of your tasks is to ensure that you comply with the Oracle licensing on your site. You can choose between *session licensing* and *named user licensing*. If you choose to use session licensing, you must track and limit the number of simultaneous database sessions. If you choose named user licensing, you must control the number of named users created on the database.

Use the LICENSE_MAX_SESSIONS and LICENSE_SESSIONS_WARNING parameters to control the number of simultaneous sessions. The LICENSE_MAX_SESSIONS designates the maximum number of simultaneous sessions, while the LICENSE_SESSIONS_WARNING parameter is used to set a threshold. A user will get a warning when he or she begins a session and the number of sessions is higher than LICENSE_SESSIONS_WARNING. This setting must always be lower than LICENSE_MAX_SESSIONS.

For Oracle RAC configuration, each instance can have its own concurrent usage limit and warning limit; however, the sum of the limits set for each instance must not exceed the site license.

Alternately, you can set a limit on the number of users created on the database by setting the LICENSE_MAX_USERS parameter. Once this limit is reached, Oracle Server will not allow you to create additional users. An example is shown here:

```
SQL> create user xyz identified by abc;
create user xyz identified by abc
                          *
ERROR at line 1:
ORA-01985: cannot create user as LICENSE_MAX_USERS parameter exceeded
```

NOTE
This mechanism assumes that each person accessing the database has a unique username and that no people share a username.

The default setting for all license-related parameters is zero, meaning that unlimited sessions and users are permitted.

Optimal Flexible Architecture

Oracle provides a guideline for filenames and locations used by Oracle Servers. This is called the Optimal Flexible Architecture (OFA). It is highly recommended that you follow this architecture to avoid conflicts when you have multiple databases on your site. Some of the benefits of using OFA are

- Easier maintenance and administration of Oracle software and databases through standard file organization and naming convention

- Improved reliability through data spanning across multiple physical drives

- Higher performance through decreased I/O contention for disks

OUI places Oracle software (executables, language, and other files) in a subfolder for which the name is determined by the ORACLE_HOME chosen during the installation. Database files, on the other hand, are placed in a subfolder named oradata (releases prior to Oracle8i placed database files in a subfolder named database).

NOTE
If you have upgraded from Oracle8, you can safely delete the entire directory structure used by the old installation since the files have been moved to an OFA-compliant folder named oradata.

OFA-compliant databases also provide some additional administration benefits since the file system is more organized and it greatly simplifies the process of locating files related to a specific database. It is also easier to add files to a database without worrying about conflicting with other files.

Since Oracle software (binaries and other files) can be placed over multiple disks, disk contention is reduced. The impact of disk failure is reduced since files are spread across multiple disks. Application rollouts are easier since files can coexist. Switching users after an upgrade is also transparent to the user.

Characteristics of an OFA-Compliant Database

To be OFA compliant, you must adhere to some important guidelines. These are discussed in this section.

Independent Folders and Subfolders

Categories of files are separated into independent subdirectories so that files in one category are minimally affected by operations on files in other categories.

Consistent Naming Conventions for Database Files

Oracle Server uses a standard convention to create filenames. Database files are easily distinguishable from all other files. Files of one database are easily distinguishable from files of another database. Data files, redo log files, and control files are easily identifiable. Data files and their associated tablespaces are easily distinguishable.

NOTE
Chapter 3 of Administrator's Guide *in Oracle documentation provides a full discussion on how filenames are derived.*

Integrity of Oracle Home Directories

Entire directory structures referred to by an ORACLE_HOME can be moved or deleted without affecting applications. Information on Oracle Home is maintained in the Windows Registry. You must use the Registry Editor to change this key on Windows. As always, editing the registry is dangerous. Create a backup of the registry before editing it.

Separation of Administrative Information for Each Database

The organization and storage of administrative data can be determined easily.

Simple Algorithm for Fragmentation Elimination (SAFE)

A standardized set of guidelines referred to as *Simple Algorithm for Fragmentation Elimination* (SAFE) exists to help reduce or eliminate database fragmentation. The *locally managed* tablespace feature of Oracle9i allows DBAs to maintain flexibility in sizing database extents that are allocated to segments. The SAFE guidelines are summarized here.

- Use uniform extent sizes with locally managed tablespaces. This minimizes the time required for updating information in the data dictionary.

- Use the STORAGE clause only while issuing tablespace-related commands (CREATE TABLESPACE, ALTER TABLESPACE, and so on).

- Set the size of extents to be 160K, 5120K, or 160MB only. Group segments in tablespaces based on the nature and size of their extents.

- No single segment should exceed 128GB.

- Temporary segments must be restricted to temporary tablespaces.

- Do not place user data in the SYSTEM tablespace.

- Use dedicated tablespaces for rollback segments.

Oracle Database Configuration Assistant

Oracle *Database Configuration Assistant* (DCA) is a graphical tool that can be used to create or delete databases. It can be used as a stand-alone tool or in conjunction with OUI. DCA also allows you to create templates that can be used in database creation. Such templates can be created from previously created templates. Finally, you can create a single instance or add instances for an Oracle RAC configuration.

DCA includes a wizard that will guide you through the process of creating a database. You can choose the degree to which you can customize the database. Finally, databases created by DCA are OFA compliant.

Creating an Oracle9i Database

So far, this chapter has provided an overview of initialization parameters, OFA, and DCA. Now detailed information on the database creation process will be provided.

Oracle9i databases can be created using DCA, or they can be created manually using a SQL tool such as SQL*Plus. Several additional steps must be performed on the newly created database before it is ready for use in a production environment. These steps include those required to create users, additional tablespaces, build database dictionary views, and install other built-in packages.

You can create customized database scripts to assist you in the creation process. Oracle Server also provides you with sample scripts that you can customize to create databases.

Creating a Database with DCA

This section provides an example to illustrate the process of creating a database using DCA. Launch DCA from the Start menu by clicking Start | Programs | Oracle - Ora Home90 | Configuration and Migration Tools | Database Configuration Assistant. You will see a Welcome screen. Click the Next button to see the Operations screen, shown in Figure 4-1.

Choose the option to create a database and click the Next button to view the Templates screen, shown in Figure 4-2.

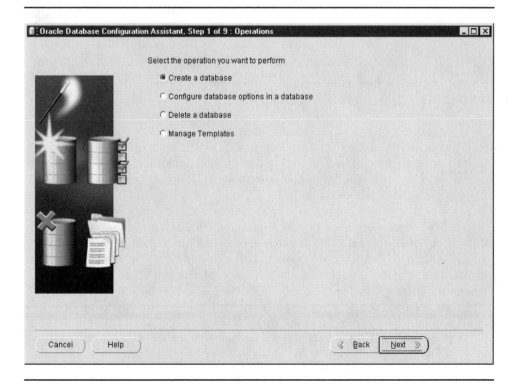

FIGURE 4-1. *Choosing a database operation*

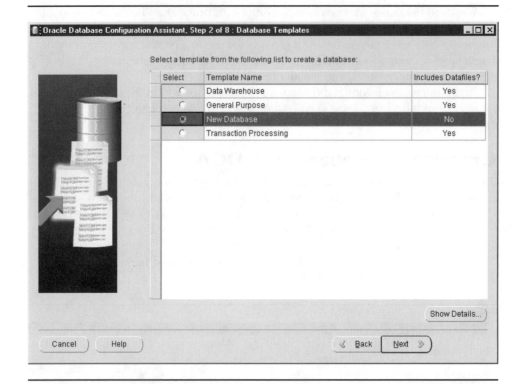

FIGURE 4-2. *Choosing a database template*

DCA allows you to view detailed information on the template. You can also create a database script based on the choices that you make and run this script later to create the database. The New Database option is chosen in this example since it provides the most flexibility.

In the next screen, you can specify the global database name. Remember that the database name must be unique on a network. Provide a global database name of the form *a.b.c*, where *a* is the system identifier and *b.c* is the domain.

You will be guided through a series of pages that allow you to further customize the database. You can set values for initialization parameters, specify locations and names for database files, log files, and control files. Pay special attention to the Initialization Parameters screen, shown in Figure 4-3. The values that you set on this screen will largely determine the performance of your database.

As seen here, the final screen of the wizard will allow you to create a database based on the selected options.

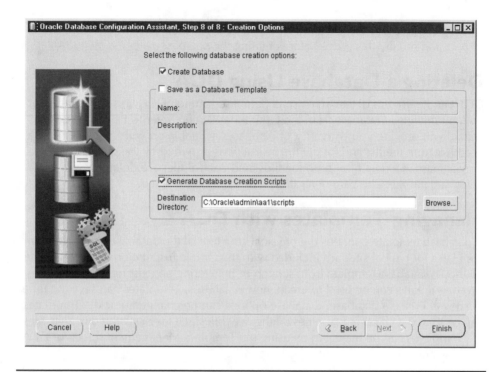

FIGURE 4-3. *Setting initialization parameters*

You can also choose to create a database script based on your choices. You can inspect and modify this script before creating the database.

Deleting a Database Using DCA

DCA can be used to delete an existing database. Launch DCA and choose the option to delete a database from the Operations screen (refer to Figure 4-1). The wizard will provide you with a list of databases available on your machine. Pick a database from the list and follow the instructions provided by the wizard to delete the database. All data files, redo log files, and control files are deleted when you delete a database. The parameter file, however, is not deleted.

Managing Templates with DCA

A database template contains the physical structure of the database. A few standard templates for typical sites are included with the Oracle installation. You can create your own database template from scratch or by altering an existing template. These saved templates can be used to create new databases. Templates can save the time needed to create a database. Database options can be changed quickly. Templates can be shared with other machines on the network since they are stored in XML files.

Templates can be managed by using the Template Management screen of DCA, as shown here:

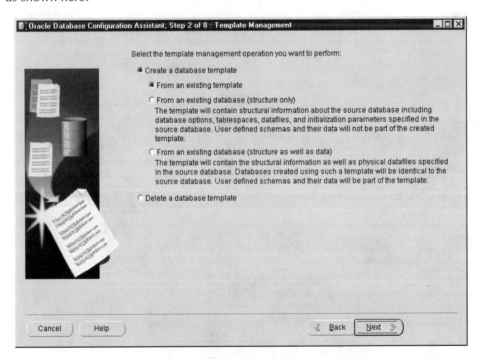

Manual Creation of a Database

While DCA allows DBAs to create a database with minimum fuss, there are situations in which you might want to maintain tighter control on the process. You might even want to gain a better understanding of the whole process. Many experienced DBAs continue to create databases manually despite the availability of DCA. In this section, we will show you how to manually create a database named projectdb.

Before creating a database, you must be clear on the type of database (size, name, and so on) that you wish to create. A few Windows-specific tasks must also be performed. These precreation tasks are covered in steps 1–3 as follows; steps 9–12 are optional, depending on the options you need to use.

Step 1: Decide on Your Site Identifier (SID) Decide on a unique Oracle SID for your database instance. Set the environment variable on the operating system. In Windows, you can set the environment variable ORACLE_SID from the Properties dialog of My Computer (right-click My Computer, click the Advanced button, and choose Environment Variables). The DB_NAME initialization parameter must match the ORACLE_SID setting. Tools and applications from Oracle do not require the ORACLE_SID setting on Windows Servers; however, some third-party applications use the ORACLE_SID setting.

Step 2: Register Oracle Services in Windows Registry Register the Oracle SID in the Windows Registry. The ORADIM utility can be used to add, modify, and delete Oracle services. We have added a service for the projectdb instance.

```
C:\> oradim -NEW -SID projectdb -INTPWD oracle -STARTMODE a
-PFILE C:\Oracle\Oracle91\database\initprojectdb.ora
```

Choose to install and start the database as a service, as shown here:

```
C:\> oradim -STARTUP -SID projectdb -USRPWD oracle
-STARTTYPE srvc
```

Step 3: Create the Initialization Parameter File Create a parameter file using a text editor. We recommend that you name it init.ora and place it in the c:\oracle\admin\projectdb\pfile folder, as per OFA standards. Create another file named initprojectdb.ora and place it in the c:\oracle\ora90\database folder. Add the parameters in the init.ora file to those in the initprojectdb.ora file using the IFILE parameter, as shown here:

```
IFILE='C:\oracle\admin\projectdb\pfile\init.ora'
```

The IFILE parameter includes the text from the included parameter file and can be placed anywhere in the initprojectdb.ora file. You can include multiple files with multiple IFILE parameters, one on each line. Here is the init.ora file used for the projectdb database.

```
# Cache and I/O
DB_BLOCK_SIZE=4096
DB_CACHE_SIZE=20971520
# Cursors and Library Cache
CURSOR_SHARING=SIMILAR
OPEN_CURSORS=300
# Diagnostics and Statistics
BACKGROUND_DUMP_DEST=C:\Oracle\Ora91\admin\projectdb\bdump
CORE_DUMP_DEST=C:\Oracle\Ora91\admin\projectdb\cdump
TIMED_STATISTICS=TRUE
USER_DUMP_DEST=C:\Oracle\Ora91\admin\projectdb\udump
# Control File Configuration
CONTROL_FILES=("C:\Oracle\oradata\projectdb\control01.ctl",
" D:\Oracle\oradata\projectdb\control02.ctl",
" E:\Oracle\oradata\projectdb\control03.ctl")
# Archive
LOG_ARCHIVE_DEST_1='LOCATION= C:\Oracle\oradata\projectdb\archive'
LOG_ARCHIVE_FORMAT=%t_%s.dbf
LOG_ARCHIVE_START=TRUE
# Shared Server
# Uncomment and use first DISPATCHES parameter below when your
# listener is
# configured for SSL
# (listener.ora and sqlnet.ora)
# DISPATCHERS = "(PROTOCOL=TCPS)(SER=MODOSE)",
#               "(PROTOCOL=TCPS)(PRE=oracle.aurora.server.SGiopServer)"
DISPATCHERS="(PROTOCOL=TCP)(SER=MODOSE)",
            "(PROTOCOL=TCP)(PRE=oracle.aurora.server.SGiopServer)",
              (PROTOCOL=TCP)
# Miscellaneous
COMPATIBLE=9.0.0
DB_NAME=projectdb
# Distributed, Replication and Snapshot
DB_DOMAIN=adkoli.com
REMOTE_LOGIN_PASSWORDFILE=EXCLUSIVE
# Network Registration
INSTANCE_NAME=projectdb
# Pools
JAVA_POOL_SIZE=31457280
LARGE_POOL_SIZE=1048576
SHARED_POOL_SIZE=52428800
# Processes and Sessions
```

```
PROCESSES=150
# Redo Log and Recovery
FAST_START_MTTR_TARGET=300
# Resource Manager
RESOURCE_MANAGER_PLAN=SYSTEM_PLAN
# Sort, Hash Joins, Bitmap Indexes
SORT_AREA_SIZE=524288
# System Managed Undo and Rollback Segments
UNDO_MANAGEMENT=AUTO
UNDO_TABLESPACE=undotbs
```

Step 4: Connect to the Instance   Start SQL*Plus and connect to your Oracle instance with SYSDBA privileges. The default password for the SYS user is CHANGE_ON_INSTALL.

```
C:\> SQLPLUS /nolog
SQL> CONNECT SYS/change_on_install AS SYSDBA
```

Step 5: Start the Instance   Start the instance using the NOMOUNT option.

```
SQL> STARTUP NOMOUNT
```

The SGA is created, and Oracle background processes are started. Note that there is no database as yet.

Step 6: Create the Database   The CREATE DATABASE command is used to create the database. The database files, control files, and redo log files are created at this time. Additionally, the SYSTEM tablespace and the SYSTEM rollback segment are also created. The database character set and time zone are set. The data dictionary is also created in the SYSTEM tablespace. Finally, the database is mounted and readied for use. The following CREATE DATABASE command was used to create the projectdb database.

```
SQL> CREATE DATABASE projectdb
MAXINSTANCES 1
MAXLOGHISTORY 1
MAXLOGFILES 5
MAXLOGMEMBERS 5
MAXDATAFILES 100
DATAFILE ' C:\Oracle\oradata\projectdb\system01.dbf' SIZE 325M REUSE
UNDO TABLESPACE undotbs DATAFILE
' C:\Oracle\oradata\projectdb\undotbs01.dbf' SIZE 200M REUSE
AUTOEXTEND ON NEXT 5120K MAXSIZE UNLIMITED
CHARACTER SET US7ASCII NATIONAL CHARACTER SET AL16UTF16
    LOGFILE GROUP 1 (' C:\Oracle\oradata\projectdb\redo01.log') SIZE 100M,
            GROUP 2 (' C:\Oracle\oradata\projectdb\redo02.log') SIZE 100M,
            GROUP 3 (' C:\Oracle\oradata\projectdb\redo03.log') SIZE 100M;
```

A database with the following characteristics is created:

- The database is named projectdb. Its global database name is projectdb.adkoli.com.

- Three control files are created, as specified by the CONTROL_FILES parameter.

- The MAXINSTANCES clause specifies that only one instance can have this database mounted and open at a given time.

- Initially, the control file is sized to hold the names of 100 data files.

- A SYSTEM tablespace, consisting of the operating system file c:\oracle\oradata\projectdb\system01.dbf, is created. If the file already exists, it is overwritten.

A tablespace named UNDOTBS is created for purposes of undo.

The US7ASCII character set will be used to store data. AL16UTF16 is specified as the *national character set* (NLS). This will be used to store data in columns of type NCHAR, NCLOB, and NVARCHAR2.

Redo log files will not be archived. The ALTER DATABASE command can be used to switch the database to ARCHIVELOG mode at a later point, when the database is in production.

Step 7: Create Additional Tablespaces   At this point, you can create other tablespaces. Here are two tablespaces added—one named USERS to hold user data and one called INDX to hold indexes:

```
SQL> CONNECT sys/change_on_install as SYSDBA
SQL> CREATE TABLESPACE users LOGGING
DATAFILE ' C:\Oracle\oradata\projectdb\users01.dbf'
SIZE 25M REUSE AUTOEXTEND ON NEXT 1280K MAXSIZE UNLIMITED EXTENT
MANAGEMENT LOCAL;
SQL> CREATE TABLESPACE indx LOGGING
DATAFILE ' E:\Oracle\oradata\projectdb\indx01.dbf'
SIZE 25M REUSE AUTOEXTEND ON NEXT 1280K MAXSIZE UNLIMITED EXTENT
MANAGEMENT LOCAL;
```

Step 8: Create Data Dictionary Views, PL/SQL Packages, and Other Scripts
At this point, you can create the data dictionary views using the CATALOG.SQL script. PL/SQL-related objects must be created using the CATPROC.SQL script. These scripts must be run as the user SYS. These two scripts are available in the c:\oracle\ora90\rdbms\admin folder. Additionally, you can run the PUPBLD.SQL

script from the c:\oracle\ora90\sqlplus\admin folder. The PUPBLD.SQL script creates the product and user profile tables. This script must be run under the SYSTEM user.

```
SQL> CONNECT SYS/change_on_install AS SYSDBA
SQL> @C:\Oracle\Ora91\rdbms\admin\catalog.sql;
SQL> @C:\Oracle\Ora91\rdbms\admin\catproc.sql;
SQL> CONNECT SYSTEM/manager
SQL> @C:\Oracle\Ora91\sqlplus\admin\pubbld.sql
```

Other scripts might be necessary based on additional options that you select. Information on these scripts is included in the remaining steps.

Step 9: Install Additional Features and Options (Optional)   Some product features and options need additional scripts. These scripts typically create tables (in some cases) and views needed by a specific feature. The scripts are included with the Oracle installation and typically reside in the c:\oracle\ora90\rdbms\admin folder or a folder named admin under the product subfolder. Table 4-3 (from Oracle documentation) summarizes these additional scripts.

Name of Script	Feature/ Option	Run As	Description
catblock.sql	Performance management	SYS	Dynamic views for lock-dependency graphs.
catclust.sql	Oracle9i RAC	SYS or other SYSDBA user	RAC views.
catexp7.sql	Exporting data to Oracle7	SYS	Creates the dictionary views needed for the Oracle7 Export utility to export data from Oracle9i in Oracle7 Export file format.
caths.sql	Heterogeneous Services	SYS	Creates packages for administering heterogeneous services.
catio.sql	Performance management	SYS	Allows I/O to be traced on a table-by-table basis.

TABLE 4-3.   *Optional Scripts for Additional Features and Options*

Name of Script	Feature/ Option	Run As	Description
catoctk.sql	Security	SYS	Package for Oracle Cryptographic Toolkit.
catqueue.sql	Advanced Queuing	User with AQ_ ADMINISTRATOR_ ROLE	Creates the dictionary objects required for Advanced Queuing option.
catrep.sql	Oracle Replication	SYS	For database replication.
catrman.sql	Recovery Manager	RMAN or any user with GRANT_ RECOVERY_ CATALOG_ OWNER role	Creates recovery catalog.
dbmsiotc.sql	Storage management	Any user	Analyzes chained rows in index-organized tables.
dbmsotrc.sql	Performance management	SYS or other SYSDBA user	Enables and disables generation of Oracle Trace output.
dbmspool.sql	Performance management	SYS or other SYSDBA user	Enables DBA to lock PL/SQL packages, SQL statements, and triggers into the shared pool.
userlock.sql	Concurrency control	SYS or other SYSDBA user	Provides a facility for user-named locks that can be used in a local or clustered environment to aid in sequencing application actions.

TABLE 4-3. *Optional Scripts for Additional Features and Options* (continued)

Name of Script	Feature/ Option	Run As	Description
utlbstat.sql and utlestat.sql	Performance monitoring	SYS	Start and stop collecting performance-tuning statistics.
utlchn1.sql	Storage management	Any user	Creates objects for storing the output of the ANALYZE command with the CHAINED ROWS option. Can handle both physical and logical ROWIDs.
utlconst.sql	Year 2000 compliance	Any user	Provides functions to validate that CHECK constraints on date columns are year 2000 compliant.
utldtree.sql	Metadata management	Any user	Creates tables and views that show dependencies between objects.
utlexpt1.sql	Constraints	Any user	EXCEPTIONS table.
utlip.sql	PL/SQL	SYS	Used primarily for migration, upgrade, and downgrade operations. It invalidates all existing PL/SQL modules by altering certain dictionary tables so that subsequent recompilations will occur in the format required by the database. It also reloads the packages STANDARD and DBMS_STANDARD, which are necessary for any PL/SQL compilations.

TABLE 4-3. *Optional Scripts for Additional Features and Options* (continued)

Name of Script	Feature/ Option	Run As	Description
utlirp.sql	PL/SQL	SYS	Used to change from 32-bit to 64-bit word size or vice versa. This script recompiles existing PL/SQL modules in the format required by the new database. It first alters some data dictionary tables. Then it reloads the packages STANDARD and DBMS_STANDARD, which are necessary for using PL/SQL. Finally, it triggers a recompilation of all PL/SQL modules, such as packages, procedures, and types.
utllockt.sql	Performance monitoring	SYS or other SYSDBA user	For lock wait-for graph in tree structure.
utlpwdmg.sql	Security	SYS or other SYSDBA user	Creates PL/SQL functions for default password complexity verification. Sets the default password profile parameters and enables password management features.
utlrp.sql	PL/SQL	SYS	Recompiles all existing PL/SQL modules that were previously in an INVALID state, such as packages, procedures, and types.

TABLE 4-3. *Optional Scripts for Additional Features and Options* (continued)

Name of Script	Feature/ Option	Run As	Description
utlsampl.sql	Examples	Any user	Creates sample (demo) tables, such as EMP and DEPT.
utlscln.sql	Oracle Replication	Any user	Copies a snapshot schema from another snapshot site.
utltkprf.sql	Performance management	SYS	Creates the TKPROFER role to allow the TKPROF profiling utility to be run by non-DBA users.
utlvalid.sql	Partitioned tables	Any user	Creates tables required for storing output of ANALYZE TABLE... VALIDATE STRUCTURE of a partitioned table.
utlxplan.sql	Performance management	Any user	Creates the table PLAN_TABLE, which holds output from the EXPLAIN PLAN statement.

TABLE 4-3. *Optional Scripts for Additional Features and Options* (continued)

The catalog and the dictionary views are created for you when you create a database using DCA. The scripts listed in Table 4-3 must be run separately.

Step 10: Create an SPFILE (Optional but Recommended)   Oracle recommends that you create an SPFILE, since it allows you to manage initialization parameters dynamically. Refer to the section titled "Server Parameter File" earlier in this chapter for more information.

Step 11: Additional Security Considerations (Optional)   A newly created database has at least three users that have the necessary privileges to administer a database. These are SYS, SYSTEM, and OUTLN (outlines are used to store execution plans for later use). To prevent unauthorized access and protect the integrity of your database, you must change the passwords for these users.

Depending on the features and options installed, other users such as MDSYS (interMedia spatial), ORDSYS (interMedia audio), ORDPLUGINS (interMedia audio), CTXSYS (Oracle text), and DBSNMP (Enterprise Manager Intelligent Agent) might have been created. Be sure to change the default passwords for these users.

NOTE
Oracle is considering several enhancements for security. In Oracle9i, Version 9.1, all database user accounts except SYS, SYSTEM, SCOTT, DBSNMP, OUTLN, AURORAJISUTILITY$, AURORA$ORB$UNAUTHENTICATED, and OSE$HTTP$ADMIN are locked by default. To activate a locked account, the DBA must manually unlock it and reassign it a new password. In future releases, DCA is also expected to prompt for passwords for the users SYS and SYSTEM. The CREATE DATABASE command will also include a clause where you can provide passwords for these users.

Step 12: Sample Schemas (Optional)   The Oracle9i Server includes a variety of SQL scripts that allow you to create sample database schemas as well as scripts that allow you to experiment with Oracle Server and learn SQL. Some of the schemas included are listed in Table 4-4.

Schema	Description
Human Resources	The Human Resources (HR) schema is a simple relational database schema. There are six tables in the HR schema: Employees, Departments, Locations, Countries, Jobs, and Job_History. The Order Entry (OE) schema has links into HR schema.
Order Entry	The Order Entry (OE) schema builds on the Human Relations (HR) schema with some object-relational and object-oriented features. The OE schema contains seven tables: Customers, Product_Descriptions, Product_Information, Order_Items, Orders, Inventories, and Warehouses. The OE schema has links into the HR schema and Product Media schema. This schema also has synonyms defined on HR objects to make access transparent to users.

TABLE 4-4.   *Sample Oracle Schemas Included with Oracle9i Server*

Schema	Description
Product Media	Product Media (PM) schema includes two tables, Online_Media and Print_Media; one object type, adheader_typ; and one nested table, textdoc_typ. The PM schema includes interMedia and LOB column types.
Sales History	The Sales History (SH) schema is an example of a relational star schema. It consists of one big range-partitioned fact table and five dimension tables: Times, Promotions, Channels, Products, and Customers.
Queued Shipping	The Queued Shipping (QS) schema is useful for the queuing feature.

TABLE 4-4.   *Sample Oracle Schemas Included with Oracle9i Server* (continued)

New Oracle9i Features

Oracle9i Server includes a few features that can make the task of creating and managing tasks simpler. An overview of these features is provided in the sections that follow.

Undo Tablespaces

Oracle Corporation recommends that you create special tablespaces to manage undo instead of using (traditional) rollback segments. To use this feature, set the UNDO_MANAGEMENT and UNDO_TABLESPACE parameters as discussed in the section "Undo Space Management" earlier in this chapter.

Default Temporary Tablespace

The CREATE DATABASE command has a new clause that can be used to create and set a default temporary tablespace. Any user that is not assigned a temporary tablespace explicitly is automatically assigned the temporary tablespace specified by the DEFAULT TEMPORARY TABLESPACE during database creation. In earlier releases, the SYSTEM tablespace was the default temporary tablespace if one was not assigned explicitly to a user. You can change the default temporary tablespace using the ALTER DATABASE DEFAULT TEMPORARY TABLESPACE command, as shown here:

```
SQL> ALTER TABLESPACE DEFAULT TEMPORARY TABLESPACE temp2;
```

You must precreate the tablespace TEMP2 before issuing this command. A temporary tablespace cannot be dropped or taken off line.

Oracle-Managed Files

Oracle9i can create and manage underlying operating system files for tablespaces, control files, and log files. The DB_CREATE_FILE_DEST and DB_CREATE_ONLINE_LOG_DEST_n parameters are used for this purpose. Oracle9i Server will automatically create and manage files if you set these parameters. Consider this example:

```
SQL> CREATE DATABASE productdb UNDO TABLESPACE undotbs DEFAULT
TEMPORARY TABLESPACE temp1;
```

Since no DATAFILE clause is specified, Oracle Server creates an Oracle-managed data file for the SYSTEM tablespace. Similarly, redo log file groups, an undo tablespace, and a default temporary tablespace are created. The DB_BLOCK_SIZE initialization parameter is used to fix the database block size.

Setting Time Zone

Oracle9i enables you to set the time zone for your database using the SET TIME_ZONE clause of the CREATE DATABASE command. The time-zone files contain the valid time-zone names and other information (such as offset from UTC, transition times for daylight savings, and so on).

In this chapter, you learned how to create databases to meet your special needs. Special features such as SPFILE and Oracle Managed Files were discussed in sufficient detail. It is best to start with DCA to create a template for your database and then tweak it manually.

CHAPTER
5

Oracle9i Database
Administration

I f you are a database administrator (DBA), completing a successful installation is only the beginning of the journey. You also need to perform regular maintenance tasks, manage users, and tune the database for optimal performance. You are responsible for the overall health of the Oracle system. This chapter contains information on all the routine tasks you need to carry out in your role as a DBA. It begins with a brief section on database theory, which is followed by an overview of the generic Oracle9i architecture. This will help beginners get a jumpstart in the role of a DBA. The second half of this chapter includes detailed information on specific administration tasks. These are designed for individuals who plan to manage Oracle9i Servers on Windows NT/2000.

Theory of Databases

A common request from readers is to include some topics on database theory to help individuals with no prior experience with databases who want to install and manage an Oracle Server on Windows NT/2000. Based on this feedback, a section on database theory is included here.

Any object or element that can hold data can be called a database. This includes common data objects that are associated with computers, such as files and personal organizers. In the field of database theory, a database is an organized collection of information. You can perform a variety of tasks with minimal effort in a database since data is organized in a manner that is conducive to queries. Data can be added, removed, and changed with equal ease. Security of data as well as its integrity is guaranteed.

An English-like language called *structured query language* (SQL) is widely used to operate on data. In today's world, a database must support data manipulation language (DML) as well as data definition language (DDL) in addition to queries. SQL commands that are defined for adding, removing, and changing data are classified as DML. SQL commands that are used to define objects are categorized as DDL. Software that manages data intelligently with all the above ingredients is termed a *database management system* (DBMS). While many approaches to managing data exist, storing data in a relational database management system (RDBMS) is currently accepted as the best methodology. Most commercial database software vendors, including Oracle, IBM, and Microsoft, use the relational approach to store data.

A DBMS can qualify as a relational database system if it adheres to 12 rules defined by E. F. Codd in 1970. The rules are listed here for your benefit, but a full discussion on Codd's rules is available in any book on database theory. The 12 rules are:

1. **Information**   Data is stored within columns and rows. This is the fundamental requirement for an RDBMS.

2. **Guaranteed Access**   All data values can be identified and accessed by an identity that is provided by a table name, column name, and key.

3. **Treatment of Null Values**   An RDBMS must handle missing data. This is typically termed *null* data in an RDBMS. Note that null is not equivalent to zero or an empty string. The keyword NULL is used to refer to null data in Oracle Server.

4. **Online Catalog**   An RDBMS must include an online catalog that contains information on the database itself. Users can query this catalog. Oracle Server includes a data dictionary that acts as the online catalog.

5. **Comprehensive Data Sublanguage**   A data sublanguage that can be used interactively and embedded within programs is defined for data definition, manipulation, and other operations. In today's world, this is provided by SQL. Oracle Server supports both ANSI SQL-92 and SQL-99 standards. These standards are also referred to as SQL-2 and SQL-3.

6. **View Update Rule**   Table *views,* or virtual tables, must be supported. Views behave like conventional tables; however, they are built dynamically by queries and, therefore, always provide an up-to-date view of data.

7. **Transaction Support**   Transaction support must be included. A transaction ensures that all data modifications are collectively applied or discarded. Sets of statements between successive COMMITs or ROLLBACKs define the boundaries of a transaction. Transactions have four properties: atomicity, consistency, isolation, and durability (ACID). Atomicity is the property that a transaction either completes fully or does nothing. The consistency property requires that a database be transformed from one consistent state to the next with every transaction. Transactions must be isolated from each other, meaning that changes made during a transaction are not visible to other users until the transaction completes. Finally, durability demands that the changes made by a transaction must be persistent.

8. **Physical Data Independence**   The physical storage of data is not relevant to the user. A user is concerned only with the logical database structure. In Oracle Server, the user is not concerned with the physical organization of data files.

9. **Logical Data Independence**   The logical structure of the data can be modified with minimal impact on users and programs. Tablespaces, segments, and extents in Oracle Server provide this support. These are discussed later in this chapter.

10. **Integrity Independence**   Integrity rules are to be stored in the catalog. Any alterations made to these rules must not affect application programs. Constraints are used to implement integrity rules in Oracle Server.

11. **Distribution Independence**   Applications must be able to work in a distributed environment (where data is stored in different locations). The distributed option of Oracle9i Server provides support for this feature.

12. **Nonsubversion**   Finally, an RDBMS should ensure security and integrity of the database. No backdoor entries must be available to bypass the security imposed by the RDBMS.

Codd also defined a rule that said that an RDBMS must be able to manage databases entirely through its relational capabilities. This important rule in database theory is known as *Codd's Rule Zero*.

NOTE

An Introduction to Database Systems, *by C.J. Date, is an excellent resource for more information on database theory. Oracle Server is one of the most highly evolved and widely used databases. Like any other RDBMS, it adheres to all Codd's rules. In addition, Oracle9i Server also supports the notion of objects. It is therefore described as an object relational database management system (ORDBMS). A very simplistic description of the Oracle Server is included in the next section. If you are just entering into the Oracle world, read this section before proceeding further. If you are an experienced Oracle DBA already, you may skip the next section.*

Overview of Oracle9i Architecture

The Oracle Server architecture has evolved over two decades and is extremely complex. If you are just beginning your journey as an Oracle DBA, a high-level understanding of the Oracle Server architecture will help you perform your administration tasks better.

Database versus Instance

The Oracle9i architecture has two distinct portions: the database and the instance. The database is that part of the Oracle Server architecture that houses the data. The database can be viewed purely as a physical structure or as a logical structure. The physical structure includes data files, control files, and redo log files, whereas the logical structure refers to tablespaces, segments, and extents. Simply put, if an Oracle object can be viewed from the operating system, it is part of the physical structure; otherwise, it is part of the logical structure. Information on logical objects is obtained through database queries on the data dictionary.

The term *instance* refers to the combination of Oracle objects in memory and the processes used by Oracle. An overview of these objects and terminology is provided in the next sections.

Figure 5-1 depicts the fundamental Oracle Architecture.

Physical Database Structure

The logical and physical independence rules dictated by Codd (rules 8 and 9) apply to Oracle Server as well. The database has a physical structure that includes all the files associated with the database. From a user's standpoint, however, the database can be viewed completely as a logical structure.

The physical database structure consists of many physical files (at operating-system level). These are data files, redo log files, archived redo log files, control files, password files, and parameter files. These files, collectively referred to as the *physical database*, are described next. The files that make up the Oracle software are not considered part of the physical database.

Data Files

An Oracle9i database can consist of one to many data files. Data files actually hold the data within a database. The data can be system data (data used by Oracle Server itself) or user data. All data is stored in an Oracle proprietary binary format within these files and cannot be read by programs other than Oracle Server. You must not attempt to view or edit these files in other programs.

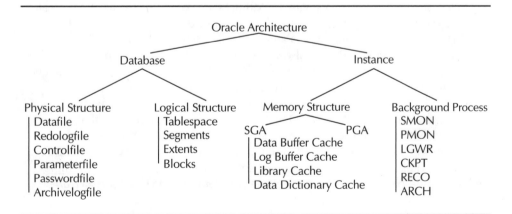

FIGURE 5-1. *Oracle Architecture*

An Oracle database typically consists of many data files. These are associated with logical objects called *tablespaces.* Each data file is associated with exactly one tablespace; however, a tablespace can be associated with multiple data files. Oracle Server requires at least one data file for every database. The first set of data files, commonly referred to as the *system data files,* are created when the CREATE DATABASE command is issued. These data files are associated with a special tablespace named SYSTEM. The SYSTEM tablespace contains the database catalog. The sizes, names, and locations of the system data files are specified when the CREATE DATABASE command is issued (Oracle Managed Files are an exception and are discussed in a separate section). Consider this example:

```
SQL> CREATE DATABASE projectdb
MAXINSTANCES 1
MAXLOGHISTORY 1
MAXLOGFILES 5
MAXLOGMEMBERS 5
MAXDATAFILES 100
DATAFILE ' c:\oracle\oradata\projectdb\system01.dbf' SIZE 325M REUSE
UNDO TABLESPACE undotbs DATAFILE
' C:\Oracle\oradata\projectdb\undotbs01.dbf' SIZE 200M REUSE
AUTOEXTEND ON NEXT 5120K MAXSIZE UNLIMITED
CHARACTER SET US7ASCII NATIONAL CHARACTER SET AL16UTF16
    LOGFILE GROUP 1 (' c:\oracle\oradata\projectdb\redo01.log')
SIZE 100M,
        GROUP 2 (' c:\oracle\oradata\projectdb\redo02.log')
SIZE 100M,
        GROUP 3 (' c:\oracle\oradata\projectdb\redo03.log')
SIZE 100M;
```

In the previous example, a single 325MB data file named **system01.dbf** is created in the folder c:\oracle\oradata\projectdb. Since this data file is created with the CREATE DATABASE command, it is automatically associated with the SYSTEM tablespace. The previous example also creates a second tablespace named UNDOTBS. The 200MB data file **undodbs01.dbf** is associated with the UNDOTBS tablespace.

It is recommended that additional tablespaces be created to hold nonsystem data (user data, indexes, temporary segments, and so on). Additional tablespaces are created with the CREATE TABLESPACE command. The data files that are associated with the tablespace being created are specified at this time. This specification includes the number of data files to be associated with the new tablespace, along with their sizes, names, and locations. The following example creates a tablespace named AA comprising two data files, **aa1.dbf** and **aa2.dbf**:

```
SQL> CREATE TABLESPACE aa
DATAFILE 'c:\oracle\oradata\aa\aa1.dbf' SIZE 50M,
'd:\oracle\oradata\aa\aa2.dbf' SIZE 50M;
Tablespace created.
```

Typically, a DBA creates the additional tablespaces after creating the database. Note that the sizes, names, and locations of the data files are explicitly defined. To get information on data files, you can query the V$DATAFILE view in the data dictionary. An example is shown here:

```
SQL> SELECT creation_time, status, bytes, block_size FROM V$DATAFILE
WHERE NAME LIKE '%AA1.DBF';
22-DEC-01 ONLINE     5242880        4096
```

You can perform additional operations on a data file with the ALTER DATABASE...DATAFILE command.

Oracle9i also supports temporary tablespaces. The data files associated with these tablespaces are called temporary data files. These are similar to other data files, except that they cannot be made read-only or renamed.

On the Windows NT/2000 platform, you can view the status of data files and modify them from Oracle Enterprise Manager (OEM). Figure 5-2 shows a sample screen of OEM with information on the **system01.dbf** data file on the sample database. You can take data files offline or bring them online from OEM. Storage characteristics can also be modified from this screen. You cannot take a data file

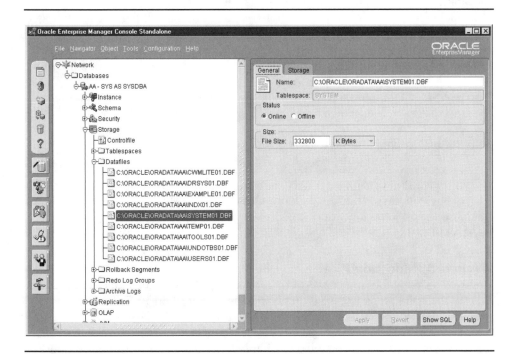

FIGURE 5-2.   *Managing data files from OEM*

belonging to the SYSTEM tablespace offline or drop the SYSTEM tablespace at any time.

By default, data files on the Windows NT/2000 platform are created in a subfolder under a folder named c:\oracle\oradata. The name of the subfolder is derived from the name of the database instance. For example, a folder named c:\oracle\oradata\aa would contain the data files belonging to a database named AA.

Redo Log Files

Redo log files are used to store changes made to the database. Redo log files contain a record of the changes made to the database. A common misconception is that the redo log files contain entire database records. In reality, they contain only information on the changes made to data. Redo log files protect a database from loss of integrity due to failures occurring from power outages, hard disk crashes, and the like. When a database needs to be recovered, the change information stored in the redo log files is applied in sequence to the latest database backup available (the undo information available in rollback segments is also used in recovery). Oracle9i Server requires at least two redo log files. The first set of redo log files is created when the CREATE DATABASE command is issued. Additional redo log files can be created, or existing redo log files can be dropped using the ALTER DATABASE command. The names, locations, and sizes of these files are specified at the time of creation.

Oracle recommends that you multiplex redo log files. Multiplexing a redo log file minimizes the probability of losing a redo log file. Redo log files are multiplexed and stored as redo log file members in redo log groups. The members within a redo log group are identical copies of each other. Members of a redo log group are stored on separate hard disks for redundancy.

The V$LOGFILE and V$LOG views in the catalog provide information on redo log groups. A sample is shown here:

```
SQL> SELECT member, status FROM V$LOGFILE WHERE group# = 1;
C:\ORACLE\ORADATA\AA\REDO01.LOG      ONLINE
D:\ORACLE\ORADATA\AA\REDO02.LOG      ONLINE
```

On the Windows NT/2000 platform, OEM can be used to view information on redo log groups. Redo log groups can also be added and removed conveniently using OEM.

Archived Redo Log File

Archived redo log files are copies of online redo log files. As the name suggests, a copy of the online redo log file is archived to secondary storage. The destination used for archiving along with the names of the archived log files are controlled by the initialization parameters LOG_ARCHIVE_DEST and LOG_ARCHIVE_DUPLEX_DEST. Database archiving can be enabled or disabled. Redo log files are archived only when the database is in ARCHIVELOG mode. By default, a database is in NOARCHIVELOG mode. You must issue the ALTER DATABASE ARCHIVELOG command to enable archiving.

You can query the views V$ARCHIVE, V$ARCHIVED_LOG, and V$ARCHIVE_DEST_STATUS for information pertaining to archiving. OEM also can be used to monitor archiving.

Control Files

Control files are used by Oracle Server to track the physical components of a database. Oracle Server uses the control file to identify all the data files and redo log files associated with a database. Other control information such as timestamps and system change number (SCN) are stored in the control file. Control files are never shared across databases. A control file is associated with only one database.

Oracle recommends that control files also be multiplexed. The CONTROL_FILES parameter provides the location and names of the control files. Oracle Server creates the control files when the database is first created. You can query the V$CONTROLFILE view for information on control files.

CAUTION

Control files are binary in nature and should not be edited at any time.

Password File

Oracle Server mostly maintains user information within the database; however, when the database is not running (or when the database is yet to be created), users with special system privileges (SYSDBA and SYSOPER) need to be authenticated. A user with SYSDBA privilege is equivalent to the SYS user (the most powerful user on Oracle Server). A user with SYSOPER privileges can start and shut down the database.

The password file is created when you create the starter database with Oracle9i installation. The password file can be re-created or modified using the Oracle Password Utility. The executable file on Windows NT/2000 is named **orapwd**. When a new database is created on Windows NT/2000 with the **oradim** utility, the password file is created with information provided by the INTPWD argument.

Parameter File

Initialization parameters used by Oracle Server to look up and assign resources are stored in this file. Parameters in this file either name resources, set limits, or define resource settings. Oracle9i Server includes a new feature that allows for a binary form of the parameter file. This feature (SPFILE) and initialization parameters are discussed in more detail in Chapter 4.

Parameter settings can also be viewed or modified by using OEM, as shown here:

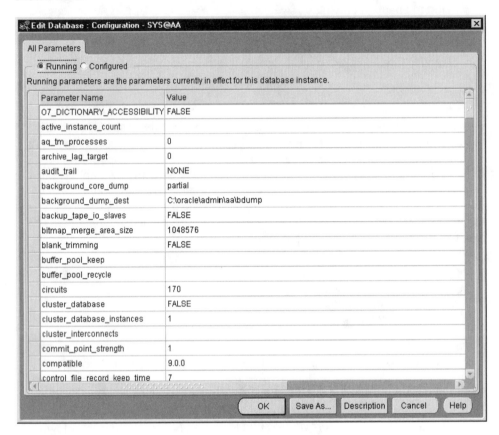

Logical Database Structure

A typical Oracle developer or end user is not usually concerned with the physical structure of the database and often is not even aware of the physical location of data; however, it is critical for a DBA to understand the correlation between the physical and logical structures of a database. It is the DBA who controls the mapping, the logical structure of a database to the physical structure.

The logical structure of an Oracle database consists of tablespaces, segments, extents, and blocks. Tablespaces are containers for a logical group of objects. For example, a tablespace might contain all database indexes or all objects belonging to the finance department of a company.

Tablespaces

An Oracle database consists of one or more tablespaces. A tablespace named SYSTEM is mandatory and is automatically created when the database is created. You can also include other tablespaces in the CREATE DATABASE command. Additional tablespaces can also be created using the CREATE TABLESPACE command. A typical Oracle database consists of the SYSTEM tablespace, a temporary tablespace (for temporary segments), an undo tablespace for storing undo, a tablespace for indexes, and other user tablespaces. Each tablespace is associated with one or more data files. When a tablespace is created, it initially has empty space that is approximately equal to the sum of the sizes of the corresponding data files. The database blocks are nulled initially. As objects keep growing or new objects get added to a tablespace, the space available in the tablespace reduces.

When you create a new user, it is good practice to associate a default tablespace to the user. A temporary tablespace must also be assigned to a user. When a user creates an object using the CREATE statement, the object is automatically created in the default tablespace. The user can explicitly choose to create the object in another tablespace if they have the required permissions on that tablespace. The temporary tablespace is used for temporary segments. Oracle9i includes a new feature that allows you to define a default temporary tablespace across all users. This feature was not available in earlier versions of Oracle Server.

You can query the V$TABLESPACE view for information on tablespaces. Information on tablespaces can also be obtained from OEM. Tablespaces can be brought offline or online with some constraints. Storage parameters for tablespaces can also be modified. Figure 5-3 shows a sample OEM screen with tablespace information for the sample database.

Segments

A segment is made of one or more extents (defined next). Segments can contain data, indexes, temporary data, and undo information. Data segments contain user or system data, whereas index segments contain indexes. Temporary segments are used as scratch areas. Undo segments contain undo information.

A tablespace can contain many segments; however, a segment is typically associated with one tablespace. Segments extend as and when required by allocating new extents.

NOTE
The partitioning feature in Oracle9i permits partitions to reside in separate tablespaces. This is an exception to the rule that a segment resides in a single tablespace.

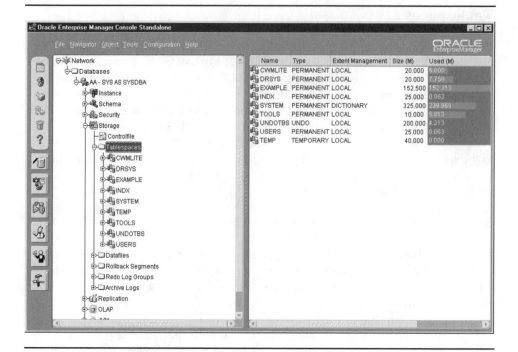

FIGURE 5-3. *OEM screen with tablespace information*

When database objects such as tables and indexes are created, Oracle Server automatically allocates extents to store this data. User applications are rarely concerned with the physical storage of segments; however, DBAs must keep a close watch and manage the growth of segments. The DBA_SEGMENTS view provides useful information on segments.

Extents
One or more extents make a segment. An *extent* is defined as a contiguous set of database blocks. Many extents form a segment. When a segment expands, space is allocated in terms of extents. The space allocated when the segment is created the very first time is defined by the INITIAL_EXTENT storage parameter. Similarly, when the segment grows, space is allocated as per the definition of the NEXT_EXTENT parameter. The INITIAL_EXTENT and NEXT_EXTENT storage parameters are provided when the object is created. The DBA_EXTENTS view provides useful information on extents.

Segments and extents are important to DBAs. When segments are created, a storage clause can be used to specify how extents are allocated. A DBA can also specify a storage clause for a tablespace. If a storage clause is not explicitly used while creating the segment, a default value is inherited from the tablespace properties. A DBA must choose appropriate values for INITIAL_EXTENT and NEXT_EXTENT for tablespace storage parameters based on the initial size of data and expected growth. If too many extents are allocated for a segment, fragmentation occurs and performance is affected; however, if an extent is too large, it can result in loss of space. The STORAGE clause of the CREATE and ALTER commands are used to control storage characteristics.

If you encounter a situation in which a segment has too many extents, you can use the Export utility to re-create the object after compressing into a single extent.

Database Blocks

A database block is the smallest unit of I/O on Oracle Server. An extent consists of several contiguous database blocks. The default block size varies across operating systems. On Windows NT/2000, the default database block size is 4,096 bytes. It can be set to a different value using initialization parameters. The size of a data block is a multiple of the OS block size.

Apart from data, a data block has a header that contains the block address. The block address is unique across the database. A data block also contains a table directory and row directory. These provide information on the tables that have rows in that block and the addresses for each row piece in the block. The unused portion of a block is maintained as free space.

It is important to understand that a row can span multiple database blocks. This situation is termed *row chaining*. In this case, Oracle Server has to combine row pieces to return records for a query. In some situations, the entire row is moved to a new database block. This is termed *row migration*. Row chaining and migration are detrimental to performance and must be curtailed as far as possible. More information on this is provided in Chapter 8.

Data Dictionary

Per Codd's rule 4, an RDBMS must have a catalog. Oracle maintains its internal system information in a catalog termed the *data dictionary*. The data dictionary consists of database objects that Oracle Server uses to manage the database. The data dictionary is maintained in the SYSTEM tablespace. This is one of the main reasons the SYSTEM tablespace is critical to Oracle databases.

The data dictionary is a read-only set of tables (also called *base tables)* that store information about the database. The data dictionary is consulted before any database transactions are performed. Such queries are called *recursive SQL queries*. All SQL queries are authenticated by a data dictionary lookup. The dictionary is automatically updated when an object is created using a DDL statement. User authentication information, space usage information, and other database structural details are also stored in the data dictionary. The information in the data dictionary can be queried through standard database views. These views are built on the base tables. The data dictionary is owned by the special user SYS, which is created automatically when the CREATE DATABASE command is issued.

Oracle Server attempts to keep the data dictionary objects that have been accessed during the course of database use in the SGA.

CAUTION
If you lose the SYSTEM tablespace, the data dictionary is lost. This is equivalent to losing the database.

Contents of the Data Dictionary

All information required by Oracle Server about an Oracle database is stored in the data dictionary. These include

- User information

- User privileges and role information

- Names and definition of schema objects (tables, indexes, clusters, synonyms, and so on)

- Integrity constraints

- Space allocation for database objects

- Information on database structure

- Functions, procedures, and packages

Note that Oracle Server maintains the data dictionary automatically. Database users are permitted only to query the data dictionary.

Data Dictionary Views

When a database is created, Oracle Server automatically executes a script named **sql.bsq** that creates the read-only tables. This script is included in the c:\oracle\ ora90\rdbms\admin folder. These base tables have a name that ends with a dollar sign. UNDO$ and TAB$ are examples of such tables. A script named **catalog.sql** is then used to create data dictionary views on top of these dollar tables. The names of data dictionary views generally begin with DBA_, ALL_, or USER_. Users who have DBA equivalent privileges can query views with names that begin with DBA_. The

DBA views provide information on all database objects. All other users can typically use the views with names that begin with ALL_ or USER_. USER_ views provide information on database objects that the user owns, whereas ALL_ views provide information on database objects that the user can access (including objects that are owned by others that the user has access to).

TIP
*If you want to create your own customized objects when the CREATE DATABASE command is issued, simply add the necessary CREATE statements to the **sql.bsq** file before creating the database.*

An example of a DBA_ view is the DBA_USERS view, which includes information on database users. Similarly, the USER_OBJECTS view provides information on all objects owned by a user, and the ALL_OBJECTS view provides a listing of all objects that a user has access to.

TIP
If you have created a DBA-level user, you should run the DBA_SYNONYMS.SQL script to create private synonyms on data dictionary views for this user.

Database Instance

Oracle Server creates and uses many data structures in physical memory to manage a database. Additionally, a set of processes is created to perform specific operations on the database. The memory combined with the processes is termed an *instance*.

Memory Structures
There are two main structures in the portion of physical memory allocated to Oracle Server by the operating system: the system global area (SGA) and the process global area (PGA). The SGA is a shared memory structure and is analogous to a bulletin board. All database users have access to a bulletin board. Some users post messages on the board, while others simply read messages on the board. Similarly, background and user processes perform a variety of special read and write operations on the SGA.

The PGA is a private area of memory and is accessed only by a specific process. In contrast to the SGA, which acts like a bulletin board, the PGA is like a book. Specific pages of the book are accessed for read and write by a particular process. User processes use the areas of the PGA as private space, hence data in the PGA is not shared.

The SGA and PGA are important structures for a DBA since many database-tuning activities are related to these structures.

System Global Area   The SGA is a shared memory region that contains data and control information for an instance. This area is allocated in physical memory when an Oracle instance is started and de-allocated when the instance is shut down. Users connected to Oracle Server share the information present in SGA. As a DBA, you should strive to keep this area as large as possible. For optimal performance, you should also keep this in physical memory (avoid swapping). The SGA contains the database block buffer cache, library cache, shared pool, large pool, and Java pool. The shared pool itself consists of the log buffer cache and data dictionary cache. The overall size of the SGA is limited to the setting of the SGA_MAX_SIZE initialization parameter.

The size of the SGA can be determined using the SHOW SGA command from SQL*Plus, as shown here:

```
SQL> SHOW SGA
Total System Global Area    80506652 bytes
Fixed Size                    282396 bytes
Variable Size               46137344 bytes
Database Buffers            33554432 bytes
Redo Buffers                  532480 bytes
```

The part of the SGA containing general information that is accessed by the background processes is termed the *fixed SGA*. The size of the fixed SGA is relatively small and is automatically determined by Oracle Server. The DBA has no control of the size of this area. You can also query the V_$SGASTAT view to get information on the SGA. A portion of the output from a query on this view is shown here:

```
SQL> select * from v_$sgastat;
POOL          NAME                             BYTES
-----------   --------------------------    ----------
              fixed_sga                         282536
              db_block_buffers                33554432
              log_buffer                        524288
shared pool   1M buffer                        1049088
shared pool   Checkpoint queue                  141152
```

Oracle9i Server allows you to size the SGA dynamically. The shared pool and the database buffer cache can be resized when Oracle Server is running. The maximum size of the SGA is still limited by the SGA_MAX_SIZE parameter.

The size of the variable areas of the SGA is determined by initialization parameters. The parameters that affect SGA size the most are summarized in Table 5-1.

Initialization Parameter	Description
DB_CACHE_SIZE	The size of the database caches in standard blocks
LOG_BUFFER	The bytes allocated for the redo log buffer
SHARED_POOL_SIZE	The size in bytes of an area devoted to shared SQL and PL/SQL statements
LARGE_POOL_SIZE	Area in bytes of the large pool
JAVA_POOL_SIZE	The area used for running Java (Java-stored procedures and Enterprise Java Beans)

TABLE 5-1. *Initialization Parameters Affecting the SGA*

The database block buffer cache (or simply, block buffers) is the major constituent of the SGA. Oracle Server reads data stored in data files into the block buffers. The block buffers in memory can contain unmodified data or modified data. Oracle modifies data in the block buffers rather than on database files. This is because read/write operations to physical memory are much faster than file I/O operations. When a query is issued, Oracle Server searches for data in the block buffers prior to retrieving them from data files. This improves efficiency. As a DBA, you must ensure that there is no contention for block buffers. The size of the block buffers is set by the initialization parameter DB_CACHE_SIZE. Data in the buffer cache is managed automatically. Oracle Server uses the most recently used (MRU) algorithm to determine which data blocks should remain in memory. The least recently used (LRU) algorithm is used to determine the data blocks that should be removed from memory. A block diagram of the SGA is shown here:

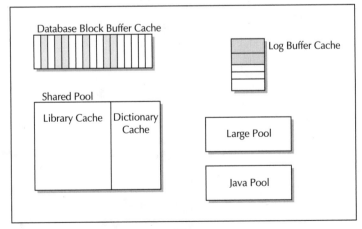

SGA

NOTE
The size of the block buffers was determined by the settings for the DB_BLOCK_BUFFERS and DB_BLOCK_SIZE in earlier releases of Oracle Server. These are retained for backward compatibility. The DB_CACHE_SIZE parameter has been introduced in Oracle9i to manage the size of the block buffers. Dynamic sizing of the block buffers is possible only if you use the DB_CACHE_SIZE parameter.

On Windows NT/2000 Server, the size of the block buffers, in bytes, can be determined by using the SHOW PARAMETER command in SQL*Plus, as shown here:

```
SQL> SHOW PARAMETER DB_CACHE_SIZE
NAME                                 TYPE         VALUE
------------------------------------ ----------- -------------
db_cache_size                        big integer 33554432
```

In Oracle9i, the size of the block buffers can be modified dynamically when the instance is running. This is done using the ALTER SYSTEM command to change the setting for the DB_CACHE_SIZE parameter. The following example sets the block buffers to 30MB.

```
SQL> alter system set db_cache_size=30000000;
System altered.
```

The instance configuration screen of OEM can also be used to view information on block buffers and also to modify the size of the cache, as shown here:

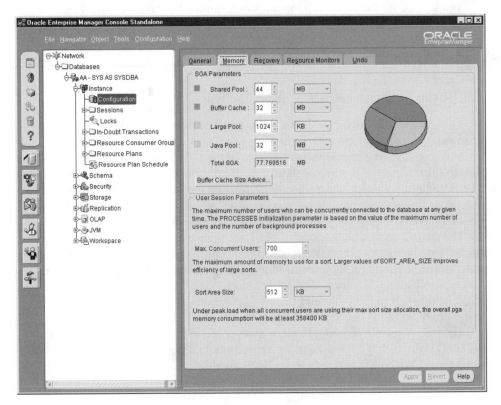

Another important piece of the SGA is the redo log buffer cache. This cache is used to store redo entries until these can be written to the online redo log files on disk. Redo entries contain information on changes made by data manipulation statements. The changes in data, along with information on how the data changed, are saved in the redo entries. Oracle Server uses this information when database recovery is required.

The size of the log buffer parameter is determined by the LOG_BUFFER initialization parameter, as shown here:

```
SQL> SHOW PARAMETER LOG_BUFFER
NAME                                     TYPE        VALUE
-----------------------------------  ----------- -------------
log_buffer                               integer     524288
```

The value of the log buffer cache is specified in bytes. This setting cannot be changed dynamically when the instance is running.

SQL and PL/SQL statements use an area in the SGA called the *shared pool area* to store parsed SQL statements along with their execution plans. When a SQL statement is issued, Oracle Server performs a lookup of the shared pool to determine if this statement has been previously executed. If so, information on the statement is already available in the shared pool and is reused.

The shared pool actually consists of two structures: library cache and dictionary cache. The dictionary cache is also called the *row cache*. While the library cache is used to store parsed SQL statements along with their execution plans, the dictionary cache purely contains information retrieved from the data dictionary. This includes information such as the table and column definitions, privileges, and so on. User session information is also stored in the shared pool if shared servers are used.

The size of the shared pool is set in bytes using the initialization parameter SHARED_POOL_SIZE. The size of the shared pool can be modified dynamically using the ALTER SYSTEM command. OEM can also be used to view and modify the shared pool size.

CAUTION
Oracle Server represents each SQL statement with a shared SQL area and a private SQL area. Two users executing the same SQL statement reuse the shared SQL area. Even if the SQL statements vary slightly, they are considered different. Even two queries with a difference in case, white spaces, or new-line characters are considered different.

The SGA also includes an area known as the *large pool*. This area of memory is used only to cater to the large memory requirements of shared servers, Recovery Manager disk I/O buffers, and so on. The initialization parameter

LARGE_POOL_SIZE is used to set the size of the large pool. The large pool is allocated only if the PARALLEL_AUTOMATIC_TUNING parameter is set to TRUE. By default, this parameter is set to FALSE on the Windows NT/2000 platform and the large pool is not allocated.

Oracle has added Java support to its database since Oracle8i. Java support in the form of Java-stored procedures and Enterprise Java Beans (EJB) is included. The JAVA_POOL_SIZE initialization parameter is used to set the size of the Java pool. If your applications do not require Java support, set this to zero. OEM can be used to manage the Java pool.

NOTE
If you do not need Java support, perform a custom installation and choose not to install the JServer.

Process Global Area   The PGA is the second largest piece of memory allocated by Oracle Server. It consists of the private SQL area and the session memory area. Information specific to user processes such as bind variable values, sort areas, and cursor information is stored in the private SQL area. Sort areas are query dependent. Cursor-related information including login information is stored in the session memory area. The size of the PGA cannot be controlled directly by the DBA. Oracle documentation also refers to the PGA as *program global area*.

Oracle Processes

Oracle Server uses several processes to manage an Oracle database. These processes have specific functions and can be classified into server processes, background processes, and slave processes. Though Oracle processes are important for the purpose of understanding the architecture, they are not directly relevant to a DBA on the Windows NT/2000 platform. A single process named **oracle.exe** is visible in the Task Manager. This is because Oracle processes are implemented as threads on Windows NT/2000. For this reason, only a very brief discussion on Oracle processes is provided here.

The Application Log of Windows Event Viewer can be used to obtain a trail of the processes. You can also query the V$BGPROCESS view to obtain information on a specific Oracle process. A sample query to obtain information on the SMON process is shown here:

```
SQL> select paddr, name, description from v$bgprocess
where name='SMON';
PADDR   NAME DESCRIPTION
-------- ----- -------------------------------------------------
6B9FEC50 SMON System Monitor Process
```

Oracle Server creates server processes to service client requests. In the dedicated server mode, a server process is created on behalf of every client. In the Shared Server configuration, client requests are serviced by a set of shared server processes. The Shared Server parameters are discussed in Chapter 6.

Several additional background processes are used to perform key tasks in Oracle Server. The process monitor (PMON), system monitor (SMON), database writer (DBWR), log writer (LGWR), and checkpoint process (CKPT) are some of the important background processes. PMON is responsible for monitoring other processes. Its job is to detect and delete unused server processes. It also keeps track of other background processes. If a background process gets terminated abnormally, PMON is responsible for restarting it.

SMON is used to perform automatic instance recovery and to manage space. It also performs the jobs of coalescing free space and shrinking rollback segments to their optimal sizes.

DBWR is responsible for flushing data from the block buffers to the data files. The DBWR performs this task whenever a checkpoint is raised. Checkpoints can be raised under several situations, for example, if a specified percentage of the database buffer cache is in use. In Oracle9i Server, you can start more than one DBWR process. The initialization parameter DB_WRITER_PROCESSES is used to set the number of DBWR processes.

The LGWR process is used to flush data from redo log buffers (from the redo log buffer cache) to the redo log files. Oracle9i Server uses a lazy writing algorithm, which tries to keep LGWR in sleep mode until it is required. LGWR is awakened at three-second intervals or whenever a COMMIT is issued. LGWR also is awakened when the redo log buffer is one-third full.

Other processes such as CKPT and the Archiver (ARCH) are not discussed in this book. *Oracle9i Database Concepts* in Oracle documentation provides excellent information on the Oracle architecture.

Oracle threads on Windows NT/2000 can be viewed using Oracle Administration Assistant for Windows NT. A section on this utility is included at the end of this chapter.

A utility named **tlist** that is available with the Windows Resource Kit can also provide useful information on Oracle threads. Windows Resource Kit can be downloaded from http://download.microsoft.com.

Database Administration

An Oracle DBA is responsible for the overall health of the Oracle system. Many sites based on the Windows NT/2000 platform expect their system administrators to take on additional responsibilities as DBAs. Oracle9i Server on Windows NT/2000 includes a variety of GUI tools and utilities that make the task of database administration simple and intuitive. In addition, the standard Oracle Server management tools such as SQL*Plus are available for the experienced DBA. The tool that you choose to perform a specific task depends on your level of experience and what you are trying to accomplish. In general, all administration tasks can be performed using a GUI as well as a command-line interface. The remainder of this chapter provides information to help you perform common database administration tasks. A wide range of the tools available for these administration tasks is included in the examples to help you become comfortable with the administration tool of your choice.

Common DBA Tasks

What exactly is the role of a DBA? What are the tasks that a DBA must learn to perform? While it is hard to enumerate all the tasks that a DBA might need to perform on a particular job, there are some tasks that almost every DBA must perform or at least have the knowledge to perform. These common tasks include

- Perform Oracle installation

- Create Oracle databases

- Perform upgrades and migrations

- Start up and shut down the database

- Manage control files, data files, and log files

- Manage tablespaces

- Manage archiving

- Manage space

- Manage users and security

- Take database backups

- Recover databases

- Tune performance

- Manage indexes

- Manage undo

The first three tasks are covered in the first four chapters of this book. This chapter covers the tasks that need to be performed after a database has been created in Windows NT/2000.

Starting Up and Shutting Down Oracle Databases

An Oracle database must be started up before users can connect to it and use it. In some situations, a database needs to be shut down to perform administration tasks. Oracle9i Server can be started up or shut down in different ways on the Windows NT/2000 platform. The method that you choose depends on your situation. The available tools are

- SQL*Plus utility

- SQL*Worksheet utility

- OEM

- Recovery Manager

- ORADIM utility

- Windows NT/2000 administrative tools

As discussed in the following sections, any one of these tools can be used to start up and shut down a database.

The SQL*Plus Utility

SQL*Plus is available in GUI as well as character mode on Windows NT/2000. SQL*Plus can be used to issue any SQL command and perform any database administration task. You must log in as a user with the required privileges to perform a given task. To launch the character mode SQL*Plus utility, execute **sqlplus.exe** from the c:\oracle\ora90\bin folder. To launch the GUI version of SQL*Plus, select Start | Programs | Oracle - OraHome90 | Application Development | SQL Plus or execute **sqlplusw.exe**. Provide your login information in the ensuing login dialog box. After you have logged in successfully, you will see the Oracle9i banner before seeing the SQL prompt.

You must log in as a user with SYSDBA or SYSOPER privileges to start up or shut down an Oracle database. The following example illustrates a database startup and shutdown.

```
C:\oracle\ora90\BIN> sqlplus
SQL*Plus: Release 9.0.1.0.1 - Production on Sun Dec 30 11:14:04 2001
```

```
(c) Copyright 2001 Oracle Corporation.  All rights reserved.
Enter user-name: sys as sysdba
Enter password: <enter password>
Connected to an idle instance.
SQL> startup
ORACLE instance started.
Total System Global Area  118255568 bytes
Fixed Size                   282576 bytes
Variable Size              83886080 bytes
Database Buffers           33554432 bytes
Redo Buffers                 532480 bytes
Database mounted.
Database opened.
SQL> shutdown immediate
Database closed.
Database dismounted.
ORACLE instance shut down.
```

The SQL*Plus Worksheet

SQL*Plus Worksheet is installed as part of the OEM. On Windows NT/2000, SQL*Plus Worksheet is a GUI front-end to SQL*Plus. There are two advantages of using SQL*Plus Worksheet. The first is that you are able to type multiple SQL commands in the command (upper) pane and execute them together. The second advantage is that SQL syntax is color-coded. This helps you type commands correctly since keywords are highlighted.

To launch SQL*Plus Worksheet on Windows NT/2000, select Start | Programs | Oracle - OraHome90 | Application Development | SQLPlus Worksheet. You can also launch SQL*Plus Worksheet from OEM. Click the Database Applications icon in OEM, and then click the SQL*Plus Worksheet icon to launch the application. If you want to launch SQL*Plus Worksheet from the command line, you can execute **oemapp.bat**, as shown here:

```
C:\oracle\ora90\BIN>OEMAPP.BAT worksheet
```

Start the sample Oracle database by typing the following commands in SQL*Worksheet.

```
connect sys/change_on_install AS SYSDBA
STARTUP NOMOUNT;
ALTER DATABASE MOUNT;
ALTER DATABASE OPEN;
```

Note that four lines of commands are typed in the command window and executed together. This is a big advantage with SQL*Worksheet over SQL*Plus. The output from the execution of the preceding four lines is shown here:

```
Connected to an idle instance.
ORACLE instance started.
Total System Global Area   118255568 bytes
Fixed Size                    282576 bytes
Variable Size               83886080 bytes
Database Buffers            33554432 bytes
Redo Buffers                  532480 bytes
Database altered.
Database altered.
```

OEM

OEM is bundled with Oracle9i Enterprise Edition on Windows NT/2000. To launch OEM, select Start | Programs | Oracle - OraHome90 | Enterprise Manager Console. You can also launch OEM from the command prompt by executing **oemapp.bat**, as shown here:

```
C:\oracle\ora90\BIN>OEMAPP.BAT console
```

To start up an Oracle database using OEM, expand the Databases node and open the configuration screen for your database, as shown in Figure 5-4.

Select the Open radio button and click the Apply button. Choose suitable startup options from the ensuing dialog box, and click the OK button. A dialog box similar to the one shown here shows you the status of the startup operation.

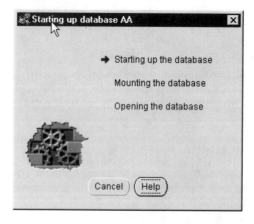

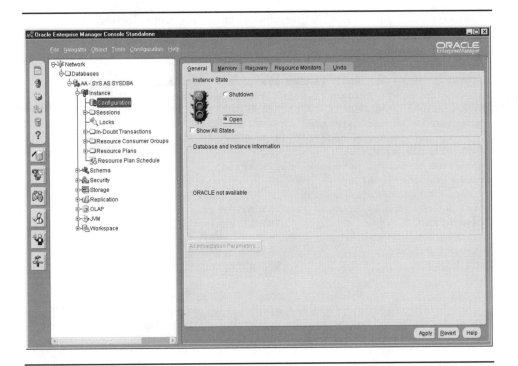

FIGURE 5-4.   *Starting up a database from OEM*

Note that the OEM Console refreshes automatically to show you the new state of the Oracle database.

NOTE
Extensive coverage of OEM is included in Chapters 7 and 8.

Recovery Manager

Recovery Manager (RMAN) is not typically used to start up and shut down Oracle databases; however, if you are already in the RMAN environment, it might be easier to use RMAN instead of switching to another tool. You can launch RMAN from OEM or execute **rman.exe** from the command line.

In a typical situation, RMAN is used for database recovery. The database is mounted, files restored, and recovery performed. The process of mounting a database is illustrated here:

```
C:\oracle\ora90\BIN>RMAN TARGET sys/change_on_install nocatalog
Recovery Manager: Release 9.0.1.1.1 - Production
(c) Copyright 2001 Oracle Corporation.  All rights reserved.
connected to target database: AA (DBID=1560084036)
using target database controlfile instead of recovery catalog
RMAN> STARTUP MOUNT;
connected to target database (not started)
Oracle instance started
database mounted
Total System Global Area      118255568 bytes
Fixed Size                       282576 bytes
Variable Size                  83886080 bytes
Database Buffers               33554432 bytes
Redo Buffers                     532480 bytes
RMAN>
```

In a typical situation, missing or corrupt files are restored at this point and the database is recovered before opening the database. The database is opened using the ALTER DATABASE command, as shown here:

```
RMAN> SQL 'ALTER DATABASE OPEN';
sql statement: alter database open
```

ORADIM Utility

The ORADIM utility is installed along with Oracle9*i* Enterprise Edition on Windows NT/2000. You can launch this utility by executing **oradim.exe** from the command line. Appropriate command-line options must be provided to start up and shut down an Oracle database.

The ORADIM utility can be used to shut down a database and start it up from the command line. This can be useful in a situation in which a full database backup is taken. Schedule a Windows task using Windows Scheduler to shut down the database, copy the necessary files for a cold backup, and then start up the database again. Windows Scheduler can be launched from the Start menu or by executing the **at** command. The following example shuts down the database AA and starts it again as a Windows service.

```
C:\oracle\ora90\BIN>oradim -shutdown -sid aa
C:\oracle\ora90\BIN>oradim -startup -sid aa -usrpwd change_on_install
-starttype srvc
```

To view all the available options, type **oradim –help** on the command line.

Windows NT/2000 Administration Tools

The Services applet included in Windows NT/2000 can be used to start up and shut down Oracle databases. Launch the Services applet from the Control Panel to manage the Oracle services. If you want to automatically start the Oracle database and services when the machine is started, set the *Startup Type* property to *Automatic.*

CAUTION
Avoid shutting down the Oracle service directly from the Services applet, as this is equivalent to performing a shutdown abort.

For example, to configure the Oracle service for the database named AA to start automatically, set the service named OracleServiceAA to start automatically, as shown here:

OracleServiceAA Properties (Local Computer)	? X
General | Log On | Recovery | Dependencies	
Service name: OracleServiceAA	
Display name: OracleServiceAA	
Description:	
Path to executable:	
c:\oracle\ora90\bin\ORACLE.EXE AA	
Startup type: Automatic	
Service status: Started	
Start | Stop | Pause | Resume	
You can specify the start parameters that apply when you start the service from here.	
Start parameters:	
OK | Cancel | Apply	

If you do not want the Oracle database to start up every time you reboot your machine, you can also manually start up the database service.

TIP
*On Windows NT/2000, also set up the Oracle
Listener to start automatically. The default Listener
service is named OracleOraHome90TNSListener.*

Database States

An Oracle9i database can be in many states. Some of the common states are

■ Instance has been created, but has not been mounted.

■ Database has been mounted but is not open.

■ Database is open for use.

■ Database is shut down.

An instance is necessary to create the database itself as seen in Chapter 4.

A database is typically mounted in a recovery situation. After performing recovery on the database, it can be opened. Normal users can connect to and use the database only when it is open. When the database is not required by user applications, a DBA can shut it down to save system resources. The database can be moved from one state to another using the appropriate STARTUP option or by issuing the ALTER DATABASE command.

Similarly, options are available to shut down the database. A database can be shut down normally if no users are connected to the database. If you want to shut down the database when users are connected to the database, as is usually the case, you can shut down with the Immediate option. In the odd situation in which your database appears to have hung, you can shut down with the Abort option. Aborting an instance dumps the instance and should be used as the last resort. Table 5-2 summarizes the various database startup options.

Startup Option	Activity	Typical Use
OPEN (default)	Sessions can be created. Export and Import. Full database backup.	Normal database use; database is open for all users
NOMOUNT	Database Creation. Control File Creation.	While creating a database

TABLE 5-2. *Common Options for Database Startup*

Startup Option	Activity	Typical Use
MOUNT	Database/data file/tablespace recovery.	Renaming data files, managing redo logs, changing archive mode, database recovery
CLOSED	None.	Add/drop/move a control file when a parameter file is modified; cold backup of database
RESTRICT	Special users with restricted session privilege can access the database.	Rebuilding indexes, database import and export
EXCLUSIVE	Normal use.	Used to start a single instance in a Parallel Server configuration
FORCE	Normal use after database comes up.	Bounce the database; instance failure
PARALLEL	Normal use.	To start multiple instances in a Parallel Server configuration
PFILE	Normal use.	Start database with a nondefault location of parameter file

TABLE 5-2. *Common Options for Database Startup* (continued)

Table 5-3 summarizes the options during shutdown.

Shutdown Option	Activity	Typical Use
NORMAL (default; do not type this clause)	Normal shutdown.	Normal shutdown; database is in consistent state
IMMEDIATE	Uncommitted transactions are rolled back. Open sessions killed.	Shut down database quickly

TABLE 5-3. *Common Options for Database Shutdown*

Shutdown Option	Activity	Typical Use
TRANSACTIONAL	Active transactions are allowed to complete. Inactive transactions terminated. New transactions not permitted.	
ABORT	Transactions are terminated abruptly. No commits or rollbacks. Users sessions aborted.	Used as last resort to shut down a database

TABLE 5-3. *Common Options for Database Shutdown* (continued)

All flavors of commands related to database startup and shutdown can be issued from SQL*Plus, SQL*Worksheet, RMAN, or OEM. The following examples illustrate these commands.

```
SQL> shutdown immediate
Database closed.
Database dismounted.
ORACLE instance shut down.
SQL> startup nomount
ORACLE instance started.
Total System Global Area   118255568 bytes
Fixed Size                    282576 bytes
Variable Size               83886080 bytes
Database Buffers            33554432 bytes
Redo Buffers                  532480 bytes
SQL> alter database mount;
Database altered.
SQL> alter database open;
Database altered.
SQL> alter database close;
Database altered.
SQL> shutdown;
ORA-01109: database not open
Database dismounted.
ORACLE instance shut down.
```

You have seen that Oracle9i Server can be started up or shut down in many ways. It is recommended that you get comfortable with one of the methods detailed in this section. If you are an experienced DBA and you need to schedule database maintenance tasks, it is advised that you write SQL scripts to perform your tasks. In this situation you are better off issuing the necessary STARTUP and SHUTDOWN commands from the script itself; however, if you are a relatively inexperienced user and you do not need to perform any maintenance operations on a regular basis, it is recommended that you use OEM to start up and shut down the database.

TIP
Use Windows Scheduler to run SQL scripts in unattended mode. For example, if you want to take a full database backup at 2:00 A.M., create a SQL script to first shut down the database. Then, take a backup and start up the database again. Finally, use Windows Scheduler to run this script at 2:00 A.M.

Restricting Database Access   Occasionally, a DBA is required to perform a maintenance operation on the database while ensuring that no users are connected to the database. An Oracle9i database can be started up in restricted mode to ensure that only users with DBA privileges can connect to the database. For example, if you want to take a full database export, you should ensure that the database is consistent. To do so, shut down the database and restart it in restricted mode, as illustrated in this example:

```
SQL> shutdown immediate
Database closed.
Database dismounted.
ORACLE instance shut down.
SQL> startup restrict;
ORACLE instance started.
Total System Global Area  118255568 bytes
Fixed Size                   282576 bytes
Variable Size              83886080 bytes
Database Buffers           33554432 bytes
Redo Buffers                 532480 bytes
Database mounted.
Database opened.
```

Note that normal database users will not be able to connect to the database when it is in restricted mode. This behavior is illustrated here:

```
SQL> connect scott/tiger
ERROR: ORA-01035: ORACLE only available to users with RESTRICTED
SESSION privilege
```

In a typical situation, a database must be shut down and restarted in restricted mode to stop user access. Oracle9i includes a new feature that can be used to restrict normal user access without shutting down the database. This feature is called *quiescing* (meaning quiet or silent). The advantage of using this feature to restrict database access is that DBA-level users can still issue queries, execute PL/SQL statements, and execute transactions. This feature disables operations only from non-DBA users.

To use this feature, Database Resource Manager must be enabled. Database Resource Manager is a new feature in Oracle9i and is discussed in the *Database Administrator's Guide* of Oracle documentation. A resource plan must be created and associated with the resource manager. Finally, the ALTER SYSTEM command can be used to put the database in quiesced mode. The steps are illustrated here.

Step 1: Create a Plan   Log in as the user SYS and execute the CREATE_SIMPLE_PLAN procedure to create a simple plan named our_plan1.

```
SQL> begin
  2   dbms_resource_manager.create_simple_plan(simple_plan => 'our_plan1',
  3     consumer_group1 => 'mygroup1', group1_cpu => 80,
  4     consumer_group2 => 'mygroup2', group2_cpu => 20);
  5   end;
  6   /
PL/SQL procedure successfully completed.
```

Step 2: Enable Database Resource Manager   Edit the parameter file and add the following parameter.

```
RESOURCE_MANAGER_PLAN = our_plan1;
```

Next, bounce (shut down and restart) the database for this parameter to take effect.

Step 3: Place the Database in Quiesced Mode   Use the ALTER SYSTEM command to place the database in quiesced mode.

```
SQL> alter system quiesce restricted;
System altered.
```

In the current mode, normal users cannot create sessions, issue queries, execute PL/SQL statements, or execute other transactions until the database is removed from the quiesced mode. If a normal user attempts any of these operations, the statement appears to hang. Control does not return to the user until the DBA removes the database from the quiesced mode. The database is removed from quiesced mode by using the ALTER SYSTEM command again.

```
SQL> alter system unquiesce;
System altered.
```

Note that the advantage of placing a database in quiesced mode is that it blocks normal users from using the database without shutting down the database. In earlier versions, a database had to be started in restricted mode to block non-DBA users from accessing the database.

Suspending a Database

Oracle9*i* includes a feature that allows a DBA to suspend a database. By doing so, all new I/O operations to data files and control files are suspended until the database is resumed. In the suspended state, the DBA can perform the necessary operations (for example, take a backup). The following example illustrates this feature.

Step 1: Suspend the Database   Log in as SYS and issue the ALTER SYSTEM command to suspend the database.

```
SQL> alter system suspend;
System altered.
SQL> select database_status from v$instance;
SUSPENDED
```

Note that the database status is updated to reflect the suspended state.

Step 2: Complete Required Operation   Perform the required operations on the database while the database is in suspended state. Normal users are not able to use the database while the database is in a suspended state. If they attempt to execute a query or other operations, the statement cannot execute and control cannot return to the user until the database is resumed again. All user requests issued when the database is suspended are queued and executed in order when the database is resumed again.

Step 3: Resume the Database   Resume the database using the ALTER SYSTEM command.

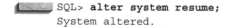
```
SQL> alter system resume;
System altered.
```

Note that a database in quiesced mode allows a DBA to transact on the database. In contrast, a suspended database stops I/O to data files and control files and therefore stops all transactions against the database.

Managing Control Files

Control files are critical to an Oracle database since they contain information on the physical structure of the database. As a DBA, you must ensure that at least one valid copy of the control file is available to Oracle Server at all times.

Use of Control Files

Information on the data files and redo log groups (and their log members) associated with a database is maintained in the control files. This information includes their physical locations and other meta information such as SCNs and timestamps. The name of the database, along with the time of creation, is also stored within the control file.

Location of Control Files

The CONTROL_FILES parameter in the initialization file is used by Oracle Server to find the control file(s) associated with a database. This parameter is read during startup, and the target control files in turn are used to find the data files and redo log files belonging to the database. The control files are created during database creation. The V$CONTROLFILE view provides information on the location of control files.

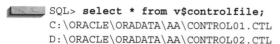
```
SQL> select * from v$controlfile;
C:\ORACLE\ORADATA\AA\CONTROL01.CTL
D:\ORACLE\ORADATA\AA\CONTROL02.CTL
```

If a control file is lost, it can be re-created using the CREATE CONTROLFILE command. If you have lost the associated redo log files, you need to open the database with the RESETLOGS option.

Multiplexing Control Files

Oracle recommends that you multiplex the control files. On Windows NT/2000, you can simply copy an existing control file to a new location and add this file to the list provided by the CONTROL_FILES parameter. You can change the name of the copy created. It is advisable that you place this control file on a separate physical disk.

Backing Up a Control File

You can create a copy of the control file with the ALTER DATABASE command. When you issue this command, Oracle Server creates a SQL script that can be used to re-create the control file. An example is included here:

```
SQL> alter database backup controlfile to trace;
Database altered.
```

Executing the preceding statement resulted in a trace file in the udump folder of the installation. The file contains the following CREATE CONTROLFILE script.

```
CREATE CONTROLFILE REUSE DATABASE "AA" NORESETLOGS NOARCHIVELOG
     MAXLOGFILES 50
     MAXLOGMEMBERS 5
     MAXDATAFILES 100
     MAXINSTANCES 1
     MAXLOGHISTORY 113
LOGFILE
   GROUP 1 'C:\ORACLE\ORADATA\AA\REDO01.LOG'  SIZE 100M,
   GROUP 2 'C:\ORACLE\ORADATA\AA\REDO02.LOG'  SIZE 100M,
   GROUP 3 'C:\ORACLE\ORADATA\AA\REDO03.LOG'  SIZE 100M
# STANDBY LOGFILE
DATAFILE
   'C:\ORACLE\ORADATA\AA\SYSTEM01.DBF',
   'C:\ORACLE\ORADATA\AA\UNDOTBS01.DBF',
   'C:\ORACLE\ORADATA\AA\CWMLITE01.DBF',
   'C:\ORACLE\ORADATA\AA\DRSYS01.DBF',
   'C:\ORACLE\ORADATA\AA\EXAMPLE01.DBF',
   'C:\ORACLE\ORADATA\AA\INDX01.DBF',
   'C:\ORACLE\ORADATA\AA\TOOLS01.DBF',
   'C:\ORACLE\ORADATA\AA\USERS01.DBF'
CHARACTER SET WE8MSWIN1252;
```

The control file can be re-created by running the preceding script. The database must not be mounted. Since the control file is binary, you can view its contents by using the preceding method.

A binary backup of the control file can also be created using the ALTER DATABASE command, as shown here:

```
SQL> alter database backup controlfile to 'c:\backup\control.bkp';
Database altered.
```

Dropping, Renaming, and Relocating Control Files

It is possible to rename or relocate a control file by using the following steps:

1. Shut down the database.

2. Rename or copy the existing control file(s) to a new name and/or location.

3. Edit the parameter file, and change the setting for the CONTROL_FILES parameter to point to the new names and locations.

4. Start up the database.

To drop a control file, simply shut down the database, edit the parameter file to exclude the dropped control file, and restart the database. You can delete the unused control file using Windows Explorer at a later time. Note that you cannot delete a control file while the database is open. If you do so, the database will not start up the next time.

Managing Data Files

Data files contain system and user data and must be managed carefully. If a data file is lost, all the data in that file is lost forever unless the data file can be recovered. Occasionally, a data file needs to be moved to another location or needs to be taken offline. Frequent DBA tasks related to data files are discussed in this section.

A tablespace is represented on the OS as one or more data files. A data file can belong to only one tablespace. Oracle Server identifies every data file with file numbers. Every file has an absolute and a relative file number. The absolute file number is a unique number assigned to a data file across the entire database. The relative file number is assigned to identify data files belonging to a tablespace.

NOTE
Earlier releases of Oracle Server had only a single file number. Oracle9i identifies a data file using the absolute file number and a relative file number.

Creating Data Files

First estimate the number of logical objects and their sizes before creating the tablespace to hold them. This will enable you to size the data files appropriately during tablespace creation.

TIP
To estimate the size of logical objects, first insert some sample data into the objects. Then determine the average row size and multiply this by the number of records that you expect to add over a given time period. Create a tablespace with a set of data files large enough to hold the objects in that tablespace.

Data files are normally created when a tablespace is created or expanded. Since the SYSTEM tablespace is created during database creation, the first set of system data files (these are listed in the CREATE DATABASE statement) are created at database creation. Other data files are typically created when a CREATE TABLESPACE or ALTER TABLESPACE command is issued. Temporary data files are created when a temporary tablespace is created using the CREATE TEMPORARY TABLESPACE command. Similarly, temporary data files are added to an existing database by issuing the ALTER TABLESPACE ADD TEMPFILE command. In a situation in which a data file is lost, an empty data file is re-created by issuing the ALTER DATABASE CREATE DATAFILE command.

The maximum number of data files that can be associated with a database is restricted by the DB_FILES initialization parameter. The default value for this parameter on Windows NT/2000 is 200. This means that a database can have 199 user data files by default since there must be at least one data file associated with the SYSTEM tablespace. Since control information on data files is stored in the SGA, it is important to tune this parameter to save space in the SGA. If you set a low value for this parameter, you will not be able to add data files beyond the set limit. If you set it too high, you will be wasting space in the SGA. Additionally, the MAXDATAFILES clause of the CREATE DATABASE command restricts the number of data files that can be created on a given database. The setting for DB_FILES must always be less than or equal to that specified by MAXDATAFILES during database creation. A few examples are included here for your reference.

```
CREATE TABLESPACE data_tab
DATAFILE 'E:/Oracle/data/data_tab01.dbf' SIZE 100M
EXTENT MANAGEMENT DICTIONARY
DEFAULT STORAGE (
      INITIAL 100K
      NEXT 100K
      MINEXTENTS 5
      MAXEXTENTS 50
      PCTINCREASE 0);
```

The previous example creates a tablespace named DATA_TAB and associates a data file named **data_tab01.dbf** with this tablespace. The extent management clause is discussed in the section titled "Locally Managed Tablespaces" later in this chapter.

```
CREATE TEMPORARY TABLESPACE temp
   TEMPFILE 'E:\oracle\oradata\temp_01.dbf' SIZE 50 REUSE  EXTENT
MANAGEMENT LOCAL UNIFORM SIZE 16M;
```

The previous example creates a temporary tablespace. Note that the TEMPFILE clause is used instead of the DATAFILE clause.

```
ALTER TABLESPACE data_tab ADD DATAFILE 'e:\oracle\data\data_tab02.dbf'
SIZE 100M;
ALTER DATABASE DATAFILE 'e:\oracle\data\data_tab02.dbf' RESIZE 150M;
```

The previous commands add a data file to an existing tablespace and resize the data file. The next example creates a data file and enables the AUTOEXTEND property. The file starts at a size of 100MB and then grows dynamically whenever additional space is required. The growth is in steps of 10MB, and the maximum size of this data file is restricted to 500MB.

```
ALTER TABLESPACE test ADD DATAFILE 'e:\oracle\data\data_tab02.dbf'
SIZE 100M AUTOEXTEND ON NEXT 10M MAXSIZE 500M;
```

On Windows NT/2000, the SYSTEM tablespace should be at least 150MB. If possible, plan to create a SYSTEM tablespace of this size with only one data file. Other OS limits must be kept in mind while designing the database. On Windows NT/2000, the maximum size of a single file is limited to 4GB if you are using the FAT32 file system; however, if you are using the NTFS file system, the maximum size of a single file is 16EB (1 exabyte = 10^{18} bytes). The maximum number of data files that can be created depends on the database block size being used. You can create up to 40,000 data files if you are using the default block size of 4,096 bytes. These limits are of academic interest for most sites.

Location of Data Files

You should try to use multiple hard disks on your machine. Place potentially contending data files across different disks. For example, the data files containing tables should be placed in a different disk from those creating corresponding indexes. Avoid placing the data files on the same disk as redo log files. Not only does this reduce I/O performance, but if you lose this hard disk, you can potentially lose your database since redo logs are critical to recovery. Remember that I/O to data files is random, whereas the write operations to a redo log file are sequential. Since random I/O is relatively slow, you should not place data files on the same disk as redo log files.

Changing Status of Data Files

Data files can be taken offline and brought online as required. This is true for all data files except those belonging to the SYSTEM tablespace. The SYSTEM tablespace has to be online at all times since it holds the data dictionary. If you are in a situation in which you know that a specific tablespace is not being accessed, you can save computer resources by taking the associated data files offline. An example is shown here:

```
ALTER DATABASE DATAFILE 'e:\oracle\data\data_tab02.dbf' OFFLINE;
```

Instead of taking individual data files offline, you can use the ALTER TABLESPACE command to take an entire tablespace offline, as shown in this example:

```
SQL> alter tablespace users offline;
Tablespace altered.
```

This command takes all the data files associated with the tablespace offline. Data files can be taken offline only if the database is running in ARCHIVELOG mode.

Renaming and Relocating Data Files

Consider a scenario wherein you have some Oracle data files on your system drive (typically C:\). Assume that you are running low on disk space and you want to move the data files to another disk (D:\) that has ample space. How do you do this? The following example illustrates this operation.

Step 1: Take the Tablespace Offline   Take the tablespace offline to ensure that no data is written to the associated data files. Your database must be in ARCHIVELOG mode to do so.

```
ALTER TABLESPACE test OFFLINE;
```

Step 2: Copy or Move the Data File to the New Location   Use an appropriate OS command to copy, move, or rename the data file(s) associated with the TEST tablespace to the new location.

Step 3: Rename the Data Files Belonging to the Tablespace   Use the ALTER TABLESPACE command to rename the data files belonging to the TEST tablespace, as shown here:

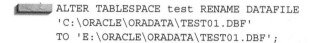

```
ALTER TABLESPACE test RENAME DATAFILE
'C:\ORACLE\ORADATA\TEST01.DBF'
TO 'E:\ORACLE\ORADATA\TEST01.DBF';
```

Step 4: Bring the Tablespace Online   Bring the tablespace online so that users can continue to access the TEST tablespace.

```
SQL> ALTER TABLESPACE test ONLINE;
```

Because the SYSTEM tablespace cannot be brought offline, you can relocate a system data file only when the database is mounted and not open.

TIP
You should take a full backup as soon as you have made any structural changes to the database.

Oracle9*i* also allows you to relocate multiple data files across many tablespaces using the ALTER DATABASE command, as shown in this example:

```
ALTER DATABASE
     RENAME FILE 'E:\ORACLE\ORADATA\PROJECT\USERS01.DBF',
'E:\ORACLE\ORADATA\PROJECT\TOOLS01.DBF'
TO 'F:\ORACLE\ORADATA\PROJECT\USERS01.DBF',
'F:\ORACLE\ORADATA\PROJECT\TOOLS01.DBF'
```

You must copy the data files to the new location prior to issuing the previous command. This is because the ALTER DATABASE RENAME FILE command does not create new data files; it simply updates the control file with the new location of the data files and updates the catalog.

Checking Data Files for Corruption

If you face a situation in which you suspect that a portion of a particular data file is corrupted, you can configure Oracle9*i* Server to check for such corruptions. Oracle Server checks each block for corruption before writing to the disk. To enable this feature, set the DB_BLOCK_CHECKSUM parameter to TRUE in the parameter file. The default setting on Windows NT/2000 is FALSE, meaning that no checking is done for corruption on nonsystem tablespaces. By default, Oracle9i Server checks the data files belonging to the SYSTEM tablespace for corruption.

Enabling this feature can degrade performance because it adds on overhead. The next time the same block is read, the checksum is used to determine if the block is corrupted. Enabling this feature can degrade performance since it adds a huge overhead. You should use this feature only on the advice of Oracle support personnel.

Viewing Data File Information

Data dictionary views provide a variety of information on data files. The DBA_DATA_FILES view provides a listing of all data files along with detailed information such as their size, location, and status. The DBA_EXTENTS view can be queried to determine which data file a specific object resides in. The DBA_FREE_SPACE view provides information on the free space available in a tablespace. The V$DATAFILE_HEADER view provides the data file header information. The following examples illustrate some queries on these views.

```
SQL> select status, recover, creation_time, checkpoint_time, bytes
from v$datafile_header where file# = 2;
ONLINE   NO   04-SEP-01 04-JAN-02   209715200
SQL> select sum(bytes) from dba_free_space where tablespace_name=
'SYSTEM';
89161728
```

OEM can also be used to manage data files and obtain relevant information on them.

Managing Redo Log Files

Redo log files are used to store changes happening on the database. Data changes are written to the online redo log file after commit. There are at least two redo log files for any database. Moreover, redo log files are multiplexed into redo log groups on many sites for redundancy. The terms *redo log files* and *redo log file groups* are used interchangeably in this book. Redo log files are used in case database or instance recovery has to be performed.

NOTE
In a RAC configuration, each instance has its own set of redo log groups. In this situation, the redo logs associated with an instance are referred to as redo log threads.

Contents of Redo Log Files

Redo log files contain redo records or change vectors. A change vector describes the changes made to a single database block. For example, when you insert a row into a table, a change is made to the database block containing this record. A corresponding change is made to the rollback segment. The corresponding headers also need to be updated. An entry in the redo log is made to describe all these changes.

Redo Log Groups and Redo Log Members

Redo log files are multiplexed (duplicated) for the sake of redundancy into redo log groups. A redo log group is a collection of redo log members. Redo log members are replicas of each other. The LGWR process concurrently writes change information to all the members of the online redo log group.

An Oracle database requires at least two redo log groups. This is to enable the Archiver (ARCH) process to archive a redo log file (the file not in use) while database changes are being written to the online file by LGWR.

Creating Redo Log Files

Redo log files are created during database creation. The clauses MAXLOGFILES and MAXLOGMEMBERS are used to restrict the number of log files and log members during database creation. Log files can be added or removed by using the ALTER DATABASE command.

As a DBA, you must choose an appropriate size for the redo log files. If you are archiving your database, you must ensure that the log files are large enough to hold the changes made to the database while the offline log files are being archived. On the other hand, if your log files are too small, frequent log switching occurs. This can degrade performance. If you decide that the sizes of your redo log files are inappropriate, you can create new log files and drop the old ones using the ALTER DATABASE command, as shown here:

```
ALTER DATABASE ADD LOGFILE GROUP 4
('C:\ORACLE\ORADATA\PROJECT\REDO04.LOG',
'D:\ORACLE\ORADATA\PROJECT\REDO04.LOG') SIZE 500K;
```

If you want to multiplex your log groups, you can add log members at a later time, as shown in the following example.

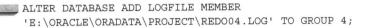

```
ALTER DATABASE ADD LOGFILE MEMBER
'E:\ORACLE\ORADATA\PROJECT\REDO04.LOG' TO GROUP 4;
```

Forcing Log Switches

Consider a situation in which you have to drop an online redo log file. You cannot drop a redo file if it is currently being used. In this case, you have to force a log switch before dropping the redo log file, as illustrated in this example.

```
SQL> select group#, sequence#, status from v$log;
          1          5 CURRENT
          2          3 INACTIVE
          3          4 ACTIVE
SQL> alter system switch logfile;
System altered.
SQL> select group#, sequence#, status from v$log;
          1          5 INACTIVE
          2          6 CURRENT
          3          4 INACTIVE
```

The log file group #1 can now be dropped.

Managing Checkpoints

The DBWR process writes modified blocks from the block buffers to the data files when a checkpoint occurs. The CKPT process signals DBWR when a checkpoint occurs. The CKPT process also updates the headers of data files and log files when a checkpoint occurs. You can force a checkpoint using the ALTER SYSTEM command.

```
SQL> alter system checkpoint;
System altered.
```

Checkpoints also occur when redo log switches occur. You can set initialization parameters to influence log switches. Imagine a situation in which you have large redo log files and not enough transactions on the database, and as a result, a log switch occurs infrequently. You can set the LOG_CHECKPOINT_INTERVAL and LOG_CHECKPOINT_TIMEOUT parameters to get better control of checkpoints. The LOG_CHECKPOINT_INTERVAL specifies the number of operating system blocks that LGWR has written to before a checkpoint occurs. The LOG_CHECKPOINT_TIMEOUT parameter designates the maximum interval between two checkpoints in seconds. Regardless of the values set for these two parameters, a checkpoint always occurs at log switch.

Renaming and Relocating Redo Log Files

Like data files, redo log files can be renamed and relocated. The database must be shut down to do so. The process is illustrated here:

```
SQL> select group# from v$logfile where member like '%REDO03%';
     GROUP#
----------
         3
SQL> select status from V$log where group#=3;
STATUS
----------------
INACTIVE
 SQL> archive log all;
ORA-00271: there are no logs that need archiving
SQL> shutdown immediate;
Database closed.
Database dismounted.
ORACLE instance shut down.
SQL> host move c:\oracle\oradata\aa\redo03.log
c:\oracle\oradata\aa\redo03copy.log
SQL> startup mount;
ORACLE instance started.
Total System Global Area  118255568 bytes
Fixed Size                   282576 bytes
Variable Size              83886080 bytes
Database Buffers           33554432 bytes
Redo Buffers                 532480 bytes
Database mounted.
SQL> alter database rename file 'c:\oracle\oradata\aa\redo03.log' to
2  'c:\oracle\oradata\aa\redo03copy.log';
Database altered.
SQL> alter database open;
Database altered.
```

Verifying Redo Log Files

Redo log files can be verified automatically for corruptions using checksums. To enable this feature, you must set the DB_BLOCK_CHECKSUM parameter to TRUE. If a block on a log member is corrupted, Oracle Server automatically tries to read the same block from another log member of the same group. If all log members are corrupted, then archiving cannot proceed. Again, there is an overhead if this feature is enabled, and performance can be degraded.

Dropping Redo Log Files

If you want to change the size of redo log files, you must drop and re-create redo log files. You can drop redo log groups with the following restrictions:

1. At least two redo log groups must be available.

2. An active redo log group cannot be dropped.

3. When the database is in archived log mode, you cannot drop a log group that is waiting to be archived.

The process is illustrated in the following example.

```
SQL> select group#, archived, status from v$log;
GROUP# ARC STATUS
---------- --- ----------------
         1 YES INACTIVE
         2 NO  CURRENT
         3 YES INACTIVE
SQL> alter system switch logfile;
System altered.
SQL> select group#, archived, status from v$log;
   GROUP# ARC STATUS
---------- --- ----------------
         1 NO  CURRENT
         2 YES INACTIVE
         3 YES INACTIVE
SQL> alter database drop logfile group 2;
Database altered.
```

With certain restrictions, a specific redo log member can also be dropped. You cannot drop the last member of a log group. If the log group is active, you must force a log file switch before dropping the member. Finally, you must ensure that the member is archived before dropping it.

```
ALTER DATABASE DROP LOGFILE MEMBER 'E:\ORACLE\ORADATA\REDO03COPY.LOG'
```

When you drop a log group or a log file member, the file is not physically deleted from the system. You must use an appropriate OS command to delete the redo log file after it is dropped from the database.

Clearing Log Files

Consider a situation in which a redo log group is corrupted when the database is open and you have only two redo log groups on the database. Since a minimum of two groups must be available, you cannot drop the redo log group. This can lead to a situation in which database activity stops. In this situation, you could add another redo log group and drop the corrupted log group. A better solution is to clear the corrupted redo logs. This is illustrated in the following example.

```
SQL> select group#, thread#, archived, status from v$log;
    GROUP#     THREAD#     ARC STATUS
---------- ---------- --- ----------------
         1          1 NO  CURRENT
         3          1 YES INACTIVE
SQL> ALTER DATABASE CLEAR LOGFILE GROUP 3;
Database altered.
```

If you are running in archived log mode, a corrupt redo log file can lead to a bad situation when the corrupted redo log file is archived. Database recovery will not be possible since you have a corrupted archived log file. To overcome this situation, you must avoid archiving the corrupted log file, as shown here:

```
SQL> ALTER DATABASE CLEAR UNARCHIVED LOGFILE GROUP 3;
Database altered.
```

Viewing Redo Log File Information

You must query data dictionary views to obtain information on redo logs files. The V$LOG view displays information on redo log files by reading this information from the control file. You can get information on redo log groups and members by querying the V$LOGFILE view. The V$LOG_HISTORY view contains a history of the logs.

```
SQL> select stamp, thread#, sequence#, first_change#, next_change#
from v$log_history;
STAMP         THREAD#    SEQUENCE#  FIRST_CHANGE# NEXT_CHANGE#
---------- ---------- ---------- ------------- ------------
449845682          1          1        267824       294197
450272694          1          2        294197       315648
450309221          1          3        315648       336870
450352998          1          4        336870       337420
450353035          1          5        337420       337421
450358668          1          6        337421       337883
450358979          1          7        337883       337886
7 rows selected.
```

Managing Tablespaces

Tablespaces and data files are like two faces of a coin. A tablespace stores logical data objects, whereas the data files provide physical storage on the hard disk for the objects. One or more data files are associated with a tablespace. The management of tablespaces is therefore very closely tied to the management of data files.

There are two types of tablespaces defined on Oracle Server: permanent and temporary. *Permanent* tablespaces store permanent data, that is, data that is kept when the instance is shut down. *Temporary* tablespaces are used to store data that is required only when the instance is running. When the database is shut down, the data in the temporary tablespace is no longer important.

A special tablespace named SYSTEM is created when a database is created. This tablespace is typically used to hold the data dictionary and other control information. Other tablespaces are created as necessary by the DBA.

Locally Managed Tablespaces

Tablespaces can be either dictionary managed or locally managed. For a dictionary-managed tablespace, space management information is stored in the data dictionary. A locally managed tablespace maintains such information within its own data files. Locally managed tablespaces can give some performance benefits since the data dictionary is not burdened with the task of managing these tablespaces.

The SYSTEM tablespace has to be managed by the dictionary. If the extents are not defined explicitly, additional permanent tablespaces are locally managed by default. Some advantages offered by locally managed tablespaces are

- Improved concurrency and speed of space management operations.

- Improved performance since recursive dictionary lookups are not required.

- Space allocation is simplified when the AUTOALLOCATE clause is used.

Types of Tablespaces

A typical Oracle database consists of many tablespaces. This section looks at some typical tablespaces.

System Tablespace

A tablespace named SYSTEM is automatically created when the database is created. This tablespace must be online and available at all times since it is used to store the data dictionary and the system rollback segment. You should configure your database such that users do not write to the SYSTEM tablespace. The following example illustrates how you can ensure that the user SCOTT can write only to the TEMP and USERS tablespaces.

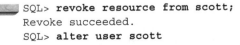

```
SQL> revoke resource from scott;
Revoke succeeded.
SQL> alter user scott
```

```
  2  quota unlimited on temp
  3  quota 20M on users;
User altered.
SQL> connect scott/tiger
Connected.
SQL> create table test(c1 number) tablespace system;
create table test(c1 number) tablespace system
             *
ERROR at line 1:
ORA-01536: space quota exceeded for tablespace 'SYSTEM'
SQL> create table test(c1 number) tablespace users;
Table created.
```

User Tablespaces

User tablespaces can be created to hold user data. The number of user tablespaces, their sizes, locations, and structures depends on your site needs. User tablespaces are created with the CREATE TABLESPACE command, as shown in the following example.

```
CREATE TABLESPACE "FINANCE"
    LOGGING
    DATAFILE 'C:\ORACLE\ORADATA\AA\FINANCE.ora' SIZE 500M EXTENT
    MANAGEMENT LOCAL;
```

Undo Tablespaces

In earlier releases of Oracle Server, undo information was stored in rollback segments. Oracle9i has a new feature that allows undo information to be created in special tablespaces called *undo tablespaces*. Figure 5-5 shows an OEM screen that illustrates the creation of an undo tablespace.

Temporary Tablespaces

Temporary tablespaces are used to create scratch areas. A typical situation when a scratch area is required is for a disk sorting operation. Oracle recommends that you create at least one temporary tablespace and assign this to a user, as shown in the following example:

```
SQL> alter user scott temporary tablespace temp;
User altered.
```

Temporary tablespaces reduce the maintenance work for a DBA. Since they do not contain any real data, there is no need to back up these tablespaces. A permanent tablespace can be converted to a temporary tablespace if there are no permanent objects in the tablespace.

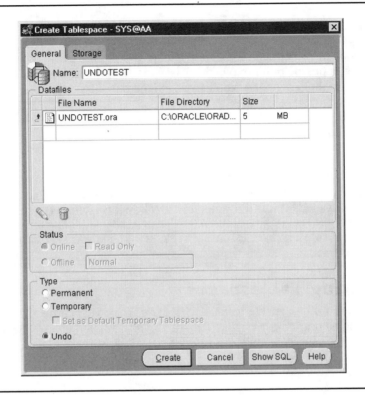

FIGURE 5-5. *Creating an undo tablespace*

Creating Tablespaces

Tablespaces are created with the CREATE TABLESPACE command. They can also be conveniently created from OEM, as shown in Figure 5-5. You should follow the Optimal Flexible Architecture (OFA) guidelines while creating a tablespace.

TIP
If you do not want to use the DB_BLOCK_SIZE setting, Oracle9i Server allows you to set a database block size explicitly while creating a tablespace.

You can define storage parameters and other properties while creating the tablespace.

Dropping Tablespaces

All tablespaces except the SYSTEM tablespace can be dropped. When you drop a tablespace, all the objects in that tablespace are lost permanently. You should take a tablespace offline before dropping it. This guarantees that there are no pending transactions on the tablespace. You can delete the data files belonging to the tablespace to reclaim disk space.

```
SQL> drop tablespace tools including contents;
Tablespace dropped.
```

After executing the preceding command, you must delete the data files at the OS level manually. Oracle9i also has an option for deleting associated data files when a tablespace is deleted. This is illustrated in the following example.

```
SQL> drop tablespace aa including contents and datafiles;
Tablespace dropped.
```

Coalescing Tablespaces

Tablespaces can get fragmented after repeated use. The SMON process automatically tries to combine unused extents into larger chunks; however, if you have set the PCTINCREASE storage parameter to zero, SMON does not coalesce the tablespace. You can manually coalesce a tablespace with the ALTER TABLESPACE command, as shown in this example.

```
SQL> alter tablespace users coalesce;
Tablespace altered.
```

Modifying Tablespaces

As new objects are created in a tablespace and existing objects grow, a tablespace runs out of space. To create additional space, you must add a new data file to the tablespace using the ALTER TABLESPACE command.

```
ALTER TABLESPACE "USERS"
    ADD
    DATAFILE 'C:\ORACLE\ORADATA\AA\USERS03.ora' SIZE 50M;
```

A tablespace can also be resized using the ALTER TABLESPACE command.

```
ALTER DATABASE
    DATAFILE 'C:\ORACLE\ORADATA\AA\USERS03.ORA' RESIZE  5M
```

Storage parameters can also be modified using the ALTER TABLESPACE command. Any changes made to storage parameters apply to new extents created after the changed settings. Existing extents are not resized. You can also allow the tablespace to grow on its own by using the AUTOEXTEND clause.

By default, a tablespace is in read/write mode; however, tablespaces can also be made read-only. This is useful in a situation in which you want to share some historical data that is not going to be modified. Read-only tablespaces are low on maintenance. Any tablespace that is online and does not contain any undo or active rollback segments can be made read-only. The following sample session makes the USERS tablespace read-only and then restores it to read/write mode.

```
SQL> alter tablespace users read only;
Tablespace altered.
SQL> alter tablespace users read write;
Tablespace altered.
```

Nonsystem tablespaces can be taken offline. A tablespace is typically taken offline for some maintenance.

```
SQL> alter tablespace users offline;
Tablespace altered.
```

Viewing Tablespace Information

Several data dictionary views can be used to obtain key information on tablespaces. The V$TABLESPACE and DBA_TABLESPACES views provide information on tablespaces. The DBA_SEGMENTS view can be used to obtain a list of objects in a tablespace. The V$DATAFILE and V$TEMPFILE views can be used to correlate tablespaces and files. User quotas on tablespaces can be obtained from the DBA_USERS view.

OEM can provide a quick overall view of tablespaces along with information on free space, as shown in Figure 5-6.

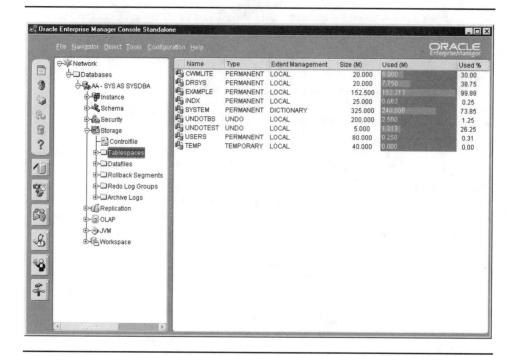

FIGURE 5-6. *Obtaining tablespace information*

Manage Database Archiving

An Oracle database can run in two modes: ARCHIVELOG and NOARCHIVELOG. When a database is running in ARCHIVELOG mode, redo log files are copied to a secondary destination (archived) in a cyclic manner. The ARCH process is responsible for this operation. In this manner, all change vectors are available in archived redo log files. Complete database recovery is possible only when the redo logs are archived.

Archiving can be automatic, meaning that the ARCH process copies redo log files to the secondary destination without the DBA's intervention. A DBA can also manually archive the log files. Automatic archiving is enabled by setting the initialization parameter LOG_ARCHIVE_START to TRUE.

Use the following steps to enable archiving:

Step 1: Take a Complete Database Backup   This is a precautionary measure and is recommended.

Step 2: Shut Down the Database   Shut down the database normally. You can also use the IMMEDIATE or TRANSACTIONAL options.

Step 3: Enable Automatic Archiving   Set the initialization parameter to enable automatic archiving.

```
LOG_ARCHIVE_START = TRUE;
```

Note that setting this parameter does not enable archiving. You must switch the database to ARCHIVELOG mode. You must also set appropriate settings for related parameters such as LOG_ARCHIVE_DEST and LOG_ARCHIVE_FORMAT. The log archive destination must point to a disk that has sufficient space to accommodate archived redo log files.

Step 4: Mount the Database   Use a tool of your choice to create an instance and mount the database.

```
SQL> startup mount
ORACLE instance started.
Total System Global Area   118255568 bytes
Fixed Size                    282576 bytes
Variable Size               83886080 bytes
Database Buffers            33554432 bytes
Redo Buffers                  532480 bytes
Database mounted.
```

Step 5: Switch the Database to Archivelog Mode   Use the ALTER DATABASE command to switch the database to archivelog mode and open the database.

```
SQL> ALTER DATABASE ARCHIVELOG;
Database altered.
SQL> ALTER DATABASE OPEN;
Database altered.
```

Step 6: Verify Archiving   Query the database to ensure that the database is in archivelog mode and that automatic archiving is enabled.

```
SQL> archive log list
Database log mode         Archive Mode
Automatic archival        Enabled
Archive destination       C:\oracle\ora90\RDBMS
Oldest online log sequence    4
Next log sequence to archive  6
Current log sequence          6
```

You must take extra care to ensure that the destination for archived log files does not get full. In this situation, the ARCH process will not be able to archive redo log files. Oracle Server will not overwrite redo log files unless they are archived. All further transactions will halt since the redo logs are not available.

Space Management

A DBA constantly has to keep a watch on how the database is growing. The amount of data and the growth rate directly affect a database's space requirements. Since data is stored in tablespaces, a DBA must ensure that there is enough room in a tablespace to hold new data.

Before looking at space management, it is useful to understand how extents are allocated. A storage parameter is associated with each database object that defines its growth. The storage parameter specifies the size of the first extent allocated, that is, the space allocated when the object is first created. This is specified by the INITIAL_EXTENT parameter of the storage clause. When the space in this extent is used up, Oracle Server allocates the second extent, then the third extent, and so on. The size of these subsequent extents is controlled by the NEXT_EXTENT and PCTINCREASE parameters of the storage clause.

NOTE

In reality, there is another parameter called MINEXTENTS that specifies the number of extents created when the segment is first created. For example, if MINEXTENTS is 5, five extents, each of size INITIAL_EXTENT, are created.

The PCTINCREASE parameter specifies the growth in terms of a percentage increase from the current size of the extent. Either of the following formulas can be used to determine the size of an extent.

```
Size = (size of previous extent) +
              (size of previous extent * PCTINCREASE/100)
Size = NEXT_EXTENT * ((1 + PCTINCREASE)^{(n-2)})/100
```

For example, if the size of the previous extent allocated was 200K and PCTINCREASE was 50 percent, the size of the next extent would be calculated as follows:

```
Size = 200 + (200'50/100) = 300K
```

If a storage clause is not used when the object is created, the storage parameter is inherited from the tablespace definition. In addition to INITIAL_EXTENT, NEXT_EXTENT, and PCTINCREASE, the storage clause for a tablespace can also specify the minimum size of an extent allocated in the tablespace. This is specified by the MINEXTENTS parameter.

The storage parameters for a tablespace can be changed with the ALTER TABLESPACE command, as illustrated in this example.

```
SQL> select initial_extent, min_extents, max_extents, pct_increase,
extent_management from dba_Tablespaces where tablespace_name='SYSTEM';

INITIAL_EXTENT MIN_EXTENTS MAX_EXTENTS PCT_INCREASE EXTENT_MAN
-------------- ----------- ----------- ------------ ----------
         12288           1         249           50 DICTIONARY
SQL> alter tablespace system default storage(pctincrease 5);
Tablespace altered.
SQL> select initial_extent, min_extents, max_extents, pct_increase,
extent_management from dba_Tablespaces where tablespace_name='SYSTEM';
INITIAL_EXTENT MIN_EXTENTS MAX_EXTENTS PCT_INCREASE EXTENT_MAN
-------------- ----------- ----------- ------------ ----------
         12288           1         249            5 DICTIONARY
```

The default storage clause can be modified only for dictionary-managed tablespaces.

Extent Allocation Methods

There are two methods to allocate extents. If you expect a tablespace to have many objects of varying sizes and growth patterns, you can choose to allocate extents automatically. Some space could be wasted in the tablespace if you choose this method; however, it is a simpler way to manage tablespaces.

If you want tighter control over unused space and you can predict the number of extents for an object, it is better to use uniform extents. The following examples illustrate the two choices.

```
SQL> create tablespace test1 datafile 'c:\oracle\oradata\aa\test1.dbf'
  2   size 50m
  3   extent management local autoallocate;
Tablespace created.
SQL> create tablespace test2 datafile 'c:\oracle\oradata\aa\test2.dbf'
  2   size 50m
  3   extent management local uniform size 64K;
Tablespace created.
```

When data files are allocated for a locally managed tablespace, some space is used to maintain the metadata on the tablespace itself.

Space Management for Locally Managed Tablespaces

Free lists have been the traditional method of managing free space within segments. A new feature called *bitmaps* provides a simpler and more efficient way to manage space in Oracle9i. Bitmaps provide better space utilization than free lists.

NOTE
Free lists are lists of database blocks that have space for new data. A bitmap is a map that describes the status of each database block with respect to space. A detailed discussion on free lists and bitmaps is beyond the scope of this book. You can refer to Oracle documentation for more information.

When you create a locally managed tablespace, a segment space management clause allows you to specify how free space and used space within a segment are managed. There are two choices: manually and automatically. In the manual mode (the default), free lists are used to manage spaces. In the automatic mode, Oracle uses bitmaps for space management within segments. The following example illustrates the use of bitmaps for space management.

```
SQL> create tablespace test datafile
  2  'c:\oracle\oradata\aa\test.dbf' size 50m
  3  extent management local
  4  segment space management auto;
Tablespace created.
SQL> select initial_extent, extent_management, segment_space_management
  2  from dba_tablespaces where tablespace_name='TEST';
INITIAL_EXTENT EXTENT_MAN SEGMEN
-------------- ---------- ------
         65536 LOCAL      AUTO
```

OEM provides information on availability of space at a quick glance (refer to Figure 5-6).

User Management and Security

Managing database security is a core task for DBAs. Database security is provided at two levels in Oracle Server: user and schema.

User-level security controls user access to the database. A DBA can control the list of users that can connect to the database and what level of access they get. Schema-level security provides methods to restrict a user's access to any given database object.

Creating and Managing Users

An Oracle database maintains a list of users who can access the database. This information is stored in the data dictionary. A user can be authenticated by a database lookup or externally by a network service or the operating system itself. You can use Oracle Administration Assistant for Windows NT to conveniently create users who are authenticated from the Windows operating system or Windows NT/2000 domain. More information on this utility is included in the "Windows NT/2000 Topics" section later in this chapter.

Using Database Authentication

The Oracle database itself can be used to authenticate users. The CREATE USER command is used to create a user. Once the user is created, necessary privileges must be given to the user. For example, the CREATE SESSION privilege is required for this user to connect to the database. A built-in role named CONNECT can also be given to the user as shown in the next example. The CONNECT role includes the CREATE SESSION privilege.

```
CREATE USER "ORATEST"  PROFILE "DEFAULT"
     IDENTIFIED BY "oracle" DEFAULT TABLESPACE "USERS"
     QUOTA UNLIMITED
     ON TEMP
     QUOTA UNLIMITED
     ON UNDOTEST
     QUOTA UNLIMITED
     ON USERS
     ACCOUNT UNLOCK;
GRANT "CONNECT" TO "ORATEST";
```

Using Operating System Authentication

You can also use the operating system to authenticate database connections. This is convenient to sites that use domain authentication. To enable OS authentication, configure the following initialization parameters:

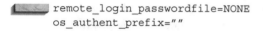

```
remote_login_passwordfile=NONE
os_authent_prefix=""
```

Next, create a database user using the OS login name. For example, if the OS-level user is ANAND, create an Oracle user as follows:

```
SQL> create user anand profile default
  2   identified externally
  3   default tablespace users
  4   account unlock;
User created.
SQL> grant connect, dba to anand;
Grant succeeded.
```

A user logged in as ANAND on the OS can now connect to Oracle Server by using a forward slash. It is not necessary to provide a username and password, as shown here:

```
SQL> connect / as sysdba
Connected.
```

In this example, the user ANAND has been given DBA privileges and is attempting to log in with the SYSDBA privilege. To do so, you must also ensure that the user ANAND is part of the ORA_DBA group at the OS level, as shown in Figure 5-7. The ORA_DBA group is created automatically when you install Oracle9i on Windows NT/2000. This feature can also be used in and Windows XP.

Managing Object Privileges

Granting specific privileges on an object controls object-level privileges. The owner of the object typically grants the privileges. Any other user who has been given the

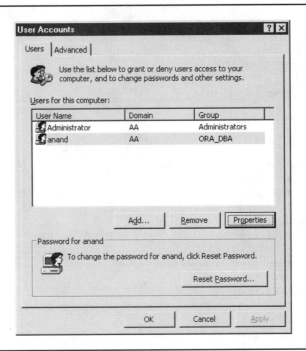

FIGURE 5-7. *Setting OS-level role*

ADMIN option on the object in question can also grant access to the object. A few examples are included to illustrate object privileges.

```
SQL> connect scott/tiger
Connected.
SQL> create table test (C1 number) tablespace users;
Table created.
SQL> insert into test values (1);
1 row created.
SQL> insert into test values (2);
1 row created.
```

```
SQL> commit;
Commit complete.
SQL> grant select on test to anand;
Grant succeeded.
SQL> connect anand/anand
Connected.
SQL> select * from scott.test;
        C1
----------
         1
         2
SQL> insert into scott.test values (4);
insert into scott.test values (4)
                  *
ERROR at line 1:
ORA-01031: insufficient privileges
SQL> connect scott/tiger
Connected.
SQL> revoke all on test from anand;
Revoke succeeded.
SQL> connect anand/anand
Connected.
SQL> select * from scott.test;
select * from scott.test
                        *
ERROR at line 1:
ORA-00942: table or view does not exist
```

Observe that the REVOKE statement is used to revoke privileges on an object. If you are a new user, refer to Oracle documentation for a complete discussion on object privileges.

Database Roles

Database roles are a convenient way to create a class of users. A role is created with the CREATE ROLE command, as seen in this example.

```
CREATE ROLE "TEST_ROLE" IDENTIFIED BY "aa";
GRANT CREATE ANY TABLE TO "TEST_ROLE"
```

When a role is created, specific database and object privileges can be assigned to that role. A database user who is assigned a role inherits the same privileges as the role.

```
GRANT "TEST_ROLE" TO "ANAND";
```

OEM can be used to create and manage database roles. Users can also be assigned to an available role. Query the DBA_ROLES view to obtain a listing of database roles available.

Database Profiles

Oracle Server also permits you to define resource limits and constraints on a user. For example, you can specify that a user cannot use more than a certain percentage of CPU on the machine running Oracle Server. A default profile named DEFAULT is automatically created when the database is created. By default, all users are assigned this profile.

You can create your own profile using the CREATE PROFILE statement and assign it to the user. The following example illustrates profiles.

```
CREATE PROFILE "TEST_PROFILE"
    LIMIT CPU_PER_SESSION DEFAULT CPU_PER_CALL DEFAULT
    CONNECT_TIME DEFAULT IDLE_TIME DEFAULT SESSIONS_PER_USER
    DEFAULT LOGICAL_READS_PER_SESSION DEFAULT
    LOGICAL_READS_PER_CALL DEFAULT PRIVATE_SGA DEFAULT
    COMPOSITE_LIMIT DEFAULT FAILED_LOGIN_ATTEMPTS 3
    PASSWORD_LOCK_TIME DEFAULT PASSWORD_GRACE_TIME DEFAULT
    PASSWORD_LIFE_TIME 30 PASSWORD_REUSE_MAX DEFAULT
    PASSWORD_REUSE_TIME DEFAULT PASSWORD_VERIFY_FUNCTION DEFAULT;
```

Once the profile is created, it must be assigned to the user, as shown here.

```
ALTER USER "ANAND"  PROFILE "TEST_PROFILE";
```

OEM can be used conveniently to manage privileges and assign them to users.

Backing Up a Database

One of the most important responsibilities of a DBA is to ensure that a database is not lost. To ensure this, it is important that good practices are followed to create a sound backup strategy. There are many ways to back up an Oracle database. This section takes a quick look at some standard methods and some specific Windows NT/2000 features.

NOTE
A full discussion on backup and recovery is beyond the scope of this book. You can refer to the Oracle8i Backup and Recovery Handbook *from Oracle Press for more information. The book is currently under revision for Oracle9i.*

What Is a Database Backup?

A database backup is best described as a copy of the critical portions of a database. The backup includes everything necessary to re-create the database in the case of a failure that results in the database being lost.

Physical versus Logical Backups

Two kinds of backups are possible for an Oracle database. A *physical* backup is one in which the required data files and database control files are backed up. The terms *backup* and *recovery* as applied to Oracle databases usually refer to physical backups. *Logical* backups are typically used to back up specific portions of a database. An export dump of a table is a good example of a logical backup.

Archiving versus Nonarchiving Mode

As a DBA, an important decision you have to make is whether you want to archive redo log files or not. You can perform full recovery only if the database is being archived. Database archiving also influences the backup strategy. If you are not archiving the database, hot backups (backups taken when the database is open) are not possible. You can take only cold backups, with the database shut down.

CAUTION
Windows NT/2000 administrators who are used to copying entire directories to backup systems should note that it is not sufficient to back up Oracle directories if the database is open.

Backup Methods

Three main methods are available for taking database backups. The first method uses Recovery Manager (RMAN). The second method uses an operating-system utility to create the backup. You can also use wizards in OEM to take backups. The method you choose depends on the situation. There are some inherent advantages to using RMAN; however, many DBAs prefer to rely on the operating system to take database backups.

Complete versus Partial Backups

A complete backup is one in which all the data files and the control files are backed up. This type of a backup is also referred to as *whole backup* or a *full backup*. It is the most common type of backup. You must shut down the database to take a full backup if the database archiving is not enabled. The database must be in a consistent state for this to be a valid backup; however, if database archiving is enabled, you can take a complete backup with the database open. An added advantage of archiving is that you can take a valid backup regardless of whether the database is in a consistent state or not.

A partial backup backs up a portion of the database. For example, you can choose to back up a specific tablespace, a specific data file, or even a control file.

Consistent versus Inconsistent Backups

A database is in a consistent state when it is shut down normally. A backup taken in this state is considered to be a consistent backup. If database archiving is not enabled (NOARCHIVELOG mode), you must take a consistent backup.

A database is in an inconsistent state when it is open and there are ongoing transactions. A database is also in an inconsistent state if it is shut down abnormally. A backup taken when the database is in an inconsistent state is called an inconsistent backup. You must be in ARCHIVELOG mode to take a valid inconsistent backup.

Hot versus Cold Backups

A hot backup is one that is taken when the database is open. In contrast, a cold backup is taken with the database shut down. A hot backup is possible only when the database is running in ARCHIVELOG mode. You can back up specific tablespaces as part of a hot backup. If archiving is not enabled, only a cold backup is possible. To take a hot backup of a tablespace, you must mark the database for backup before backing up the data files belonging to the tablespace. The following example takes a hot backup of the USERS tablespace.

```
SQL> alter tablespace users begin backup;
Tablespace altered.
SQL> HOST COPY C:\ORACLE\ORADATA\AA\USERS*.* d:\backup
SQL> alter tablespace users end backup;
Tablespace altered.
```

Backup Using Recovery Manager

Recovery Manager is a standard tool for taking database backups. Oracle recommends that you use RMAN to take backups. RMAN can be used to take cold or hot backups. RMAN is installed with the standard Oracle9i installation on Windows NT/2000.

RMAN can be used to take two kinds of backups: image and backup sets. An image backup is a copy of the data files and control files. The copied files are exact replicas of the source files. The disadvantage of an image copy is that it requires a lot of time and space to take a backup. This is because you must allocate sufficient disk space to accommodate all the data files and control files that are included in the backup. This can also be time-consuming if the files are large. You can use RMAN to restore a database from an image backup or use a standard tool such as SQL*Plus for recovery.

A backup set is a logical backup of the database. A backup set includes many pieces. Each piece is stored in Oracle proprietary format. You must use RMAN to recover a database from backup sets. The advantage of a backup set is that you can depend on RMAN to do most of the work during recovery. A backup set also allows you to take incremental backups, meaning that only incremental changes to a database are backed up. This can save a lot of time if your database does not change frequently.

A complete backup can be taken using RMAN by using the BACKUP DATABASE command or the COPY command. Partial backups can be taken with the BACKUP TABLESPACE and COPY DATAFILE commands.

Recovery Catalog

RMAN can use a special schema to maintain metadata on the target database. The metadata is derived from the control file. To avoid a situation in which the recovery catalog itself is lost, the recovery catalog is maintained in a separate database. Oracle recommends that you use a recovery catalog even though it takes additional resources. If you have multiple databases on your site, you can create a single recovery catalog and share this across all the databases. Of course, you must be extra careful to ensure that the recovery catalog itself is not lost!

The biggest advantage of using a recovery catalog is that RMAN automatically tracks information on previous backups. In a recovery situation, you are typically under a lot of stress, and this can leads to mistakes. A recovery catalog can make database recovery easy.

NOTE
It is also possible to use RMAN without a recovery catalog. Assume that a recovery catalog is available in all backup and recovery topics in this book.

Case Study: Using RMAN to Take a Full Backup

Assume that you are the DBA of a production database named AA on Windows NT. This case study will provide a step-by-step approach to using RMAN for taking a whole backup.

Step 1: Create a Database to Hold the Recovery Catalog   Use Database Configuration Assistant to create a small database called RECO that will be used for the recovery catalog as described in Chapter 4. You can select the New

Database option and create a small database. The database is created using the
following script:

```
startup nomount pfile="C:\oracle\admin\RECO\scripts\init.ora";
CREATE DATABASE RECO
MAXINSTANCES 1
MAXLOGHISTORY 1
MAXLOGFILES 5
MAXLOGMEMBERS 5
MAXDATAFILES 100
DATAFILE 'C:\oracle\oradata\RECO\system01.dbf' SIZE 200M
REUSE AUTOEXTEND ON NEXT  10240K MAXSIZE UNLIMITED
UNDO TABLESPACE "UNDOTBS" DATAFILE 'C:\oracle\oradata\RECO\undotbs01.dbf'
SIZE 10M REUSE AUTOEXTEND ON NEXT  5120K MAXSIZE UNLIMITED
CHARACTER SET WE8MSWIN1252
NATIONAL CHARACTER SET AL16UTF16
LOGFILE GROUP 1 ('C:\oracle\oradata\RECO\redo01.log') SIZE 100M,
GROUP 2 ('C:\oracle\oradata\RECO\redo02.log') SIZE 100M,
GROUP 3 ('C:\oracle\oradata\RECO\redo03.log') SIZE 100M;
```

Step 2: Create a User Named RMAN to Own the Recovery Catalog   The
recovery catalog has to be owned by a user. A user named RMAN on the RECO
database is created, as shown here. Note that the RECOVERY_CATALOG_OWNER
role is assigned to the user.

```
SQL> connect sys/change_on_install@reco as sysdba;
Connected.
SQL> create user rman identified by rman
  2  temporary tablespace temp
  3  quota unlimited on system;
User created.
SQL> grant connect, resource to rman;
Grant succeeded.
SQL> grant recovery_catalog_owner to rman;
Grant succeeded.
```

Step 3: Create the Recovery Catalog   Create the recovery catalog in the RMAN
schema of the RECO database using RMAN.

```
c:\>rman catalog rman/rman@reco
Recovery Manager: Release 9.0.1.1.1 - Production
(c) Copyright 2001 Oracle Corporation.  All rights reserved.
connected to recovery catalog database
recovery catalog is not installed
RMAN> create catalog;
recovery catalog created
```

Step 4: Register the Production Database in the Recovery Catalog Use
RMAN to register the production database AA in the recovery catalog.

```
c:\> rman target sys/change_on_install@aa catalog rman/rman@reco
Recovery Manager: Release 9.0.1.1.1 - Production
(c) Copyright 2001 Oracle Corporation.  All rights reserved.
connected to target database: AA (DBID=1560084036)
connected to recovery catalog database
RMAN> register database;
database registered in recovery catalog
starting full resync of recovery catalog
full resync complete
```

You can double-check that the target database was registered with the REPORT
SCHEMA command.

```
RMAN> report schema;
```

You should see a listing of the tablespaces belonging to the target database
along with information on the corresponding data files. To save space, the output
of this command is omitted.

Step 5: Take a Full Backup Using RMAN Use the BACKUP DATABASE
command of RMAN to take a complete backup.

```
RMAN> backup database;
Starting backup at 06-JAN-02
allocated channel: ORA_DISK_1
channel ORA_DISK_1: sid=9 devtype=DISK
channel ORA_DISK_1: starting full datafile backupset
channel ORA_DISK_1: specifying datafile(s) in backupset
including current controlfile in backupset
input datafile fno=00001 name=C:\ORACLE\ORADATA\AA\SYSTEM01.DBF
input datafile fno=00002 name=C:\ORACLE\ORADATA\AA\UNDOTBS01.DBF
input datafile fno=00005 name=C:\ORACLE\ORADATA\AA\EXAMPLE01.DBF
input datafile fno=00007 name=C:\ORACLE\ORADATA\AA\TEST.DBF
input datafile fno=00011 name=C:\ORACLE\ORADATA\AA\USERS03.ORA
input datafile fno=00006 name=C:\ORACLE\ORADATA\AA\INDX01.DBF
input datafile fno=00008 name=C:\ORACLE\ORADATA\AA\USERS01.DBF
input datafile fno=00003 name=C:\ORACLE\ORADATA\AA\CWMLITE01.DBF
input datafile fno=00004 name=C:\ORACLE\ORADATA\AA\DRSYS01.DBF
input datafile fno=00009 name=C:\ORACLE\ORADATA\AA\USERS02.DBF
input datafile fno=00010 name=C:\ORACLE\ORADATA\AA\UNDOTEST.ORA
channel ORA_DISK_1: starting piece 1 at 06-JAN-02
channel ORA_DISK_1: finished piece 1 at 06-JAN-02
piece handle=C:\ORACLE\ORA90\DATABASE\02DDHD71_1_1 comment=NONE
```

```
channel ORA_DISK_1: backup set complete, elapsed time: 00:05:37
Finished backup at 06-JAN-02
```

Similarly, a specific tablespace can be backed up with a BACKUP TABLESPACE command. This is useful in a situation in which a new tablespace has been added to the database or to back up a database that is subjected to heavy activity.

Case Study: Using RMAN to Take a Backup of a Specific Data File

Consider a situation in which you have just recovered a data file and you want to take a backup of this data file. Assuming that the recovery database and recovery catalog are available (see the previous case study for details), you can use the COPY command to create a backup of the required data file.

```
RMAN> copy datafile 9 to 'c:\tmp\users02.bkp';
Starting copy at 06-JAN-02
using channel ORA_DISK_1
channel ORA_DISK_1: copied datafile 9
output filename=C:\TMP\USERS02.BKP recid=2 stamp=450410447
Finished copy at 06-JAN-02
```

The file number of the data file to be backed up can be obtained from the output of the REPORT SCHEMA command or by querying the V$DATAFILE view. Observe that the COPY command has been used here to take the backup. Since this is an image copy, this file can be restored from the operating system using an appropriate COPY command. It is not necessary to use RMAN to restore the backed up file.

Backup Using Windows NT/2000 Operating System

Many sites can afford to shut down the database at the end of a working day and take a full backup. You can take a full database by just copying the data files, control files, parameter files, and archived log files to a new destination. The steps involved are listed here.

Step 1: List the Files to Be Backed Up   Query the data dictionary and get a listing of all the data files, control files, archived redo log files, and parameter file. These are the files that need to be backed up. It is not necessary to back up the online redo log files.

Step 2: Shut Down the Database   Shut down the database normally to ensure that it is in a consistent state.

Step 3: Copy Files to Secondary Storage   Use an appropriate OS copy command to copy the necessary files to an alternate location. This location can even be a tape.

Step 4: Start Up the Database   Start the database after the copying process is complete.

Oracle9i on Windows NT also includes an OCOPY utility that can be used for taking a hot backup of the database. A backup of the data file **users02.dbf** is illustrated here.

```
C:\> ocopy c:\oracle\oradata\aa\users02.dbf c:\tmp\users02.bkp
```

Scheduling a Backup Using Windows Scheduler

You can use Windows Scheduler to run a batch file that will perform the backup tasks for you. The necessary steps are listed next.

Step 1: Create a Script for Shutting Down the Database   Create a script named **shutdown.sql** that will be used to shut down the database, as shown here:

```
connect sys/change_on_install@aa as sysdba;
shutdown immediate
startup restrict
shutdown normal
exit
```

Step 2: Create a Script That Will Be Used to Start Up the Database
Create a script named **startup.sql** that will be used to start up the database with the following contents:

```
connect sys/change_on_install@aa as sysdba;
startup
exit
```

Step 3: Create a Batch File to Take the Backup   Create a batch file named **oraback.bat** that will be used to do a normal shutdown, back up the database, and then start it up again. To ensure that the database is in a consistent state, a normal shutdown is done.

```
c:\oracle\ora90\bin\sqlplus.exe -s /nolog @shutdown.sql
copy c:\oracle\oradata\aa\*.dbf c:\tmp\.
copy c:\oracle\oradata\aa\*.log c:\tmp\.
copy c:\oracle\oradata\aa\*.ctl c:\tmp\.
c:\oracle\ora90\bin\sqlplus.exe -s /nolog @startup.sql
```

You can also use the ORADIM utility to start up and shut down the database.

Step 4: Schedule the Script for Execution   Use Windows Scheduler to run the **oraback.bat** file, and schedule a run at midnight, four times a week.

```
C:\>at 00:00 /every:m,w,f,su oraback.bat
Added a new job with job ID = 1
C:\>at
Status ID   Day                    Time            Command Line
----------------------------------------------------------------
        1   Each M W F Su          12:00 AM        oraback.bat
```

Backup Using OEM

It is possible to take a backup from OEM with the GUI to RMAN. More information on this is included in Chapter 8.

Logical Backup

A logical backup is useful when a specific portion of the database needs to be backed up. You can back up specific database tables or schemas using the Export utility. Since it uses the SQL layer, a logical backup is possible only when the database is open. A logical backup is time-consuming in comparison to a physical backup.

The Export utility can be used in an interactive mode or a noninteractive mode. In an interactive mode, Export prompts you for inputs. In a noninteractive mode, you must provide all the information at the command line. Create a logical backup of the schema belonging to the user SCOTT using an interactive session.

```
C:\> exp
Export: Release 9.0.1.1.1 - Production on Sun Jan 6 10:08:53 2002
(c) Copyright 2001 Oracle Corporation.  All rights reserved.
Username: system@aa
Password: <enter password>
Connected to: Oracle9i Enterprise Edition Release 9.0.1.1.1 - Production
With the Partitioning option
JServer Release 9.0.1.1.1 - Production
Enter array fetch buffer size: 4096 >
Export file: EXPDAT.DMP > scott.dmp
(1)E(ntire database), (2)U(sers), or (3)T(ables): (2)U > 2
Export grants (yes/no): yes > <RETURN>
Export table data (yes/no): yes > <RETURN>
Compress extents (yes/no): yes > <RETURN>
Export done in WE8MSWIN1252 character set and AL16UTF16
 NCHAR character set
About to export specified users ...
```

```
User to be exported: (RETURN to quit) > SCOTT
User to be exported: (RETURN to quit) > <RETURN>
. exporting pre-schema procedural objects and actions
. exporting foreign function library names for user SCOTT
. exporting object type definitions for user SCOTT
About to export SCOTT's objects ...
. exporting database links
. exporting sequence numbers
. exporting cluster definitions
. about to export SCOTT's tables via Conventional Path ...
. . exporting table                    BONUS          0 rows exported
. . exporting table                     DEPT          4 rows exported
. . exporting table                      EMP         14 rows exported
. . exporting table                 SALGRADE          5 rows exported
. . exporting table                     TEST          3 rows exported
. exporting synonyms
. exporting views
. exporting stored procedures
. exporting operators
. exporting referential integrity constraints
. exporting triggers
. exporting indextypes
. exporting bitmap, functional and extensible indexes
. exporting posttables actions
. exporting materialized views
. exporting snapshot logs
. exporting job queues
. exporting refresh groups and children
. exporting dimensions
. exporting post-schema procedural objects and actions
. exporting statistics
Export terminated successfully without warnings.
```

The same export operation could have been performed in a noninteractive mode, as shown here.

 `C:\>exp userid=system/manager@aa file=scott.dmp owner=scott`

Type **exp help=yes** on the command line to get help on the Export utility.

Database Recovery

Database recovery is required whenever a portion of the database or the entire database is lost. This can be due to a hardware failure, such as a corrupted hard disk, or a user error. If you have a valid backup, you can recover the database in its entirety if you are running the database in ARCHIVELOG mode. If archiving is not

enabled, you can recover the database only until the last complete backup that
is available.

There are many complex recovery situations. A complete discussion is beyond
the scope of this book. Recovery using RMAN is illustrated with two case studies.
A separate case study for tablespace point-in-time recovery is provided in Chapter 12.

Case Study: Tablespace Recovery Using RMAN

Assume that a data file named **users02.dbf** belonging to the USERS tablespace has
been corrupted. The database is unable to open because of this, as shown here:

```
SQL> startup
ORACLE instance started.
Total System Global Area   118255568 bytes
Fixed Size                    282576 bytes
Variable Size               83886080 bytes
Database Buffers            33554432 bytes
Redo Buffers                  532480 bytes
Database mounted.
ORA-01157: cannot identify/lock data file 9 - see DBWR trace file
ORA-01110: data file 9: 'C:\ORACLE\ORADATA\AA\USERS02.DBF'
```

A whole backup of the database has been taken using RMAN and is available.
The lost data file from this backup must be restored and the database recovered.

Step 1: Take the Missing Data File Offline   As a DBA your topmost priority
must be to maintain high availability for the database. Since the database cannot
be opened because of the missing data file, you must take this data file offline. This
will enable you to open the database.

```
SQL> alter database datafile 'c:\oracle\oradata\aa\users02.dbf' offline;
Database altered.
```

Step 2: Open the Database   Open the database. Users can continue to use the
other portions of the database. You can recover the lost data file after ensuring
partial use of the database.

```
SQL> alter database open;
Database altered.
```

Step 3: Confirm That Valid Backup Is Available   Query the recovery catalog
to check that a valid backup of the data file is available. You can use the LIST
BACKUP command to obtain a list of available backup sets. To conserve space, the
output is omitted here. You can confirm that the backup set is valid. In this example,
backup set #33 is validated.

```
RMAN> validate backupset 33;
allocated channel: ORA_DISK_1
channel ORA_DISK_1: sid=11 devtype=DISK
channel ORA_DISK_1: starting validation of datafile backupset
channel ORA_DISK_1: restored backup piece 1
piece handle=C:\ORACLE\ORA90\DATABASE\02DDHD71_1_1 tag=null params=NULL
channel ORA_DISK_1: validation complete
```

Step 4: Restore the Missing File   Restore the lost data file using RMAN.
Note that RMAN automatically queries the catalog, locates the backup of the file,
and restores it.

```
RMAN> restore datafile 9;
Starting restore at 06-JAN-02
using channel ORA_DISK_1
channel ORA_DISK_1: restoring datafile 00009
input datafilecopy recid=2 stamp=450410447
filename=C:\TMP\USERS02.BKP
destination for restore of datafile 00009:
C:\ORACLE\ORADATA\AA\USERS02.DBF
channel ORA_DISK_1: copied datafilecopy of datafile 00009
output filename=C:\ORACLE\ORADATA\AA\USERS02.DBF recid=3
stamp=450413580
Finished restore at 06-JAN-02
```

Step 5: Recover the Data File   Media recovery is necessary on this data file.
Again, RMAN can be used to accomplish this task.

```
RMAN> recover datafile 9;
Starting recover at 06-JAN-02
using channel ORA_DISK_1
starting media recovery
media recovery complete
Finished recover at 06-JAN-02
```

Step 6: Bring the Data File Online   Use the ALTER DATABASE command to
bring the recovered data file online again.

```
SQL> alter database datafile 'c:\oracle\oradata\aa\users02.dbf' online;
Database altered.
```

This could have also been done from within the RMAN environment using the
SQL command to execute the ALTER DATABASE command.

Step 7: Take a Backup   Schedule a database backup at the earliest opportunity.

Case Study: Database Recovery Using RMAN

Assume that all the data files have been lost due to a hardware failure. You can recover the entire database using RMAN.

The steps for recovering the database are almost identical to the previous case study. The only difference is that RMAN is used to recover the database instead of a specific data file. The steps are detailed here.

Step 1: Start the Instance   Launch RMAN and mount the database. Note that since data files are missing, you cannot open the database.

```
C:\>rman target sys/change_on_install@aa catalog rman/rman@reco
RMAN> startup nomount;
connected to target database (not started)
Oracle instance started
Total System Global Area      118255568 bytes
Fixed Size                       282576 bytes
Variable Size                  83886080 bytes
Database Buffers               33554432 bytes
Redo Buffers                     532480 bytes
RMAN> sql 'alter database mount';
sql statement: alter database mount
```

Step 2: Restore the Database   Recover the missing data files and perform media recovery, as shown here.

```
RMAN> restore database;
Starting restore at 06-JAN-02
using channel ORA_DISK_1
channel ORA_DISK_1: restoring datafile 00009
input datafilecopy recid=2 stamp=450410447 filename=C:\BACKUP\USERS02.BKP
destination for restore of datafile 00009: C:\ORACLE\ORADATA\AA\USERS02.DBF
channel ORA_DISK_1: copied datafilecopy of datafile 00009
output filename=C:\ORACLE\ORADATA\AA\USERS02.DBF recid=4 stamp=450414584
channel ORA_DISK_1: starting datafile backupset restore
channel ORA_DISK_1: specifying datafile(s) to restore from backup set
restoring datafile 00001 to C:\ORACLE\ORADATA\AA\SYSTEM01.DBF
restoring datafile 00002 to C:\ORACLE\ORADATA\AA\UNDOTBS01.DBF
restoring datafile 00003 to C:\ORACLE\ORADATA\AA\CWMLITE01.DBF
restoring datafile 00004 to C:\ORACLE\ORADATA\AA\DRSYS01.DBF
restoring datafile 00005 to C:\ORACLE\ORADATA\AA\EXAMPLE01.DBF
restoring datafile 00006 to C:\ORACLE\ORADATA\AA\INDX01.DBF
restoring datafile 00007 to C:\ORACLE\ORADATA\AA\TEST.DBF
restoring datafile 00008 to C:\ORACLE\ORADATA\AA\USERS01.DBF
restoring datafile 00010 to C:\ORACLE\ORADATA\AA\UNDOTEST.ORA
restoring datafile 00011 to C:\ORACLE\ORADATA\AA\USERS03.ORA
```

```
channel ORA_DISK_1: restored backup piece 1
piece handle=C:\ORACLE\ORA90\DATABASE\02DDHD71_1_1 tag=null params=NULL
channel ORA_DISK_1: restore complete
Finished restore at 06-JAN-02
RMAN> recover database;
Starting recover at 06-JAN-02
using channel ORA_DISK_1
starting media recovery
media recovery complete
Finished recover at 06-JAN-02
```

Step 3: Open the Database   Now that the database has been recovered, it can be opened. Note that the database has been opened from within the RMAN environment.

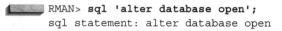

```
RMAN> sql 'alter database open';
sql statement: alter database open
```

Step 4: Take a Full Backup   Schedule a complete backup as soon as possible.

Recovery Using OEM

Database recovery can be done from OEM. More information on this is included in Chapter 8.

Logical Database Recovery

The Export utility can be used to take a logical backup of a specific portion of the database. If a valid export dump is available, the Import utility can be used to recover a specific object or schema.

Case Study: Recovering a Full Schema

Assume that the user SCOTT was dropped inadvertently and you want to recreate the schema. Assume that the export dump is available in a file named **scott.dmp**.

Step 1: Create the User SCOTT   If the user SCOTT does not exist, create the user and assign appropriate roles to the user. Assign a default and temporary tablespace.

Step 2: Import from the Dump File   Use the Import utility to import the entire schema from the SCOTT.DMP file.

```
C:\>imp userid=system/manager@aa file=scott.dmp full=y
Import: Release 9.0.1.1.1 - Production on Sun Jan 6 10:50:33 2002
(c) Copyright 2001 Oracle Corporation.  All rights reserved.
Connected to: Oracle9i Enterprise Edition Release
 9.0.1.1.1 - Production
With the Partitioning option
JServer Release 9.0.1.1.1 - Production
Export file created by EXPORT:V09.00.01 via conventional path
import done in WE8MSWIN1252 character set and AL16UTF16
NCHAR character set
. importing SYSTEM's objects into SYSTEM
. importing SCOTT's objects into SCOTT
. . importing table               "BONUS"          0 rows imported
. . importing table               "DEPT"           4 rows imported
. . importing table               "EMP"           14 rows imported
. . importing table            "SALGRADE"          5 rows imported
. . importing table               "TEST"           3 rows imported
About to enable constraints...
Import terminated successfully without warnings.
```

Case Study: Recovering a Lost Table

Assume that a user has inadvertently dropped a table. The quickest way to recover this table is to import it from an available export dump. The following example illustrates this situation.

```
SQL> connect scott/tiger@aa
Connected.
SQL> drop table emp;
Table dropped.
C:\>imp userid=system/manager@aa file=scott.dmp tables=emp
fromuser=scott touser=scott
Import: Release 9.0.1.1.1 - Production on Sun Jan 6 11:00:25 2002
(c) Copyright 2001 Oracle Corporation.  All rights reserved.
Connected to: Oracle9i Enterprise Edition Release 9.0.1.1.1 - Production
With the Partitioning option
JServer Release 9.0.1.1.1 - Production
Export file created by EXPORT:V09.00.01 via conventional path
import done in WE8MSWIN1252 character set and AL16UTF16
 NCHAR character set
. importing SCOTT's objects into SCOTT
. . importing table                    "EMP"         14 rows imported
About to enable constraints...
Import terminated successfully without warnings.
```

As seen in the case studies, recovery from an export dump is a convenient way to recover a small portion of the database. If an export dump were not available, the entire tablespace containing the schema for SCOTT would have to be recovered.

Performance-Tuning

As a DBA, you must strive to obtain the best performance from your database. Performance-tuning a database requires a lot of skill and experience. A full discussion on performance-tuning is beyond the scope of this book. This section focuses on using the available GUI tools to monitor database performance.

OEM on Windows NT/2000 is bundled with several tools that can be used for monitoring the performance of a database and general troubleshooting. These tools can be launched from the Tools menu of OEM or from the Start menu under the shortcut folder Enterprise Management Packs. The important tools are overviewed here.

Performance Manager

Oracle Performance Manager (PM) can be used to obtain real-time information that is useful to monitor the performance of databases, web servers, and other services. PM can provide information on CPU usage, response times, the I/O, locks, and so on. Figure 5-8 shows a sample chart that provides information on CPU load.

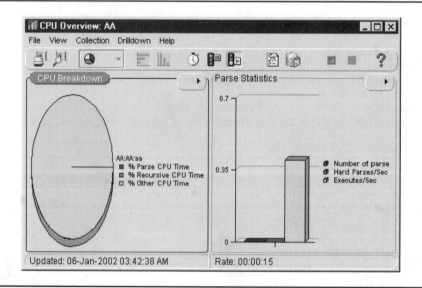

FIGURE 5-8. *CPU usage chart*

The chart here provides an example of a graphical view of the number of tablespaces, data files, schemas, and users.

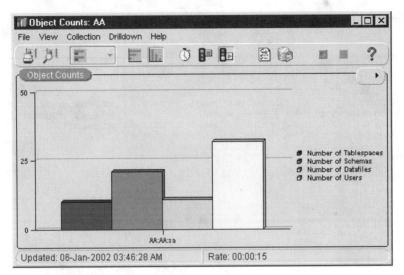

Lock Monitor

Locks are critical to a database. Use Lock Monitor to get an overview of the locks for current sessions. Lock Monitor creates charts by querying data dictionary views such as V$LOCK and V$SESSION. You can get information on the locks obtained by a specific session.

Performance Overview

Many times it is useful and sufficient to get an overall performance overview. A chart that provides information on the overall health of the database can be obtained using OEM. Select Performance Overview from the Diagnostics Pack. A sample screen is shown in Figure 5-9. Note that a summary of the CPU activity, database I/O, and memory use is available in this chart. You can also obtain session information. In this example, there is a total of 14 sessions, of which 8 are active and 6 are inactive. Information on resource contention is available at the bottom of the screen.

Analyzing Tablespaces

If you are concerned about tablespace fragmentation, you can analyze a tablespace using OEM. Select the Tablespace Map option from the available tuning packs.

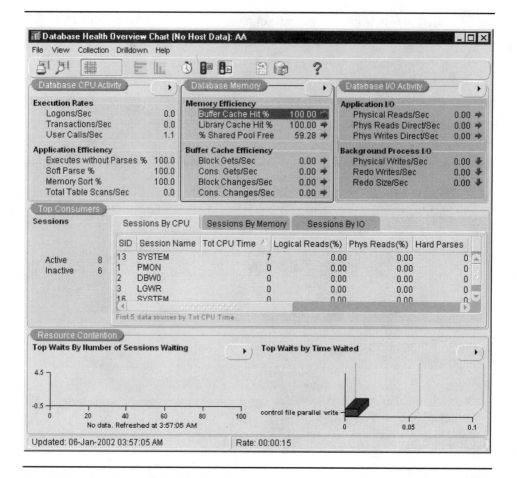

FIGURE 5-9. *Overall health of a database*

A full report on the segments belonging to the tablespace along with their space usage is provided. A graphical view of the database blocks being used is also available. Figure 5-10 provides a sample tablespace map for the SYSTEM tablespace.

Oracle Expert

Oracle Expert can help you tune instance structures and database structures. Oracle Expert analyzes specific portions of the database as requested and uses its tuning rules to suggest changes to be made to the database. These changes can be applied

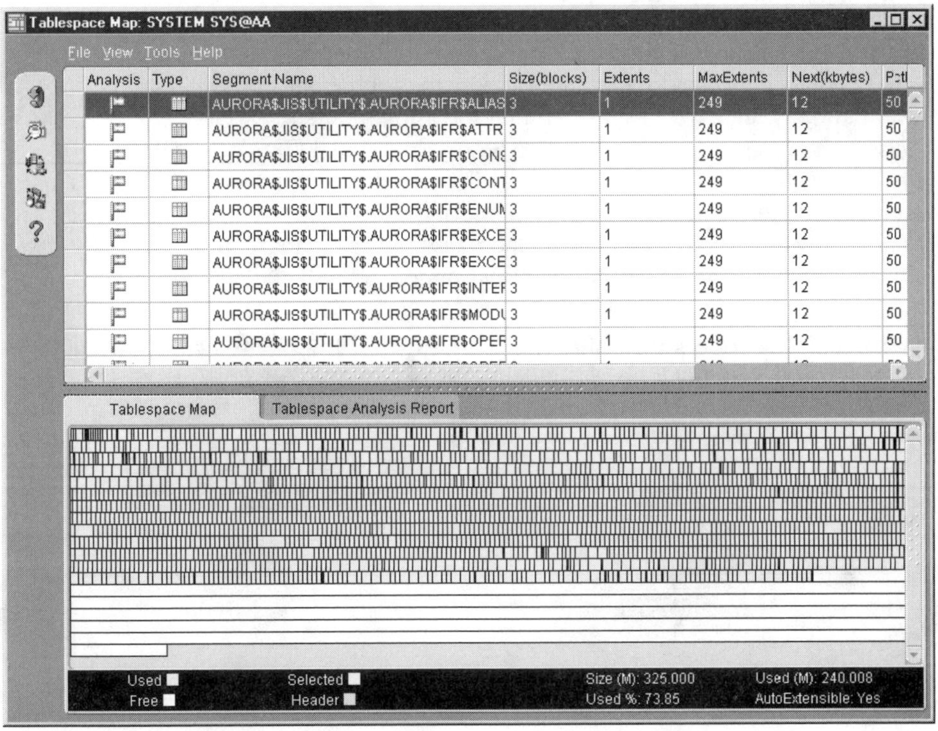

FIGURE 5-10. *A sample tablespace map*

to the database from Oracle Expert itself. Alternatively, you can view the implementation scripts and then run them manually. The use of Oracle Expert (OE) is illustrated by tuning the database.

Step 1: Create SQL History   OE analyzes and suggests changes that can be made to the database to improve performance. The analysis is based on the set of SQL statements that have been run against the database. Before using OE to assist you with performance-tuning, you must let the database age (run the normal SQL statements and applications against the database over a period of time). This will build a history that OE uses to collect performance statistics.

You can view the SQL history. Right-click the node SQL History Session in the navigator. Create a new history. Click the Collect button and then review the history by selecting the Review tab.

Step 2: Create a Tuning Session A tuning session is required to use OE. In a typical tuning session, you begin by specifying the areas of the database that you wish to analyze. OE then collects statistics on these areas of interest and recommends changes. You can either apply these changes from OE itself or apply them manually after viewing and editing the implementation scripts.

Launch Oracle Expert by choosing Start | Programs | Oracle - OraHome90 | Enterprise Management Packs | Tuning | Expert. A repository is created on first use when you log in. Launch the Tuning Session Wizard from the Tools menu and create a new tuning session. Provide the name of the database and a name for the tuning session. The session is called book_sample.

Step 3: Select a Scope for Tuning In a given tuning session, you can request OE to focus on specific areas of the database for tuning. This session focuses on tuning the instance. Click the Scope tab and select Check for Instance Optimizations, as shown here:

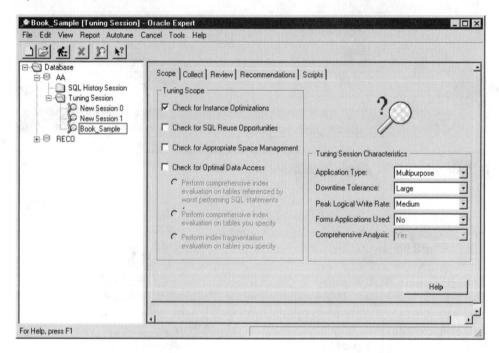

Step 4: Collect Statistics   Click the Collect tab and select the option to collect information on the instance. Click the Options button. Set the time interval for collecting sample data, as shown here:

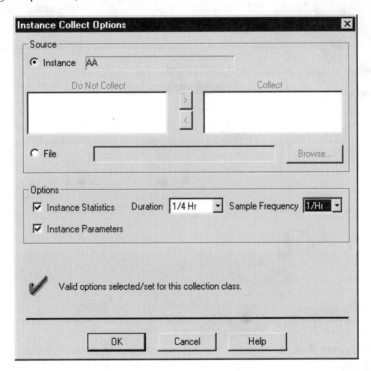

Click the OK button to return to the main screen. Click the Collect button to collect information on the instance. You must collect sample data over a period of time to capture sufficient data and get good results.

Step 5: Generate Recommendations   Select the Recommendations tab and click the Generate button to generate recommendations for instance tuning. OE will generate a bunch of recommendations and display them. Review the recommendations. You can get details for each of the recommendations by clicking the View Detail button. A sample screen from the tuning session is shown here:

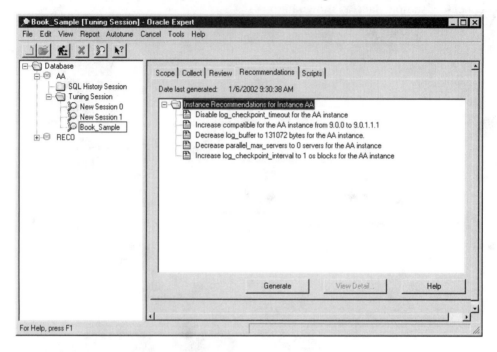

Step 6: Generate Script Select the Scripts tab and click the Generate button to generate a script that will make the changes recommended by OE. You can make changes to this script before running it.

Remember that performance-tuning is an iterative process. You must constantly analyze performance of various portions of a database. OE will help you tune your database with minimum fuss.

Performance-tuning an Oracle database is a highly complex subject. Performance issues must be considered from the design stages of the application. Most of the performance bottlenecks in real life pertain to bad design choices, not database configuration.

Managing Indexes

Indexes can offer performance benefits in a situation in which a majority of the queries on a table return less than 10–15 percent of the rows. Indexes also offer benefits when queries contain joins or WHERE clauses. Managing indexes is important from the DBA's standpoint. If you have many indexes, it is best to create a separate tablespace for them. You must keep this tablespace on a different disk from the one that holds data. Since indexes can be rebuilt from SQL statements, there is no need to back up tablespaces containing indexes. It is sufficient to maintain SQL scripts that can re-create the indexes in case the index tablespace is lost.

Creating Indexes

There are many types of indexes. Indexes are created using the CREATE INDEX statement. A majority of the index types are stored in a single tablespace. Partitioned indexes are an exception (partitioned tables are also an exception to this rule). Oracle creates a B-tree index by default. Other index types such as bitmapped indexes are available for special situations.

 If you are populating a table using SQL*Loader or any other mechanism, you must create the required indexes after the data is loaded. If you create the index before loading data, an index is created every time a row is added to the table. This can be very time-consuming.

 If you are creating large indexes, the sort area used can grow rather quickly. To avoid this situation, you can create a special temporary tablespace and assign this to the user creating the index. This avoids a situation in which the shared temporary tablespace has to grow to hold the sort areas for the large index creation. After the index is created, you can drop this temporary tablespace and reassign the user to the original temporary tablespace.

Dropping and Rebuilding Indexes

Since indexes do not affect data, they can be dropped at any time. As a DBA, you must keep track of indexes that are not used and drop them. Of course, if your data is growing rapidly, you must rebuild the index. Indexes can be rebuilt using the ALTER INDEX statement. An ALTER INDEX...REBUILD statement uses existing indexes to build the new index and is faster than dropping and re-creating an index.

```
SQL> alter index scott.pk_emp rebuild;
Index altered.
```

Monitoring Indexes

Because indexes can take a lot of space, you should constantly monitor indexes. Indexes that are not frequently used must be dropped. The following steps can be taken to monitor the use of an index.

Step 1: Begin Monitoring   When you monitor the usage of an index, the information is stored in the data dictionary. You must issue the ALTER INDEX statement to begin monitoring an index.

```
ALTER INDEX <index> MONITORING USAGE;
```

Step 2: Collect Data   Continue to monitor the use of the index in question for a sufficient period of time. Data on the use of the selected index accumulates in the data dictionary. The V$OBJECT_USAGE view can be used to query the usage data.

Step 3: Stop Monitoring   Since index monitoring itself adds to the overhead, you must discontinue monitoring as follows:

```
ALTER INDEX <index> NOMONITORING USAGE;
```

Step 4: Analyze Use of Index   Query the V$OBJECT_USAGE view and analyze the data to understand how the index is being used. If an index is growing too fast, you must change its storage characteristics.

Index Fragmentation

If a table has too many inserts and deletes, the index segment itself can get fragmented. You can coalesce or rebuild the index to overcome this problem.

```
SQL> alter index scott.pk_emp coalesce;
Index altered.
```

Managing Undo

Oracle Server has to maintain information that can be used to undo or roll back changes made to data. The ROLLBACK statement uses undo records to undo changes made in the transaction. Database recovery also uses undo information in the recovery process.

Previous versions of Oracle Server used rollback segments to store undo records exclusively. Rollback segments (RBS) can be quite difficult to manage as they can grow and shrink at alarming rates. Recovery of a tablespace containing an active RBS can be quite an involved procedure. In Oracle9i, undo can also be stored in a special tablespace called the *undo tablespace*. This is a much-improved way of providing storage for undo. RBS are still supported for backward compatibility.

Oracle9i still retains a special rollback segment called the *system* rollback segment. This rollback segment resides in the SYSTEM tablespace and is mandatory.

Choosing Undo Mode

An instance can be set to use RBS or an undo tablespace for undo. These are mutually exclusive, so the same instance cannot use both RBS and an undo tablespace. The initialization parameter UNDO_MANAGEMENT is used to control the undo mode. If you choose to use an undo tablespace for undo, you must also specify the tablespace (this is a special tablespace) that must be used for undo records. For example, to set an instance to use an undo tablespace named UNDOTBS, set the following initialization parameters:

```
UNDO_MANAGEMENT = auto
UNDO_TABLESPACE = UNDOTBS
```

To use the traditional RBS, set the following initialization parameters:

```
UNDO_MANAGEMENT = manual
ROLLBACK_SEGMENTS = <list of user rollback segments>
```

You must ensure that the specified RBS are online.

Managing Undo Tablespaces

The tablespace used for undo is a special tablespace that can be created when the database is created or by using the CREATE UNDO TABLESPACE command. Managing Undo tablespaces is similar to managing other tablespaces. Undo tablespaces can be expanded by adding new data files. Storage characteristics can also be changed. An undo tablespace can also be dropped.

Since the UNDO_TABLESPACE parameter is dynamic, you can switch an undo tablespace dynamically using the ALTER SYSTEM command.

Managing Rollback Segments

RBS are created using the CREATE ROLLBACK SEGMENT statement and dropped using the DROP ROLLBACK SEGMENT statement. One special RBS named SYSTEM is automatically created when the database is created. You can take an RBS offline when the database is running if it is not active. The system rollback segment cannot be taken offline at any time. You must choose the size and storage parameters for RBS based on the number of transactions on your database. It is best to create a separate tablespace to hold RBS.

Viewing Undo Information

Data dictionary views are available to get statistics on undo segments. Views are available to get information on undo tablespaces and RBS. These views include V$TRANSACTION, V$UNDOSTAT, V$ROLLSTAT, DBA_ROLLBACK_SEGS, and V$ROLLNAME.

Additional Topics

There are several additional features provided by Oracle9i. The sections that follow provide information on these features and other miscellaneous topics.

Log Miner

Log Miner (LM) is a utility that allows you to query redo log files using the SQL interface. Recall that redo log files contain change vectors, i.e. a history of changes made to the database. LM reads the specified log file and populates the V$LOGMNR_CONTENTS view with information. You can query this view to analyze redo log files. The V$LOGMNR_LOGS view provides one row of information for each redo log file that has been analyzed.

A typical scenario where LM is useful is a situation in which you have to do a time-based or SCN-based recovery. You can get the SCN information by querying the redo log file. The information obtained through LM can also be helpful for capacity planning.

Log Miner Dictionary

A LM dictionary translates internal object identifiers and datatypes to a human readable format. If the LM dictionary is not available, LM displays log file information using internal IDs and hex bytes. This is not human-friendly. Compare the following SQL statements:

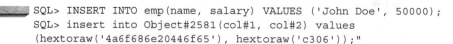

```
SQL> INSERT INTO emp(name, salary) VALUES ('John Doe', 50000);
SQL> insert into Object#2581(col#1, col#2) values
(hextoraw('4a6f686e20446f65'), hextoraw('c306'));"
```

The first statement is a human-readable form of the second! To obtain a human-readable format, you must create an LM dictionary.

The LM dictionary can be extracted to a flat file or the redo log file itself. If you extract the dictionary to a flat file, you can conserve system resources. The problem is that if other users are issuing DDL statements at the same time, the extracted file might contain inconsistent data. In contrast, you will get consistent data if you extract the dictionary to a redo log file.

Another option of using the database catalog for storing dictionary information is available. In all cases LM builds its own internal dictionary from the source dictionary specified at startup (flat file, dictionary in redo logs, or dictionary in online catalog). LM updates this internal dictionary automatically.

NOTE

Log Miner does not support LOBs, abstract data types, index-organized tables, or VARRAYs.

Log Miner Packages

Two PL/SQL packages are provided with Oracle9i for LM support. The DBMS_LOGMNR package contains procedures to initialize and run LM. These procedures include interfaces to specify log filenames, filter criteria, and other session characteristics. The DBMS_LOGMNR_D package creates the LM dictionary file. The SYS schema owns both LM packages.

Using Log Miner

The quickest way to understand LM is to go through an example. A step-by-step example follows.

Step 1: Extract a Dictionary   You can extract the dictionary to a flat file, the redo log file, or the catalog. In this case, the dictionary is extracted to a flat file.

First, verify if the initialization parameter UTL_FILE_DIR is set and is pointing to a valid directory. If it is not set, you must set it and bounce the database.

```
SQL> show parameter utl_file_dir
NAME                                     TYPE        VALUE
---------------------------------- ----------- -------------
utl_file_dir                             string      c:\tmp
```

Execute the PL/SQL procedure DBMS_LOGMNR_D.BUILD to extract the LM dictionary to a flat file named **dictionary.ora** in the directory specified by UTL_FILE_DIR.

```
SQL> begin
  2     dbms_logmnr_d.build('dictionary.ora',
  3     'c:\tmp',
  4     OPTIONS => DBMS_LOGMNR_D.STORE_IN_FLAT_FILE);
  5  end;
  6  /
PL/SQL procedure successfully completed.
```

The resultant dictionary file **dictionary.ora** is fairly large (in this case, more than 8MB).

Step 2: Specify the Redo Log for Analysis   Add a list of redo log files for analysis.

```
SQL> begin
  2     dbms_logmnr.add_logfile (LOGFILENAME =>
  3        'c:\oracle\oradata\aa\redo01.log',
  4        OPTIONS => DBMS_LOGMNR.NEW);
  5  end;
  6  /
PL/SQL procedure successfully completed.
```

Step 3: Launch Log Miner   You can execute the START_LOGMNR procedure to start the Log Miner. The dictionary file must be fully qualified, as shown here:

```
SQL> begin
  2     dbms_logmnr.start_logmnr (
  3     DICTFILENAME => 'c:\tmp\dictionary.ora');
  4  end;
  5  /
PL/SQL procedure successfully completed.
```

Step 4: Analyze Output   You can query the V$LOGMNR_CONTENTS view to analyze the output of LM.

```
SQL> select operation, sql_redo from v$logmnr_contents;
```

To conserve space, the output of the previous command is omitted.

Step 5: Perform Object-Level Recovery   You can use the information gathered in step 4 to perform object-level recovery.

Step 6: End Session   An LM session must be ended properly, as shown here:

```
SQL> execute dbms_logmnr.end_logmnr;
PL/SQL procedure successfully completed.
```

Authentication Using Password File

On Windows NT/2000, a password file is maintained for the purpose of authenticating users with SYSDBA or SYSOPER privileges. This external authentication is necessary to authenticate a user who will start up the database (since the database is not open, the user cannot be authenticated from the database).

The password file is maintained in the c:\oracle\ora90\database folder by default. The name of the password file is of the form *pwd<database name>.ora*. For example, the password file is named **pwdaa.ora** for a database named AA. The password file is created automatically when the database is created; however, it can also be created and modified with the Oracle password utility. You must protect the password file from users. You can do so using Windows NT/2000 file permissions; however, if you are using a FAT file system this is not possible since anyone with access to the console can access the file. In this situation, you can move the **orapwd.exe** file to a secure location or delete it entirely.

Adding New Users to Password File

The password file is automatically updated when you create a user and assign the SYSDBA or SYSOPER privileges. You must first ensure that the initialization parameter REMOTE_LOGIN_PASSWORDFILE is set to EXCLUSIVE.

```
SQL> show parameter remote_login_passwordfile;
NAME                                     TYPE        VALUE
-------------------------------------- ----------- -----------
remote_login_passwordfile                string      EXCLUSIVE
SQL> connect sys/change_on_install@aa as sysdba;
Connected.
SQL> create user admin identified by admin;
User created.
SQL> grant sysdba to admin;
Grant succeeded.
SQL> shutdown
Database closed.
Database dismounted.
ORACLE instance shut down.
SQL> connect admin/admin@aa as sysdba;
Connected to an idle instance.
SQL> startup
ORACLE instance started.
Total System Global Area  118255568 bytes
Fixed Size                   282576 bytes
Variable Size              83886080 bytes
Database Buffers           33554432 bytes
Redo Buffers                 532480 bytes
Database mounted.
Database opened.
```

Observe that the new user ADMIN is now able to start up the database.

Oracle Managed Files

Oracle9i supports a new feature called Oracle Managed Files that reduces the maintenance required on data files, log files, and control files. The feature eliminates the need for a DBA to manage files at the OS level directly. Internally, Oracle Server uses a standard file system interface to create and delete the files as needed.

The Oracle Managed Files feature can be used with operating systems that support large and extensible files. In addition, databases that use a logical volume manager (LVM) and support redundant array of inexpensive disks (RAID) can benefit. Databases that use raw disks cannot use this feature.

NOTE
An LVM makes a combination of physical hard disks appear like a single disk to an application. It enhances performance, reliability, and availability of data as compared to a combination of hard disks. LVM is available for most operating systems. The Veritas Volume Manager is a popular commercial LVM.

It is acceptable to have a mixture of manually managed files (traditional Oracle files) and Oracle managed files.

Initialization Parameters for Oracle Managed Files

To use Oracle Managed Files, you must specify the default destination for the data files, temp files, and redo log files. The DB_CREATE_FILE_DEST parameter is used to define the location of the data files and temp files. The DB_CREATE_ONLINE_LOG_DEST_n parameter specifies the location for the redo log files and control files. The *n* is used for multiplexing. You can multiplex up to five copies of redo log files and control files. If this parameter is not set, the setting for DB_CREATE_FILE_DEST is used for redo log files and control files as well.

```
DB_CREATE_FILE_DEST = 'E:\Oracle\AA'
```

This setting by itself controls the destination for all data files, temp files, redo log files, and control files (since DB_CREATE_ONLINE_LOG_DEST_n is not set). If you want to locate the redo log files and control files to another location, you can add the DB_CREATE_ONLINE_LOG_DEST_n parameter, as shown here:

```
DB_CREATE_ONLINE_LOG_DEST_1 = 'E:\Oracle\AA'
DB_CREATE_ONLINE_LOG_DEST_2 = 'F:\Oracle\AA'
```

Note that the log files and control files are multiplexed because of the previous setting. Two copies of the files are created. You can also use the ALTER SYSTEM or ALTER SESSION command to set these initialization parameters dynamically. These parameters are used only if you do not explicitly name the files during creation.

Advantages and Disadvantages of Oracle Managed Files

The administration of the database is easier since there is no need to specify a filename or location for each individual file. There is also no need to specify storage parameters since Oracle Server manages these files. Oracle Server automatically deletes files if they are not in use. This feature is especially useful for less-experienced DBAs since they do not have to worry about wasting space. This feature can also be very useful in a test or development environment. Third-party applications can be developed easily as they do not need to put OS-specific filenames in their SQL scripts. This can be a pain since every OS has its own filenaming conventions.

Oracle Managed Files is designed for use with a logical volume manager. Since LVM makes a combination of disks look like one disk, it is easy to provide settings for the two initialization parameters. If you are not using an LVM, the files will not be striped since they will all be created in one location. This can lead to I/O contention.

Using Oracle Managed Files

Once the initialization parameters are set, they will be used to generate files automatically when a data file, temp file, redo log file, or control file is created. This feature is illustrated with a CREATE DATABASE statement. The following initialization parameters have been set:

```
DB_CREATE_FILE_DEST = ' E:\oracle\ora90\oradata\anand\'
DB_CREATE_ONLINE_LOG_DEST_1 = ' E:\oracle\ora90\oradata\anand\'
DB_CREATE_ONLINE_LOG_DEST_2 = ' F:\oracle\ora90\oradata\anand\'
```

The database is created with the following statement.

```
SQL> CREATE DATABASE anand;
```

Oracle Server automatically creates the data file required for the SYSTEM tablespace and the redo log groups. For the most part, Oracle Managed Files behave as normal files. The filenames are stored in the control file. Information on the files is available in the data dictionary views. The files can be backed up with RMAN; however, there are a few differences. One is that the data file is automatically deleted from the file system when the associated tablespace or the data file is dropped.

Naming Convention for Oracle Managed Files

The filenames comply with OFA rules. The names assigned to data files, control files, and redo log files are identifiable clearly. The name chosen for a data file depends on the tablespace that it is associated with. The association is clearly indicated.

Transportable Tablespaces

This feature allows you to transport a subset of an Oracle database to another database. You can move dictionary-managed or locally managed tablespaces from one database to another. Why would you want to do this? Imagine that you have a database that has technical bulletins published by the Customer Support department. You can publish these bulletins to external customers using this feature.

NOTE
In past releases you would have to export the data and then import it into other databases.

There are some limitations that you must be aware of. For example, you can transport tablespaces only across databases on the same operating system. Secondly, the source and the target database must have the same character set and national character set. Finally, the target database cannot have a preexisting tablespace with the same name.

Using the Transportable Tablespaces Feature

You must set compatibility to 8.1 or higher to use this feature. If your tablespaces use nonstandard block sizes, compatibility must be set to 9.0 or higher. You can transport a tablespace from Oracle8i to Oracle9i. There are four steps that must be taken to transport a tablespace. These are detailed here.

Step 1: Check if the Tablespaces Are Self-Contained   You can transport only a self-contained set of tablespaces. A self-contained set simply means that there are no references from inside the set to a tablespace not in the set. For example, if a table has an index in a separate tablespace, you must include both tablespaces to create a self-contained set.

You can verify if a set of tablespaces is self-contained by using the TRANSPORT_SET_CHECK procedure included in the DBMS_TTS package. The user must have the EXECUTE_CATALOG_ROLE privilege to execute this procedure. For example, to check if a tablespace named USERS is self-contained, you can execute the procedure as follows:

```
SQL> execute dbms_tts.transport_set_check ('users',true);
PL/SQL procedure successfully completed.
```

The first parameter is a set of tablespaces (in this case there is only one tablespace) that is to be transported. The second parameter indicates that referential integrity constraints must be taken into consideration. The procedure populates the TRANSPORT_SET_VIOLATIONS view with a report that indicates violations, if any.

```
SQL> select * from transport_set_violations;
no rows selected
```

Since no rows are returned, there are no violations. The tablespace USERS can be transported since it is self-contained. If rows are returned by this query, they will indicate the violations. You must resolve these before transporting the tablespace.

Step 2: Generate a Transportable Tablespace Set   First, the tablespaces that are to be transported must be made read-only.

```
SQL> alter tablespace users read only;
Tablespace altered.
```

Use the Export utility to export the structural information about the tablespace. Note that the data is not exported. You must use an account with SYSDBA privileges.

```
C:\>exp transport_tablespace=y tablespaces=users triggers=y
constraints=y grants=n file=c:\tmp\userxfer.dmp
Export: Release 9.0.1.1.1 - Production on Sun Jan 6 18:42:53 2002
(c) Copyright 2001 Oracle Corporation.  All rights reserved.
Username: sys/change_on_install@aa as sysdba
Connected to: Oracle9i Enterprise Edition Release 9.0.1.1.1 - Production
With the Partitioning option
JServer Release 9.0.1.1.1 - Production
Export done in WE8MSWIN1252 character set and AL16UTF16
NCHAR character set
Note: table data (rows) will not be exported
Note: grants on tables/views/sequences/roles will not be exported
About to export transportable tablespace metadata...
For tablespace USERS ...
. exporting cluster definitions
. exporting table definitions
. . exporting table                           TEST
. exporting referential integrity constraints
. exporting triggers
. end transportable tablespace metadata export
Export terminated successfully without warnings.
```

Step 3: Transport the Tablespace Set   Transport the data files belonging to the USERS tablespace and the export file to a location accessible to the target database. You can use normal OS commands or a network utility such as **ftp** to transport the files.

Step 4: Import the Tablespace into Target Database   Use the Import utility to import the tablespace into the target database, as shown here:

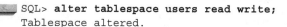

```
C:\>imp transport_tablespace=y file=c:\tmp\userxfer.dmp
datafiles=('c:\oracle\oradata\aa\users01.dbf',
'c:\oracle\oradata\aa\users02.dbf',
'c:\oracle\oradata\aa\users03.ora') tablespaces=users
Import: Release 9.0.1.1.1 - Production on Sun Jan 6 18:54:45 2002
(c) Copyright 2001 Oracle Corporation.  All rights reserved.
Username: sys/change_on_install@reco as sysdba
Connected to: Oracle9i Enterprise Edition
Release 9.0.1.1.1 - Production
With the Partitioning option
JServer Release 9.0.1.1.1 - Production
Export file created by EXPORT:V09.00.01 via conventional path
About to import transportable tablespace(s) metadata...
import done in WE8MSWIN1252 character set and AL16UTF16
 NCHAR character set
. importing SYS's objects into SYS
. importing SCOTT's objects into SCOTT
. . importing table                        "TEST"
Import terminated successfully without warnings.
```

Step 5: Restore the Tablespace to Read-Write Mode

```
SQL> alter tablespace users read write;
Tablespace altered.
```

Windows NT/2000 Topics

This section includes a few topics that pertain to Oracle9i on Windows NT/2000.

ORA_DBA Group

A special group called ORA_DBA is automatically created on the operating system when you install Oracle9i Server. If you are using external authentication (OS authentication), the OS user must be included in the ORA_DBA group. The Windows user that installed Oracle9i Server is automatically included in the ORA_DBA group.

Monitoring a Database

You can monitor a database on Oracle using OEM's data management packs. In addition to these, you can use Event Viewer to monitor database events. Launch Event Viewer and open the application log. Review the Oracle Server events in the application log. Pay special attention to warning notifications.

Oracle alert files should be monitored regularly for any abnormal behavior. The alert log on Windows NT/2000 is written to the c:\oracle\admin\<instance name>\bdump folder by default. A quick way to check for abnormal behavior is to perform a case-sensitive search for the string **ORA-** in this file. In Chapter 7, you can see how OEM can be used to track critical alerts written to the alert log file.

HTTP Server

Oracle9i for Windows NT/2000 is bundled with the Apache HTTP Server. This is the standard Apache Server with Oracle extensions such as mod_perl and mod_ssl. More information is available in Chapter 9.

Starting and Shutting Down HTTP Server

You can start up and shut down the server from the Start menu. Click Start | Programs | Oracle – OraHome90 | Oracle HTTP Server and choose the appropriate shortcut. You can also manage the HTTP service from the Services applet.

Configuring HTTP Server

The standard configuration files are located in the c:\oracle\ora90\apache\apache\ conf folder. The file **httpd.conf** is used for configuring Apache Server. Table 5-4 summarizes important configuration parameters.

Parameter	Description
Port	This is the port on which HTTP Server will listen. Use the default value of 80, unless you have another HTTP Server using this port.
DocumentRoot	This is the root folder for HTML documents. The default is set to the c:\oracle\ora90\Apache\Apache\htdocs folder.
ServerAdmin	E-mail ID of System Administrator.

TABLE 5-4. *Important Apache Configuration Parameters*

Windows NT/2000 Tuning

Windows NT/2000 provides very little room for tuning as far as using it for an Oracle Server is concerned; however, there are a few things that you can do to improve performance. Consider these issues if you are using the machine as a dedicated database server.

Avoid using the machine running Oracle Server as a primary domain controller (PDC) or to manage file and print services since these can create performance problems. Also avoid using the machine for network management (such as a proxy server or a router) and Active Directory Services.

By default, foreground applications are given priority on Windows NT/2000. Since a majority of Oracle tasks are performed in the background, you should change this setting. Start the System applet from Control Panel. Choose the Performance tab. Move the Application Boost slider to None.

In Windows 2000, the procedure is slightly different. Choose the Advanced tab in the System Applet and click the Performance button to view the current priority settings. Set the priority for background processes.

On a typical Windows NT/2000 Server, there are scores of services that are running. Some of these services are not required to run Oracle Server. You can disable services such as plug and play and telephony since these are rarely needed. If you are not using remote access services (RAS), disable these services also.

You can improve performance of a Windows NT/2000 Server by removing unnecessary network protocols that are installed on the machine. Many sites of today use only TCP/IP protocols. Remove other protocols such as NetBEUI if you do not need them.

Prioritize network bindings so that the primary protocol is given the highest priority. To do so, perform these steps:

1. Open the Network applet from Control Panel.

2. Choose the Bindings tab.

3. Select All Services from the Show Bindings drop-down list to obtain a list of available protocol adapters.

4. Select the primary protocol and move it to the top.

5. Click the OK button. You will need to reboot your machine for this setting to take effect.

Similar settings can be configured for Windows 2000 and Windows XP from the Network properties dialog box.

Try to use a logical volume manager such as Logical Disk Manager on your server. Also configure your server for RAID if possible.

You should configure the virtual memory so that the swap file(s) are created across multiple physical disks rather than just one disk.

Close unnecessary applications that are running on the server. Common applications that use resources such as screen savers should be closed. The MS-DOS command prompt should be avoided. Finally, remove unnecessary applications that are placed in the Startup folder.

Initialization Parameters

Several initialization parameters are either not supported on the Windows NT/2000 platform or have some limitations. Refer to *Administrators Guide for Windows* in Oracle documentation for information on initialization parameters (Table 7-1 in our documentation set).

Raw Partitions

Windows NT/2000 supports raw partitions. These can be used instead of a file system for Oracle files. A raw partition can give a performance benefit of 10–20 percent.

Raw partitions are of two types on Windows NT/2000: physical disk and logical partition. A physical disk represents an entire hard disk. Each physical disk is identified by a symbolic link (an addressable name) that is created automatically. For example, if you have two physical disks, these are identified by the symbolic links \\.\PhysicalDrive0 and \\.\PhysicalDrive1. Internally these names are mapped to the physical disk as follows:

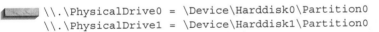

```
\\.\PhysicalDrive0 = \Device\Harddisk0\Partition0
\\.\PhysicalDrive1 = \Device\Harddisk1\Partition0
```

Note that Partition0 is special as it represents the entire physical disk. As a DBA, it is recommended that you create and use logical partitions instead of physical disks. This is because a logical partition does not represent an entire disk; it represents only a specific partition on a disk. A logical partition is created using Disk Administrator on Windows NT/2000. A logical partition cannot point to Partition0. Logical partitions are assigned names with drive letters initially. You can reassign symbolic link names to logical partitions. Symbolic link names are of the form \\.*symbolic link name*. Consider the following examples:

```
\\.\E:= \Device\Harddisk3\Partition1
\\.\Oracle_1 = \Device\HardDisk4\Partition2
```

The first example addresses a logical partition with a drive letter, and the second example addresses a logical partition using a symbolic name.

Creating Tablespaces in Raw Partitions

To create a tablespace in a raw partition, you must use the symbolic link name in the data file definition. Consider the following example:

```
Create tablespace test1 datafile '\\.\E' size 400m;
create tablespace test2 datafile '\\.\Oracle_1' size 200m;
```

Observe that both naming conventions for raw partitions can be used.

Administrative Assistant for Windows NT

The Oracle Administration Assistant for Windows NT (OAA) is a tool that is mainly used to create database administrators, operators, users, and roles on the Windows NT/2000 platform. The tool can also be used to manage Oracle services and view information on Oracle processes. OAA is integrated with Microsoft Management Console (MMC).

You can launch OAA by choosing Start | Programs | Oracle - OraHome90 | Configuration and Management Tools | Oracle Administration Assistant for Windows NT. A variety of tasks can be performed from OAA. An overview is included here for your benefit.

Managing Oracle DBAs, OS Operators, and Roles

Oracle DBAs and OS operators can be easily managed using OAA. Expand the node Oracle Managed Objects in OAA. Find the computer where Oracle Server is running from the navigator. Select the node titled OS Database Administrators - Computer in the navigator. You will see a list of all the OS-level DBAs. You can add or remove a DBA using the context menu (right-click menu).

Select the database of interest and right-click it. You will see an option to Connect to the Database. You will also see a list of roles and OS users (including Administrators and Operators) in the navigator. Right-click any of these to add or remove a role or an OS user. A wizard will guide you through the process of creating an Oracle user who is authenticated using Windows or the NT domain. Figure 5-11 shows a sample screen from OAA. Note that a user named ANAND is authenticated from a Windows login on the computer AA (the string OPS$ is the default setting for OS_AUTHENT_PREFIX).

Starting and Stopping Database Services

Find the computer running Oracle Server in the navigator and expand the Databases node. Select the database that you want to manage. Use the right-click menu to start the database service if it is not running or to stop the database if it is running.

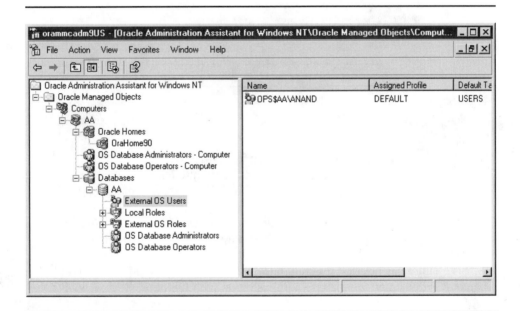

FIGURE 5-11. *External authentication using Administrative Assistant*

Configuring a Database to Start or Stop with the Service

You can choose to start the database when the database service is started and/or shut down the database when the service is stopped. Again right-click the database you are interested in and set the required Startup/Shutdown options, as shown here:

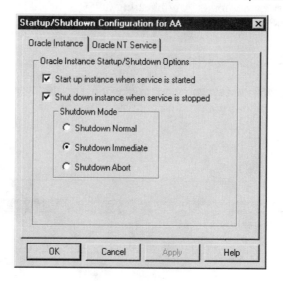

You can also configure the service to start automatically from here.

Viewing Oracle Process Thread Information

Select the database of interest from the navigator. Right-click and select Process Information to view a list of Oracle processes along with thread information. You can kill a specific thread (process) from here.

Remember that Windows Task Manager does not show all the Oracle processes running on Windows NT/2000. You will see only a process named **oracle.exe** in Task Manager.

This chapter has covered the minimum tasks that a DBA is required to perform. Chapter 8 is dedicated to database administration with OEM.

CHAPTER
6

Oracle Net Services

he present era of the Internet requires companies to manage and provide end-to-end scalable and reliable network services. Oracle databases and network components play a major role since they are required to handle thousands of concurrent sessions on a 24×7 basis. These sessions are spread across local area networks and the Web. Oracle9i is bundled with many tools and methods to handle the entire gamut of business needs. This chapter is dedicated to Oracle Net Services.

NOTE
Oracle Net Services replace Net8 of Oracle8/8i. A comparison of features is provided in the "Enhancements in Oracle Net Services" section.

Oracle Solution and Services

Oracle Net Services provide enterprise-wide network connectivity solutions in a distributed and heterogeneous computing environment. Oracle Net Services ease the complexities of network configuration and management, maximize performance, and improve network diagnostic capabilities. The main components are

- Oracle Net
- Listener
- Connection Manager
- Networking Tools
- Oracle Advanced Security

Oracle Net

The Oracle Net component provides connectivity for a client application to an Oracle database. The connection can use a two-tier (client/server) or three-tier model. For each session, Oracle Net acts as a data courier, moving data in both directions between the client and the database. Oracle Net is responsible for establishing and maintaining a session as well as exchanging messages (data) between the client application and database. Oracle Net is installed on the computer running the client application as well as the computer running Oracle Server and consists of two subcomponents: Oracle Net Foundation Layer and Oracle Protocol Support.

Client applications communicate with Oracle Net Foundation Layer to establish connections. The Foundation Layer communicates with an industry-standard network protocol to communicate with the machine housing Oracle Server. The Oracle Protocol Support layer enables this communication. Correspondingly, the Oracle Net Foundation Layer on the server machine communicates with Oracle Server. The Foundation Layer communication stack is depicted in Figure 6-1.

Oracle Protocol Support maps the Foundation Layer functions to industry-standard protocols in a two-tier architecture. Common protocols such as TCP/IP, Named Pipes, and LU6.2 can be used. TCP/IP with SSL and Virtual Interface (a new thin protocol) is also supported.

Listener

Oracle Listener is a process that is continuously listening for new connection requests on the database server. It acts as a broker between the client application and Oracle Server. New connection requests are handed off to the database for authentication. On authentication, a server process acts as the intermediary between the client and Oracle Server for subsequent requests. Listener does not play an active role in that session once a connection is established. It simply returns to its listening mode and continues to wait for new connection requests.

The listener process is aware of all the services available to a client. These services are the database and external procedure (EXTPROC) services available on the Server. Listener is configured to await connection requests on specific protocols.

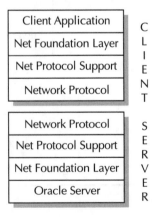

FIGURE 6-1. *Oracle Net Foundation Layer communication stack*

The address configuration depends on the protocol. For example, the address information for the TCP/IP Protocol would include the UDP port information on which the Listener process is listening. The block diagram in Figure 6-2 illustrates this architecture. More information on how connections are established is provided in the "Oracle Net Connections" section later in this chapter.

Connection Manager

Connection Manager acts as a proxy for client requests. It is also responsible for session multiplexing and protocol conversion. Connection Manager can be installed on the machine running Oracle Server or a separate machine such as an application server. Connection Manager appears like a server for clients and

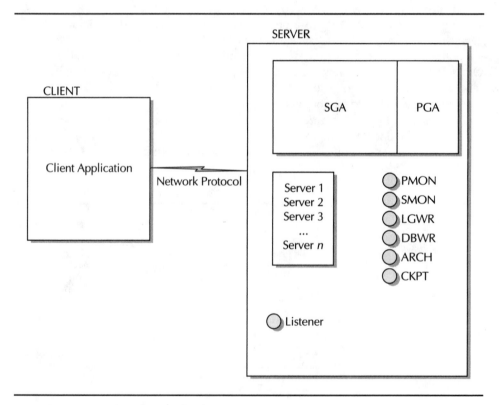

FIGURE 6-2. *Client/server database connection*

appears like a client for Oracle Server. A firewall can be configured using Oracle Net Firewall Proxy.

Session multiplexing, if configured, funnels multiple connections to a database service through a single transport protocol connection. This minimizes the system resources required to manage sessions between the end points.

It is possible to control access to the database server based on a service identifier. Access Control provides support for this feature. Sometimes, you might have a situation in which the client machine and the server machine are using different networking protocols. Connection Manager can be configured so that database sessions can be established across networking protocols.

Networking Tools

Even though Oracle Net Services software is complex, it can be easily configured and managed using simple tools included with Oracle Server. Both GUI and command-line tools are available.

Oracle Net Configuration Assistant is a graphical tool that can be used to configure networking components. Listener, directory services, and naming methods can be configured using this, too. Oracle Net Manager adds to the features of Oracle Net Configuration Assistant. Many wizards are included to help you configure and test connections. Command-line utilities are also available to configure and administer components.

Oracle Advanced Security

Oracle Advanced Security provides comprehensive security features. It is meant to protect sessions across corporate networks and the Internet. Data encryption, authentication solutions, and single sign-on facility are possible with Advanced Security. Advanced Security is covered in more detail in Chapter 11.

NOTE
Advanced Security is a separately licensable product on Windows NT/2000.

Enhancements in Oracle Net Services

Readers who have been using Oracle software in the past will be familiar with SQL*Net and Net8. Oracle Net Services replaces Net8. New features, changes, and enhancements in Oracle Net Services are discussed in this section.

New Nomenclature

A small but necessary change has been made to the nomenclature. Components of Oracle Net Services have been named to be in line with Oracle9i Server (see Table 6-1).

Changes in Multithreaded Server (MTS)

As seen in Table 6-1, MTS has been renamed Shared Server. MTS parameters and dictionary views have also been renamed in Oracle9i. All old initialization related to MTS except the MTS_MAX_SERVERS parameter are supported for backward compatibility. This is expected to change in the next version. Oracle recommends that you modify your parameter file to use these new parameters. Table 6-2 summarizes changes relevant to MTS.

Except for V$MTS, which is a view, all entries in Table 6-2 are initialization parameters. Other views such as V$CIRCUIT, V$QUEUE, V$SHARED_SERVER, V$DISPATCHER, and V$DISPATCHER_RATE remain from earlier versions.

Load-Balancing

In the case of Oracle Parallel Server—replaced by the Real Application Clusters (RAC) feature on Oracle9i—load-balancing was available only for shared server configurations in Oracle8/8i. Load-balancing is also available for dedicated servers.

Multiple Oracle Contexts

Net Configuration Assistant allows you to create multiple Oracle Contexts that facilitate the management of a complex naming structure in a directory server. An Oracle Context contains all information pertaining to Oracle software in a directory. An Oracle Context has a relative distinguished name (RDN) of (cn=OracleContext) and consists of entries for naming and features such as Oracle Advanced Security.

Oracle8i Name	Oracle9i Name
Multithreaded Server (MTS)	Shared Server
Net8	Oracle Net
Net8 Communication Stack	Oracle Foundation Layer
Net8 Configuration Assistant	Oracle Net Configuration Assistant

TABLE 6-1. *Summary of New Nomenclature in Oracle Net Services*

MTS Parameter or View	New Oracle9i Name
MTS_CIRCUITS	CIRCUITS
MTS_DISPATCHERS	DISPATCHERS
MTS_MAX_DISPATCHERS	MAX_DISPATCHERS
MTS_MAX_SERVERS	MAX_SHARED_SERVERS
MTS_SERVERS	SHARED_SERVERS
MTS_SESSIONS	SHARED_SERVER_SESSIONS
V$MTS	V$SHARED_SERVER_MONITOR

TABLE 6-2. *Changes in Shared Server (MTS) Parameters and Views*

Oracle Names LDAP Proxy Server

Oracle Names has been deprecated in favor of directory naming with Lightweight Directory Access Protocol (LDAP). If you have Oracle8/8i clients, you can use Oracle Names LDAP Proxy Servers instead of managing Oracle Names and directory servers separately and simultaneously.

Virtual Interface Protocol Support

Virtual Interface (VI) is an emerging thin protocol. It performs better than TCP/IP since the messaging burden is carried by specialized hardware, thus freeing the CPU. VI provides maximum benefits for Application Servers and interdatabase communication across small networks.

Obsolete Features

With the advent of the Internet, many features are no longer needed. High-level features that were included in Net8 and have been discontinued in Oracle Net Services are

- **Prespawned dedicated servers** You should use shared servers instead of dedicated servers.

- **Support for SPX Protocol** Migrate to a protocol such as TCP/IP, which has become ubiquitous.

- **PROTOCOL.ORA file** Parameters such as TCP.NODELAY can be merged into the SQLNET.ORA file. On Windows NT/2000, Oracle Net Manager automatically merges information from an existing PROTOCOL.ORA into SQLNET.ORA for you when you launch it the first time.

- **Identix and SecurID authentication**   You can now authenticate using CyberSafe, RADIUS, Kerberos, SSL, or Novell's NDS.

- **Net8 OPEN**   This API is no longer available for programmers to develop their own applications.

- **Trace Assistant**   Trace files must be inspected and analyzed manually.

Oracle Net Connections

An Oracle database can be accessed by one or more instances. In addition to the memory and Oracle processes discussed in Chapter 5, an instance can also manage other services, including Oracle9*i* JVM (Java Virtual Machine) and Oracle Servlet Engine. An instance is identified by the INSTANCE_NAME parameter. The default setting for this parameter is the Oracle *system identifier* or *site identifier* (SID) of the instance. In a RAC configuration, many instances can share a single database. So it is not possible to use the instance name to identify the service. You must use the database name to identify the service.

Consider the situation illustrated in Figure 6-3. Two databases, db1 and db2, are running on the same machine. Each is assigned a service name using the SERVICE_NAMES initialization parameter. The service name db1.company.com identifies the database db1, and the service name db2.company.com identifies the database db2. If the SERVICE_NAMES parameter is not explicitly defined, the service name is derived from the combination of the DB_NAME and DB_DOMAIN parameters. Assume that you have the following settings:

```
DB_NAME = prod
DB_DOMAIN = yourcompany.com
```

The default setting for the SERVICE_NAMES parameter would be prod.yourcompany.com.

The service name can also be changed dynamically using the ALTER SYSTEM command.

```
SQL> ALTER SYSTEM SET SERVICE_NAMES = "db3.company.com, db4.company.com";
System Altered
```

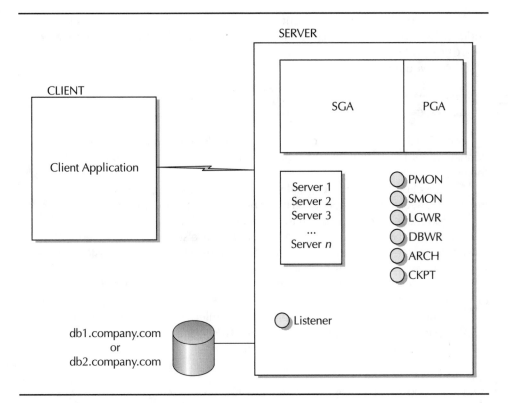

FIGURE 6-3.   *Database instances and services*

Client applications must use a connect descriptor to establish a session against a given database service. The descriptor provides the location of the database and identifies the service. A sample descriptor for the database service is shown here:

```
(DESCRIPTION=
  (ADDRESS=(PROTOCOL=tcp)(HOST=db-server)(PORT=1521))
  (CONNECT_DATA=
    (SERVICE_NAME=db1.company.com)))
```

Note that the address portion of the connect descriptor is the protocol address of the listener. Clients must first contact the listener to get authenticated before establishing a session.

The listener also needs to be configured to accept client requests at a protocol address. The protocol address provides protocol-specific information—for example, the TCP/IP port number. The protocol address corresponding to the sample client descriptor would be

```
(DESCRIPTION=
  (ADDRESS=(PROTOCOL=tcp)(HOST=db-server)(PORT=1521)))
```

Port 1521 has been assigned by IANA to Oracle (http://www.iana.org). Clients configured for the TCP/IP Protocol must use this protocol address to connect to the listener.

A connect descriptor also explicitly specifies a database service name to which the client is seeking a connection. This is necessary because a listener can service connection requests to many database services. For this to happen, database services must be registered with the listener. When a database service is registered with the listener, associated database service handlers are registered with the listener. These service handlers are responsible for passing data back and forth between the client and the database during the session. Service handlers can either be dedicated servers or shared servers.

A client can request for a specific service handler. This is done by using the SERVER parameter in the connect descriptor. The connect descriptor in the following example requests for a shared server.

```
(DESCRIPTION=
  (ADDRESS=(PROTOCOL=tcp)(HOST=db-server)(PORT=1521))
  (CONNECT_DATA=
    (SERVICE_NAME=db1.company.com)
(SERVER=shared)))
```

You can request for a dedicated server by modifying the same connect descriptor.

```
(DESCRIPTION=
  (ADDRESS=(PROTOCOL=tcp)(HOST=db-server)(PORT=1521))
  (CONNECT_DATA=
    (SERVICE_NAME=db1.company.com)
(SERVER=dedicated)))
```

By default, a shared server is requested.

Connection Process

When the listener receives a client request, it selects one of the service handlers that has been previously registered. Depending on the type of handler selected, the communication protocol used, and the operating system of the database server, the listener performs one of the following actions:

- Hands the connect request directly off to a dispatcher.

- Sends a message back to the client with the location of the dispatcher or dedicated server process. The client then connects directly to the dispatcher or dedicated server process.

- Spawns a dedicated server process and passes the client connection to the dedicated server process.

Once the listener has completed the connection for the client, the client communicates with the Oracle database server via the server process. The listener resumes listening for new connection requests.

Naming

A client can request a connection to a database by passing a *connect string* that includes the login and connect descriptor information as shown here.

```
CONNECT scott/tiger@(DESCRIPTION=(ADDRESS=(PROTOCOL=tcp)
(HOST=db-server1)(PORT=1521)) (CONNECT_DATA=
     (SERVICE_NAME=db1.company.com)))
```

It is obviously very tedious to type the connect descriptor every time a connection request has to be made. A connection descriptor can be identified by a connect identifier. A connect identifier can be specified in many ways. A common way is to provide a net service name or an alias that maps to the connect descriptor. The following example creates a connect identifier named ourdb for the sample connect descriptor:

```
ourdb=
  (DESCRIPTION=
    (ADDRESS=(PROTOCOL=tcp)(HOST=db1)(PORT=1521))
    (CONNECT_DATA=
      (SERVICE_NAME=db1.company.com)))
```

You can now initiate the same connection by using this:

```
CONNECT scott/tiger@ourdb
```

Naming Methods

Connection identifiers are mapped to connect descriptors using naming methods. When a naming method is used, the following steps are performed during client connection:

- The client initiates a connect request providing a connect identifier.

- The connect identifier is mapped to a connect descriptor by a naming method. This information is returned to the client.

- The client makes the connect request to the address provided in the connect descriptor.

- A listener receives the request and directs it to the appropriate database server.

- The database server accepts the connection.

Five separate naming methods are available:

- Local naming

- Directory naming

- Oracle Names

- Host naming

- External naming

Local Naming   Connection identifiers are resolved from a file named tnsnames.ora. This file is located on the client machine. When a connect string has to be resolved, information in this file is used to map a connection identifier to a connect descriptor. Though a simple method to resolve names, it is quite difficult to manage a site using this method. This is because it is hard to maintain a current copy of this file on all clients. Every time a change is made to this file, it has to be made available to all clients. Furthermore, users might tamper with their local copies of the file.

Directory Naming   A central LDAP-compliant directory server is used to store net service names and database service names. A site using this naming method can be managed easily since connection identifiers are managed centrally. There is, however, an overhead of maintaining a directory server if you don't already have one.

Oracle Names   This method for naming uses Oracle proprietary software to store the names and addresses of database services on the network. This method is deprecated in Oracle9i. If you are using this method, you should consider switching to one of the other naming methods.

Oracle Names uses a database to store information on database services. The database that maintains this information is identified in a client file named SQLNET.ORA.

Host Naming   If you are using the TCP/IP Network Protocol, your network is already configured for hostname resolution using domain name services (DNS), network information service (NIS), or a local HOSTS file. Oracle Net is able to use the hostname to resolve a service name. The listener must be configured on port 1521 for this to work.

External Naming   Oracle Net can look up net services from third-party software. NIS External Naming is an example of a third-party external naming service.

Oracle Net Services Architecture

Oracle Net is primarily necessary to establish and maintain Oracle client sessions. Clients and database servers use different communication mechanisms to share data. You must choose a suitable architecture for your site from the options described in the sections that follow.

Client/Server Architecture

This client/server communication architecture is based on the standard Open Systems Interconnection (OSI) reference model. Communication between the two computers occurs in a stack-like fashion with information passing from one node to the other through several layers of code.

The client machine uses proprietary software called Oracle Call Interface (OCI) to interact with the database server during a session. OCI provides an interface between the client and the SQL languages used by Oracle Server. An additional layer called *two task common* (TTC) in the presentation layer is responsible for character-set and data-type conversion. This is necessary when the client and database server use different character sets.

The Oracle Net Foundation Layer is responsible for establishing and maintaining the connection between the client application and database server. Messages are exchanged between the client and database server using transparent network substrate (TNS), an Oracle proprietary technology. TNS provides a single and common interface functioning over all industry-standard protocols. In other words,

TNS enables peer-to-peer connectivity so that the client application and database server can communicate with no intermediary points. The tasks performed by Foundation Layer on the client side are

- Locates the destination database server
- Handles interrupts between the client and database server

Additionally, Foundation Layer works with the listener on the server side to receive incoming connection requests. Oracle Net Foundation Layer communicates with naming methods to resolve connect strings and also with security services to ensure secure connections.

Oracle Protocol Support is a layer in between Foundation Layer and the network protocol layer. It maps TNS functions to industry-standard protocols that are supported for client/server connections. The network stack is necessary to establish the network-level communication between two computers to transfer data.

A similar architecture exists on the database server. The only difference is that the process is reversed. Data flows from the network to Oracle Protocol Support to Foundation Layer and then the database via Oracle Program Interface (OPI). OPI can be thought of in the same way as OCI except for the fact that OPI functions respond to OCI requests. Rows are fetched from the database by OPI in response to OCI requests.

Network Protocols

A network protocol is necessary to transport data between the client and database server. An overview of the supported network protocols is provided here.

TCP/IP Protocol   The TCP/IP Protocol with Secure Sockets Layer (SSL) supports a client to communicate with remote Oracle databases through TCP/IP and SSL. Oracle Advanced Security is required to use TCP/IP with SSL. SSL stores authentication data, such as certificates and private keys, in an Oracle Wallet. Oracle Wallet can also be stored in the Windows Registry on the Windows NT/2000 platform. When the client initiates a connection to the database server, SSL performs a handshake between the two using the certificate. During the handshake, the two machines negotiate a cipher suite. The database server then sends its certificate to the client with the client's public key. The client decrypts the message sent by the database server using its private key to verify the database server's certificate. The database server may also request the client for a certificate to verify that it bears the certificate authority's signature. An example of authentication with a digital certificate is provided in Chapter 12.

Named Pipes Protocol   The Named Pipes Protocol is a high-level interface providing interprocess communications between clients and database servers using distributed applications. The server creates a named pipe that is then opened by the client. Many PC LANs, including Windows NT/2000–based networks, still use Named Pipes.

LU6.2 Protocol   The Logical Unit Type 6.2 (LU6.2) Protocol is part of the IBM Advanced Program-to-Program Communication (APPC) architecture. APPC provides peer-to-peer communication for the SNA (System Network Architecture) network. SNA is a network model similar to OSI and is IBM-proprietary. Oracle Server must be running on a machine that supports APPC.

Virtual Interface Protocol   The Virtual Interface (VI) Protocol (http://www.viarch.org) can be used for communication between an application web server and a database server. VI is the de facto communication protocol for clustered server environments. VI reduces the burden on the CPU by transferring the messaging overheads to specialized networking hardware.

Java-Client Application Architecture

Oracle Server supports Java database connectivity (JDBC). Included JDBC drivers provide Java applications access to an Oracle database. Two JDBC drivers are included with Oracle9i. The JDBC OCI driver (level 2 JDBC driver) can be used by Java-based client/server applications. This driver converts JDBC calls to OCI calls, which are then processed by Oracle Net. The second driver, the JDBC Thin driver (level 4 JDBC driver), is meant for Java applets. Connections are established to an Oracle database using Java sockets.

The JDBC OCI driver uses a communication stack similar to a standard client/server communication stack. The JDBC Thin driver uses a Java implementation of the Oracle Net Foundation Layer called *JavaNet* and a Java implementation of TTC called *JavaTTC*.

Web Clients Architecture

The Oracle database can be configured to accept requests from web clients over the Hypertext Transfer Protocol (HTTP) or Internet Inter-ORB Protocol (IIOP). HTTP is used to access Oracle Internet File System, IIOP for Enterprise Java Beans (EJBs), and common object request broker architecture (CORBA) applications.

Oracle Listener

Oracle Listener is a key component of Oracle Net Services since it is responsible for client connections. As the name suggests, Oracle Listener waits, or listens, for new connection requests from clients. When a connection request comes in, the request is handed off to the requested service handler.

Many listener processes can be used on the database server. Each listener is configured with one or more protocol addresses that specify the listening end points. Client machines must have at least one matching protocol address to send a connection request to the listener.

Each listener is configured with one or more protocol addresses that specify its listening end points. Clients configured with one of these protocol addresses can send connection requests to the listener.

A set of database services is registered with the listener process. During registration, the PMON process provides the listener with the names of the database services provided by the database as well as the name of the instance. The service handlers are also made known to the listener process. The listener is able to route a client's connection request based on the information available from registered services.

Since PMON is responsible for registering services with the listener process, you should start the listener process before starting the instance. If you start the listener after starting the instance, you might have to wait up to 60 seconds for PMON to wake up and perform the registration. In this situation, you can use the ALTER SYSTEM REGISTER command to have PMON wake up and register the service immediately. This command takes no additional clauses, as shown here:

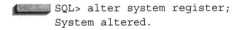

```
SQL> alter system register;
System altered.
```

Database Server Processes

Database Server Processes are used to service client requests to the database server. Two strategies are available. The dedicated server approach entails using one process for each client session. The shared server approach shares server processes between many clients. The default service handler is the shared server. The client can request for either a dedicated or a shared server explicitly.

Shared Servers

In shared server configuration, client processes connect to an intermediary process called a *dispatcher*. The database server can be configured to run many dispatchers.

The least-loaded dispatcher is automatically used to handle the request. A single dispatcher can support multiple clients concurrently. Each client is bound to a piece of shared memory by the dispatcher. This piece of shared memory, called a *virtual circuit,* is then placed on a common request queue. The next available shared server picks up a client request from the head of the queue and services it. The virtual circuit is returned to the pool at this time. This approach to handling client requests allows a small number of shared servers to service a large number of clients.

Shared Server configuration is better suited for OLTP applications in which transaction size is small and server processes are not kept busy for long periods of time. A block diagram of the Shared Server configuration is shown in Figure 6-4.

Dedicated Servers

In dedicated server architecture, a unique server process is spawned to manage client sessions. This architecture is not recommended for large sites since hundreds or thousands of server processes might be necessary. Furthermore, HTTP and IIOP

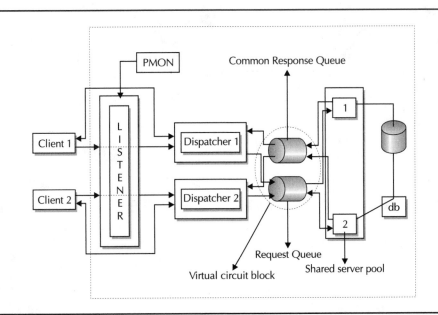

FIGURE 6-4. *Shared server architecture*

clients cannot use dedicated server. The dedicated server architecture is illustrated here:

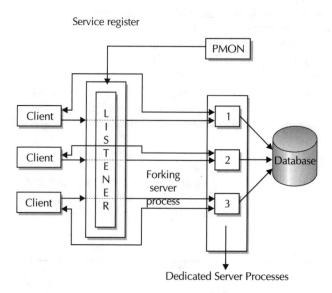

A dedicated server configuration could be a better choice for large DSS applications in which a server process is kept busy for a long time.

NOTE
Dedicated servers are a spillover from Oracle Version 7 and Oracle8. Oracle recommends that you use shared servers.

Oracle Connection Manager

Oracle Connection Manager is the equivalent of a network router. Clients who route connection requests through an Oracle Connection Manager can take advantage of the connection multiplexing, access control, and protocol conversion features configured on Oracle Connection Manager.

Connection Manager maintains a gateway process and an administrative process. The gateway process (CMGW) receives a client request and uses a set of rules to evaluate whether the client should be allowed or denied access. If access is granted, the gateway process forwards the client request to the next hop, usually the database server. CMGW is also capable of multiplexing or funneling multiple client connections through a single protocol connection. This conserves network resources and can be very beneficial to large sites.

As the name suggests, the administrative process (CMADMIN) is responsible for all administrative functions of Connection Manager. This includes registration of CMGW and maintaining a list of listeners and route information to CMGW processes and listeners. Connection Manager also refreshes Oracle Names Servers. The Connection Manager architecture is illustrated here:

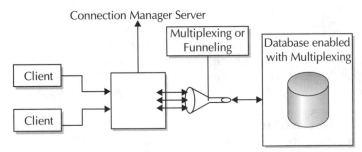

This shows the CMGW process registering with the CMADIN process. Note that the CMGW process handles client requests. The requests from the first three clients are funneled through a single network protocol connection while the fourth client has been rejected.

Oracle Net Tools

Oracle Net Services can be configured using GUI or command-line tools. Oracle recommends that you use these tools to create and edit configuration files for Net Services rather than using a text editor.

Oracle Net Manager

Oracle Net Manager is an integrated environment for configuring and managing Oracle Net. It has a GUI and can be used to manage Oracle Net Services on the client or the server. Oracle Net Manager is integrated with OEM and can be used to configure the following:

- **Naming** You can define connect identifiers and map them to connect descriptors. The connect descriptors can be stored in a local TNSNAMES file, a directory service, or Oracle Names Server.

- **Profiles** Preferences can be created for enabling and configuring Net features on both the client and server.

- **Listeners** Listeners can be configured on the server side.

- **Names Server Management** An existing Oracle Names Server can be managed. The Names Server can be started or stopped. Performance statistics can be gathered and analyzed, and Names Server can be tuned.

Launching Oracle Net Manager

Oracle Net Manager can be launched from OEM or independently from the Start menu. Click Start | Programs | Oracle - OraHome90 | Configuration and Migration Tools | Oracle Net Manager to launch Net Manager on Windows NT/2000. Wizards in Net Manager guide you through the configuration process.

Net Service Name Wizard   Net Service Name Wizard is used to create basic net names in a local TNSNAMES file or a directory server. Select the required node in the navigator and click the + icon to launch this wizard. You can create a TNSNAMES file for the client or the server using this tool.

> **NOTE**
> *The tnsnames.ora file lives in the c:\oracle\ora90\network\admin folder on Windows NT/2000/XP.*

Names Wizard   The Names Wizard guides you through creating and configuring an Oracle Names server. Select the node Oracle Names Servers in the navigator and click the + icon to launch the Names Wizard.

Oracle Net Configuration Assistant

Oracle Net Configuration Assistant is primarily used to configure basic network components. Listener names, protocol addresses, and net service names can be configured using Net Configuration Assistant. Net Configuration Assistant is used during Oracle9i installation to configure Net components.

Launching Oracle Net Configuration Assistant

Click Start | Programs | Oracle - OraHome90 | Configuration and Migration Tools | Net Configuration Assistant to launch this tool on Windows NT/2000. The wizard guides you through the steps to configure an Oracle Net Service. A sample screen from the utility is shown here:

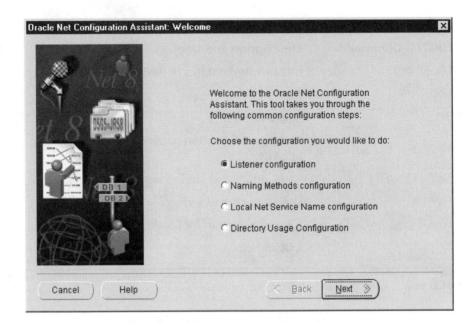

Oracle Net Control Utilities

Command-line utilities are also available to configure and manage Net components.
These are discussed briefly here.

Listener Control Utility

The Listener Control utility (LSNRCTL) is used solely to administer listeners. The
general syntax of LSNRCTL is

```
lsnrctl <command> [listener name]
```

The default name for a listener is LISTENER. You can have multiple listeners
configured together. The LSNRTCL utility can also be used to start up and shut
down the listener. The current status of the listener can also be obtained. The
listener configuration file LISTENER.ORA lives in the c:\oracle\ora90\network\
admin folder on Windows NT/2000. Table 6-3 summarizes LSNRCTL commands.

NOTE
*If the default listener name (LISTENER) cannot
be resolved to a protocol address using TCP/IP,
port 1521 is assumed.*

LSNRCTL Command	Description and Use
STATUS	Obtain current status of listener
START	Start a listener
STOP	Stop a listener
SET	Modify configuration parameters, for example, SET TRC_LEVEL
SHOW_LOG_FILE	Show information in listener log file
SHOW	Display a current setting
CHANGE_PASSWORD	Change password for LSNRCTL
HELP	Obtain help

TABLE 6-3. *Common LSNRCTL Commands*

The following example illustrates a startup of the default listener:

```
C:\oracle\ora90\network\ADMIN>lsnrctl start
LSNRCTL for 32-bit Windows: Version 9.0.1.1.1
- Production on 09-JAN-2002 13:22:
01 Copyright (c) 1991, 2001, Oracle Corporation.  All rights reserved.
Starting tnslsnr: please wait...
TNSLSNR for 32-bit Windows: Version 9.0.1.1.1 - Production
System parameter file is C:\oracle\ora90\network\admin\listener.ora
Log messages written to C:\oracle\ora90\network\log\listener.log
Listening on: (DESCRIPTION=(ADDRESS=(PROTOCOL=ipc)
(PIPENAME=\\.\pipe\EXTPROC0ipc)))
Listening on: (DESCRIPTION=(ADDRESS=(PROTOCOL=tcp)(HOST=aa)
(PORT=1521)))
Connecting to (DESCRIPTION=(ADDRESS=(PROTOCOL=IPC)(KEY=EXTPROC0)))
STATUS of the LISTENER
------------------------
Alias                   LISTENER
Version                 TNSLSNR for 32-bit Windows:
                        Version 9.0.1.1.1 - Production
Start Date              09-JAN-2002 13:22:04
Uptime                  0 days 0 hr. 0 min. 2 sec
Trace Level             off
Security                OFF
SNMP                    OFF
```

```
Listener Parameter File   C:\oracle\ora90\network\admin\listener.ora
Listener Log File         C:\oracle\ora90\network\log\listener.log
Listening Endpoints Summary...
   (DESCRIPTION=(ADDRESS=(PROTOCOL=ipc)
       (PIPENAME=\\.\pipe\EXTPROC0ipc)))
   (DESCRIPTION=(ADDRESS=(PROTOCOL=tcp)(HOST=aa)(PORT=1521)))
Services Summary...
Service "PLSExtProc" has 1 instance(s).
  Instance "PLSExtProc", status UNKNOWN,
      has 1 handler(s) for this service...
Service "aa.liqwidkrystal.com" has 1 instance(s).
  Instance "aa", status UNKNOWN, has 1 handler(s) for this service...
The command completed successfully
```

Note that the instance is reported as "UNKNOWN" in the previous output. This is because the instance has not been created as yet. You should start the listener before the instance.

You can also use the Services applet in Control Panel to start up and shut down the listener. You should configure the listener service to start automatically at system startup.

Listener Security   You should configure a password to restrict access to the listener. This is to ensure that malicious users cannot perform privileged operations such as configuration changes. You can set a password using the CHANGE_ PASSWORD command from LSNRCTL or by using Net Manager. The encrypted password is stored in the LISTENER.ORA file.

On Windows NT/2000, you should ensure that the c:\oracle\ora90\network\ admin folder is protected. Again, if you are using the NTFS file system, you can accomplish this by setting OS-level security.

The following sample session illustrates the process of setting the password and using it for the purpose of authentication before shutting down the listener.

```
LSNRCTL> change_password
Old password: <old password>
New password: <new password>
Reenter new password: <new password>
Connecting to (DESCRIPTION=(ADDRESS=(PROTOCOL=IPC)(KEY=EXTPROC0)))
Password changed for LISTENER
The command completed successfully
LSNRCTL> stop
Connecting to (DESCRIPTION=(ADDRESS=(PROTOCOL=IPC)(KEY=EXTPROC0)))
TNS-01169: The listener has not recognized the password
```

Note that the listener did not shut down because the user is not authenticated. The SET PASSWORD command is used for authentication as shown here:

```
LSNRCTL> set password
Password: <password>
The command completed successfully
LSNRCTL> stop
Connecting to (DESCRIPTION=(ADDRESS=(PROTOCOL=IPC)(KEY=EXTPROC0)))
The command completed successfully
```

TIP
If you are administering the listener remotely over an insecure network and require maximum security, configure the listener with a secure protocol address that uses the TCP/IP with SSL Protocol. Ensure that the protocol address for TCP/IP with SSL Protocol is listed first in the listener.ora file.

CAUTION
The password is ignored if someone attempts to start up or shut down the listener service from the Console using Services Applet. The listener service is managed by the built-in SYSTEM account on Windows NT/2000.

Connection Manager Control Utility

Oracle connection manager control utility (CMCTL) is used to administer connection managers. Configuration parameters can be viewed and set. The CMGW and CMADMIN processes can be started or shut down. The general syntax to use this utility is

```
cmctl command [process]
```

The *process* clause specifies the type of process to be started. The options are

- *cman* specifies both processes (CMGW andCMADMIN).

- *cm* specifies the CMGW process.

- *adm* specifies the CMADMIN process.

The following command starts both the CMGW and CMADMIN processes:

```
CMCTL START cman
```

NOTE
Oracle recommends using the cman *option. Use the* cm *option when it is necessary to conserve resources. The CMGW process performs Oracle Connection Manager basic functions and can run without the CMADMIN process.*

Like LSNRCTL, you can issue commands at the CMCTL prompt. Use the HELP command to get a listing of all the commands and their usage within this utility.

Names Control Utility

The Oracle names control utility enables you to administer Oracle Names Servers. You can use its commands to perform basic management functions on one or more Oracle Names Servers. Additionally, you can view and change parameter settings. The general syntax for this utility is

```
namesctl <command> [names_server]
```

In the preceding code listing usage, *names_server* is the name of the Oracle Names Server to be administered. Commands can be issued at the command prompt.

When you launch the NAMESCTL utility, it starts a session with an Oracle Names Server. A session on the Names Server listed in the discovery file is started. This file is named sdns.ora on Windows NT/2000. Optionally, the NAMES.PREFERRED_ SERVERS parameter can be set in sqlnet.ora. You can use the SET SERVER command to start a session on a specific Names Server.

Like other utilities, NAMESCTL can be used to start up and shut down the Names Server. The SET and SHOW commands are also available to set and view configuration settings.

Distributed Operations   The Oracle Names control utility can be used against a local or a remote Oracle Names Server. This feature is useful when a single administrator is managing all Names Servers from a central location. All operations except starting a Names Server are allowed remotely.

When issuing commands, specify the name of the Oracle Names Server as an argument, for example,

```
NAMESCTL> SHOW SYSTEM_QUERIES db1.company.com
```

You can also use the protocol address of the Names Server, for example:

```
NAMESCTL> SHOW SYSTEM_QUERIES
(ADDRESS=(PROTOCOL=tcp)(HOST=db1.company.com)(PORT=1575))
```

Oracle Names Server Security   Password protection can be configured in the names.ora file or the sqlnet.ora file.

TIP
All Oracle Net Service command-line utilities can be executed in a batch mode. Place the commands in a standard text file, one command on each line. You can use the # character to mark a comment line. Pass the name of the file containing the commands as an argument to the utility.

Planning for Oracle Net Services

Today's business requires database applications to run on a wide variety of networks. Database applications are being widely used on the Web. Security and other issues need to be taken into consideration.

Scalability

The three-tier architecture (database, application server, and client) is increasingly being deployed in the industry. Scalability can be improved with shared servers and connection pooling. Session multiplexing must be used between application server and database server.

Availability

Availability and uptime are crucial for business applications. Redundancy can be increased by configuring multiple listeners for a given database service. You should deploy at least two Connection Manager firewalls or Oracle Net Firewall Proxies.

Naming Methods

Local or host naming is sufficient for small-sized networks. Large sites with several databases should use directory naming in a centralized LDAP-compliant server.

Security

Databases and applications within the intranet should be behind the firewall. Access control for Internet applications is crucial. Access control can be provided through a firewall on the database. Oracle Connection Manager should be used to create a firewall. Clients can be granted or denied access to a specific database service or computer based on a set of rules. The sqlnet.ora file should be configured to allow or deny clients access based on the protocol being used. The VI Protocol is inherently more secure than TCP/IP since there are no utilities such as FTP or Telnet available.

Performance Tuning for Oracle Net Services

Oracle Net Services offers a number of features that can help reduce round-trip time across the network, increase listener performance, and reduce the number of protocols used. For example, you can configure multiple listeners on a server, or you can increase the listener queue size. Such performance-related features are discussed next.

VI Protocol

You can reduce round-trip time between application servers and the database server with the VI Protocol, which has a significantly lower messaging overhead. The VI Protocol is unsuitable for your site if you need utilities such as FTP and Telnet.

Managing Session Data Unit Size

Before sending data across the network, Oracle Net buffers and encapsulates data into a session data unit (SDU). Oracle Net transmits data stored in this buffer when the buffer is full or flushed, or when the database server tries to read data. When large amounts of data are being transmitted or when the message size is consistent, adjusting the size of the SDU buffers can improve performance because of better network use and lower memory consumption. You can deploy SDU at the client, the application server, or the database server.

Listener Queue Size and Number of Listeners

If you anticipate receiving a large number of simultaneous connection requests, you can increase the size of the listener queue or configure multiple listeners on the server. If you choose to run multiple listeners on your server, each must ensure that there are no conflicts. For example, two listener processes cannot listen on the same UDP port. If you run multiple listeners, you must segregate your clients to balance the load on the listeners.

   If your listener requests come in bunches, you can increase the listener queue size. The size of the listener queue is set in the listener.ora configuration file, as shown in the sample configuration here:

```
LISTENER =
   (DESCRIPTION_LIST =
```

```
(DESCRIPTION =
  (ADDRESS_LIST =
    (ADDRESS = (PROTOCOL = IPC)(KEY = EXTPROC3))
  )
  (ADDRESS_LIST =
    (ADDRESS = (PROTOCOL = TCP)(HOST = aa)(PORT = 1521)
        (QUEUESIZE=10))
  )
)
)
```

Protocol Conversion

The database needs to be configured to listen on only one protocol address, even though clients may use other protocols. Oracle Connection Manager provides a protocol conversion feature that enables a client and database server configured with different networking protocols to communicate with one another.

Setting Up Oracle Directory Server

Many Oracle products include support for an LDAP-compliant directory server. For example, Oracle Net and Advanced Security Enterprise User can use directory servers. To use these features, you must establish a directory server for them, as well as enable your computers to use the directory server.

Configuring Directory Usage During Installation

Oracle Universal Installer launches Oracle Net Configuration Assistant during Oracle9i software installation to configure Oracle Net. Directory servers can be configured at this time depending on the type of installation being performed.

Directory Usage Configuration During a Custom Installation

During a custom installation on the server, Oracle Net Configuration Assistant prompts you to configure a directory server. Oracle Database Configuration Assistant can be used to register a database service entry in the directory server. Oracle Net Manager is also launched during a custom installation. This can be used to create net service names in the directory server.

NOTE
Directory usage configuration is not performed if you choose to install the Enterprise Edition or Standard Edition of Oracle9i.

During directory server usage configuration, Oracle Net Configuration Assistant prompts you to select the type of directory server. You can choose between Oracle Internet Directory and Microsoft Active Directory Services (MS-ADSI). You should identify the location of the directory server. The Oracle Context (cn=OracleContext) is the root of a directory subtree that is used to store information related to Oracle software. The ldap.ora file is used to locate the directory server and access Oracle entries.

If an Oracle Context does not exist in the directory under the selected administrative context, then Oracle Net Configuration Assistant prompts you to create it. During the Oracle Context creation, you are prompted for directory administrator authentication credentials. If the Oracle Context is created successfully, then the authenticated user is added to the OracleDBCreators and OracleNetAdmins groups. As a member of the OracleDBCreators group, a user can use Oracle Database Configuration Assistant to register a database service entry. As a member of the OracleNetAdmins group, a user can use Oracle Net Manager to create, modify, and delete net service names, as well as modify Oracle Net attributes of database services.

```
OracleDBCreators (cn=OracleDBCreators,cn=OracleContext)
OracleNetAdmins (cn=OracleNetAdmins,cn=OracleContext)
```

A directory administrator can add other users to these groups. Oracle Net Configuration Assistant then verifies that the Oracle schema was created. The Oracle schema defines the Oracle entries and their attributes. If the schema does not exist or is an older version, you are prompted to create or upgrade it. During Oracle schema creation, you are prompted for authentication credentials.

After Oracle Net Configuration Assistant completes configuration, Oracle Database Configuration Assistant creates the database. The service name for the database is automatically created under the Oracle Context.

Directory Usage Configuration During a Client Installation

During an Oracle client installation, Oracle Net Configuration Assistant prompts you to configure the use of a directory server. Directory server usage configuration enables the client to look up connect identifier entries in the directory. If directory server access is not configured, the client cannot use directory naming. Oracle Net Configuration Assistant typically performs the necessary directory server usage configuration during client installation and stores it in the ldap.ora file. This file is created in the c:\oracle\ora90\network\admin folder. During directory server access configuration, Oracle Net Configuration Assistant prompts you for the following:

- To specify the type of directory server
- To identify the location of the directory server

■ To select a location in the directory that contains an Oracle Context from which this client can look up connect identifiers

In addition, Oracle Net Configuration Assistant verifies that the Oracle schema is installed. If the Oracle Context or the Oracle schema is unavailable, you cannot complete directory server usage configuration on the client.

Configuring Directory Usage After Installation

Directory usage can be configured with Oracle Net Configuration Assistant at any time. Follow the steps describe here to configure directory usage.

Launch Oracle Net Configuration Assistant from the Start menu. Choose the Directory Service Usage Configuration option from the first screen of the wizard to view the available options for directory usage configuration, as shown in Figure 6-5.

As seen in Figure 6-5, the following options are available:

Option 1: Select the Directory Server You Want to Use   Select this option to use a directory server that is already configured to use directory-enabled features. This option is ideal for clients that use a directory server that has already been

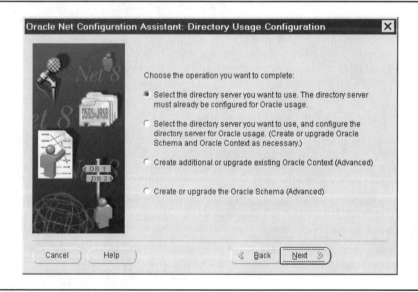

FIGURE 6-5.   *Directory usage configuration options*

configured for these features. Once configuration is complete, this option enables this computer to look up entries in the directory. This option prompts you for the type and location of the directory server. If no Oracle Context or Oracle schema exists, you cannot use this option. Use the next option instead.

Option 2: Select the Directory Server You Want to Use and Configure the Directory Server for Oracle Usage Select this option to configure a directory server for directory-enabled features and enable this computer to use that directory. This option is designed for first-use. Once configuration is complete, this computer can then look up entries in the directory server. This option also prompts you to select the type and location of the directory server; however, if an Oracle Context is not found, you are prompted to create one. Similarly, if an Oracle Schema is not found, or an older version is found, you are prompted to create or upgrade the schema. You are prompted for directory administrator's authentication. If the Oracle Context is created successfully, then the authenticated user is added to the OracleDBCreators and Oracle NetAdmins groups.

Option 3: Create Additional or Upgrade Existing Oracle Context Select this option to create an additional Oracle Context in the directory or to upgrade the Oracle Context to the current release. A directory entry under which the Oracle Context is to be created and Oracle Schema must exist. You will be asked for directory administrator's credentials. Again, if the Oracle Context is created successfully, the authenticated user is added to the OracleDBCreators and Oracle NetAdmins groups.

Option 4: Create or Upgrade the Oracle Schema Select this option to create Oracle Schema in the directory or upgrade the Oracle schema to the current release. During Oracle schema creation or upgrade, you are prompted for directory administrator's credentials.

Select the appropriate option and follow the instructions from the wizard to complete the directory usage configuration.

Adding Users to and Removing Users from the OracleNetAdmins Group

The directory user who creates the Oracle Context is a member of the OracleNetAdmins (cn=OracleNetAdmins,cn=OracleContext) group. Using a directory tool such as LDAPMODIFY, a directory administrator (or the directory user who created the Oracle Context) can manage users in this group.

Adding a User to the OracleNetAdmins Group with **LDAPMODIFY**

First create an LDAP data interchange format (LDIF) file that specifies that you want to add a user to the OracleNetAdmins group. Use the appropriate distinguished name (DN) for cn=OracleNetAdmins and the user that you want to add. You can use the sample test.ldif file shown here:

```
dn: cn=OracleNetAdmins,cn=OracleContext,dc=company,dc=com
changetype: modify
add: uniquemember
uniquemember: Admin
```

Use LDAPMODIFY to add the user:

```
ldapmodify -h ld.company.com -p 389 -D cn=orcladmin -w welcome
-f test.ldif
```

Removing a User from the OracleNetAdmins Group with **LDAPMODIFY**

Again, create an LDIF file and use LDAPMODIFY to delete the user. The following sample LDIF file deletes a user named Admin.

```
dn: cn=OracleNetAdmins,cn=OracleContext,dc=company,dc=com
changetype: modify
delete: uniquemember
uniquemember: Admin
```

Use the LDAPMODIFY command to delete the user. A case study in Chapter 12 illustrates the configuration of enterprise-level security with Oracle Internet Directory.

Configuring Oracle Naming Methods

Oracle clients use a simple name called the connect identifier in the connect string when requesting a connection to a database. This section discusses the available naming methods and the process of configuration.

Configuring the Order of Search for Naming Method

You can configure an Oracle client to use more than one naming method. The order in which naming methods are used is specified in the sqlnet.ora file. The parameter NAMES.DIRECTORY_PATH is used to specify the order in which naming methods are used to resolve connect identifiers. You can configure this parameter from Oracle Net Manager.

Launch Oracle Net Manager, expand the Local node, and select Profile. Select Naming from the drop-down list and choose the Methods tab. From the list of available methods, add the naming methods to your configuration and arrange the order in which you want to use them. Be sure to save the configuration when you are done. The sqlnet.ora file is updated. A sample entry is shown here:

```
NAMES.DIRECTORY_PATH=(ldap, tnsnames, onames, hostname)
```

Configuring Local Naming Method

The local naming method uses a local tnsnames.ora file for naming. Every net service name is mapped to a connect descriptor. The tnsnames.ora file lives in the c:\oracle\ora90\network\admin folder on Windows NT/2000. Local naming can be configured during or after installation using Oracle Net Configuration Assistant or Oracle Net Manager.

Configure Local Naming Using Net Manager

Launch Net Manager and expand the Local node. Choose Service Naming and click the + icon to add a service. You can also select Edit | Create. The Net Service Name Wizard appears. Enter a name for the net service and domain information.

TIP
If the NAMES.DEFAULT_DOMAIN parameter is set in sqlnet.ora, the domain is automatically qualified and it does not have to be specified in the connect string.

In the next screen, select the protocol information for the listener. The network protocol must already have been installed prior to using Net Services.

Click the Next button to view the Protocol Settings screen. Complete the information required for the protocol. On the next page, enter the destination service and (optionally) a database connection type as shown in the illustration here:

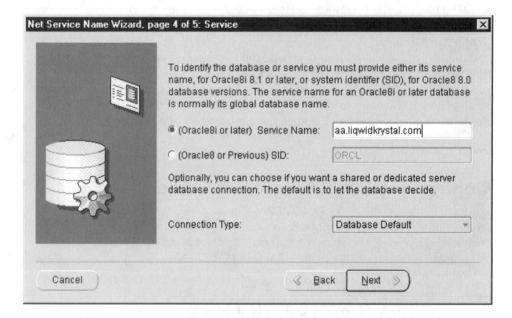

If you are using Oracle9i, set the destination service to Oracle8i or Later. Enter a service name.

NOTE
If you are using Oracle8, set the destination to Oracle8 or Previous and enter an Oracle System Identifier.

Choose to use the default setting for the connection type. Shared servers or dedicated servers are used based on configuration parameters in the initialization parameter file. (The SHARED_SERVERS parameter is set to 1 for shared servers and 0 for dedicated servers.) Click the Next button to view the Test page. You can verify if the service name works. Both the listener and the database must be up and running to test the connection. Click the Finish button and save your configuration.

Configure Local Naming with Oracle Net Configuration Assistant

Oracle Net Configuration Assistant can also be used to configure local naming. Again the wizard takes you through the necessary steps. The steps are almost identical to Net Manager and so are repeated here.

You can view the tnsnames.ora file to verify that the service name was added to it. A sample entry is shown here:

```
ourdb =
(DESCRIPTION=
   (ADDRESS=(PROTOCOL=tcp)(HOST=db-server)(PORT=1521))
   (CONNECT_DATA=
      (SERVICE_NAME=db1.company.com)))
```

The connect identifier **ourdb** is mapped to the connect descriptor.

Configuring Directory Naming Method

While local naming is simple to configure, it can be quite tedious to use on large sites since every client has to maintain an updated tnsnames.ora file. The directory naming method uses a central directory server to look up a net service name. Connect identifiers are mapped to connect descriptors in an LDAP-compliant directory server. Oracle Internet Directory, Microsoft Active Directory, or Novell Directory Services can be used.

You can configure database service entries and net service entries using Oracle Database Configuration Assistant during installation. Net Manager can be used to modify net service entries at any time. To add database services and net service names to a directory, the directory access configuration must be completed. This process has been described in the "Setting Up Oracle Directory Server" section earlier in this chapter.

To create a net service name in a directory server, launch Net Manager on a computer that has been configured with directory access. Choose the Directory node in the navigator pane and select Service Naming. Click the + icon to launch the Net Service Name Wizard. Provide the service name and protocol information. In the following screen provide the database service information and connection type. Test the service name and save the configuration.

Configuring Oracle Names LDAP Proxy Servers

If you are not in a position to upgrade Oracle client machines to use directory naming, you can use Oracle Names LDAP Proxy Servers. You must use Version 9.0 or later of Oracle Names Servers to use this feature. The Oracle Names Server configuration file ckptop.ora is stored in the c:\oracle\ora90\network\names folder on Windows NT/2000 by default. If you want to use an alternative location, set the NAMES.TOPOLOGY_CHECKPOINT_FILE parameter in the names.ora file. Topology data consists of definitions for all parent domains and Oracle Names Servers in the region. This information is used by Oracle Names Servers to understand the structure of the domain.

First, ensure that you have populated the directory server and exported the existing name server data to the populated directory server. Stop each Oracle Names Server using NAMESCTL. Set the NAMES.ADMIN_REGION parameter in the names.ora file to the directory server's DN, or read it from an LDIF file. The syntax for an Oracle Names LDAP Proxy Server to load the data from a directory server is

```
NAMES.ADMIN_REGION=
    (REGION=
      (TYPE=ldap)
     [(USERID=user_dn)]
     [(PASSWORD=password)]
      [(HOST=host)]
      [(PORT=port)]
     [(SUBTREE_LIST=]
       [(SUBTREE=(BASE=base_DN)[(SCOPE=sub|one))]
       [(SUBTREE=(BASE=base_DN)[(SCOPE=sub|one))]
     [)])
```

Values from the ldap.ora file are used as defaults for the USER, HOST, and SUBTREE parameters. The following example shows an Oracle Names LDAP Proxy Server configured to load the data from an Oracle Context that is directly under the DN (dn:dc=company,dc=com) and all Oracle Contexts under the DN subtree (dn:dc=company,dc=com).

```
NAMES.ADMIN_REGION=
    (REGION=
      (TYPE=LDAP)
      (HOST=ld.company.com)
      (PORT= 389)
      (SUBTREE_LIST=
         (SUBTREE=(BASE=dc=company,dc=com)(scope=sub))
      )
    )
  )
```

The following example shows an Oracle Names LDAP Proxy Server configured to load data from LDIF file named onames.ldif.

```
NAMES.ADMIN_REGION=
   (REGION=
   (TYPE=LDIF)
   (FILE=d:\onames.ldif))
```

The TYPE parameter specifies how Oracle Names LDAP Proxy loads data from a directory. You can load data directly from a directory server (TYPE=LDAP) or from an LDAP Data Interchange Format file (TYPE=LDIF).

The following LDIF file excerpt shows a DN of (dn: cn=db1, cn=OracleContext, dc=company, dc=com) that contains net service names db1 and db2.

```
dn: cn=db1,cn=OracleContext,dc=company,dc=com
objectclass: top
objectclass: orclNetService
cn: db1
orclNetDescString:
(DESCRIPTION=(ADDRESS_
LIST=(ADDRESS=(PROTOCOL=tcp)(Host=db-server)(Port=1521)))
(CONNECT_DATA=(SERVICE_NAME=db1.company.com)))
dn: cn=db2,cn=OracleContext, dc=company,dc=com
 objectclass: top
objectclass: orclNetService
cn: db2
orclNetDescString:
(DESCRIPTION=(ADDRESS_LIST=(ADDRESS=(COMMUNITY=TCP_COMMUNITY)
(PROTOCOL=tcp)(Host=db2-server)(Port=1521)))
(CONNECT_DATA=(SERVICE_NAME=db2.company.com)))
```

Restart the Oracle Names Servers.

Configuring the Host Naming Method

In TCP/IP-based networks host naming can be used to establish simple connectivity. This eliminates the need for a naming method; however, host naming does not work for large or complex environments where advanced features such as connection pooling and external procedures are used.

Oracle clients use the server's global database name in the connect string to connect to the database. The global database name is equivalent to a hostname or an alias in an existing name resolution service. The hostname must be resolved using DNS, NIS, or a local hosts file on the client. A sample entry in the hosts file is shown here:

```
#IP address of server      host name        alias
192.168.200.1            db1-server     db1.company.com
192.168.200.2            db2-server     db2.company.com
```

The domain section of the global database name must match the network domain. The listener process must be configured to listen on port 1521.

Exporting Naming Data

You can export service names from other naming methods to a directory server. In this manner an existing configuration, say from a local TNSNAMES file, can be uploaded to a directory server. This section describes the methodology.

Exporting Service Names from Local Names to Directory Server

You can export service names from a tnsnames.ora file to a directory server. The steps necessary are as follows.

Step 1: Create Structure in Directory Server   In the directory server, create the directory information tree (DIT) with the structure in which you want to import net service names. Create a structure as needed. For example, if the tnsnames.ora file supports a domain structure company.com, you create domain component entries of dc=company and dc=com in the directory.

Step 2: Create Oracle Contexts   Create an Oracle Context under each DIT location. The Oracle Context has a relative distinguished name (RDN) of (cn=OracleContext). The Oracle Context stores network object entries, as well as other entries for other Oracle components.

Step 3: Export Objects from TNSNAMES.ORA to Directory Server   Launch Net Manager and choose Command I Directory I Export Net Service Names from the menu to launch the Directory Migration Wizard.

If multiple domains were detected in the tnsnames.ora file, the Select Domain page appears. Else, the Select Net Service Names page appears. Choose the network domain that you want to export (if you have multiple domains) and then the net service names that you want to export. In the ensuing Select Destination Context page, select the directory entry that contains the Oracle Context from the Directory Naming Contexts list. Click the Next button to start the operation. A status screen shows the status of the export. Dismiss the wizard when migration is complete.

Exporting Names from Oracle Names Server to Directory Server

Database services and net service names stored in Oracle Names Server can be exported directly to a directory server. Alternatively, you can first export to an LDIF file, which can then be used to load the directory server. Data is exported from a specified domain. If the domain has authority for delegated domains, the data from the delegated domains can also be exported.

First ensure that the directory server is configured with the required DIT and Oracle Context structure. Use the DUMP_LDAP command of NAMESCTL to export objects directly to a directory server on an LDIF file. The LDIF file can later be loaded with LDAPADD or LDAPMODIFY. The following example exports a single domain to the same DIT node:

```
NAMESCTL> DUMP_LDAP company.com -f sample.ldif
```

The following example exports data from the domain company.com and its delegated domains to the configured DIT structure:

```
NAMESCTL> DUMP_LDAP company.com -R -f sample.ldif
```

NOTE
Use the HELP command to obtain help for the NAMECTL utility.

Configuring Profiles

A *profile* is a collection of parameters that specifies preferences for enabling and configuring Oracle Net features on the client or the database server. A profile is implemented in the sqlnet.ora file. A profile is typically used to specify a client domain for unqualified names or to prioritize naming methods. Logging and tracing can be enabled or disabled using a profile. Advanced Security is also configured using a profile. Net Manager can be used to configure profiles. A sample profile is shown here:

```
TRACE_DIRECTORY_CLIENT = c:\tmp
SQLNET.AUTHENTICATION_SERVICES= (NTS)
LOG_DIRECTORY_CLIENT = c:\tmp
TRACE_LEVEL_CLIENT = ADMIN
TCP.EXCLUDED_NODES= (192.168.1.3)
TRACE_LEVEL_SERVER = ADMIN
TCP.VALIDNODE_CHECKING = YES
```

In this profile tracing and logging is enabled. Also note that connections from a specific IP address can be blocked with the TCP.EXCLUDED_NODES parameter.

Setting a Default Domain for a Client

A client can be configured for a default domain. If the default domain is configured, a client does not have to explicitly provide the domain name in the connect string. For example, if the default domain is company.com, and the client wants to connect to a service named db1, the connect string would normally be userid/password@db1.company.com. By configuring a default domain, the user could use a connect string of the form userid/password@db1 instead.

Use Net Manager to set a default domain. In the navigator pane of Net Manager, expand the Local node. Select Profile and choose Naming from the drop-down list. Select the Oracle Names tab and set the default domain. Save the network configuration. Your sqlnet.ora file should contain an entry similar to the one shown here:

```
NAMES.DEFAULT_DOMAIN=company.com
```

Prioritizing Naming Methods

Available naming methods are listed in the sqlnet.ora file. The order in which naming methods are to be used can also be specified. Use Net Manager to set the order in which naming methods are to be used. Oracle Net attempts to use the first naming method provided in the list. If this fails, the next entry in the list is used automatically. Net Manager is used to manage this list. A sample entry in the resulting sqlnet.ora is shown here:

```
NAMES.DIRECTORY_PATH=(ldap, tnsnames, onames, hostname, cds, nis)
```

Configuring and Administering Listener

A listener is configured with one or more listening protocol addresses, information about supported services, and parameters that control its run-time behavior. The listener configuration is stored in a configuration file named listener.ora. Because all the configuration parameters have default values, it is possible to start and use a listener with no configuration. This default listener has the name LISTENER, supports no services upon startup, and listens on port 1521.

Services supported by a listener must be registered prior to use. The PMON process automatically registers the database services. You can add other services to listener.ora using Net Manager. Service registration is recommended since it offers some inherent benefits such as fail-over support and load-balancing. Since the listener is always aware of the state of an instance, automatic fail-over of a client connect request to another instance is possible. Similarly, the listener can forward a client connect request to the least loaded instance or dispatcher.

NOTE
Static configuration in the listener.ora file with the SID_LIST_LISTENER_NAME parameter is still required if you are managing the databases with OEM.

A listening IPC protocol address for external procedures is automatically configured during installation. The following sample listener.ora file defines the protocol address for the default listener named LISTENER. The SID_LIST_LISTENER parameter provides information about the supported services.

```
LISTENER=
   (DESCRIPTION=
     (ADDRESS_LIST=
       (ADDRESS=(PROTOCOL=tcp)(HOST=db1-server)(PORT=1521))
       (ADDRESS=(PROTOCOL=ipc)(KEY=extproc))))
SID_LIST_LISTENER=
   (SID_LIST=
     (SID_DESC=
       (GLOBAL_DBNAME=db1.company.com)
       (ORACLE_HOME=c:\oracle\ora90)
       (SID_NAME=db1))
     (SID_DESC=
       (SID_NAME=plsextproc)
       (ORACLE_HOME=c:\oracle\ora90)
       (PROGRAM=extproc)))
```

Oracle Net Manager or Net Configuration Assistant can be used to configure the listener.

Configuring Listening Protocol Addresses

You can add as many protocol addresses as you need. Follow these steps to configure additional protocol addresses for the listener:

Step 1: Select the Listener to Be Configured　　Launch Net Manager and expand the Local node. Select a listener. If a listener is not listed, exit Net Manager, start the listener from LSNRCTL, and restart Net Manager.

Step 2: Create a Listener if Needed　　If a listener has never been created, click the + icon and create a unique listener.

Step 3: Create a Protocol Address   Choose Add Address, select the required protocol, and enter the appropriate parameters for the selected protocol.

TIP
If the computer has more than one IP address and you want the listener to listen on all available IP addresses, configure TCP/IP or TCP/IP with SSL and enter the hostname of the computer in the Host field.

Step 4: Save Configuration   Be sure to save the new configuration before restarting the listener. A sample screen is shown in Figure 6-6.

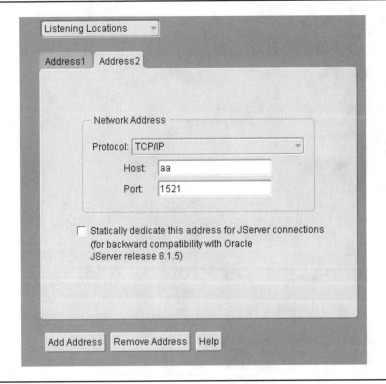

FIGURE 6-6.   *Configuring listener addresses from Net Manager*

Protocol Addresses for Oracle9i JVM

On Oracle9i, you are no longer required to configure the JServer protocol address. This configuration occurs dynamically during service registration.

Handling Large Volumes of Concurrent Connection Requests

If you expect the listener to handle large volumes of concurrent connection requests, you might need to specify a listen queue size for its listening end points. To specify a queue size for a protocol address, enter a value for the QUEUESIZE parameter at the end of the protocol address, for example:

```
LISTENER=
  (DESCRIPTION=
   (ADDRESS=(PROTOCOL=tcp)(HOST=db1-server)(PORT=1521)(QUEUESIZE=20)))
```

Currently, you can configure only the queue size for listeners operating on TCP/IP. The default queue size is system specific (5 for Windows NT 4.0 Workstation and 50 for Windows NT 4.0 Server).

Configuring Static Service Information

In order for the listener to accept client connect requests to previous Oracle releases (Oracle Version 7 and Oracle8), you must configure with static information. Static configuration is also required for external procedures and OEM. Services for Oracle8i/9i are dynamically configured. An excerpt of a statically configured database service is shown here:

```
SID_LIST_listener=
(SID_LIST=
 (SID_DESC=
  (GLOBAL_DBNAME=db1.company.com)
  (SID_NAME=db1)
  (ORACLE_HOME=c:\oracle8)))
```

Configuring Password Authentication for the Listener

It is important to provide security through a password for the listener. If configured, privileged operations such as configuration changes and stopping the listener require password authentication.

Use the LSNRCTL CHANGE_PASSWORD command, or use Net Manager to set or change an encrypted password. The password is stored in the listener.ora file.

Configuring Service Registration

To ensure that dynamic service registration works properly, the following parameters must be set properly in the initialization file:

```
SERVICE_NAMES
INSTANCE_NAME
```

The SERVICE_NAMES parameter defaults to the global database name, which is a combination of the DB_NAME and DB_DOMAIN parameters.

Registering Information with the Default Local Listener

By default, the PMON process registers service information with its local listener on the default local address of TCP/IP, port 1521. This is the port registered by Oracle with IANA. However, you can change this port by modifying the initialization parameter file.

Registering Information with a Nondefault Listener

If you want PMON to register with a local listener that does not use TCP/IP and UDP port 1521, configure the LOCAL_LISTENER initialization parameter to provide the name of the local listener. If you are using shared server, you can also use the LISTENER attribute of the DISPATCHERS initialization parameter file to register the dispatchers with a nondefault local listener. The LISTENER attribute overrides the LOCAL_LISTENER parameter. More information on the DISPATCHERS parameter is available in the "Shared Servers" section earlier in this chapter.

Registering Information with a Remote Listener

You can register services to remote listeners. This is especially useful in RAC configuration. Use the LISTENER attribute of the DISPATCHERS initialization parameter or the REMOTE_LISTENER initialization parameter to register services in a shared server environment. Use the REMOTE_LISTENER parameter if you wish to use a dedicated server. For example, if two remote listeners are configured on remote servers named db1-server and db2-server to listen on port 1521, you can set the REMOTE_LISTENER parameter in the initialization file for the instance on host db1-server as

```
REMOTE_LISTENER=listener_db2
```

Set the same parameter in the initialization file for the instance on host db2-server as

```
REMOTE_LISTENER=listener_db1
```

The tnsnames.ora file would have the following entries:

```
listener_db2=
  (DESCRIPTION=
    (ADDRESS=(PROTOCOL=tcp)(HOST=db2-server)(PORT=1521)))
listener_db1=
  (DESCRIPTION=
    (ADDRESS=(PROTOCOL=tcp)(HOST=db1-server)(PORT=1521)))
```

In a shared server configuration, you can use the following setting:

```
DISPATCHERS="(PROTOCOL=tcp)(LISTENER=listeners_db)"
```

In this case, the tnsnames.ora file would contain

```
listeners_db=
  (DESCRIPTION=
    (ADDRESS=(PROTOCOL=tcp)(HOST=db1-server)(PORT=1521))
    (ADDRESS=(PROTOCOL=tcp)(HOST=db2-server)(PORT=1521)))
```

Configuring a Naming Method

The listener name alias specified for the initialization parameter such as LOCAL_LISTENER and REMOTE_LISTENER is resolved using the tnsnames.ora file or Oracle Names Server.

Listener Administration

Once the listener is configured, the listener can be administered with LSNRCTL. For example, you can enable or disable logging with LSNRCTL.

Starting and Stopping the Listener

Use the START command to start the listener and the STOP command to stop it. On Windows NT/2000, you can control the listener from the Services applet of Control Panel.

Monitoring Runtime Behavior

Use the STATUS command to obtain the status of listener. The Services applet also shows you if the listener is running or not.

```
LSNRCTL> STATUS <listener name>
```

Use the SERVICES command to get a listing of services known to the listener.

Monitoring Log Files

Listener logs can provide useful information on the listener's health. If you are experiencing long delays in establishing a connection or connections are being refused, you can obtain listener logs. The listener log file on Windows NT/2000 is named listener.log and is created in the c:\oracle\ora90\network\log folder.

You can also obtain trace files for a specific user session or across the system. The following sample session demonstrates this feature:

```
LSNRCTL> help trace
trace OFF | USER | ADMIN | SUPPORT [<listener_name>] : set tracing
to the specified level
LSNRCTL> trace user
Connecting to (DESCRIPTION=(ADDRESS=(PROTOCOL=IPC)(KEY=EXTPROC0)))
Opened trace file: C:\oracle\ora90\network\trace\listener.trc
The command completed successfully
```

Trace information is continuously written until it is turned off. Note that tracing is an expensive operation and should not be used in a production environment.

Configuring Oracle Connection Manager

The cman.ora file maintains the configuration for Oracle Connection Manager. It lives in the c:\oracle\ora90\network\admin directory on Windows NT/2000. Four parameters are necessary for Connection Manager:

- The listening end point list for CMGW process

- The listening end point list for CMADMIN process

- Access control rule

- Parameter list

A sample entry from cman.ora is shown here.

```
CMAN=
     (ADDRESS=(PROTOCOL=tcp)(HOST=proxysvr)(PORT=1630))
  (ADDRESS=(PROTOCOL=tcps)(HOST=192.168.201.1)(PORT=2484))
```

```
CMAN_ADMIN=
(ADDRESS=(PROTOCOL=tcp)(HOST=proxysvr)(PORT=1830))
CMAN_RULES=
    (RULE=(SRC=192.168.200.1/27)(DST=db1-server)(SRV=*)(ACT=accept)))
CMAN_PROFILE=
(PARAMETER_LIST=
(LOG_LEVEL=2)
    (TRACING=on))
```

Listening End Point Lists

The listening end point list specifies protocol addresses for the gateway and administrative processes. Both processes can be configured with multiple protocol addresses. The following example shows the listening end point list for CMGW on TCP/IP and TCP/IP with SSL.

```
(ADDRESS=(PROTOCOL=tcp)(HOST=proxysvr)(PORT=1630))
(ADDRESS=(PROTOCOL=tcps)(HOST=192.168.201.1)(PORT=2484))
```

Access Control Rule List

The access control rule list specifies which connections are accepted, rejected, or dropped. For example, the following rule accepts connections from a range of IP addresses.

```
(RULE=(SRC=192.168.200.1/27)(DST=db1-server)(SRV=*)(ACT=accept)
```

Parameter List

The parameter list sets attributes for an Oracle Connection Manager. Typically, tracing and logging configuration is included here.

```
CMAN_PROFILE=
    (PARAMETER_LIST=
        (LOG_LEVEL=2)
        (TRACING=on))
```

Configuring Clients for Oracle Connection Manager

You can configure clients to use Connection Manager by using a connect descriptor that specifies the protocol address of Connection Manager. You can use Net Manager to configure the client using the steps describe here.

NOTE
Do not choose to test the connection until the protocol address is added to the listener.

Step 1: Configure an Oracle Connection Manage Protocol Address Launch Oracle Net Manager. In the navigator pane, expand the Directory or Local node, and then select Service Naming. Choose + from the toolbar to launch the Net Service Name Wizard. Create a Net Service Name named oracm. Click Next to view the Protocol Settings page. Select a protocol on which Connection Manager is configured. Enter appropriate protocol settings. The default port for Connection Manager is 1630. Provide the database service information. Save the Protocol Address when done.

CAUTION
Do not click Test yet.

Step 2: Configure a Listener Protocol Address Create an address for the listener. Select the net service oracm that you just created. Create a protocol address using the default port of 1521. In the Address Configuration box, click the Advanced button to view the Address List Option window shown here:

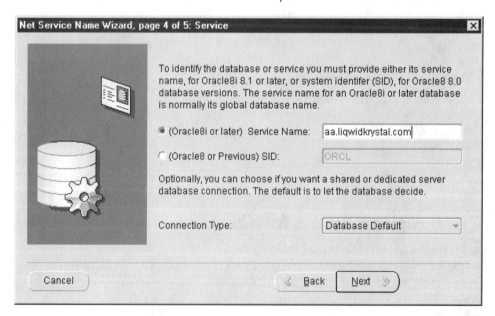

Select the option Use Each Address in Order Until Destination Reached; then click OK. This option sets SOURCE_ROUTE to ON. Save the Network Configuration. Following is a sample tnsnames.ora file for a client set to use Connection Manager.

```
ourdb=
    (DESCRIPTION=
        (SOURCE_ROUTE=yes)
(ADDRESS=
(PROTOCOL=tcp)
(HOST=proxysrv)
(PORT=1630))
(ADDRESS=
        (PROTOCOL=tcp)
        (HOST=db1-server)
        (PORT=1521))
    (CONNECT_DATA=
        (SERVICE_NAME=db1.company.com)))
```

Enabling Oracle Connection Manager Features

Features such as Session Multiplexing can be enabled once Connection Manager is configured.

Enabling Session Multiplexing

To enable Connection Manager to take advantage of session multiplexing, use the MULTIPLEX attribute of the DISPATCHERS initialization parameter as shown:

```
DISPATCHERS="(PROTOCOL=tcp)(MULTIPLEX=on)"
```

Enabling Address Control

To add filtering rules so that Connection Manager can allow or deny requests from specific clients, configure a cman.ora file. You can create one manually if it does not exist. Add the CMAN_RULES parameter as shown:

```
    (CMAN_RULES=
      (RULE_LIST=
        (RULE=(SRC=source_host)
              (DST=destination_host)
              (SRV=service)
              (ACT=accept | reject | drop))))
```

The access rules are summarized in Table 6-4.

Parameter	Description
SRC	Specify the source hostname or IP address of the client
DST	Specify the destination hostname or IP address of the database server
SRV	Specify the service name of the Oracle9*i* database obtained from the SERVICE_NAME initialization parameter
ACT	Accept, reject, or drop incoming requests based on the SRC, DST, and SRV parameters

TABLE 6-4. *Access Control with Connection Manager*

You can define multiple rules in the rule list. The action in the first matched rule is applied. If no rules match, all connections are accepted. In the following example, client computer *client1-pc* is denied access to the service *db,* but any client with the IP address *192.168.201.10* is granted access.

```
(RULE_LIST=
    (RULE=(SRC=client1-pc)(DST=db1-server)(SRV=aa.liqwidkrystal.com)
    (ACT=reject))
    (RULE=(SRC=192.168.201.10)(DST=192.168.200.1)(SRV=db1)(ACT=accept)))
```

Enabling Protocol Conversion Support

Oracle Connection Manager provides support for protocol conversion, enabling clients and a database server configured with different network protocols to communicate with each other. An Oracle Connection Manager can listen on any protocol that Oracle supports. Without this kind of support, a client that uses Named Pipes cannot connect to a database server that uses TCP/IP. If Oracle Connection Manager is configured for TCP/IP, the client can connect to Oracle Connection Manager using Named Pipes, and Oracle Connection Manager can connect to the database server using TCP/IP. As the following example shows, the cman.ora file must be configured with a protocol address for each protocol that the client uses.

```
(CMAN=
(ADDRESS=(PROTOCOL=tcp)(HOST=proxysvr)(PORT=1630)))
(ADDRESS=(PROTOCOL=nmp)(SERVER=proxysvr)(PIPE=cmanpipe)))
(ADDRESS=(PROTOCOL=tcps)(HOST=192.168.200.1)(PORT=2484)))
```

Oracle Shared Server

Shared Server is an architecture that enables a database server to share server processes. A process named *dispatcher* directs multiple incoming network session requests to a common queue. An idle shared server process picks up the request from the queue and hands.

NOTE
The Shared Server feature was called Multithreaded Server in earlier versions of Oracle Server.

Configuring Shared Server

Use the initialization parameter DISPATCHERS to enable shared server configuration. Database Configuration Assistant allows you to set this during database creation.

Required Attributes of the DISPATCHERS Parameter
The DISPATCHERS parameter has a combination of mandatory and optional attributes. The required attributes are listed here.

- **ADDRESS (ADD or ADDR)**   Used to specify the network protocol address of the end point on which the dispatchers listen.

- **DESCRIPTION (DES or DESC)**   Specifies the network description of the end point on which the dispatchers listen, including the network protocol address.

- **PROTOCOL (PRO or PROT)**   Specifies the network protocol for which the dispatcher generates a listening end point.

Optional Attributes of the DISPATCHERS Parameter
The optional attributes are summarized here:

- **CONNECTIONS (CON or CONN)**   Specifies the maximum number of network connections to allow for each dispatcher. The default is operating system specific and is 1,024 on Windows NT/2000.

- **DISPATCHERS (DIS or DISP)**   Specifies the initial number of dispatchers to start when the instance is started. The default is 1.

■ **LISTENER (LIS or LIST)**   Specifies an alias name for the listener(s) with which the PMON process registers dispatcher information. The alias must be set to a name that can be resolved through a naming method. This attribute overrides the initialization parameters LOCAL_LISTENER and REMOTE_LISTENER.

■ **MULTIPLEX (MUL or MULT)**   Used to enable the Oracle Connection Manager session multiplexing feature. You can enable session multiplexing for both incoming and outgoing sessions by setting this parameter to the value ON. You can enable session multiplexing for incoming sessions only or outgoing sessions only by setting this parameter to IN and OUT, respectively. Finally, a setting of OFF disables session multiplexing.

■ **POOL (POO)**   Used to enable connection pooling. If this is set to a number, it enables connection pooling for both incoming and outgoing idle network connections. The number specified is the timeout in ticks for both incoming and outgoing idle network connections. If this is set to ON, it enables connection pooling with a default of 10 ticks for both incoming and outgoing connections. A setting of IN enables pooling for incoming connections at 10 ticks, and a setting of OUT enables pooling for outgoing idle connections at 10 ticks. You can also explicitly specify the number of ticks for IN and OUT attributes. A setting of OFF turns off connection pooling.

■ **SERVICE (SER or SERV)**   Specifies the service name(s) the dispatchers registered with the listeners. If no values are specified, then service names specified by the SERVICE_NAMES initialization parameter are used.

■ **TICKS (TIC or TICK)**   Specifies the length of a network tick in seconds. A tick is the amount of time it takes for a message to be sent and processed from the client to the database server or from the database server to the client.

Setting the Initial Number of Dispatchers

The number of dispatchers started at instance startup is controlled by the DISPATCHERS attribute. You can calculate the optimal setting for this attribute using the formula:

```
# of dispatchers = CEIL (max. number of concurrent sessions /
connections for each dispatcher
```

Assume that a system is expected to have 4,000 concurrent connections through the TCP/IP Protocol and supports 1,000 connections/process. In addition, there are another 2,500 sessions on TCP/IP with SSL. Again, each process supports 1,000 connections. There should be a minimum of four dispatchers for TCP/IP and three for TCP/IP with SSL. The DISPATCHERS attribute can be set as shown here:

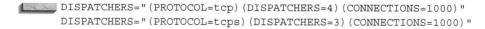

```
DISPATCHERS="(PROTOCOL=tcp)(DISPATCHERS=4)(CONNECTIONS=1000)"
DISPATCHERS="(PROTOCOL=tcps)(DISPATCHERS=3)(CONNECTIONS=1000)"
```

Enabling Connection Pooling

Connection pooling is a resource utilization feature that enables you to reduce the number of physical network connections to a dispatcher. This can be achieved by sharing a set of connections among the client processes. Use the POOL attribute to configure connection pooling. A sample setting for the DISPATCHERS initialization parameter with pooling enabled is shown here:

```
DISPATCHERS="(PROTOCOL=tcp)(DISPATCHERS=4)(POOL=on)(CONNECTIONS=1000)"
DISPATCHERS="(PROTOCOL=tcps)(DISPATCHERS=3)(POOL=on)(CONNECTIONS=1000)""
```

Allocating Resources

An Oracle database can be represented by multiple service names. Because of this, a pool of dispatchers can be allocated exclusively for clients requesting a particular service. This way, the mission-critical requests may be given more resources. This produces the same effect as increasing priority.

Testing Oracle Net Services

As a DBA you might run into a situation in which you have to isolate a connection issue or a performance issue. A few utilities that can help you in this situation are discussed next.

TNSPING Utility

The TNSPING utility is used to test whether a specific service can be reached. The service can be a database, a Names Server, or any other service. This utility (much like TCP/IP ping) provides an estimate for the amount of time taken to complete the round trip (to the specified Net Service and back). This estimate is provided in milliseconds. An error message is displayed if TNSPING fails. The following example uses TNSPING to check if a database can be reached using the Net Service Name *aa*.

```
C:\>tnsping aa
TNS Ping Utility for 32-bit Windows: Version 9.0.1.1.1 -
Production on 10-JAN-20
02 04:15:33
```

```
Copyright (c) 1997 Oracle Corporation.  All rights reserved.
Used parameter files:
C:\oracle\ora90\network\admin\sqlnet.ora
C:\oracle\ora90\network\admin\tnsnames.ora
Used TNSNAMES adapter to resolve the alias
Attempting to contact (DESCRIPTION = (ADDRESS_LIST =
(ADDRESS = (PROTOCOL = TCP)
(HOST = aa)(PORT = 1521))) (CONNECT_DATA =
(SERVICE_NAME = aa.liqwidkrystal.com)))
OK (130 msec)
```

TNSPING can be very useful if you are using third-party applications using ODBC or JDBC. If you do not have any Oracle utility on your machine, you can still check connectivity using TNSPING since it is installed with Oracle Client. Note that TNSPING does not actually establish a connection. Using TNSPING does not isolate authentication issues.

TRACERT Utility

The trace route utility (TRACERT) enables administrators to discover the path or route a connection is taking from a client to a server. If TRACERT encounters a problem, it returns an error stack to the client instead of a single error. These additional error messages make troubleshooting easier. TRACERT is installed on Windows NT/2000 with the TCP/IP stack and lives in the c:\windows\system32 folder.

Net Manager

Net Manager can be used to create a connection identifier using a GUI. At the end of this process you can test the connection with Net Manager.

LSNRCTL and NAMESCTL

The Listener Control utility and Names Control utility can be used to obtain a status on Listener and Names Server.

This chapter covered the features and configuration of Oracle Net Services. The GUI configuration tools make it easy for you to configure Net Service components.

CHAPTER
7

Oracle Enterprise
Manager Basics

he Oracle family of products is designed to provide solutions for small and large business needs. A combination of Oracle9i Server, Oracle Net Services, Oracle9i Application Server, and Oracle HTTP Server can be quite daunting to manage from a DBA's point of view. Oracle Enterprise Manager (OEM) is a single-point administration tool that can be used to manage all Oracle services across the Enterprise. OEM can also communicate with the Windows operating system as well as third-party administration tools. This chapter includes topics related to installation and configuration of OEM. The GUI and common features are also introduced. The practical use of OEM is left for Chapter 8.

All administrative tasks including those described in Chapters 5 and 6 can be performed through OEM. Some of the common tasks are

- **Oracle database administration** Common DBA tasks such as starting up and shutting down databases, performance-tuning, creating database backups, and database recovery are made easy by OEM. The status and health of an Oracle database on the network can be obtained from OEM Console. User management and space management are possible.

- **Oracle Application Server and HTTP Server administration** Oracle Application Servers and Oracle HTTP Servers across the network can be managed from OEM.

- **Oracle Net Services administration** Oracle Net Listeners can be started up and shut down using OEM. Since Net Manager is integrated with OEM, all configurations necessary for Oracle Net Services are possible.

- **Schedule management tasks** Many administrative tasks must be performed regularly and repetitively. For example, you might need to take a database backup every week. This task can be scheduled via OEM.

- **Monitor events** DBAs can monitor events that can lead to outage or malfunction of Oracle components using OEM. Automated alerts can be generated based on a specified set of conditions.

- **Launch applications** Oracle and third-party applications can be launched from OEM.

Benefits of Using Oracle Enterprise Manager

It is true that OEM requires a little effort during configuration; however, the benefits outweigh this effort. These benefits include

- **Single-point administration**   OEM allows you to manage all databases and applications from a centralized location using OEM Console.

- **Shared administration**   Large sites that have several administrators can share tasks and responsibilities across the enterprise.

- **Unattended administration**   OEM permits DBAs to schedule routine administration tasks. Additionally, OEM can track events that can generate email and pager alerts in case a problem arises. In case of an outage or an abnormal condition, corrective measures can be taken without user intervention.

- **Autonomous administration**   Network failures do not affect scheduled tasks because local processes called *Oracle Intelligent Agents* (OIAs) execute them. Once a task is scheduled successfully on the target machine, you can be assured that it will be executed regardless of network availability.

- **Simple administration interface**   The simple GUI allows DBAs to perform virtually any administration task using OEM.

Services Offered by Oracle Enterprise Manager

OEM includes a bunch of services that make administration tasks simpler. These services work behind the scene, and administrators interact with them only through OEM Console. The main services are summarized in Table 7-1.

Why Use Oracle Enterprise Manager?

Old habits die hard! If you have been an Oracle DBA for several years and worked with older versions of Oracle Server, you will likely be tempted to persist with old techniques and tools for the purposes of database administration; however, OEM is a very sophisticated, simple-to-use tool, and you are encouraged to use it for database administration activities. Once you have OEM configured on your site, you will experience the benefits yourself.

It is useful to understand the basic architecture of OEM before attempting to use it on your site. The next few sections include topics related to OEM architecture and OEM configuration on Windows NT/2000/XP. OEM can be effectively used only after it is installed and all its features have been configured.

Service	Description/Use
Job System	Schedule tasks for one-time or repeated execution.
Event System	Abnormal conditions can be monitored remotely or in absentia.
Discovery	Available services can be found using Discovery Wizard.
Notification	Administrators can be notified of the status of jobs. Alerts can be generated and sent via email and pager message to target administrators.
Reporting	OEM generates reports that provide a quick status on all monitored systems.
Security	Two classes of OEM administrators are defined. A *Super Administrator* defines access and privileges of other administrators.

TABLE 7-1. *Services Offered by Oracle Enterprise Manager*

Oracle Enterprise Manager Architecture

OEM can be configured for use with a two- or three-tier architecture. You can choose to use either based on the needs of your site; however, only the three-tier architecture provides support for all the OEM features. A big benefit of the three-tier architecture is that you can take advantage of the Job System and Event System. A limitation of the two-tier architecture is that it can be used only to manage databases. If you want to manage other targets such as Oracle Net Listeners and HTTP Servers, you must use the three-tier architecture.

Two-Tier Architecture of Oracle Enterprise Manager

A two-tier architecture allows a DBA to connect to a database from OEM Console and perform administrative tasks against the database. OEM Console acts as the client application and manages the database directly. To use the two-tier architecture, you must run OEM in stand-alone mode from the first dialog box shown after OEM is launched. A sample screen is shown in Figure 7-1.

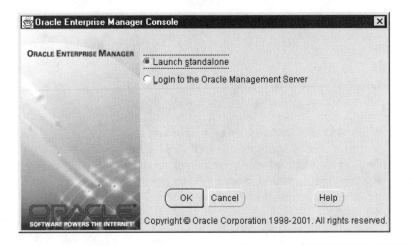

FIGURE 7-1.   *Choosing Enterprise Manager mode*

In stand-alone mode, you can administer only Oracle databases. Additional limitations are:

- You cannot share administrative data with other administrators on the network.

- You cannot schedule jobs to perform tasks.

- Event notifications are not available.

- You cannot use OEM Console from a web browser.

Three-Tier Architecture of Oracle Enterprise Manager

The three-tier architecture of OEM uses Oracle Management Servers in the middle tier and OIA to manage nodes in the third tier.

Being the client, OEM Console is the first tier. Oracle Management Server (OMS) implements the middle tier of the OEM architecture. One or more Management Servers in the middle tier are used in conjunction with a repository to manage administrative functions, jobs, and events. All dataflow between the client and the managed nodes occurs through Management Servers. Management Servers direct OIA processes on the managed nodes to perform tasks. All the intelligence of

OEM comes from the middle layer. You should dedicate a separate machine to act as an OMS. The size of the machine and the number of Management Server processes can be increased for purposes of scalability.

NOTE
In this book, the term Management Server is used to refer to the machines that manage the middle tier or the processes that run on these machines and perform the tasks required by OEM. The context in which the term is used should make it obvious if the reference is to the machine or the processes. In most cases, it is acceptable to understand the term to include both the machine and the processes.

The third-tier consists of *managed nodes.* Managed nodes are the target machines on which services have to be managed. OIAs are running on the target machines and perform tasks that have been assigned by OMS. These tasks can be performed against databases or other services such as Oracle HTTP Server. For example, an OIA might be instructed to shut down a database on the target node.

OIAs also monitor services on target nodes for any problems that might come up. If OIAs are terminated prematurely, they are restarted automatically. It is important to note that OIAs run independently of the OEM Console and Management Servers. Figure 7-2 shows the three-tier architecture of OEM.

Observe that the first tier consists of OEM Consoles, the middle tier of several Management Servers, and OIAs run on managed nodes in the third tier and can manage databases and other services such as HTTP Server. You should configure at least two Management Servers on your network configured for redundancy.

Installation and Configuration of Oracle Enterprise Manager

OEM Console can be run as an application or as a web client on Windows NT/2000. The web client can be used only in the three-tier architecture.

Requirements for OEM Console

OEM Console can be run on Windows NT/2000/XP and Windows 98. You must install Service Pack 6a on Windows NT and Service Pack 1 on Windows 2000. Management Server is not supported on Windows 98.

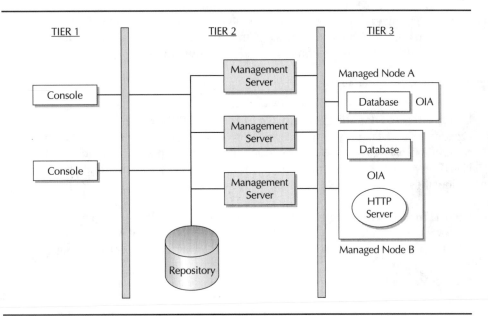

FIGURE 7-2. *Three-Tier architecture of Oracle Enterprise Manager*

NOTE
OEM Console is implemented in Java. The Java Runtime Environment is installed with Oracle9i software installation.

Web Client Requirements

OEM can be launched from a standard web browser. Again, Windows NT with Service Pack 6a and Windows 2000 with Service Pack 1 are supported. You can use Netscape Navigator 4.7 and higher or Microsoft Internet Explorer 5.0 and higher. You can use Oracle's HTTP Server (version 1.3.12), Apache HTTP Server (1.3.9 and higher), or Microsoft's Internet Information Server 4.0 and higher to run the web client.

Some components are not supported on the web client. These include Oracle Management Pack for SAP R/3, Directory Manager, Net Manager, SQL Analyze, Oracle Expert, Trace Data Viewer, Capacity Planner, and Index Tuning Wizard.

Installation of OEM Console

OEM Console Application is installed automatically when you install Oracle9i Enterprise Edition on Windows NT/2000. If OEM is not installed on your machine, use Oracle Universal Installer to perform a custom installation and choose to install OEM. You can launch OEM from the Windows Start menu or by executing the **oemapp** batch file from the command line, as shown here:

 `c:> oemapp.bat console`

Web Client Installation on Oracle HTTP Server

Optionally, you can choose to launch OEM Console as a web client from a browser. Most of the configuration is already done during the standard installation. Oracle HTTP Server is one of the components installed during the standard installation. Follow these steps to use the web client feature from the Oracle HTTP Server:

Step 1: Install Supported Web Browser on the Client   Install Netscape Navigator 4.7 or Internet Explorer 5.0 or higher on your client machine. OEM web client is not supported on a Windows machine on which Active Desktop is enabled.

Step 2: Verify Installation   Verify that the folder c:\oracle\ora90\ oem_webstage exists on your machine. In this folder, you should have two files named emwebsite.html and oem.conf. The first file is the HTML page used to launch OEM Console web client. The second file has configuration information for Oracle HTTP Server.

> **NOTE**
> *In reality, Oracle HTTP Server is the Win32 Apache HTTP Server. Oracle has secured a license to distribute the Apache HTTP Server with Oracle9i media. Oracle Extensions to Apache HTTP Server are discussed in Chapter 9.*

The entire configuration required for OEM components should have been completed automatically during the installation; however, if you have other web servers previously installed on your machine, you must double-check the configuration settings for Oracle HTTP Server. Web servers such as Microsoft Internet Information Server and Apache HTTP Server are typically configured to listen for HTTP requests on port 80 and secure-HTTP requests on port 443. If you install Oracle HTTP Server on a machine that is running another web server on port 80, OUI attempts to configure Oracle HTTP Server on port 7777. The following discussion will help you resolve potential conflicts.

The Oracle HTTP Server configuration is stored in a file named httpd.conf in the folder c:\oracle\ora90\Apache\Apache\conf. Verify that this file contains an entry for an Oracle-specific include file. A line similar to the one shown here should exist:

`include "C:\oracle\ora90\Apache\Apache\conf\oracle_apache.conf"`

The oracle_apache.conf file contains Oracle Server–specific configuration for Apache HTTP Server. For OEM, an entry similar to the one shown here must exist in this file:

```
include "C:\oracle\ora90/oem_webstage/oem.conf"
```

NOTE
Apache Server treats forward and backward slashes as backward slashes on Win32 platforms.

Finally, verify that OEM-specific additions to Apache HTTP Server configuration are available in the file oem.conf. The default port (3339) is configured in this file.

Step 3: Launch Oracle HTTP Server   If you chose to install Oracle9i Enterprise Edition on Windows NT/2000, the Oracle HTTP Server is already installed on your machine. Launch Oracle HTTP Server from the Start menu or from the Services applet.

Step 4: Launch OEM Console   Point your web browser to the URL of the form *<machine>:3339* to see a page similar to the one shown here. Port 3339 is the port configured during installation.

Launch the Oracle Enterprise Manager Console

The Enterprise Manager Console allows you to centrally manage and administer your environment. To launch the Console, enter the machine name on which your Oracle Management Server runs and then click the button labeled "Launch Console".

Oracle Management Server:

| aa | (Launch Console)

Enter the name of the machine and click the Launch Console button. If this is the first time you are using the web client, you are prompted to install the Jinitiator plug-in if you are using Netscape Navigator. Install this plug-in before proceeding. This takes several minutes.

If you are using Internet Explorer, you must download the plug-in manually. Use the Download Plug-In link on the emwebsite.html page to download and install the plug-in.

NOTE
You might have to lower your browser security settings to install the plug-in.

If the plug-in installation fails, execute **jinit11810.exe** from the c:\oracle\ora90\ oem_webstage\java-plugin folder. Restart your browser after installing the plug-in.

Step 5: Connect to OEM Console   Connect to OEM Console as the user *sysman*. This user is created automatically during installation. The initial password for this user is set to *oem_temp*.

Web Client for Apache HTTP Server and Internet Information Server   You can configure other web servers to use OEM web client. Oracle has certified Apache Server and Microsoft's Internet Information Server (IIS).

Use these steps to configure Apache HTTP Server to run OEM web client.

1. Perform a custom installation and install OEM without Oracle HTTP Server.

2. Install Apache Web Server 1.3.9 or higher for Windows.

3. Modify the Apache configuration file httpd.conf and add a **ScriptAlias** directive, as shown here:

```
ScriptAlias /cgi-bin/ "c:\oracle\ora90/oem_webstage/cgi-bin/"
ScriptAlias /oem_webstage/cgi-bin/ "c:\oracle\ora90/
oem_webstage/cgi-bin/"
```

4. Modify the path information as required by your installation. Add as many aliases as you want. A sample is shown here:

```
Alias /oem_webstage/ "C:\oracle\ora90/oem_webstage/"
```

5. Modify the directory for CGI scripts. This is typically done using c:\Program Files\Apache\Apache\cgi-bin. Modify it as shown here:

```
<Directory "C:\oracle\ora90/oem_webstage/cgi-bin/">
    AllowOverride all
    Allow from all
</Directory>
```

6. Restart Apache Server.

Restart Apache Server from the Start menu or by using the **apachectl** utility.

 `apachectl restart`

You can also configure Microsoft's IIS 4.0/5.0 to run the web client. Use these steps:

1. Perform a custom installation and install OEM without Oracle HTTP Server.

2. Install IIS 4.0/5.0 as per Microsoft documentation (IIS 6.0 is not officially certified by Oracle).

3. Launch Internet Service Manager from the Start menu. Select Default Web Site and right-click it to view the associated properties sheet.

4. Create a new virtual directory named OEM_WEBSTAGE (you can use any name convenient to you). Set the following:

```
Alias: /oem_webstage
Path: c:\oracle\ora90\oem_webstage
Access: Read, Execute
```

5. Save the settings and expand the Default Web Site node to display the newly created virtual directory. Click the Action button and add a new virtual directory with the following settings:

```
Alias: cgi-bin
Path: c:\oracle\ora90\oem_webstage\cgi-bin
Access: Read, Execute
```

6. Create another virtual directory with the following settings:

```
Alias: java-plugin
Path: c:\oracle\ora90\oem_webstage\java-plugin
Access: Read-only
```

7. Restart IIS Web Server.

You can use Microsoft Management Console to configure IIS. Refer to IIS documentation for information on this utility.

CAUTION

*Most web servers are configured to listen on UDP port 80. If you have multiple web servers on your machine, you must ensure that there is no conflict on this port. Use the **netstat** utility to get information on the ports being used on your server. The advantage of using port 80 is that you do not have to explicitly provide port information in the URL.*

Oracle Enterprise Manager Repositories

Some OEM components, including Recovery Manager, Oracle Expert, and Tablespace Manager, require a repository to store information. You must create a separate Oracle user who will own this repository. Oracle recommends that you also create a separate tablespace to hold the repository.

NOTE
A repository is a set of database objects that are used by an application. The necessary schema is created when the repository is created.

The structure of the repository is different for the two-tier and three-tier architectures. You must create a separate repository depending on the OEM architecture that you plan to deploy.

Stand-Alone Repository

Use the following steps to create the stand-alone repository. This repository can be used only for the two-tier architecture of OEM.

Step 1: Create a Separate Tablespace for the Repository   Create a separate tablespace to hold the repository. A tablespace named OEM_REPOSITORY has been created to hold the repository.

```
SQL> CREATE TABLESPACE "OEM_REPOSITORY"
  2   LOGGING
  3   DATAFILE 'C:\ORACLE\ORADATA\AA\OEM_REPOSITORY.ora' SIZE 5M
  4   REUSE AUTOEXTEND
  5   ON NEXT  5M MAXSIZE  2000M EXTENT MANAGEMENT LOCAL;
Tablespace created.
```

Step 2: Create an Owner for the Repository   Create an Oracle user that will own the repository. Be sure to provide necessary quotas on the tablespace OEM_REPOSITORY created in step 1. In the following example, a user called OEM_REP has been created.

```
SQL> CREATE USER "OEM_REP"  PROFILE "DEFAULT"
  2   IDENTIFIED BY "oem" DEFAULT TABLESPACE "OEM_REPOSITORY"
  3   TEMPORARY TABLESPACE "TEMP"
  4   QUOTA UNLIMITED
  5   ON OEM_REPOSITORY
  6   QUOTA UNLIMITED
  7   ON TEMP
  8   ACCOUNT UNLOCK;
User created.
```

Step 3: Grant Necessary Privileges   The user needs certain privileges to manage the OEM repository. The following script can be used to grant the necessary privileges for the user OEM_REP.

```
SQL> GRANT CREATE PROCEDURE TO "OEM_REP";
Grant succeeded.
SQL> GRANT CREATE TRIGGER TO "OEM_REP";
Grant succeeded.
SQL> GRANT CREATE TYPE TO "OEM_REP";
Grant succeeded.
SQL> GRANT EXECUTE ANY PROCEDURE TO "OEM_REP";
Grant succeeded.
SQL> GRANT EXECUTE ANY TYPE TO "OEM_REP";
Grant succeeded.
SQL> GRANT SELECT ANY DICTIONARY TO "OEM_REP";
Grant succeeded.
SQL> GRANT SELECT ANY TABLE TO "OEM_REP";
Grant succeeded.
SQL> GRANT "CONNECT" TO "OEM_REP";
Grant succeeded.
SQL> GRANT "SELECT_CATALOG_ROLE" TO "OEM_REP";
Grant succeeded.
```

Step 4: Create Repository   Launch OEM Console in stand-alone mode and supply the login information for the user OEM_REP. The repository is created automatically.

CAUTION
The stand-alone repository cannot be used for the three-tier architecture.

Management Server Repository
If you are planning to deploy the OEM three-tier architecture, you must create a separate repository. Again, it is recommended that a separate tablespace and owner are created for the repository. Use the following steps to create the repository.

Step 1: Create a Separate Tablespace   Create a separate tablespace to hold the repository. In the following example, a tablespace named OEM_REPOSITORY has been created to hold the repository.

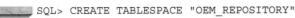

```
SQL> CREATE TABLESPACE "OEM_REPOSITORY"
  2    LOGGING
  3    DATAFILE 'C:\ORACLE\ORADATA\AA\OEM_REPOSITORY.ora' SIZE 5M
  4    REUSE AUTOEXTEND
  5    ON NEXT  5M MAXSIZE  2000M EXTENT MANAGEMENT LOCAL;
Tablespace created.
```

Step 2: Launch Oracle Enterprise Manager Configuration Assistant   Launch Oracle Enterprise Manager Configuration Assistant (EMCA) from the Start menu or by executing **emca.bat** to configure OEM's Management Server. You should see a Welcome screen, as shown in Figure 7-3.

Step 3: Create and Configure Repository   If the repository is not available, Configuration Assistant guides you through the process of creating one. You can use an existing repository or create a new one. Configuration Assistant gives you the option of creating the repository in an existing database or in a new database that can be created as part of this process.

Since there already is a tablespace to hold the repository, we have chosen to create a custom repository. Additionally, we have chosen to create a new repository that is owned by the Oracle user OEM_AA, as shown in Figure 7-4.

If you follow this procedure, the Recovery Manager catalog is not created. You must create it separately as documented in Chapter 5; however, if you choose to create a new database to hold the repository, OEM automatically creates a database named OEMREP with two tablespaces named OEM_REPOSITORY and CATTBS.

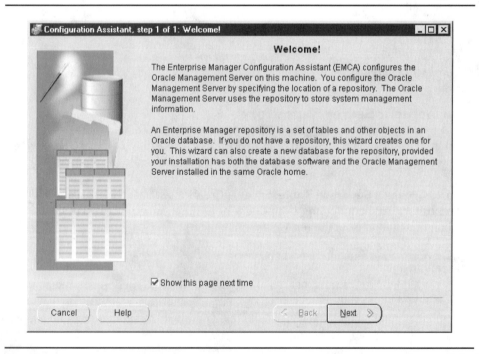

FIGURE 7-3.   *Welcome screen of OEM Configuration Assistant*

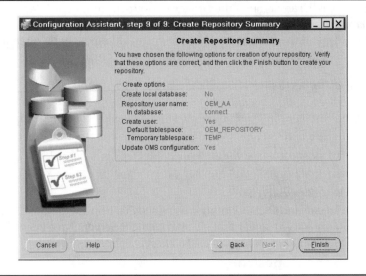

FIGURE 7-4.   *Creating a new repository*

The OEM repository is created in the OEM_REPOSITORY tablespace, and the Recovery Manager catalog is created in the CATTBS tablespace.

CAUTION
You will be prompted to provide the password for the user SYS during the repository creation process. EMCA assumes that the password for SYS is the default password change_on_install. *If you have altered the password for this user, you must reset it to the default before creating the repository with EMCA. Remember to change the password soon after creating the repository.*

Do not create the OEM repository in the SYSTEM tablespace or a temporary tablespace. It is also recommended that the tablespace containing the OEM repository not have any rollback segments.

Click the Finish button to create the repository. A progress window is displayed.

Step 4: Verify Management Server   EMCA should have created an OMS automatically at this point. Verify that the service exists and is running by using the Services applet. The name of the service is of the form *Oracle<Oracle Home>ManagementServer.*

You can verify that the repository has been created properly by querying the data dictionary. On this installation, 667 objects were created in the repository.

```
SQL> connect oem_aa/aa@aa
Connected.
SQL> select count(*) from user_objects;
  COUNT(*)
----------
       667
```

Dropping the Repository

You can drop an existing OEM repository using EMCA. Choose the option Drop an Existing Repository after ensuring that all Management Servers have been shut down.

Backing Up the Repository

You can back up the repository by taking a backup of the database or by using the Export utility to create a logical backup of the Repository owner schema.

Oracle Enterprise Manager Console

OEM Console is available as an application on the Windows NT/2000 platform. OEM Console can also be launched from a standard web browser. OEM Console has a GUI to perform several administrative tasks. A set of system management packs and applications is also included. Table 7-2 summarizes the major components that can be launched from OEM Console.

Category	Name of Tool/Pack	Description
GUI	Console	Provide a GUI for single-point administration
Integrated Applications	Oracle Net Manager	Configure Oracle Net Services
	Data Manager	Export/import databases and load external data using SQL*Loader

TABLE 7-2. *Oracle Enterprise Manager Components*

Category	Name of Tool/Pack	Description
	Recovery Manager	Take database backups, perform recovery
	SQL*Plus Worksheet	Issue SQL commands
	Spatial Index Advisor	Analyze and tune spatial indexes on data
	Text Manager	Text-search facility for database
	Security Manager	Manage user security across the enterprise
Database Management Tools	Instance Management	Start up and shut down databases, view and modify initialization parameters
	Security Management	Manage users, roles, and profiles
	Schema Management	Manage schema objects
	Storage Management	Manage tablespaces, data files, and rollback segments
	Replication Management	Configure and manage replication environment
System Management Packs	Diagnostics Pack	Monitor overall health of Oracle Server
	Tuning Pack	Database performance tuning tools
	Change Management Pack	Track changes made to database objects
	Management Pack for Oracle Applications	Monitor and diagnose with Oracle applications in the middle tier

TABLE 7-2. *Oracle Enterprise Manager Components* (continued)

Category	Name of Tool/Pack	Description
	Management Pack for SAP R/3	Monitor and manage SAP R/3 system
	Standard Management Pack	Combination of tools for workgroup environment
Wizards	Backup and Recovery	Back up databases; restore and recover tablespaces, data files, and databases
	Table Wizard	Create tables
	View Wizard	Create views
	Resource Plan Wizard	Group users who have similar resource requirements
	Analyze Wizard	Analyze data and collect statistics
	Data Management Wizard	Assist in export/import and data loading
Others	Oracle9i JVM	View EJB and CORBA components, change permissions
	OLAP Services	Java API for OLAP
	Workspace Management	Maintain table versions

TABLE 7-2.   *Oracle Enterprise Manager Components* (continued)

There is some overlap between some components in OEM. Components are clubbed into logical categories in Table 7-2. All the components listed can be launched from OEM Console.

Console User Interface

OEM Console has a GUI that allows for easy navigation and administration of objects across the Enterprise. Like Windows Explorer, OEM Console has two panes. The Master pane (on the left) contains a Navigator that controls the contents displayed in the Detail pane (on the right). A sample screen is shown in Figure 7-5.

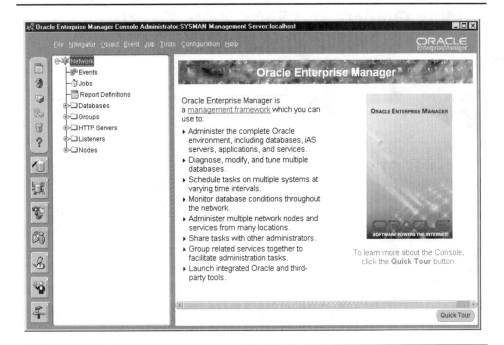

FIGURE 7-5.   *OEM Console*

Observe that objects and services are grouped into logical categories in the Master pane. The same object might appear in more than one node. For example, you can expand the Listeners node to get a list of all listener processes and the Databases node to get a list of all databases. Alternately, you can find a specific machine in the list of nodes and find the same database or listener.

Navigator

The Navigator has an Explorer-like interface that displays a view of the nodes and services on the network. The nodes and services on the network are either manually or automatically added to Navigator.

The Master pane lists all the objects or services in the managed environment. It provides a view of all services grouped logically. By expanding any node in Navigator, you can view all the objects available in that category of objects. You can navigate to a service or an object and launch an appropriate tool or property sheet to work with the selected object. You can right-click a selected item to view a context-sensitive menu.

The Navigator menu allows you to launch tools, wizards, and property sheets that can be used on the selected object. The menu is context sensitive.

Adding Objects and Services to Oracle Enterprise Manager

You can add objects and services that you want to manage from OEM Console. If you are running in stand-alone mode, you must do this manually; however, if you are running in Management Server mode, services on the network can be added automatically and added to OEM Console.

Adding Services Manually

You can add a database service manually to OEM Console if it was not discovered automatically for some reason or if you are running in stand-alone mode. Launch OEM Console and choose Navigator | Add Database to Tree. Provide identification information on the database, including Net Service Name, and click the OK button. The database is added to the Navigator pane. You cannot add other services such as Listeners or HTTP Servers in stand-alone mode.

Discovering Services

OEM is capable of automatically discovering services across the enterprise and adding them to the console. To do so, you must use the Management Server configuration (the three-tier architecture). Follow these steps to discover services on the network:

Step 1: Ensure that OIA Is Running   OIA must be running on all nodes that you want to search for services. On Windows NT/2000, you can start OIA from the Services applet. The service is named *OracleOraHome90Agent* on the test installation. Start OIA if it is not running.

Step 2: Launch OEM   Launch OEM in management server mode. The Discovery Wizard should start automatically, as shown here:

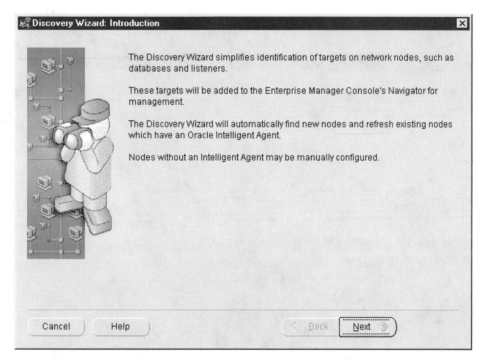

Step 3: Discover Services   Follow the steps suggested by the Discovery Wizard to discover all the services on the nodes of your interest. You are asked to supply a

list of nodes that you want to probe for services. OEM automatically discovers services, as illustrated in the sample screen shown here:

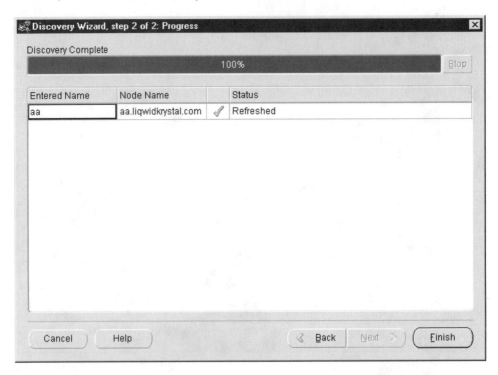

Click the Finish button when you're done.

Step 4: Verify Discovered Services   OEM Console adds all the discovered services to the Navigator. A sample screen is shown in Figure 7-6. Observe that the database services, Listener, and Oracle HTTP Server running on the test machine have been added to the list.

How the Discovery Wizard Works   The Discovery Wizard searches the network for the targets you specify. If that target has an OIA running, services running on that target are added to the Navigator. The listener.ora and tnsnames.ora files are read to get a list of services. If an OIA is not running on the target node, the Discovery Wizard gives you the option of performing a manual configuration. You can add Oracle databases on that target so that they appear in Navigator.

When refreshing an existing target, the Discovery Wizard verifies and updates the list of services that had been previously discovered. If the target was previously configured manually, the Discovery Wizard checks if the target is now running an OIA.

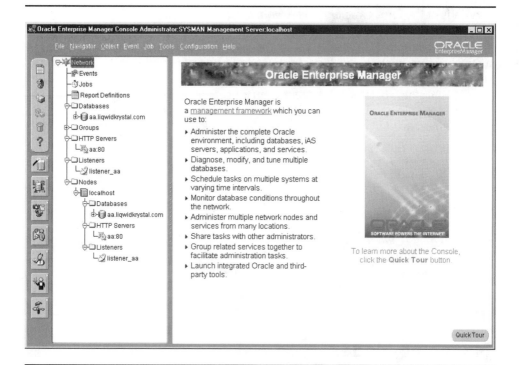

FIGURE 7-6. *Discovered services in OEM Console*

If an OIA is found, you have the option of discovering the services running on the target or updating the previous configuration.

The services running on the machines acting as Management Servers are automatically discovered when you start OEM Console.

Refreshing a Target   You can update the list of services on a target node that has been previously discovered. Select the target from the Navigator and choose Navigator | Refresh from the menu.

Removing a Target   To remove a target from the Navigator, select the object and right-click it. Choose the Delete option from the menu.

Troubleshooting Discovery-Related Issues   This section includes tips that you can use if you are unable to use the automatic discovery feature.

First of all, ensure that OIA is running on the target machine. You can use the Services applet from Control Panel to check the status of OIA. The name of the service is of the form *Oracle<Oracle Home>Agent*. For example, if you used the default installation, the service is named *OracleOraHome90Agent*.

Next, ensure that you can reach the target machine using a TCP/IP network. Use a utility such as **ping** to check connectivity to the target machine from the machine running OEM Console.

If this is a new database, ensure that an entry for this database exists in the tnsnames.ora file on the target machine running OIA. The list of discovered services is maintained in a file named services.ora in the c:\oracle\ora90\network\agent folder. If your service does not exist in this file, try restarting OIA.

Finally, view the log file maintained by OIA in the c:\oracle\ora90\network\log folder. The default name for this file is OracleOraHome90Agent.nohup.

CAUTION
If you change the hostname of the machine or change its TCP/IP domain, OIA stops functioning, and you must drop discovered nodes manually and rediscover them. Contact Oracle support to obtain technical bulletin No. 167775.1 for more information.

Managing Nodes

If you select the Nodes item in the Navigator, OEM Console displays a list of all known nodes on the network. You can expand this node in Navigator to get a list of services running on the node.

Removing a Node

Consider this situation: You have registered an event with OIA on a managed node. OIA goes down for some reason. If you remove the node from Navigator without removing the event, the node is rediscovered when OIA comes up again.

You can remove a node from the control of OEM with a little care. First, you must ensure that all jobs and events on the node have completed or have been removed. This is to ensure that OIA does not get out of sync with the Management Server. Remove the node from Navigator after you have ensured that there are no pending jobs or events. Be sure to check the Management Server log (oms.log) if you encounter any problems. This file lives in the c:\oracle\ora90\sysman\log folder.

TIP
*If you encounter a situation in which you are unable
to remove a node, try to dump all events and jobs
manually. To do so, shut down OIA and delete all
files with the extension .q, .jou, or .inp in the
c:\oracle\ora90\network\agent folder. Jobs and
events are maintained in these files. Also delete the
services.ora file before restarting OIA. Refer to Oracle
Technical Bulletin No. 62463.1 for more information.*

Managing Groups

You can organize objects into logical categories called groups. Groups can be
created using any criteria that you choose. You can create groups out of functions,
geographic locations, or departments. The created groups can be placed on a map
or a graphical view of your network so that you can quickly determine the location
of a service or an administrator who is responsible for a node. You can also assign
jobs to groups and monitor them.

To create a group, select the Groups node in OEM Navigator. Right-click and
select Create from the menu, or click the Create icon to create a group. OEM does
not create any default groups, so initially, this node is empty.

Choose the General tab, provide a name for the group, and add members from
the list of available targets, as shown here.

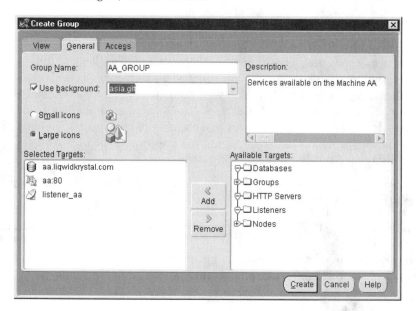

You can create a group out of any combination of databases, listeners, nodes, and HTTP Servers. Once created, you can drag and drop objects within Navigator into a group. You can also merge groups or add an existing group to a new group being created.

CAUTION
Jobs and events created for an object before it was added to a group are applied to the group retroactively. You must create new jobs and events that you want to apply to the group.

Jobs and events apply only to discovered targets, so any jobs or events applied to a heterogeneous group consisting of manually configured and discovered objects apply only to the discovered objects.

Modifying Groups
You can modify groups and their properties. Select the group in Navigator and choose the General tab. You can modify access rights and the group description, but you cannot rename an existing group. Targets can also be added to or removed from the group.

Deleting Groups
You can delete groups or subgroups within a group from OEM Navigator.

Obtaining the Status of a Group
You can obtain the current status of a group from OEM Console. You can associate a background image with a group. You can use one of the standard geographical image files or your own image. To use your own image, place the associated file in GIF or JPG format in the folder C:\oracle\ora90\classes\oracle\sysman\resources\images. To obtain the status of a member of the group, right-click the object and use the appropriate command from the context menu. Figure 7-7 shows a sample screen to obtain the status of a listener.

Managing Objects Within a Group
You can manage objects within a group from OEM Console. Select a target from the Group View and right-click it to get the context menu. Pick the appropriate action on the object.

For example, to start up a database, pick the database from the Group View and right-click it. Choose Startup from the menu.

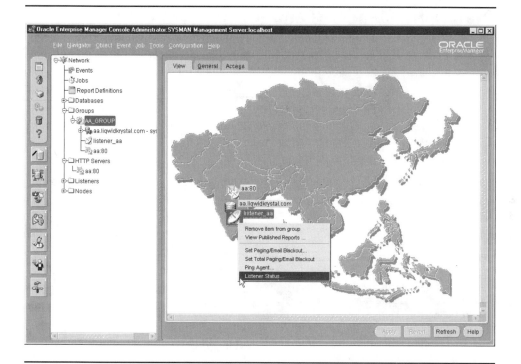

FIGURE 7-7. *Obtaining object status from OEM Console*

Oracle Management Servers

In the three-tier architecture of OEM, one or more Management Servers provide the middle-tier support. This layer provides all the intelligence necessary for OEM.

Management Servers on Windows NT/2000 are installed as services. You can control them with the Services applet or the OEMCTL utility. The service is automatically created when you create the OEM repository using EMCA as described in the "Management Server Repository" section earlier in this chapter.

Installation of Oracle Management Servers

Management Servers are services on the Windows NT/2000 platform. They are created automatically when you create an OEM repository using EMCA.

Managing Oracle Management Servers

You can start up Management Servers using the Services applet or the **net** command. Alternately, you can use the OEMCTL utility to manage the service or obtain its status, as shown in the sample session here:

```
C:\>oemctl ping oms
OEMCTL for Windows NT: Version 9.0.1.0.0
Copyright (c) 1998, 1999, 2000, 2001 Oracle Corporation.
All rights reserved.
The management server is running.
c:\>oemctl stop oms
OEMCTL for Windows NT: Version 9.0.1.0.0
Copyright (c) 1998, 1999, 2000, 2001 Oracle Corporation.
All rights reserved.
Stopping the Oracle Management Server...
c:\>oemctl start oms
The OracleOraHome90ManagementServer service is starting..........
The OracleOraHome90ManagementServer service was started successfully.
c:\>oemctl status oms
OEMCTL for Windows NT: Version 9.0.1.0.0
Copyright (c) 1998, 1999, 2000, 2001 Oracle Corporation.
All rights reserved.
The Oracle Management Server on host [aa] is functioning properly.
The server has been up for 0 00:00:46.337
  Target database session count: 0 (session sharing is off)
  Operations queued for processing: 1
  Number of OMS systems in domain: 1 (aa)
  Number of administrators logged in: 0
  Repository session pool depth: 15
  Repository session count: 7 in-use and 4 available,
       pool efficiency: 35%
```

You must provide Super Administrator credentials to stop OMS or obtain its status using OEMCTL.

Managing Administrators

OEM has two kinds of administrators: super and regular. Super administrators have full access to all objects and are authorized to discover, add, and remove targets.

The precreated user SYSMAN is a super administrator. You can create other super administrators or regular administrators using OEM Console.

To manage OEM administrators, launch OEM Console and choose Configuration | Manage Administrators. Click the Add button to create an administrator. Choose the privileges for the user, as shown here:

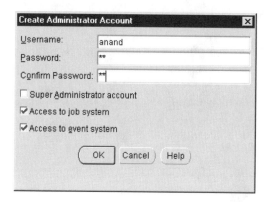

You can create a regular administrator to access the Job System and/or Event System. To modify an administrator's privilege, click the Edit button.

Controlling Access to Objects

Super administrators can control what regular administrators see in OEM Console. This feature is useful for large sites where multiple administrators are available and each is responsible for a specific area or department. By customizing the Navigator, the super administrator can ensure that an uncluttered view of the objects that an individual is responsible for is created. Use the following steps to create a customized view:

1. From OEM Console, choose Configuration | Manage Administrators.

2. Select an existing user or create a new user and click the Grant Access to Targets button.

3. Expand the available targets and grant the required access to the user by selecting the appropriate check boxes. As seen here, you can choose the targets that a given administrator can manage.

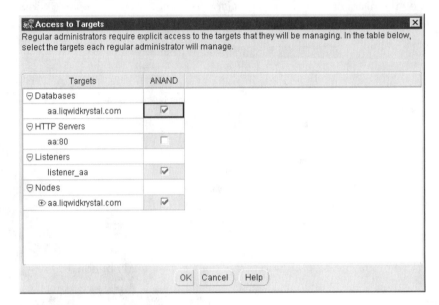

4. Click OK, and then click the Close button.

Changing Administrator Preferences

A super administrator can change the preferences for his or her own account as well as other regular administrators. Choose Configuration | Manage Administrators from OEM Console, select a specific user, and click the Edit button to set or change preferences from the Preferences screen, shown in Figure 7-8. The following tasks can be performed:

- **Change administrator password** As a super administrator, you can modify the password of any other administrator on the system. Choose the General tab from the Preferences dialog box shown in Figure 7-8.

- **Control administrator access** You can change an existing regular administrator to a super administrator, and vice versa. Access to the Job System and Event System can also be controlled from the General tab of the Preferences dialog box.

- **Specify work schedule** For large sites that have many administrators who work in shifts, it is useful to route alert notifications to the administrator(s)

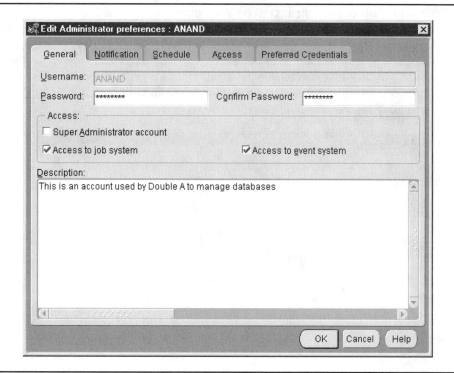

FIGURE 7-8.   *Setting administrator preferences*

on call or on duty. You can define the work schedule and assign
responsibilities for specific objects using the Schedule tab of the Preferences
dialog box shown in Figure 7-8.

■ **Control access level for new objects**   On large sites, new objects including
databases, web servers, and listeners can be added quite frequently. It can
be tedious to go back and reassign access rights to these objects to existing
administrators. You can specify the access rights that you wish to give
existing administrators for new objects by selecting the Access tab.

■ **Set preferred credentials**   You can set the preferred credentials to each
object for every administrator on the system. This allows you to exercise
further control on the access available to each administrator. To set
credentials, choose the Preferred Credentials tab.

SYSMAN Super Administrator Account

During installation of OEM, a super administrator account named SYSMAN is automatically created. The default password for this user is OEM_TEMP. When you launch OEM and attempt to connect to OMS, you are prompted to change the password for this user. To change the password for this user at a later time, choose Configuration | Manage Administrators and click the Edit button. Change the password from the ensuing dialog box, as shown here:

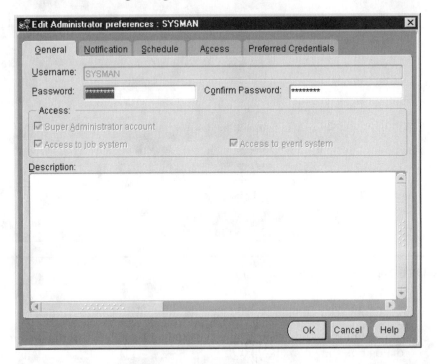

As a rule, you should not use a super administrator account for daily use. Create a regular administrator account to manage jobs and events.

Resetting SYSMAN Password   The password for the SYSMAN user is stored in the OEM repository. If you forget the password for this user, you can reset it using a built-in PL/SQL package. You must be logged in as the repository owner to accomplish this task.

```
SQL> connect oem_aa/aa
Connected
SQL> execute smp_maintenance.reset_sysman();
PL/SQL procedure successfully completed.
```

When you execute the preceding procedure, the password for SYSMAN is reset to OEM_TEMP. When you connect to OEM Console again as this user, you are prompted to change the password.

CAUTION
If you are not careful, the OEM repository can be a potential loophole in security. You must protect the OEM repository and super administrator accounts.

Setting Preferred Credentials

Some services such as databases require login information. To administrate such services from OEM Console, you can save preferred credentials that OEM can use. From OEM Console, choose Configuration | Preferences and select the Preferred Credentials tab. Select a service from the list and set the preferred credentials, as shown in Figure 7-9.

Target Name	Target Type	Credentials
<DEFAULT>	Database	
aa.liqwidkrystal.com	Database	
<DEFAULT>	HTTP Server	
aa:80	HTTP Server	
<DEFAULT>	Listener	
listener_aa	Listener	

Database <DEFAULT> Credentials:

Username: system
Password: *******
Confirm Password: *******
Role: NORMAL

FIGURE 7-9.   *Setting preferred credentials for OEM*

Changing Database Password for Repository Owner

You can use the ALTER USER command to change the database password for the repository owner.

```
SQL> alter user oem_aa identified by aa;
User altered.
```

To notify OEM about this change, launch EMCA and select the Configure Local Management Server option. Click the Next button. OEM displays the current repository login information. Click the Edit button, and provide the new password for the repository owner.

Management Regions

If you have a large site consisting of multiple nodes, you can split it up into subsets called *management regions*. This feature allows you to partition the nodes in a repository and assign them to specific Management Servers. The advantage of defining management regions is that cross-traffic between regions is eliminated during fail-over and automatic load-balancing.

Management regions are created and managed from OEM Console. You can share an OEM repository between regions; however, a particular node can belong to only one region. A Management Server can also belong to only one region. You can log on to a Management Server belonging to one region to access nodes in other regions. On large networks, management regions can provide benefits in performance by limiting network traffic to within a region.

Defining Management Regions

You can define management regions from OEM Console or EMCA. A management region named Default is automatically created by EMCA. All Management Servers using the repository are automatically placed in the Default management region. You must create additional management regions and then move existing nodes and Management Servers to these regions. To create a new management region, perform the following steps:

1. Log on as a super administrator from OEM Console to a Management Server within the Default region.

2. To bring up the Management Regions property sheet, choose Configuration | Define Management Regions.

3. To view the Regions page, select the Regions tab.

4. Click the Add Regions button.

5. Type the name of the new management region. The sample screen shown here adds a management region named WEST_COAST.

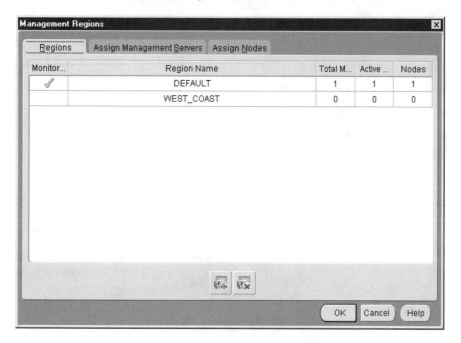

You can assign existing Management Servers to the newly created management region. To do so, perform the following steps:

1. To access the Management Regions property sheet, from OEM Console, choose Configure | Configure Management Regions.

2. To view the available Management Servers, select the Assign Management Servers tab. To assign a management server to a region, select the appropriate radio button. Click the OK button.

You can also assign existing nodes to a specific management region. To do so, perform the following steps:

1. To access the Management Regions property sheet, from OEM Console, choose Configure | Configure Management Regions.

2. To view the discovered nodes, select the Assign Nodes tab. To assign a node to a management region, select the appropriate radio button. Click the OK button. A sample screen is shown in Figure 7-10 for your reference.

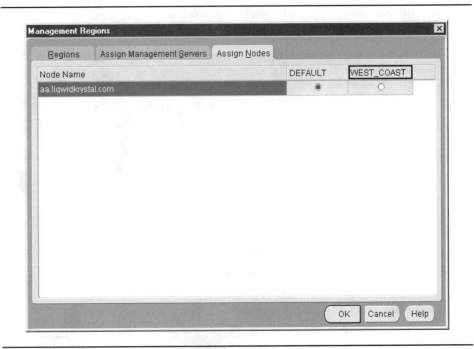

FIGURE 7-10. *Assigning nodes to management regions*

Removing a Management Region

You can remove only an empty management region. Ensure that there are no nodes or Management Servers in the region and use OEM Console to delete the region using the following steps:

1. Log on as a super administrator from OEM Console to a Management Server within the Default region.

2. To bring up the Management Regions property sheet, choose Configuration | Define Management Regions.

3. To view the Regions page, select the Regions tab.

4. Select the region that you wish to remove. Click the Delete Region button. Confirm your intent to delete the region, and click the OK button to delete the region. Objects existing in the region must be moved to another region. If you attempt to delete a region that has objects in it, a warning dialog box appears.

Tuning Oracle Management Servers

If you have a large site consisting of many nodes, you should look into the performance of Management Servers. Parameters in the omsconfig.properties file are used to configure Management Servers. This file lives in the c:\oracle\ora90\sysman\ config folder.

Setting Maximum Connections

You can configure the simultaneous maximum connections that Management Servers maintain. Incoming and outgoing connections can be managed separately. The number of outgoing connections defines the number of connections that the Management Server can maintain to OIA. Use the following parameters to set the maximum number of outgoing and incoming connections:

```
oms.vdg.max_out_conns =32;
oms.vdg.max_in_conns =16;
```

The default values for these settings are 64 on Windows NT and 32 on Windows 2000 and Windows XP. In general, you should configure the maximum number of incoming connections to be half the maximum outgoing connections.

Setting Ping Intervals

The Management Servers are constantly monitoring all the services that they are aware of. This operation is called *pinging*. By default, Management Servers are configured to ping all known services every 2 minutes. If you have a large site, it might take more than 2 minutes to ping all services. In this case, you should increase the time interval between pings. A sample setting for pinging services every 5 minutes is shown here.

```
oms.vdg.ping_interval = 5;
```

Repository Connection

Since a Management Server uses a repository to store information, it needs to maintain a constant connection to the database. If the connection is lost for any reason, OEM automatically tries to reestablish a connection. Two parameters are available to control this behavior.

```
oms.repository.connect_timeout=120
oms.repository.connect_numTries=12
```

The preceding two parameters together control the time interval and the number of retry attempts. In this case, OEM tries to connect to the database repository 12 times at 10-second intervals (120/12) before giving up.

If your network is prone to delays and slowdowns, you can make the Management Server more tolerant to these failures by adding a delay between attempts to reconnect. The following setting introduces a delay of 3 seconds between retries.

```
oms.repository.conn_retries_delay = 3;
```

Diagnosing Issues with Oracle Management Servers

If you encounter an error condition or abnormal behavior with Management Servers, you can try to isolate the issue by obtaining information from three different sources.

Windows Event Viewer

Alerts related to the Management Servers are logged in Event Viewer. Launch Event Viewer and choose to view Application Log. Find the alert(s) logged for Management Server, and view it to obtain useful information on the service. Event Viewer can be launched from Control Panel | Administrative Tools.

Log Files

Management Server log files are written to the folder c:\oracle\ora90\sysman\log. The file oms.nohup provides useful information on Management Servers.

Information from JRE

You can obtain additional information from JRE itself. Modify the oemctl.bat file in the c:\oracle\ora90\bin folder, and set JRE to run in verbose mode. The following change was made on line 56 of this file in the test installation:

```
SET JRE=jre -nojit -mx32m -verbose
```

Tracing

You can enable tracing for Management Servers. The following setting enables admin-level tracing for Management Servers.

```
TRACING.ENABLED=true
TRACING.LEVEL=5
```

By default, only critical errors are reported to the trace file oms.nohup. Set the tracing level to 3 to obtain all user trace and warnings. Use a setting of 2 to obtain complete information on Management Servers. Use tracing only in development or temporarily to isolate issues, as it affects performance.

Oracle Managed Nodes

Managed nodes are target nodes running Oracle databases, Oracle Net Listeners, Oracle Application Servers, and HTTP Servers. The services on the target node are managed by OIA. These are processes that execute tasks in response to requests made by Management Servers. Once a task is scheduled, the agent(s) performs this task independently on the target node. The advantage of this architecture is that these agents are not affected by the availability of the network or Management Servers. OIA also provides support for SNMP services and automatic discovery features of OEM. Specifically, OIA is responsible for

- Making calls to the operating system for services necessary on the target node, for example, to copy a data file during backup

- Running jobs scheduled by OEM

- Tracking events on targets

- SNMP support

Installation of Oracle Intelligent Agents

OIA is installed as a service on the Windows NT/2000 platform when you install Oracle9i Software. If the service is not installed, perform a custom installation and choose to install OIA from the component named Oracle Enterprise Manager Products.

Managing Oracle Intelligent Agents

The default name for OIA is OracleOraHome90Agent. You can set up this service to start automatically or manually start it using the Services applet in Control Panel. Alternatively, use the **net** command to start up and shut down the service.

An agent control utility is also available on Windows NT/2000 to manage the agent. It can be used to start up, shut down, and determine the status of an agent.

```
C:\>agentctl start
DBSNMP for 32-bit Windows: Version 9.0.1.0.1 -
Production on 14-JAN-2002 23:03
Copyright (c) 2001 Oracle Corporation.  All rights reserved.
Starting Oracle Intelligent Agent.......
Agent started
```

If you have a large site and want to discover services and refresh targets in OEM, you should configure OIA to start up automatically on system startup.

Operating System Account for Jobs

If you are scheduling OEM jobs on a target node, you must run OIA on that node. The scheduled jobs must be run under a Windows NT/2000 user who has the Logon As a Batch Job privilege.

On Windows NT, launch User Manager and create a new user. Choose Policies | User Rights. Select the Show Advanced User Rights check box. Select the Logon As a Batch Job privilege. Click the OK button.

On Windows 2000, choose Control Panel | Administrative Tools | Local Security Policies from the Start menu. Expand the Local Policies node. Select User Rights Assignment. In the right pane, double-click Log on As Batch Job. Add the user that will execute jobs. Click OK to close the dialog box.

You can also choose to use a domain user to run jobs.

Database User for Oracle Intelligent Agent

OIA uses the database user DBSNMP (default password of DBSNMP) to connect to the database. You should alter the password for this user on your production system. Follow these steps to change the password for the DBSNMP user.

1. Use OEM or SQL*Plus to alter the user's password.

   ```
   SQL> alter user dbsnmp identified by aa;
   User altered.
   ```

2. Edit the snmp_rw.ora file, and add the following entry to reflect the new password:

   ```
   snmp.connect.OracleOraHome90Agent.password = aa;
   ```

3. Restart OIA.

   ```
   C:\>net stop OracleOraHome90Agent
   The OracleOraHome90Agent service is stopping..
   The OracleOraHome90Agent service was stopped successfully.
   C:\>net start OracleOraHome90Agent
   The OracleOraHome90Agent service is starting........
   The OracleOraHome90Agent service was started successfully.
   ```

If you want to use a different database user altogether, use the following steps:

1. Create the new database user. Use OEM or SQL*Plus to create the user, say AA with password AA. Grant the CREATE SESSION privilege to the user.

2. Create the required database objects. Modify and execute the **catsnmp.sql** script, as shown here:

   ```
   SQL> connect sys/change_on_install as sysdba
   Connected.
   SQL> @c:\oracle\ora90\rdbms\admin\catsnmp.sql
   ```

3. Add these settings to the snmp_rw.ora file:

```
SNMP.CONNECT.OracleOraHome90Agent.NAME = aa
SNMP.CONNECT. OracleOraHome90Agent.PASSWORD = aa
```

Be sure to control read/write access to the c:\oracle\ora90\network\ admin folder.

Auto Discovery

OIA must be running to perform automatic discovery from OEM. OIA uses the files listed in Table 7-3 to discover services.

In order for automatic discovery to work, a valid listener.ora file must be available. You must also ensure that OIA has read/write access to the c:\oracle\ora90\ network\admin folder.

On startup, OIA first reads the Windows Registry, then the listener.ora file, and finally the tnsnames.ora file to get a list of services running on the machine. On Windows, the ORACLE_SID and ORACLE_HOME settings in the Registry are used first to discover database services. Further, this information is used to get corresponding listeners from the listener configuration file. If a setting is not found for the GLOBAL_ DBNAME parameter, OIA then reads the tnsnames.ora file and attempts to get this information.

The snmp_ro.ora, snmp_rw.ora, and services.ora files are either read or updated with the services found on the target node.

Blackouts

Since OIA is constantly monitoring targets, it is difficult to perform maintenance operations on these targets without notifying the agent. You can temporarily suspend OIA by creating a blackout. Blackouts are created to suspend events, jobs, and data collection. When a target is under a blackout, OIA registers no events on the target. Similarly, no jobs are executed on the target node during a blackout. This

Filename	Use/Description
snmp_ro.ora	This read-only file is created and managed by OIA.
snmp_rw.ora	This file consists of settings used by OIA. Database user information and trace settings are provided here.
services.ora	The services currently being monitored by OIA are listed here.

TABLE 7-3. *Files Used by Oracle Intelligent Agent*

feature is especially useful during a scheduled downtime. For example, if a database has been deliberately shut down for some maintenance, you can define a blackout to ensure that email or pager alerts are not generated during this scheduled maintenance.

You can define a blackout by using the agent control utility. You can set only one blackout at any given time, though multiple blackouts can exist simultaneously. This example starts a blackout on the node AA.

```
C:> agentctl start blackout aa
```

When you have completed the maintenance task and restored the service, you should stop the blackout.

```
C:> agentctl stop blackout aa
```

Troubleshooting Oracle Intelligent Agent

If you are having trouble with discovery, jobs, or events, first verify if OIA is running. You can use the System applet to get information on the OIA service. By default, the service is named *OracleOraHome90Agent*. If OIA is unable to start up, use Event Viewer to get additional information on the issue.

Ensure that the listener.ora and tnsnames.ora files are valid. You can do so by restarting the listener on the target node and attempting to connect to a database using a connection identifier defined in the TNSNAMES file.

OIA maintains log files in a folder named c:\oracle\ora90\network\agent\log. There are two log files of interest. The dbmsnmp.log contains a log of the OIA. If you want to obtain information on a specific job being executed, view the dbsnmpj.log file.

You can enable tracing at different levels by setting parameters in the snmp_rw.ora file. For example, to enable tracing at the highest level, use the following setting:

```
AGENTCTL.TRACE_LEVEL = 16
```

Trace files are quite cryptic and voluminous. You need assistance from Oracle support personnel to decipher them.

Simple Network Management Protocol Support

Simple Network Management Protocol (SNMP) is a popular protocol that is used by system administrators to manage databases and networks on large sites. Hewlett-Packard's HP-Open View and Tivoli Net View and Sun's SunNet Manager are common SNMP management tools in use. Oracle9i Server does not directly interact with SNMP tools; however, it can support SNMP through Oracle Net Services.

Overview of SNMP Components

SNMP tools have standard components. These include management tools and processes (agents) that allow for system-wide discovery and management of services.

Management Applications

The management applications are the tools integrated with the management framework to accomplish specialized network or database tasks.

Managed Node

The platform being managed is called a *managed node.* Oracle Server would be a managed node.

Agents

A process that runs on the managed node and accepts queries from the other parts of the framework is called a *master agent.* Each master node has one master agent.

A process called the *subagent* exists for every managed element on the managed node. These subagents receive queries from the master agent and respond with appropriate answers. OIA acts as a subagent for Oracle database services.

Management Information Base

A management information base (MIB) is a text file that describes the variables containing the information that SNMP can access. There is only one MIB for each element being monitored. OIA is responsible for providing access to a database's MIB.

SNMP Support on Oracle9i Server

OIA provides SNMP support on Oracle Server. It also provides direct access to a database's MIB.

Installation of SNMP Service on Windows NT 4.0

Use the steps described in this section to configure SNMP Service on Windows NT 4.0.

Step 1: Install SNMP Service   You must install the SNMP Service first. Start the Network applet in Control Panel. Choose the Services tab, and click the Add button. From the available list of network services, select SNMP Service, and click the OK button. You are prompted for the original Windows NT 4.0 media. The required SNMP files are copied to your machine. Now to coerce Windows NT into recognizing service changes, choose the Bindings tab. Finally, reinstall Windows NT Service Pack (6.0a or later), and reboot the machine. The SNMP service is available on Windows 2000 and can be configured in the same fashion.

Step 2: Configure SNMP Support　You must configure SNMP services. Again, start the Network applet from Control Panel, and choose the Services tab. Select the SNMP services, and click the Properties button. Choose the Agent tab, and set the following:

- **Contact**　Contact information for this computer.

- **Location**　Physical location of this computer.

- **Service**　Select all service types (physical, applications, datalink/subnetwork, Internet, and end-to-end).

Select the Traps tab, and set the following:

- **Community Name**　Set this to PUBLIC.

- **Trap Destinations**　Specify either the hostnames or IP addresses for all machines running SNMP-aware products.

Step 3: Integrate SNMP with Oracle Intelligent Agent　OIA is required to support SNMP. Verify that the services Oracle Peer SNMP Master Agent and SNMP Encapsulator Agent are running on your machine. These services are named OracleOraHome90SNMPPeerEncapsulator and OracleOraHome90SNMPPeerMasterAgent on the test installation. If these services do not exist, use Oracle Universal Installer to perform a custom installation and install them.

Step 4: Configure the Services File　You must specify the port on which the Microsoft SNMP Service must listen. This is port 161 by default. Edit the services file from the c:\windows\system32\drivers\etc folder, and add or modify the SNMP entries to read as here:

```
snmp            1161/udp      snmp
snmp-trap       1162/udp      snmp
```

NOTE
You might already have these entries in the Services file.

Step 5: Configure the Master Peer Agent Configuration File   Edit the file master.cfg from the c:\oracle\ora90\network\admin folder. Add or modify the section named **transport** as follows:

```
TRANSPORT   ordinary      SNMP
   OVER UDP SOCKET
   AT PORT 1161
```

Add or modify the section named **community** as follows:

```
COMMUNITY public
   ALLOW ALL OPERATIONS
   USE NO ENCRYPTION
```

If you need to send traps, specify the IP address of that computer in the section named **manager** as follows:

```
192.168.1.9
   SEND ALL TRAPS
   WITH COMMUNITY public
```

If you have more than one Master Peer Agent, edit the file encaps.cfg in the c:\oracle\ora90\network\admin folder and add at least one agent entry including MIB subtrees. See the example here:

```
AGENT AT PORT 1161 WITH COMMUNITY public
SUBTREES 1.3.6.1.2.1.1,
         1.3.6.1.2.1.2,
         1.3.6.1.2.1.3,
         1.3.6.1.2.1.4,
         1.3.6.1.2.1.5,
         1.3.6.1.2.1.6,
         1.3.6.1.2.1.7,
         1.3.6.1.2.1.8,
         1.3.6.1.4.1.77
         1.3.6.1.4.1
FORWARD ALL TRAPS;
```

All the files described in this step should already have the required entries.

Step 6: Verify That the Configured UDP Port Is Free   Verify that UDP port 1161 is unused on the machine using the **netstat** command. All used UDP ports are listed in the example here:

```
C:\>netstat -p udp -a
Active Connections
```

```
Proto   Local Address          Foreign Address        State
UDP     aa:epmap               *:*
UDP     aa:microsoft-ds        *:*
UDP     aa:1026                *:*
UDP     aa:ntp                 *:*
UDP     aa:1900                *:*
```

Note that UDP port 1161 is free on the machine.

Step 7: Verify That SNMP Services Are Not Running   Start Windows Task Manager, and select the Process tab. Verify that the processes named **agent.exe** and **encaps.exe** are not running. Kill these processes if they are running. Use the Services applet to ensure that Oracle SNMP and OIA are not running.

Step 8: Start SNMP Services   Start the SNMP Services in the following order:

1. SNMP service

2. Master Peer Agent

3. Encapsulator

4. OIA

You can also start SNMP services from a batch file similar to the one shown in the example here:

```
NET START "SNMP"
NET START "SNMP Trap Service"
start c:\oracle\ora90\bin\agent.exe c:\oracle\ora90\network\
admin\master.cfg c:\ORACLE\ORA90\NETWORK\LOG\master.log
NET START "OracleOraHome90Agent"
```

Step 9: Test the SNMP Environment   You can test the SNMP environment using the SNMPUTILG tool. You can download this tool from http://download.microsoft.com.

Installation of SNMP Service on Windows 2000

All the steps listed in the previous section apply to Windows 2000. The only difference is that, to use SNMP, you must install Windows 2000 Service Pack 1 or 2. If you already have one of these service packs installed, you do not have to reinstall it after installing SNMP services.

Scheduling Jobs

In Chapter 5, you saw how common DBA tasks can be scheduled as batch commands using Windows Scheduler. OEM includes a Job System that can be used to automate standard and repetitive tasks. These tasks can be the execution of simple SQL scripts, operating system commands, or common database administration tasks such as taking a database backup. The Job System allows you to create and manage jobs, share them with other administrators, and schedule them for execution. A job can be scheduled on any node that is running OIA.

Setting Credentials

A job can be viewed as a task that is executed on your behalf by OIA. You must provide the necessary credentials to execute a task. The credentials that you supply must be sufficient to perform the task.

You should set node-level credentials by providing login information for a Windows NT/2000 user as detailed in the "Operating System Account for Jobs" section earlier in this chapter. If you are scheduling a job against a specific service, say a database, then you must provide credentials for a database user who has the necessary privileges to perform the task in question. For example, if you want to shut down a database, take a backup, and start it up again, you must provide credentials for a user who has SYSDBA or SYSOPER privileges.

To set the preferred credentials, from OEM Console, choose Configuration | Manage Administrators. Select the Preferred Credentials tab, and set the preferences for the necessary services, as shown in Figure 7-11.

Creating Jobs

A variety of jobs can be scheduled. These jobs are grouped by the target against which the job is to be executed. These are database, node, listener, and HTTP Server. Some of the common tasks that can be performed via jobs are

- SQL scripts can be executed.

- Databases can be started up and shut down.

- Listeners can be started up and shut down.

- HTTP Servers can be started up and shut down.

Jobs are created using TCL (tool command language). Oracle has added some extensions to the standard TCL syntax and created a variant called *OraTcl* with OEM.

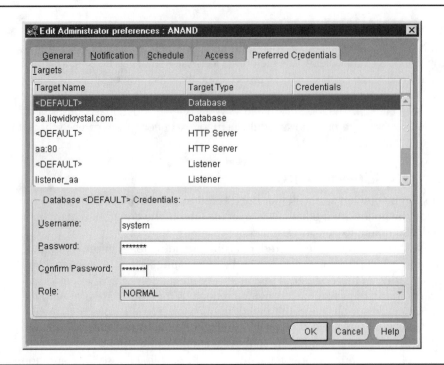

FIGURE 7-11. *Setting preferred credentials*

Built-In Jobs

Oracle has bundled TCL scripts for common tasks with the installation. You can create your own scripts or extend existing scripts quite readily. The built-in scripts are available in three categories: Database Tasks, Node Tasks, and Listener Tasks.

Database Tasks

Common database tasks can be performed with scripts from this category. You can use the Preferred Credentials set on OEM Console or override them with credentials that you supply while running the task. This section looks at the tasks available in this category.

Run SQL*Plus Script   You can run any SQL script using this task. You can pass parameters to the SQL script and trap error conditions. The success or failure of a script depends on the exit condition from the execution of the script. You should make it a habit to trap the exit condition so that you can take appropriate corrective measures if the execution of the script fails. For example, include the following EXIT statement at the end of the script:

```
EXIT sql.sqlcode
```

To create a job of this type, choose Job | Create Job from OEM Console. You see the Create Job screen, as shown here:

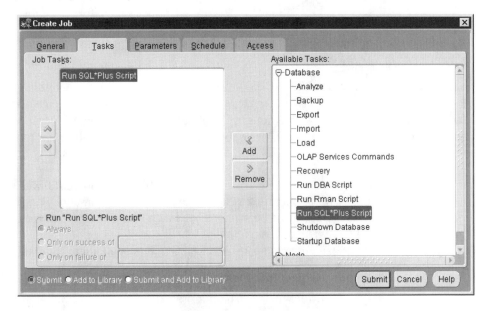

Provide a name and description for the job in the General Information. Specify a target against which the script will be executed. Optionally, you can override the credentials set in the preferences.

Select the Tasks tab, and include the Run SQL*Plus Script task. You can also choose to run other scripts based on the exit condition of your script. Choose the Parameters tab, and type or import the text for the SQL script. Specify any parameters that the script might need. Set the access rights for the user scheduling the job, and schedule it from the Schedule tab. You can choose to run the script immediately or schedule it for execution later.

Run DBA Script   This category is meant to run scripts using Server Manager. Since Server Manager is obsolete in Oracle9i, this category is not useful. All DBA tasks can be performed using SQL*Plus scripts in Oracle9i.

Start Up Database   Use this job type to schedule a database startup. You can choose options to just create an instance, mount the database, or open it for users.

Other options, including starting up the database in restricted mode, are available. You can execute this only if the credentials belong to a user who has SYSDBA or SYSOPER privileges.

Shut Down Database   Use this job to shut down a database. You can optionally choose to shut down the database in immediate mode or abort the instance.

Node Tasks

Typical node tasks are operating-system commands. You can execute third-party applications by creating a task of this kind.

Broadcast Message   You can broadcast a message to all users on the network using this task. Typically, this task is used to warn users of an impending outage. On Windows NT/2000, you can use the **net send** command to broadcast messages to specific users. The **net** command can be scheduled using a task of the Run OS Command type.

Run OS Command   You can run OS commands using this task. You must have appropriate permissions on the operating system to execute the command. OS commands on Windows NT/2000 can be executables, batch files, or command files.

Run TCL Script   You can create custom TCL scripts and execute them using this task. Oracle has extended the standard syntax to include some common database requirements by defining the OraTcl language. Orastart, Orastop, and Oracommit are examples of Oracle extensions to TCL. The oramsg extension is especially useful since it can be used to retrieve Oracle Server messages. Refer to *Oracle Intelligent Agent User's Guide* in Oracle documentation for information on these extensions.

Halt Jobs   A job can include multiple tasks. Normally, the job is considered complete when all tasks defined in the job are completed in sequence. If you want to halt the execution of a job prior to completing all tasks listed in the job, you can use this script. Typically, you would use this if a task fails to complete and you want to terminate the job without executing the remaining tasks in the job.

Listener Tasks

Predefined tasks for shutting down and starting up listeners are available. These are called Shutdown Listener and Startup Listener, respectively.

OEM Wizard Tasks

You might have noticed other built-in tasks such as export and import in the Job System. These are used by OEM Wizards such as Data Manager and are for internal use by wizards only. The following tasks cannot be used in your jobs:

- Export and import
- Load
- Analyze
- Backup and recovery

Jobs Task List

OEM Console provides a complete lists of jobs that have been scheduled for execution as well as a status on tasks that have been completed. Select the Jobs node in OEM Navigator to view the jobs task list. A sample is shown in Figure 7-12.

Select the Active tab to view currently active jobs. You can get a history of the execution of all jobs by choosing the History tab.

Clearing Job History   A history log is maintained for all jobs executed from OEM. From time to time, you should clear the history to avoid clutter. To clear the job history, choose Job | Clear Job History.

Job Libraries

You can add jobs that you have created to a job library. By doing so, you can manage all the scripts on your site in one location. To add a job to the library, perform the following steps:

1. Launch OEM Console and choose Jobs | Create Job from the menu to view the Create Job screen.

2. Provide the necessary information to complete the job definition.

3. Select the radio button Add to Library at the bottom of the screen, and click the Add button. The job is added to the job library.

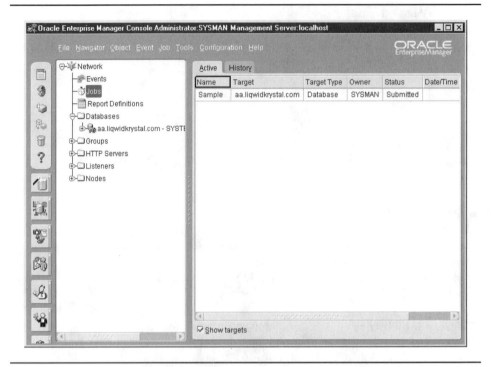

FIGURE 7-12. *Jobs task list of OEM*

Once a job is added to the library, you can modify it or submit it for execution. Choose Job | Job Library to view the Job Library screen to manage jobs in the library.

Monitoring Events

As a DBA, one of the primary concerns that you have is to keep the database and other services running on your site. If you are responsible for many databases, listeners, and HTTP Servers, how do you monitor them effectively 24×7? The Event System of OEM includes features that allow you to monitor services on your network. OIA can monitor performance and outages in your absence and alert you if there is a critical issue. You can define threshold values to define what is a critical issue.

Scope of Events

Each administrator on the site can define a set of events of interest to himself or herself. In this manner, an administrator can monitor specific services within an area of responsibility and not worry about getting flooded with reports for other services. Of course, it is possible to share an event with other administrators on the network.

Creating Events

Events can be created from OEM Console. Once an event is created with the required properties and submitted, OIA is responsible for monitoring the target and generating alerts whenever a certain condition is met or not met. The conditions along with relevant threshold values are specified as *event tests*. In addition, you can also specify a corrective action in an event handler to handle issues as they arise. The event handler is written as a *fixit job* and is executed automatically when the event is raised. A fixit job is a special job that is designed to take corrective measures when an issue is reported. Any job can be registered as a fixit job by setting a property in the job's property dialog box. For example, if you create an event to track free space in a tablespace, you could write a fixit job that expands the tablespace (by adding a data file) when the tablespace is nearly full.

Event Types

Tests for five types of events are provided with the installation. These tests cover almost all the normal needs for a site.

Fault Management Tests

Fault management tests are tests for critical conditions. Two kinds of tests are built in: UpDown and Alert. The UpDown test can be used to test if a database, listener, node, or HTTP Server is up or down. Typically, a fixit job is defined to bring up the service that has gone down.

An Alert test is used to check for any database alerts added to the alert.log file. Oracle Server writes alerts (critical ORA-xxxx errors) to the alert.log. As a DBA, you want to keep track of alert entries to this log file and take corrective measures as soon as possible.

Space Management Tests

A space management test checks for availability of disk space. Many typical tests are included with Oracle Server. For example, a test is available to check the available physical disk space. Another test is available to check for a condition in which the destination for archived log files is full. Both these space conditions are critical to an Oracle database. Other examples of tests in this category include checks for a tablespace being full, extents reaching MAXEXTENTS, and the alert.log getting too big.

For space management tests to be useful, you should configure these events to raise an alert when a threshold value is reached. For example, raise an alert in the event that the disk space falls below 200MB.

Resource Management Tests

Resource management tests are available to check for conditions in which resources are getting used up beyond expectations. A common resource that you want to track is the CPU usage. Another example of a resource management test is a license check. If you are reaching the limit of your licenses, you want to be alerted of the situation. Again, it is useful to configure these events with threshold values such that an alert is raised before a critical situation arises.

Performance Management Tests

This category of tests checks for performance bottlenecks. For example if it is taking abnormally long to establish a database condition, you want to be alerted. Tests are available to monitor the health of important functions of a database, such as disk I/O.

Unsolicited Events

An unsolicited event is tested by a third-party process and is outside the purview of OIA. Use this to integrate OEM with third-party utilities.

Registering Events

Once an event is created and necessary tests have been added to the event, you must register the event. When you register an event, you specify the target on which you want the event monitored. OIA is responsible for actually monitoring the event and informing Management Server when the test condition triggers an event.

Notifications

When an event occurs, a notification via email or a pager message can be sent to the administrator(s) who has registered the event. If a fixit job has been defined, OIA executes the job automatically.

Note that an event test can terminate in many end results. For example, an event might raise a critical alert and the DBA has to do something. It is possible that an event could result in a warning, and when the condition has passed, the alert is cleared.

TIP
OEM displays a small icon next to the alert in the Alert page. This icon gives a quick indication on the nature of the alert. Critical alerts are marked with a red flag, while warnings are marked with a yellow flag. If an alert is clear (because the event has passed), it is marked with a green flag. Make it a habit to view the Alerts page and quickly isolate the critical issues.

Event Handling

Events are actually handled by Oracle Management Server. OIA sends an event notification to Oracle Management Server, and alerts are raised and actions taken based on these notification events.

Obtaining System Reports

A big part of a DBA's job is to generate and analyze reports that contain information on the performance, availability, and configuration issues. Reports can be generated by collating data on performance and availability across all targets including databases, nodes, listeners, and HTTP Servers.

OEM has a built-in reporting system. The reporting system can be used to generate and publish reports to a chosen audience. In fact, reports can be published to a web server directly at regular intervals. You can also obtain reports on demand.

Configuration of Reports System

The Oracle Management Server and the Reporting Web Server are the two main components of a reports system. Two-way communication occurs between the Management Server and Web Server.

On Windows NT/2000, the Reporting Web Server and Management Server are automatically installed when you install Oracle9i Enterprise Edition. The Reporting Web Server (Oracle HTTP Server) is automatically aware of the Management Server and has the necessary repository information; however, a few additional tasks are necessary to complete the configuration. Follow these steps to configure the Reports System:

1. Ensure that Oracle HTTP Server and Management Server are running. Use the Services applet to ensure that Oracle HTTP Server and Management Server are running.

2. Change the password for REPORTS_USER. A built-in super administrator named REPORTS_USER is created when you install OEM. The default password for this user is OEM_TEMP. Change this password before proceeding.

3. Launch OEM Console and choose Configure | Manage Administrators. Select the user REPORTS_USER and change the password. This password is required in step 3.

4. Configure Reporting Web Server. Configure Reporting Web Server using the OEMCTL utility, as shown here:

```
c:\>oemctl configure rws
Configuring the reporting web server...
This command line utility configures a web server on this machine
```

```
so that it can be used for Enterprise Manager reporting.  Answer
each prompt and hit return.  After you answer each prompt, you will
be asked for confirmation
before the web server is configured.
To quit this utility, hit CTRL-C.
For Help, see EM_ReportingConfig.HTML.
Webserver Name [default is aa]: aa
Port number [default is 3339]: 3339
Oracle Management Server [default is aa]: aa
Password for the REPORTS_USER Administrator: aa
You have provided all of the information required to configure the
web server.
Configure the web server now? [Y/N, default is Y]: Y
CONFIGURATION COMPLETED: The web server has been successfully
configured.
You can now access the Enterprise Manager Reporting Home Page
using the URL http://aa:3339/em/OEMNavigationServlet.
You can also access the Reporting Home page using the View
Published Reports menu command in the Enterprise Manager Console.
```

Viewing and Modifying Existing Reports

From OEM Console, select the Report Definitions node. From the list of reports in the Detail pane, select a report, right-click it, and choose Edit from the context menu. Modify the settings for the report from the ensuing Edit Report dialog box. A sample is shown here:

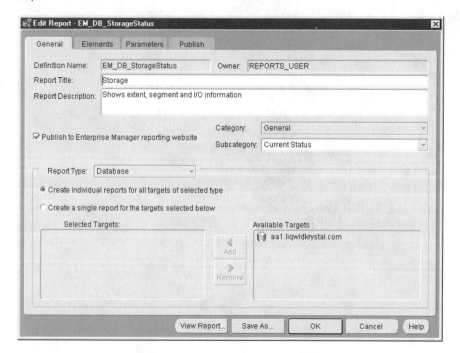

You can also execute and view a report from OEM Console on demand. Select a report, right-click it, and choose View Report to execute the necessary queries to generate the report. You are prompted for the name of the target against which the queries must be run. The report can be viewed from Console or, if the property is set, published to the reporting web site.

To view a report, point your browser at the URL for OEM (http://*<server>*:3339, by default) and click the Access Reports button. You can also view the report directly at the URL http://*<server>*:3339/em/OEMNavigationServlet.

Creating Reports

Use OEM Console to create a new report. Select the Report Definitions node, choose Object | Create, and choose to create a new report definition. Provide the necessary information (such as the queries to run and the headers to be created for the report) from the Create Report screen, shown here:

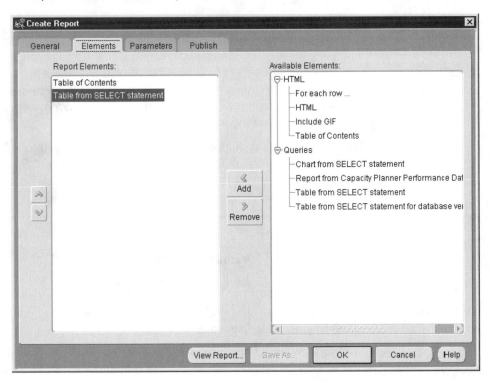

Making Events, Jobs, and Reports Work for You

Now that you have sufficient information on configuring OEM, it is time to see how jobs, events, alerts, event notifications, fixit jobs, and reports work together to give you complete control of your Oracle system.

Assume that you are an administrator for a small company with 100 employees. You have a production database named AA that is used by critical applications across the enterprise. You want to create a job for taking a database backup at midnight and also monitor the availability of the database. Additionally, you want to monitor a critical condition in which the database or the listener shuts down for some reason. Following are step-by-step instructions on how you might manage this site using OEM.

1. Configure OEM to use Management Server. Maintain a second database OEMREP to house OEM's repository.

2. Ensure that Management Server and OIA are running.

3. Define the following jobs:

   ■ **Backup_AA**   From OEM Console, choose Object | Create, and choose to create a new job. Select the General tab and enter information, as shown in Table 7-4. Submit the Job Backup_AA.

   ■ **START_DB**   If the database shuts down for some reason, this fixit job brings it back up. Create the job with the settings shown in Table 7-5. Submit the job START_DB.

OEM Create Job Screen Tab	Field/Setting	Value	Comment
General	Job Name	Backup_AA	Name for the job.
	Description	Any text	Optional.
	Target Type	Database	
	Override Node Preferred Credentials for entire job	Not required	It is assume that you have set proper preferred credentials.
	Selected Target	AA	Choose your target node.

TABLE 7-4.   *Settings for a Job to Back Up the Database*

OEM Create Job Screen Tab	Field/Setting	Value	Comment
	Submit	Selected	Radio button setting to submit the job.
Tasks	Job Tasks	Backup	To back up the database using RMAN
	Run Backup	Always	
Parameters	Not applicable		
Schedule	Radio Button On Interval	Selected	To run the job every day
	Start Execution	1/12/2002	Starting date for the job (current date)
	Time	02:00 A.M.	
	Radio button Every Days	1	Run the job every day
Access	SYSMAN	Full	Super administrator

TABLE 7-4.   *Settings for a Job to Back Up the Database* (continued)

Tab in Create Job Screen of OEM	Field/Setting	Value	Comment
General	Job Name	START_DB	Name for the job.
	Description	Any text	Optional.
	Target Type	Database	
	Override Node Preferred Credentials for entire job	Not required	It is assume that you have set proper preferred credentials.
	Selected Target	AA	Choose your target node.
	Submit	Selected	Radio button setting to submit the job.

TABLE 7-5.   *Settings for a Fixit Job*

Tab in Create Job Screen of OEM	Field/Setting	Value	Comment
Tasks	Job Tasks	Startup Database	To start up the database.
Parameters	Not applicable		
Schedule	Radio Button As a Fixit Job	Selected	To run the job only in the event the database has shut down.
Access	SYSMAN	Full	Super administrator.

TABLE 7-5. *Settings for a Fixit Job* (continued)

4. Define an event to trap the condition when the database goes down. Choose Object | Create, and create a new event with the settings shown in Table 7-6. Register the event DB_Down.

5. Check modem configuration. Ensure that a modem is attached to the node and is configured properly. If the modem is not configured properly, the pager service will not start.

Tab in Create Event Screen of OEM	Field/Setting	Value	Comment
General	Event Name	DB_Down	Name for the event.
	Target Type	Database	
	Event Description	Any text	Optional text.
	Monitored Targets	AA	Name of your target node.
	Radio button Register	Selected	To register the event.
Tests	Selected Tasks	Database UpDown	From Fault group.

TABLE 7-6. *Event for Monitoring Database Availability*

Tab in Create Event Screen of OEM	**Field/Setting**	**Value**	**Comment**
Parameters	Selected Tests	Database UpDown	Leave as is.
Schedule	Radio button On Interval	Selected	
	Event Test Evaluation	Immediately after registration completes	We want to start monitoring immediately.
	Every	0 hours and 5 minutes	
Access	SYSMAN	Full	
Fixit Jobs	If ANY test triggers, run a fixit job	Selected	
	Selected Tests	Database UpDown	
	Fixit Job	START_DB	Created earlier.

TABLE 7-6. *Event for Monitoring Database Availability* (continued)

6. Start the pager service. Start the service responsible for paging. Use the Services applet to start the service named OracleOraHome90PagingServer.

7. Configure the email and paging configuration. Choose Configuration | Configure Paging/Email. Provide the settings shown in Table 7-7.

8. Configure Reports. You should ensure that the backup job that you have configured has actually been executed. From OEM Console, pick the existing report named Completed Jobs from Last 24 hours, and publish it to the Reporting Web Server.

Oracle Enterprise Manager has evolved over the last two years into a comprehensive management tool. As a DBA, you should take the time to get familiar with the various features of OEM. In the next chapter, you will see how OEM can be used for end-to-end database administration.

Node in Configure Paging/Email Screen	Field	Value	Comment
Email Configuration	SMTP Mail Gateway	mail.liqwidkrystal.com	Your mail server
	Sender's SMTP Mail Address	Jobs	Create a special email ID for alerts
Paging Configuration	Servers	AA	Add a paging server for your site

TABLE 7-7. *Email/Pager Configuration*

CHAPTER
8

Oracle Enterprise Manager for Database Administration

s seen in Chapter 7, OEM is a comprehensive platform for managing an enterprise. Oracle databases, Oracle Net Listeners, HTTP servers, and machines can be managed and monitored from OEM Console. In this chapter you will see how OEM can help DBAs perform end-to-end administration of Oracle databases.

The first half of this chapter matches common DBA tasks with OEM functions. Wizards in OEM perform most DBA functions. These wizards in turn issue a series of SQL commands to the database to perform the function requested. The second half of this chapter focuses on utilities and tools that help you monitor and improve the overall health of the database. Before beginning, take a quick look at what makes OEM a compelling tool for database administration.

Enterprise Manager Console for Database Administration

OEM Console and OEM Navigator were introduced in Chapter 7. Table 8-1 summarizes features of OEM Console that enable you to perform tasks quickly and easily.

Information on managing administrators, setting preferred credentials, and the like is included in Chapter 7, and so is not repeated here. Next you will see how specific DBA tasks are performed using OEM.

Feature	Comments/Description	Example/Illustration
Property sheets	Properties for the selected object in Navigator are shown in the Detail pane.	Expand the folder Databases | Database SID | Security | Users | Scott in OEM Navigator to view user properties for the user SCOTT.
Column lists	Obtain a list of all objects of a certain type or category.	Expand the folder Databases | Database SID | Security | Users to view a list of all database users in the Detail pane.

TABLE 8-1. *OEM Console Features for Database Administration*

Feature	Comments/Description	Example/Illustration
Changing order of lists	When viewing a column list, click any column header to sort the list in ascending or descending order based on values in that column.	Obtain a list of users on the database. Click the column head Username to obtain a list of users sorted in ascending order by name. Click the column head again to view the same list in descending order by name.
Context menus	Right-clicking a selected item displays a context-sensitive menu.	Expand the folder Databases	Database SID	Security/Users. Right-click the Users folder to obtain a context-sensitive menu for user management.
View data definition language (DDL)	View the DDL of an object.	Expand the folder Databases	Database SID	Schema	Table	Scott/EMP. The Detail pane shows the structure of the EMP table.
View associated objects	Obtain a list of database objects associated with a given object, for example, a list of indexes associated with a table.	Expand the folder Databases	Database SID	Schema/Table	Scott	EMP. The Navigator shows the PK_EMP index under the list of associated indexes.
Generate/hide SQL	Cut and paste SQL for actions performed in OEM and create SQL scripts.	Use Navigator to obtain the property sheet for the user SCOTT. In the Detail pane, type a new password for the user in the two password fields. Click the Show SQL button to view the text of the corresponding ALTER USER command. Click the Hide SQL button to hide the SQL text box.

TABLE 8-1.   *OEM Console Features for Database Administration* (continued)

Feature	Comments/Description	Example/Illustration
Search	Search for a specific object.	Select the Users folder. Choose Navigator | Find from the menu, enter the string SCO, and click OK. The user SCOTT is selected in Navigator.
General database information sheets	Provides general information on the database including name of node, OS and version, listener information, etc.	Expand the Databases folder and select an available database. The Detail pane displays general information on the database.
Quick help	Get an overview of functions and operations possible on the chosen folder.	Select the Security folder. The Detail pane gives you a quick overview of security management.
Online help	Context-sensitive help with F1.	View the property sheet for the user SCOTT. Select the Role tab in Detail pane and press F1 to view help on Privileges and Roles in the Help Topics window.
SQL logging	Obtain a SQL Log for your operations.	Choose Configuration | SQL Logging from the menu. Select the Enable SQL Logging check box. Create a table named TEST in the schema owned by the user SCOTT. Choose Configuration | View SQL Log from the menu. Click the Report icon to obtain an HTML report of the SQL used.

TABLE 8-1. *OEM Console Features for Database Administration* (continued)

Feature	Comments/Description	Example/Illustration
Cross-reference views	Obtain a list of objects organized in a variety of views.	Expand the folder Databases | Database SID | Storage | Tablespaces/Datafiles to view a list of all data files. The reverse information (the tablespace associated with a data file) can be obtained from the property sheet for the data file.
SQL history	Obtain a history of SQL statements issued by OEM Console. In contrast to the SQL logging feature, this feature shows the SQL issued by the OEM application itself.	Choose Navigator | Application SQL History from the menu.

TABLE 8-1.   *OEM Console Features for Database Administration* (continued)

Managing Database Security

Database-level security on Oracle databases is provided through users, roles, and profiles. Using a combination of these security features, you can authenticate users as well as control their access and the resources that they use on the database.

Users, roles, and profiles can inherit from other roles and profiles, meaning that new definitions can be created from existing definitions. Furthermore, roles can include other roles, and profiles can include other profiles.

Managing Users

User-level security entails that every database user session is authenticated with a user login and a password. The user information is stored within tables in the database catalog. A user wanting to create a session against the database is authenticated by the database itself. This means that the database must be open before new sessions can be established. Views are provided on top of tables in the catalog. DBAs can query these views to obtain helpful information on users.

The following tasks pertaining to user management can be performed:

- Creating a new user

- Deleting an existing user

- Changing a user's password

- Assigning and reassigning roles to a user

- Setting system- and object-level privileges

- Setting tablespace quotas for a user

- Assigning default and temporary tablespaces for a user

- Defining user proxies

To view the user property sheet, expand the Users folder in OEM Navigator and select the user. A sample is shown in Figure 8-1. Choose the appropriate tab and set the necessary properties for an existing user.

To create or delete a user, right-click the Users folder and pick the appropriate option from the context menu.

Managing Roles

Roles allow DBAs to manage a group of users conveniently. A database role is very similar to a role on operating systems such as Windows NT/2000 and UNIX. A database role is identified by a unique name and is assigned a set of rights and privileges on the database. A set of users can be clubbed together and assigned one or more roles. A user who is assigned the role automatically inherits the privileges assigned to the role. By redefining a role, a DBA can quickly modify the privileges that are assigned to a large community of users.

Information about a database role is stored within the database. You can assign more than one role to a user. The user can assume any role from the list of assigned roles in a session. The SET ROLE command can be used to switch from one role to another in the same session. Roles can also be protected by passwords. In this case, a user has to fulfill two levels of security checks: the first level to validate the user, the second level to assume a role. As with user authentication, roles can also be authenticated externally by the operating system. This allows you to match role names defined in the operating system with database roles.

The following SQL statement switches the user to a role named MYROLE.

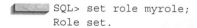

```
SQL> set role myrole;
Role set.
```

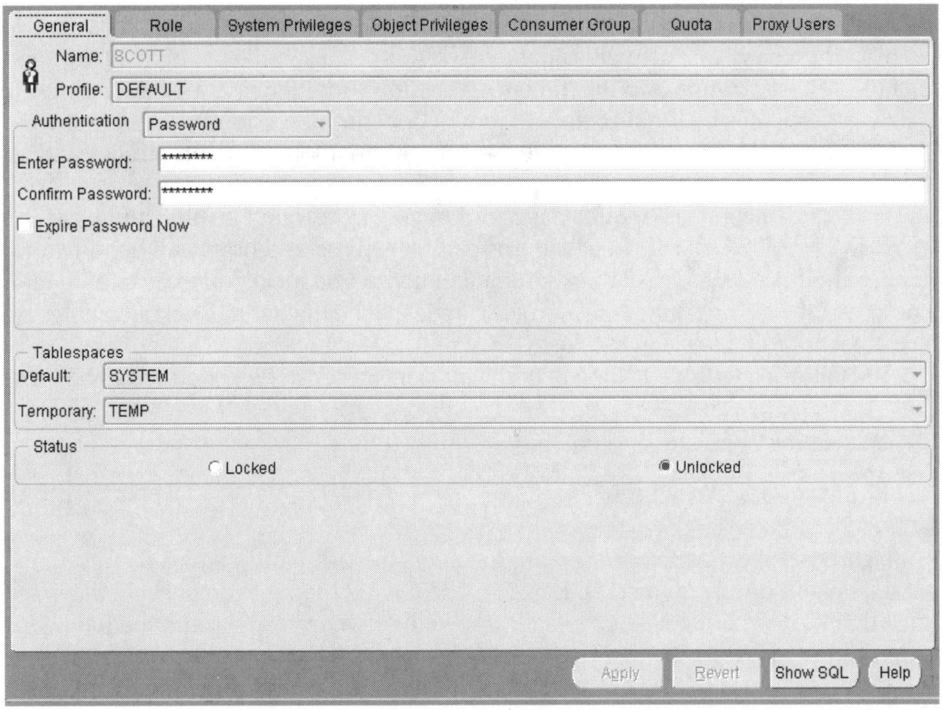

FIGURE 8-1. *Setting user properties*

You can query the DBA_ROLES view to obtain a complete list of precreated database roles.

The following tasks pertaining to role management can be performed with OEM:

■ Creating new roles

■ Removing roles

■ Assigning and modifying object and system privileges

■ Setting and unsetting role authentication

Expand the Role folder and choose a role to view its property sheet. You can modify the assigned privileges or set a password for an existing role. Right-click the Role folder and use the context menu to create a new role or delete a role.

Managing Profiles

Profiles allow DBAs to control the resources used by a database user. Limits can be placed on hardware as well as database resources. Examples of hardware limits include CPU utilization and idle time for a session. Additionally, a DBA can control database resources by limiting the number of concurrent sessions a user can create and the size of the PGA. Refer to Chapter 5 for more information on profiles and sample usage.

Profiles can also be used for password management. In a fashion similar to Windows NT/2000, database passwords can be expired and users can be forced to change their passwords. Database user accounts can be locked after a set number of unsuccessful login attempts. A set of rules can define the minimum level of complexity that a password must have.

The following tasks pertaining to profile management can be performed using OEM:

■ Setting hardware and database resource limits

■ Managing passwords

Figure 8-2 shows a sample screen that alters the password management scheme for the default profile (named DEFAULT). The password management scheme is set such that the account gets locked after three failed login attempts and the password expires in 60 days.

Complexity of Passwords   You can define the minimum level of complexity for user passwords. For example, you can set up the following minimum guidelines for a user password:

■ The password cannot match the Oracle username.

■ The password cannot be a common word. You can create a list of common words that are not permitted as passwords.

■ The password must have a minimum length of eight characters.

Passwords can be managed using a password verification function. A password verification function is like any other database function except that it is assigned to a profile. Use the following steps to configure password management:

1. Create a function to check the complexity of a password. You can use the sample function included in the file utlpwdmg.sql as a starting point. Like all other administration-related scripts, this file lives in the c:\oracle\ora90\rdbms\admin folder.

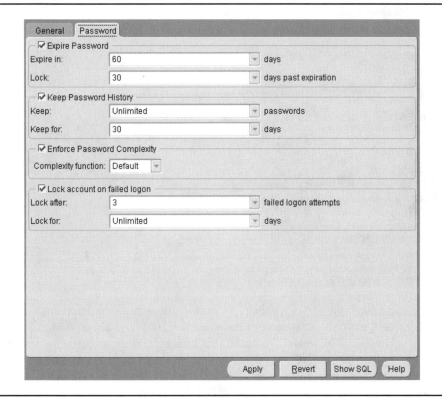

FIGURE 8-2. *Password management*

2. Create or alter an existing profile and assign the password verification function that you have created to the profile. Ensure that the Enforce Password Complexity property is selected in the profile property sheet. Alternatively, you can use the PASSWORD_VERIFY_FUNCTION clause of the CREATE PROFILE and ALTER PROFILE commands.

NOTE
The sample script utlpwdmg.sql alters the default profile. If you use this script, all existing users assigned the default profile have to adhere to the password rules that you have set.

3. Assign the profile to the user with the ALTER USER command.

The following sample session illustrates the effect of the password complexity function.

```
SQL> connect sys/aa as sysdba;
Connected.
SQL> @utlpwdmg.sql
Function created.
Profile altered.
SQL> alter user scott identified by abc;
alter user scott identified by abc
*
ERROR at line 1:
ORA-28003: password verification for the specified password failed
ORA-20002: Password length less than 4
SQL> alter user scott identified by welcome;
alter user scott identified by welcome
*
ERROR at line 1:
ORA-28003: password verification for the specified password failed
ORA-20002: Password too simple
```

Note that the password complexity function applies only to passwords that are set subsequent to enabling password management. If a user already has a poor password, it will not be tested. To avoid this situation, you can force the user to change the password. Of course, you should give them some time to do so! The new password rules apply when the user attempts to change the password. The following sample session illustrates this technique.

```
SQL> connect system/manager@aa
Connected.
SQL> ALTER PROFILE "DEFAULT" LIMIT PASSWORD_LIFE_TIME 7;
Profile altered.
SQL> CONNECT scott/tiger@aa
ERROR:
ORA-28002: the password will expire within 7 days
Connected.
SQL> ALTER USER SCOTT IDENTIFIED BY welcome;
ALTER USER SCOTT IDENTIFIED BY welcome
*
ERROR at line 1:
ORA-28003: password verification for the specified password failed
```

Note that the user SCOTT is allowed to create a session before a warning message referring to the password expiration is displayed.

Auditing Users

OEM can be used to track users connecting to the database. An event can be registered to monitor sessions of a specific user or a set of users.

Consider a situation in which you want to keep track of logins by the privileged user SYS. You can do so by using OEM to create an event, as follows:

I. Launch OEM Console and log on to the Management Server.

2. Choose Event | Create Event from the menu.

3. Specify a name and other settings for the event. Select the Tests tab and add the test Audit | User Audit.

4. Select the Parameters tab and modify the filter to include the SYS user (the default).

5. Select the Schedule tab and schedule the event.

Whenever someone connects as the user SYS to your database, an alert is generated. You can obtain information on the session from OEM Console. A sample screen is shown here:

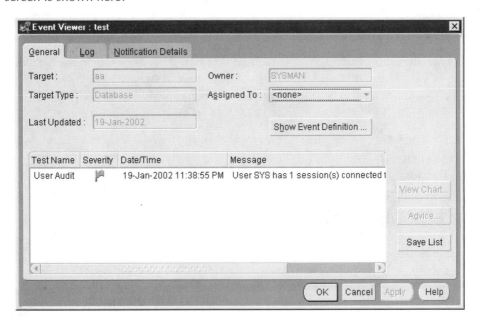

Oracle Server also includes an auditing feature that permits DBAs to monitor all activities against the database. Even though it is not within the realm of OEM, a brief discussion on this useful security feature is included here.

Auditing Database Activities

Oracle Server's auditing feature allows you to monitor database activity. Some of the actions that you can audit include the following:

- Database startup and shutdown

- Access with SYSDBA or SYSOPER privileges

- The database session identifier that is performing a task

- The operating system user and machine name accessing the database

- Name of the schema object accessed

- Whether a specific action failed or succeeded

A complete list of auditable operations can be obtained by querying the AUDIT_ACTIONS View. Oracle Server records a timestamp for all operations being audited. Auditing is enabled or disabled using the AUDIT_TRAIL initialization parameter. The audit information, called the *audit trail,* is logged in the database or to the Application Log. Table 8-2 summarizes the possible settings for this parameter.

On Windows NT/2000, you should choose to write the audit trail to the database. This is because the AUDIT_FILE_DEST parameter is not supported on Windows NT/2000. If you choose to write the audit trail to the operating system, the trail is written to the Application Log. On other operating systems, the audit trail is written to a file when you set AUDIT_TRAIL=OS.

CAUTION
The Application Log can grow very quickly if you choose to write the audit trail to the OS. You should increase the size of the Application Log using the properties dialog box in Event Viewer.

Setting for AUDIT_TRAIL Parameter	Description
NONE	Auditing disabled
DB	Audit trail is written to the SYS.AUD$ table
OS	Audit trail is written to Application Log; use Event Viewer to view Application Log

TABLE 8-2. *Initialization Parameter Settings for Auditing*

Once auditing is enabled, you can use the AUDIT command to specify a list of operations that you want to audit. Whenever a user performs an operation being audited, the audit trail is updated. You can query the data dictionary or see the log file to get the audit trail.

```
SQL> audit delete on scott.emp
  2  by access
  3  whenever successful;
Audit succeeded.
SQL> connect scott/tiger
Connected.
SQL> delete from emp where ename like 'K%';
1 row deleted.
SQL> commit;
Commit complete.
SQL> connect sys/aa as sysdba
Connected.
SQL> select sessionid, userid, to_char(timestamp#,'DD-MON-YY,HH:MI')
from aud$;
SESSIONID USERID                          TO_CHAR(TIMESTAMP#)
--------------- ------------------------------ ---------------
      287 SCOTT                           19-JAN-02,12:43
```

If you have enabled auditing to the operating system, the Application Log shows the audit trail. A separate entry is made for each database operation. A sample screen is shown in this illustration.

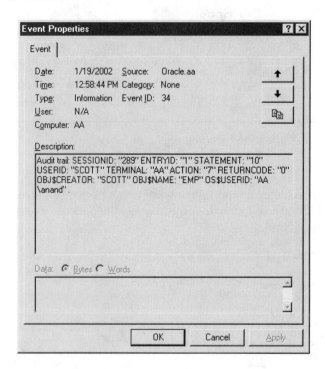

You must constantly monitor the AUD$ table and the Application Log to ensure that they do not get too big. Use the TRUNCATE command to clean up the AUD$ table and Event Viewer to clear the Application Log. Remember that database auditing is an expensive operation. Because of this you should enable auditing only if you suspect unauthorized activity on the database.

Schema Management

OEM can be used to manage database schema objects, including tables, views, clusters, indexes, partitioned tables and indexes, PL/SQL and Java subprograms, and materialized views. Schema objects can be created, dropped, and modified using simple property sheets and wizards.

Viewing Schema Objects

OEM Navigator provides a tree view of all schema objects organized by object type. Select an object type in the Navigator to view a listing of all objects of that type in the Detail pane. Expand the node for an object type to view a listing of database objects organized by schema. Select a specific object to view its property sheet. You can also obtain a tree view of schema objects by owners.

Schema Management Features of OEM

All operations on a schema object can be performed from OEM Console. In OEM Navigator, select an object and right-click it to view a context menu similar to that shown in Figure 8-3.

The context menu displayed in Figure 8-3 is available for table objects. The context menu for other objects differs to accommodate possible actions on the selected object. An overview of each menu item in the context menu shown in Figure 8-3 is provided to familiarize you with operations possible from context menu. You should be able to extend this information to other schema objects readily.

FIGURE 8-3.   *Operations on schema objects*

Creating Objects

The first two menu items can be used to create a new object. OEM provides two convenient methods of creating a new object. Use the Create option to define a new object from scratch. Alternately, use the Create Like option to create an object by deriving its definition from an existing object.

The Create option displays the Create Object screen. You can specify the object definition in this screen. The Create Like option displays a list of existing objects in the database. Pick an object from the list to create an object similar to it. At the very minimum, you must provide a new name for the object or create it in another schema to avoid name conflicts.

The Create Object Wizard is also included with OEM for creating objects. The third menu item in the context menu, Create Using Wizard, launches the wizard. You can create the object by following instructions provided by the wizard.

Viewing and Modifying Object Definitions

To modify an object definition, use the View | Details option in the context menu. In addition to viewing information on the object, you can change its storage definitions and enable or disable constraints.

Modifying Data

Data within some types of objects (such as tables) can be modified using OEM. Launch the Table Data Editor from the context menu and edit data directly. If you have experience with Microsoft Access, you will see that the interface is very similar.

You can also edit, compile, and save PL/SQL subprograms directly in OEM using the built-in editor.

Deleting Objects

To delete an object permanently from the database, select the Remove option. You will be provided an opportunity to confirm the deletion of the object. Use this option with caution becase a deleted object is permanently dropped from the database.

Viewing Dependencies

You can get a list of all dependencies on an object. Select the Show Dependencies option to get a list of all dependents on the object and object dependencies. The sample screen shown here displays the dependencies on the SCOTT.DEPT table.

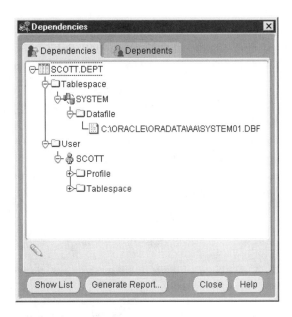

Granting Privileges

You can grant privileges on a schema object by choosing the Grant Privileges On option. A dialog box showing current privileges and additional possible privileges is displayed. You can add or remove assigned privileges.

Creating Synonyms

You can create synonyms (aliases) for schema objects by choosing the Create Synonym For option. Both private and public synonyms are possible. This is equivalent to the CREATE SYNONYM command in SQL.

Reorganizing Objects

You might want to move an object to another tablespace or resolve fragmentation issues. The Reorganize option launches the Reorg Wizard to help you with such tasks.

The Reorg Wizard is useful to resolve fragmentation issues relating to chained or migrated rows and indexes. A separate section on the Reorg Wizard is included later in this chapter.

Collecting Statistics

Oracle Server includes an analyze feature that can be used to collect statistics on certain objects. For example, you can estimate the average length of a row in a table. Use the analyze option in the context item to submit a job to analyze the selected object. Once an object has been analyzed, you can view statistics on the object from its property sheet. Figure 8-4 shows a sample screen with statistics on the SCOTT.DEPT table. This function is similar to the ANALYZE SCHEMA command in SQL.

NOTE
*The statistics on an object are populated after you have analyzed it. Until then the Statistics property page displays blank fields or zeroes. The statistics are updated only when you explicitly use the **analyze** command. Oracle Server does not maintain these statistics dynamically.*

Edit Table : SCOTT.DEPT - SYSTEM@aa					
General	Constraints	Storage	Options	Statistics	Constraints Storage

Last Analyzed:	20-JAN-2002 00:38
Empty Blocks:	0
Average Space:	0
Number of Rows:	4
Sample Size:	4
Average Row Length:	20
Continued Row Count:	0
Average Space Freelist Blks:	0
No. of Freelist Blks:	0

OK   Cancel   Apply   Show SQL   Help

FIGURE 8-4. *Statistics on a table*

PL/SQL Subprograms

You can use OEM to obtain the status of an existing PL/SQL stored procedure, function, package, or package body. Amongst other information, you can view the source for a PL/SQL subprogram and compile it from OEM. Editing is disabled for system procedures and packages since they are read-only.

Storage Management

Storage management is critical for a DBA. A DBA must constantly monitor and optimize storage for control files, redo log files, archive log files, data files, rollback segments, and tablespaces. OEM can be used conveniently to manage storage. A DBA can track storage and use the Jobs and Event systems to generate alerts when available space drops below a critical threshold value.

Tablespace Management

You can obtain complete information on tablespaces belonging to a database from OEM. Choose the Tablespaces node from the Storage folder of OEM's Navigator. The Detail pane displays a list of tablespaces, along with their current statuses and properties. You can graphically view the amount of space used along with the percentage of space used in the tablespace.

You can obtain the property sheet for a specific tablespace by choosing it in the Navigator. The property sheet displays information on the data files belonging to the tablespace as well as the current storage attributes. You can add or remove data files, take the tablespace offline, bring it online, and alter its storage parameters.

Expand the Tablespaces node further to view all the data files and rollback segments belonging to the tablespace.

Control File Information

OEM Console provides information on the database control files. Expand the Storage folder and select Control File to view all the control files belonging to the database. You can view the contents of the control file in a tabular form by selecting the Record Section tab in the control file property sheet.

Data File Information

Expand the Storage folder to view a listing of the data files. Select a data file from the list and to obtain its property sheet in the Detail pane. You can take a data file offline, bring it online, and change its storage characteristics from the associated property sheet.

Rollback Segments

Expand the Rollback Segments folder to obtain a list of rollback segments along with the number of extents allocated by them. A rollback segment can be brought on line or taken offline.

NOTE
Oracle recommends that you use the new Undo tablespace feature of Oracle9i instead of rollback segments.

Redo Log Groups

Expand the Redo Log Groups folder to obtain a list of redo log groups. All conceivable tasks to manage redo log groups can be performed from OEM. You can add or remove redo log groups and log members. You can switch the current log group and force a checkpoint.

Archive Logs

A list of archived log files can be displayed from OEM Console. The list provides information on the archived log file including SCN (system change number) and timestamp information. The SCN and timestamp information is useful for point-in-time recovery.

Managing Instances

OEM is a one-stop tool for instance management. The important instance-management tasks that can be performed from OEM Console are discussed in the following sections.

Starting Up and Shutting Down a Database

Choose a database from the list of databases in OEM Console and expand the Instance folder. Choose Configuration in Navigator to view the current configuration of the instance in the Detail pane. A portion of the Detail pane is shown in Figure 8-5.

Note the five tabs in the property sheet. Choose the General tab. The current state of the database instance is displayed. If the database is open, you can select the Shutdown radio button and click the Apply button to shut down the database. If the database is currently closed, you can open it from the same page.

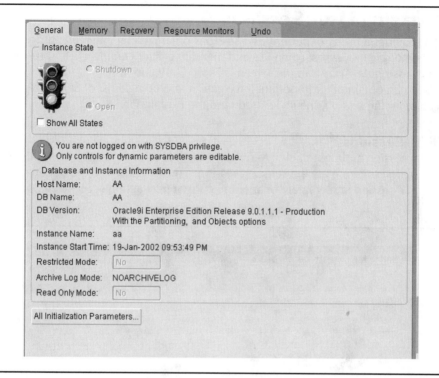

FIGURE 8-5. *Configuring an instance*

Viewing and Modifying Initialization Parameters

You can view the initialization parameters in effect by clicking Initialization Parameters. Many of the parameters can be modified here directly. The tabular view also indicates whether a parameter can be modified dynamically (without needing to restart the database). If you modify a static parameter and click Apply, OEM automatically brings up a dialog box to bounce the database.

Select the Memory tab to configure the SGA. You can set the size of the shared pool, buffer cache, Java pool, and large pool. You can also define the size of the sort area and the maximum number of concurrent users. All these settings are stored in the initialization file.

Archiving information is displayed if you select the Recovery tab. The Resource Monitors tab displays information on CPU resources and the average wait time to get CPU. The last tab provides a graphical view of how space has been used in the UNDO tablespace.

Managing User Sessions

OEM provides a listing of current user sessions organized by their CPU usages. You can reorganize this list based on I/O and memory usage. Double-click a session to obtain session details. A sample screen is shown in Figure 8-6.

You can obtain other important information, including a list of SQL statements executed in the session, the locks used, and the Explain Plan.

Killing Sessions

Select a session and right-click it to obtain the context menu. Select the Kill Session menu option to terminate the selected session. You will be given the option of killing the session immediately or after the current transaction is completed.

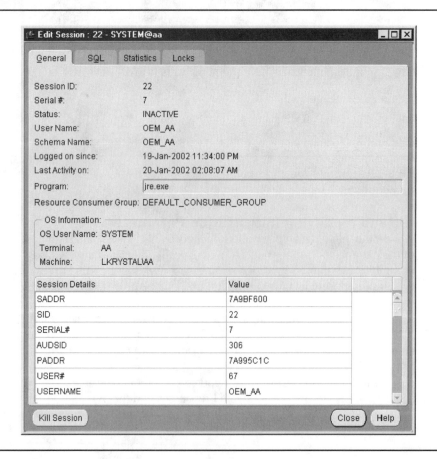

FIGURE 8-6. *Session information*

Managing In-Doubt Transactions

Pending commits in a distributed database configuration can be viewed here. You can obtain information on why the transaction failed and take suitable action.

Locks

Choose the Locks node to obtain a list of all the locks held by Oracle Server. A list of pending requests for locks can also be obtained by setting the appropriate filter. You can determine which process is holding the lock and use this information to take suitable action on the process.

Stored Configuration

Oftentimes, DBAs are presented a situation in which a database has to be started with special settings for initialization parameters. For example, at the end of a month you might need to run an application that requires a larger sort area. It can be cumbersome to maintain many initialization parameter files. The stored configuration feature allows you to save a set of initialization parameters as a named configuration in OEM repository. You can use a specific stored configuration to bring up the database. This feature is available only with the Management Server configuration of OEM.

Managing Resources with Resource Plans

Oracle9i Server includes a feature known as Resource Manager that can be used to control resources used by a database user. A typical example is a situation in which you want to ensure that DBAs get more CPU than a normal user. More information on resource management is provided in the next few sections.

Creating Consumer Groups

You can group a set of users who have similar resource needs into a consumer group. A consumer group is identified by a unique name. You can add database users or roles to a consumer group. In OEM Console, expand Databases | Database SID | Instance | Resource Consumer Groups to view existing consumer groups. You can modify or create new consumer groups. Resource plans can be assigned to the available consumer groups with resource plan schedule.

Resource Plans

You can create multilevel resource plans and specify how resources must be distributed for each resource plan. Again OEM Console can be used to view, create, and modify resource plans.

Resource Plan Schedule   Once you have created resource consumer groups and resource plans, you can build a resource plan schedule. The resource plan schedule simply assigns consumer groups to available resource plans at specified times.

The RESOUCE_LIMIT initialization parameter must be set to TRUE to enable Resource Manager.

A complete discussion on Resource Manager is beyond the scope of this book. Chapter 27 of *Database Administrator's Guide* in Oracle documentation provides complete information on Resource Plan Manager.

Backup and Recovery

Oracle Recovery Manager (RMAN) is integrated with OEM. The Jobs System is used to schedule backup and recovery tasks, which are then executed by Oracle Intelligent Agent. All features of RMAN can be used from OEM Console. These include the following:

- **Creating and managing a recovery catalog**   You can create a recovery catalog using OEM or use an existing recovery catalog. The recovery catalog must be in a separate database from the one being managed.

- **Taking backups**   OEM allows you to schedule full and incremental backups. Incremental backups are quicker since RMAN backs up only the database blocks modified since the previous backup. You can choose to back up specific tablespaces, data files, and archived log files.

- **Performing recovery**   Recovery is performed via the Recovery Wizard. Information in the recovery catalog is used to recover and restore lost portions of the database.

NOTE
Even though RMAN can be used to take backups of databases without a recovery catalog, this is not recommended. Throughout the discussion, assume that a recovery catalog is available.

Wizards are available to perform all tasks related to backup and recovery. To launch the required wizard, choose Tools | Database Wizards | Backup Management from the OEM menu. Alternatively, you can choose a target object for backup (a tablespace, data file, and so on), right-click it, and access the Backup Management menu.

The overall process for using OEM Backup Management features follows.

Step 1: Configure OEM for Management Server Mode   OEM must be used in Management Server mode to use all the wizards. The Jobs and Event systems must be configured properly. Refer to Chapter 7 for more information on these topics. SYSDBA credentials are necessary to use backup wizards.

Step 2: Configure TNSNAMES   The service names of the databases to be backed up must be included in the tnsnames.ora file. Chapter 6 provides information on configuring TNSNAMES.

Step 3: Create a Recovery Catalog   If you have chosen to create the default OEM repository using EMCA, a separate database to hold the OEM repository and the recovery catalog has already been created. If you chose to create the OEM repository using a custom method, you must ensure that the recovery catalog is created properly (see Chapter 5). A recovery catalog must reside in a separate database from the one being backed up. This ensures that the recovery catalog is available in a recovery situation.

Step 4: Create a Backup Configuration   A backup configuration provides necessary information for RMAN to take backups. To create a backup configuration, choose Tools | Database Wizards | Backup Management | Create Backup Configuration from OEM menu. Table 8-3 summarizes the information included in a backup configuration. The column named Example illustrates a backup configuration on the test installation. Click the Create button to create a backup configuration.

Element	Description/Comment	Example
Name	A backup configuration is identified by a unique name. Select the General tab to provide the information.	AA_BKP
Description	A description is optional; include information on the backup, for example, Backup of USER tablespace of database AA.	Backup of the USERS tablespace in AA database

TABLE 8-3.   *Elements of a Backup Configuration*

Element	Description/Comment	Example
Channel information	Choose to use a Backup Set or Image File copy; take the backup to a disk or a tape; provide a format for the filenames.	Select the Backup Set radio button Select Disk as the destination for the backup Channel Name—c1
Recovery Catalog	Information on how to access recovery catalog.	Choose to use a recovery catalog Username—RMAN Password—RMAN Service Name—RCV
Backup parameters	Define the size of the backup sets; it is recommended that you use the default.	Use default settings
Preferred credentials	SYSDBA privilege is required.	Set preferred credentials for the user SYS

TABLE 8-3.   *Elements of a Backup Configuration* (continued)

Step 5: Enable Archiving   The target database must be running in ARCHIVELOG mode. Follow these steps to ensure that archiving is enabled.

1. Choose the target database in OEM Navigator.

2. Expand the Configuration folder to view the current configuration of the target database.

3. In the Detail pane, select the General tab to view general information on the database. Verify that the database is running in ARCHIVELOG mode.

4. If archiving is not enabled, shut down the database using the IMMEDIATE option.

5. Mount the database. You might need to select the check box Show All States.

6. Select the Recovery tab and select the check box Archive Log Mode. It is recommended that you also enable Automatic Archival.

7. Select the General tab and open the database. OEM shows a confirmation dialog box before enabling archiving.

Step 6: Register the Database   You must register the database(s) being backed up in the recovery catalog. Use the Catalog Maintenance Wizard to register the target database in the recovery catalog. Choose Tools | Database Wizards | Backup Management | Catalog Maintenance to launch this wizard. Select the option to register the database and click OK.

NOTE
You can also resynchronize the catalog or reset the catalog using the Catalog Maintenance Wizard. Refer to RMAN documentation for more information on these topics.

Step 7: Schedule a Backup   Use the Backup Wizard to choose the objects that you want to back up. You can selectively back up tablespaces, data files, and archive logs. You can choose to back up the entire database. Launch the Backup Wizard from the Backup Maintenance menu. You are given two options:

- Use a predefined backup strategy.

- Customize the backup strategy. Select the option to use a predefined strategy to see a screen similar to the one shown here:

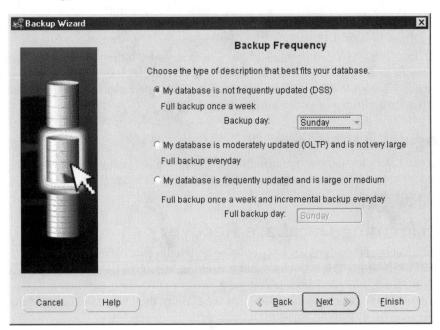

Select the options that best match your site. In the next screen, you can choose the time at which you want to start the backup. The wizard also allows you to choose a backup configuration and the target(s) that you want to include in the backup. Click the Finish button to schedule a backup job.

If you want to take partial backups of specific tablespaces, data files, and archive log files, create a custom backup strategy. The wizard guides you through a process that allows you to select the objects you want to back up.

CAUTION
The Backup Wizard submits a backup job to OEM's Jobs System. You should verify that a backup was completed successfully by viewing the job history in OEM Console.

Full versus Incremental Backups

The Backup Wizard allows you to take a full backup or an incremental backup of an object. A full backup includes all the database blocks belonging to the object. For example, if you take a full backup of a tablespace, all the database blocks in all the data files belonging to the tablespace are backed up. In contrast, an incremental backup takes a backup only of the database blocks that have changed since the previous backup. An incremental backup takes less space and time; however, recovery from an incremental backup takes longer since data contained in several backup sets is used in recovery.

You can create a comprehensive backup strategy by setting increment levels. Increment levels can be defined in the Backup Wizard, as seen in the sample screen shown in Figure 8-7. Refer to Recovery Manager documentation for more information on creating an incremental backup strategy.

Logical Backups

You can take a logical backup using Data Manager. A logical backup uses the SQL layer to take a consistent image of an object. Data Manager is discussed later in this chapter.

Performing Database Recovery

OEM's Recovery Wizard can be used to recover tablespaces and data files or the entire database itself. It is obvious that a valid backup must be available for this to work properly. The recovery catalog must also contain information on the target database. The Recovery Manager Wizard is a GUI for the Oracle Recovery Manager.

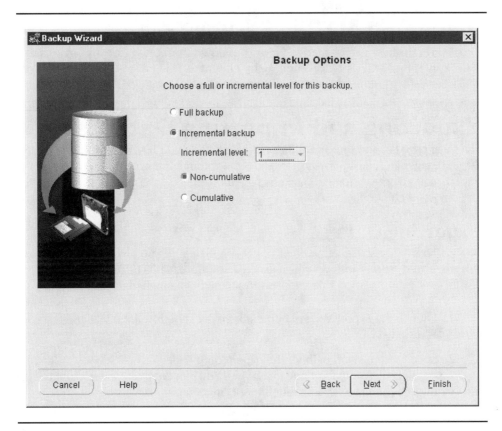

FIGURE 8-7.   *Backup options*

Launch the Recovery Wizard from the Backup Management menu to perform a recovery. The Recovery Wizard guides you through the recovery process. You can choose to recover a specific tablespace or data file. If you want to recover the entire database, the database must be in a mounted state. You should schedule a backup soon after performing the recovery.

Viewing Listener Information

You can obtain the status of Oracle Net Listeners from OEM Console. In addition to this, you can start and stop a blackout for a chosen listener process. Blackouts are discussed in Chapter 7.

Managing HTTP Server

Oracle HTTP Server can be started up or shut down from OEM Console. You can also verify if the HTTP Server is running by pinging it. The current configuration of HTTP Server, including the UDP port being used, can be viewed.

Exporting and Importing Databases

The Oracle Export and Import utilities are integrated into OEM's Data Manager. Data Manager includes wizards that guide you through the process of export and import. You can create logical backups by exporting a database or specific schemas and objects within a database.

Exporting Data

Choose Tools | Database Wizards | Data Maintenance | Export to launch the Export Wizard. The wizard guides you through the export process. The following steps illustrate an export session that exports the schema of a single database user.

1. Launch the Export Wizard and click the Next button if the Welcome screen is displayed.

2. Specify the file and path for the export (dump) file. You can choose to create multiple files instead of one export file. You can configure the maximum size of each dump file and provide file specifications for the files.

3. On the next screen, choose the option to export a user.

4. On the next screen, you can select the options to export grants, constraints, and indexes. You can also choose to export the object definitions without exporting the data by clearing the Rows of Table Data check box.

5. Click the Advanced button to specify a location for the export log file.

6. In the next screen, you can schedule the export job. The export job can be run once, or it can be scheduled to run repeatedly at chosen intervals.

7. Confirm the options that you have chosen and click Finish to submit the export job. Be sure to monitor the job and verify that it was executed successfully.

Importing Data

You can import data into a target database using Data Manager. Launch the Import Wizard from the Data Maintenance Menu and follow the steps recommended. Again the SQL layer is used to import data. If you are importing large amounts of data, you must enable the COMMIT option to avoid rapid growth of rollback segments.

When to Use Export and Import
You should use Export and Import utilities in the following situations:

■ **Compress extents**   If a schema object has allocated several extents, you can use Export and Import to compress the object into one extent. To compress an object into one extent, click the Advanced options button in the Export Wizard, select the Tuning tab, and select the radio button Merge Extents for Import.

■ **Logical backups**   Export can be used to take a logical backup. A logical backup can provide benefits in some recovery situations. For example, an export file of a specific table can be used to recover from a situation in which the table was dropped accidentally.

■ **Migration**   The export file created by Export utility is platform independent. An export file created on one operating system can be imported into an Oracle database on another operating system. Generally, you can import a dump file created on the same or earlier version of Export.

■ **Checking database blocks for corruption**   Export performs checks on each database block and each row to ensure that it is not corrupted before exporting it. This is a useful feature of Export to check for database corruption. The DBVERIFY utility (dbv.exe) can also be used to check the condition of data files.

Loading Data
Data Manager in OEM provides a GUI to the SQL*Loader utility. With this utility, you can load external data from files into an Oracle database. The Jobs System performs the load operation as per instructions in a control file (this control file pertains to SQL*Loader and is not the same as the database control file). The control file includes information on the data source and the tables into which the data must be loaded. The table(s) into which the data needs to be loaded can be preexisting or can be created with DDL commands included within the control file. The data to be loaded can exist in a separate file or can be part of the control file itself (inline).

A brief example illustrates the use of Data Manager for loading external data.

I. Verify that the sample files listed in Table 8-4 exist in the folder c:\oracle\ora90\demo\schema\sales_history.

2. Run the four SQL scripts listed in Table 8-4 to create tables named Customers, Sales, Promotions, and Products in your test schema.

3. From OEM Console, launch the Load Wizard.

Name of File	Description
sh_cre.sql	Creates all the tables and indexes for the demo
sh_cust.ctl	Control file to load data into Customers table
sh_prod.ctl	Control file to load data into Products table
sh_sales.ctl	Control file to load data into Sales table
sh_promo.ctl	Control file to load data into Promotions table
sh_cust.dat	Data to be loaded into Customers table
sh_prod.dat	Data to be loaded into Products table
sh_sales.dat	Data to be loaded into Sales table
sh_promo.dat	Data to be loaded into Promotions table

TABLE 8-4. *Sample Files Used in Data Load Example*

4. Use the control file sh_cust.ctl as the input control file for appending data in the sh_cust.dat file to the CUSTOMERS table.

5. Select the option to load data from an external file. Specify sh_cust.dat as the file containing the data.

6. In the Job Information screen (the last screen of the wizard), be sure to override the preferred credentials and provide the user information for the owner of the tables.

7. Schedule the job to run once immediately. Submit the job.

8. Ensure that the job was executed successfully.

9. Repeat steps 3–8 for the Products, Sales, and Promotions tables.

   Data Manager can be used in three ways:

   ■ Conventional path

   ■ Direct path

   ■ Parallel load

You must pick a load method in the Load Wizard, as shown in Figure 8-8.

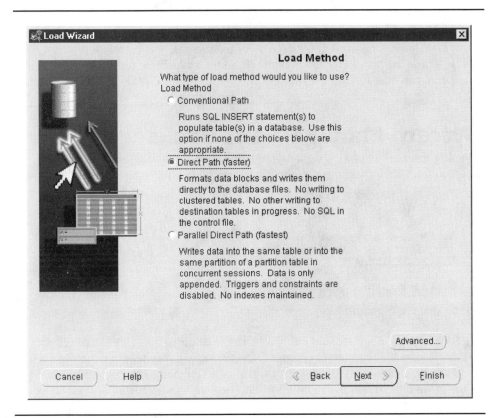

FIGURE 8-8. *Picking a load method*

The conventional method uses the SQL layer to load data using INSERT statements. This method is slow and cumbersome for large data sets since the size of the transaction is large. A large overhead in terms of redo and undo must be maintained for large transactions.

The direct path method writes data directly to database blocks and can provide performance benefits as compared to the conventional load method. You can use this method if no other process is writing to the same database blocks. This method cannot be used if your control file contains SQL statements since the SQL layer is not available.

The parallel method is the fastest of the three methods. Multiple processes are used to load data in parallel; however, it cannot be used to create indexes and enforce constraints since the processes are working asynchronously. Refer to Oracle documentation to get complete information on Data Manager options.

Other Features

OEM Console can be used to manage other features such as Oracle9i JVM, OLAP Services, and Workspace Management. These topics are beyond the scope of this book. You can refer to *Oracle Concepts, Java Developer's Guide,* and *Administrator's Guide* in Oracle documentation for more information.

System Management Packs

Oracle provides optional system management packs that can enhance OEM's functionality. These packs are automatically installed when you perform the default installation of Oracle9i Enterprise Edition. The following packs are discussed later in this chapter:

- Oracle Diagnostics Pack
- Oracle Tuning Pack
- Oracle Change Management Pack
- Oracle Standard Management Pack

Each of these packs consists of several applications. The applications can be launched from the Start menu or from OEM Console. Other features such as Event Tests can be used within OEM. DBAs can use these management packs to obtain a status of the Oracle system using OEM's GUI and then take appropriate corrective measures.

Oracle Diagnostics Pack

Oracle Diagnostics Pack consists of applications and event tests that can be used to diagnose problems. You can also obtain trends to help you plan for growth. Performance issues can be detected and corrected with Diagnostics Pack. The main components of Diagnostics Pack are discussed next.

Oracle Advanced Events

This component consists of advanced event tests that can be used to detect abnormal use of resources and performance issues. These tests can be used to detect problems before they become critical enough to impact the system. Threshold values are used to define critical boundaries for specific resources.

Oracle Advanced Events are available to monitor events on Oracle databases, listeners, nodes, and Microsoft SQL Server.

Database Event Tests   Database event tests are designed for use against Oracle databases. The event tests, along with examples of situations in which they can be used effectively, are summarized in Table 8-5.

Event Test	Description/Comment	Example
Audit management	Monitor database connections.	Track sessions created by the SYS user. An alert is raised whenever the user SYS logs in.
Performance management	Detect performance issues.	Track the percentage of sorts that are occurring in physical memory. Set a threshold value such that an alert is raised when more than 90% of the physical memory assigned for sorting is used. You can increase SORT_AREA_SIZE to resolve this issue.
Resource management	Track resources such as number of users.	Configure an event to generate an alert when 90% of your Oracle licenses are in use.
Fault management	Monitor critical Oracle Server problems.	Generate an alert when the archiver process hangs.
Space management	Track space issues.	Generate an alert when the archive destination is running out of space.
User SQL	Write your own SQL script to evaluate a specific condition.	Track the growth of the AUD$ table and generate an alert when the AUD$ has more than 100,000 rows; then back up the table before truncating it.

TABLE 8-5.   *Database Event Tests Included in Diagnostics Pack*

All the event tests described in Table 8-5 must be used within OEM's Event System. Create a new event or modify an existing event and add the appropriate event test(s).

Listener Event Tests   Listener event tests can check the status of a listener. You can use these tests in conjunction with a Fixit Job that restarts the listener if it goes down.

Microsoft SQL Server Event Test   This test is designed to test the status of Microsoft SQL Server. An alert can be generated if a target SQL Server is not running.

Node Event Test   Events on the target machine can be tracked using a node event test. These tests are typically used with third-party tools. For example, you can generate an alert if a user with administrator privileges logs in to Windows Console.

Oracle HTTP Server Test   This event test can be used to monitor the status of Oracle HTTP Server. A Fixit Job can be used to start an HTTP server if it is not running.

Oracle Performance Manager

Oracle Performance Manager is used to track the performance of databases, nodes, and web servers. You can configure Performance Manager to collect statistics on a specific target at regular time intervals. These statistics are used to generate performance reports in a text or graphical format. A variety of charts can be obtained on performance.

You can launch Performance Manager from the Start menu or the Tools menu of OEM. The Navigator shows a listing of objects that can be monitored. Select an object to get an overview of the statistics being recorded and the charts being displayed.

Click the Show Chart button in the Detail pane to view a chart. The displayed chart is automatically refreshed as per the refresh interval set. The following illustration shows a sample chart of the performance of Oracle HTTP Server on the test machine.

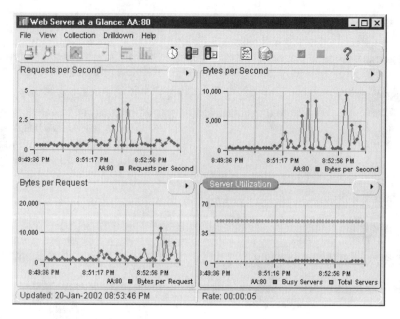

You can select the type of chart that you want from the View menu or the taskbar.

Oracle Capacity Planner

Performance Manager can be configured to collect historical data on the performance of a target database. This historical data is then used to identify trends that allow you to predict future resource requirements.

Choose Drilldown | Hist from the Performance Manager menu. If you see a warning dialog box that no historical data is available, choose to start data collection from a dialog box similar to the one shown here:

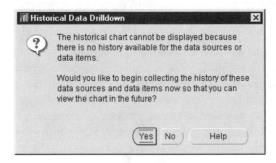

Historical data is periodically pushed into a history database. Once the history database is updated, you can obtain a graphical view of historical performance. The charts help you quickly identify performance bottlenecks due to resource problems. For example, if your HTTP server is busy a majority of the time, you might need to add another HTTP server to balance the load.

Oracle Top Sessions

Performance-related issues can often be tied to specific sessions against the database. Oracle Top Sessions can be used to obtain a listing of sessions that are using the database heavily. The algorithm used to choose these sessions takes into consideration a variety of database resources including sort areas, CPU usage, I/O, and the like. You can configure Top Sessions to display the top *n* (default is 10) sessions. You can set filters to restrict the report to parameters of your interest. Top Sessions provides a tabular output of resources used by the top sessions. The table can be displayed in a horizontal or vertical format.

Oracle Tuning Pack

Oracle Tuning Pack includes applications to help you tune all aspects of database performance. These applications can be useful in planning for space management and also performance. An overview of the applications is included next.

Index Tuning Wizard

It is critical to define proper indexes for efficient data retrieval from tables. Oftentimes, application developers create improper indexes for applications, and it is left to the DBA to determine whether those indexes are being efficiently used. In earlier versions of Oracle Server, the EXPLAIN PLAN command was used to understand how indexes were being used in a specific situation. Oracle9*i* includes an application called the Index Tuning Wizard that can be used to analyze how indexes are being used. The Index Tuning Wizard can even make recommendations on how tables can
be reindexed for better performance.

Select a target database that you want to analyze and launch the Index Tuning Wizard from the Tools menu. Choose to analyze a specific schema or analyze all schemas. Click the Generate button to start the index evaluation process. The progress of the evaluation is displayed, as shown in Figure 8-9.

After analyzing the specified schemas, the Index Tuning Wizard launches a report with recommendations on improving indexes. A SQL script is automatically generated. You can optionally run this script to implement the recommendations made by the Index Tuning Wizard.

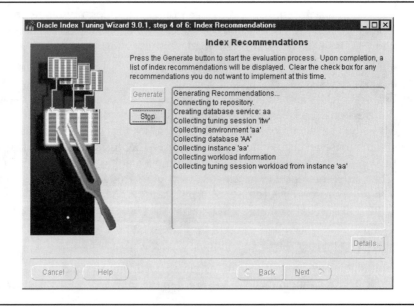

FIGURE 8-9. *Analyzing indexes*

Oracle Tablespace Map

Use this application to get a map of how segments are organized in a tablespace. The map provides an overview of extents allocated sequentially within a tablespace. A built-in Tablespace Analysis tool can be used to detect space management problems.

Launch Tablespace Map to obtain graphical information on how extents and segments are allocated within a tablespace. Once a tablespace map is generated, you can analyze the tablespace and obtain a report by choosing Tools | Tablespace Analysis. Statistics on row chaining, fragmentation, and space usage are provided in the report. The report can be viewed by choosing the Tablespace Analysis Report tab. A portion of the tablespace analysis report is shown in this illustration.

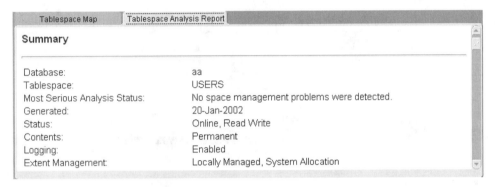

Oracle SQL Analyze

In earlier releases of Oracle Server, it was cumbersome to obtain information on how a SQL statement was being executed. It was difficult to analyze the access path being used and the indexes being used without having intimate knowledge of the schema. SQL Analyze is a utility that can help you quickly isolate the top SQL sessions and isolate performance bottlenecks in SQL statements. Specifically, its features allow you to

- Obtain a history of SQL statements that have been executed

- Obtain information on the execution plan used

- Analyze the SQL statements and obtain recommendations on how performance can be improved by modifying the same SQL statement

- Add hints to SQL statements

- Create virtual indexes to help you test if an index would help performance before actually creating the index

Launch SQL Analyze from the Tools menu and select TopSQL to obtain a listing of top SQL statements on the database. You can obtain a list of top SQL statements based on the number of parse calls or executions. A sample report is shown in Figure 8-10.

You can sort the report by any column in the report. The Explain Plan can be obtained from the SQL menu.

Reorg Wizard

Fragmentation issues can crop up over time in a tablespace. Schema objects can get fragmented, and rows can get chained or migrated to other blocks. Data retrieval

SQL Text	Parse Calls	Buffer Gets	Disk Reads	Executions
SELECT VALUE FROM NLS_INSTANCE_PARA...	54	119	17	54
select distinct SID from V$MYSTAT	53	62	11	53
select username,count(username),machine ...	262	63	6	131
SELECT BANNER FROM V$VERSION WHERE ...	39	65	5	39
SELECT ATTRIBUTE,SCOPE,NUMERIC_VALU...	13	110	3	13
INSERT INTO SMP_VDM_ADDRESS ...	3	284	2	61
UPDATE smp_vdm_session_notiftype_pair S...	5	1168	1	382
SELECT DISTINCT principal_name FROM smp_...	78	359	1	78
SELECT notification_type, last_notif_sequence ...	6	5630	0	469
SELECT notification_type, last_notif_sequence	367	1023	0	367
INSERT INTO SALES (PROD_ID,CUST_ID,TIM...	102	1820	0	102
SELECT notifications.sequence_num, notification...	102	1218	0	102
SELECT sequence_num, notification_type ...	6	739	0	102
SELECT COUNT(*) FROM smp_vdm_session_not...	5	129	0	43
DELETE FROM smp_vdm_notification WH...	5	1907	0	33
SELECT targetname,targettype,masid	18	54	0	18

Statistics | SQL Text

Name	Value
Sharable Memory	6588
Persistent Memory	624
Runtime Memory	2512
Sorts	0
Version Count	1
Loaded Versions	1
Open Versions	0
Users Opening	0
Executions	367
Users Executing	0
Loads	1
First Load Time	2002-01-20/11:48:25
Invalidations	0
Parse Calls	367
Disk Reads	0
Buffer Gets	1023
Rows Processed	2202
Command Type	3
Optimizer Mode	CHOOSE
Parsing User ID	67
Parsing Schema ID	67
Kept Versions	0
Address	7993A4E4

FIGURE 8-10. *Obtaining top SQL commands being executed*

can slow down considerably due to slower physical access. The Reorg Wizard can be used to reorganize data to resolve issues related to space usage. Specifically, it can be used to

■ Re-create tables, indexes, and other objects with optimal storage attributes

■ Repair migrated rows

■ Relocate objects to another tablespace

Because the Reorg Wizard physically moves data during reorganization, this is a very expensive operation and should be avoided during normal business hours. TheReorg Wizard provides a report on issues along with a script that can reorganize data. The script can be scheduled directly to the Job System for execution at a later time.

Outline Management

Execution plans can be stored in outlines and reused at a later time. Outlines are used to guarantee the stability of execution plans in quickly changing environments. The Oracle optimizer creates an execution plan based on statistics. These statistics might not be current for a database that has been reorganized. Stored outlines allow you to use an old execution plan. Outlines can be edited using Outline Editor in OEM.

Oracle Expert

Oracle Expert is an application that can recommend changes to your existing database for better performance. Oracle Expert collects performance statistics on the database and generates scripts that can be used to implement the suggested changes.

Launch Oracle Expert from the Tools menu and create a tuning session. Choose the scope for tuning. Oracle Expert collects only the statistics relevant to the defined scope. Samples are collected at regular intervals. You can define the intervals at which samples are collected. Oracle Expert uses the historical data to make tuning recommendations. These recommendations include changes for initialization parameter settings and hardware configuration changes. You can review these recommendations before applying the changes. Oracle Expert can be used to run the scripts to make the necessary changes.

Oracle Change Management Pack

A new feature available on Oracle9i allows you to track and make changes to database object definitions. You can compare two objects in different schemas or different databases. Changes can be tracked on the same object over time. You can compare the existing state of an object with a previous state called a *baseline*.

Creating a Baseline

A baseline captures the state of an object (a baseline can also be created on a set of objects, a schema, or the entire database) at a specific point in time. A baseline is associated with a timestamp. You can select an object and create a baseline for that object from the context menu.

Comparing a Baseline

You can compare the existing version of an object with an available baseline. By doing so, you can get a summary of changes made to the object since creating the baseline.

Comparing Objects across Schemas and Databases

Change Manager allows you to compare two objects belonging to different schemas within the same database or two objects residing in separate tablespaces.

A simple example illustrates Change Manager. Consider a situation in which you have to compare a schema between two databases. You want to quickly pinpoint any differences in definitions of schema objects. Change Manager can help you in this situation.

Launch the Change Manager Wizard and follow the instructions. Choose the schema and the database that you want to compare. Change Manager analyzes all the schema objects and provides you with a report on the comparison, as illustrated here.

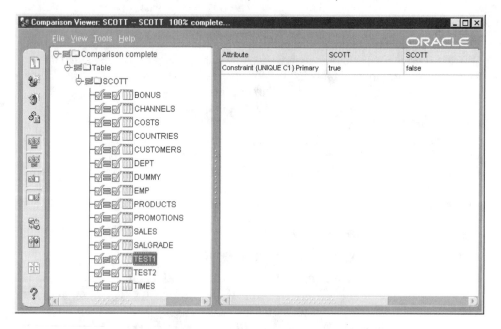

It is clear that all objects except the table named TEST1 are equal to each other (note the green equal signs). The difference in the definition of TEST1 on the two databases is also reported. In this case, the difference between the two objects is a constraint definition.

Oracle Standard Management Pack

The Oracle Standard Management pack can be optionally installed on Oracle9i Standard Edition. These tools can be used to monitor, diagnose, and tune your Oracle9i database. A lengthy description of these tools is not included here since many of them have already been described earlier in this chapter. Table 8-6 summarizes the tools available with Standard Management Pack.

Chapters 7 and 8 provided comprehensive coverage of Oracle Enterprise Manager. It is clear that OEM is an administration tool that can be used to manage a variety of services on your site locally and remotely.

Tool/Utility	Description
Oracle Performance Manager	Obtain a variety of performance charts
Oracle Index Tuning Wizard	Optimize your indexes
Oracle Change Manager	For change management
Oracle Compare Database Objects	Compare objects in two schemas
Oracle Top Sessions	Identify top sessions on the database
Oracle Create Baseline and Baseline Viewer	To create and view baselines

TABLE 8-6. *Tools with Standard Management Pack*

CHAPTER
9

Oracle9i Application
Server Basics

racle's three-tier architecture is designed to meet the special requirements of e-business. The three-tier architecture comprises a thin client, middleware, and database layer. The thin client, typically a web browser, provides an interface to applications that are spread across the network. The middleware manages all the complexity required by client applications, while the data is managed in the third layer. Figure 9-1 provides a schematic diagram of this architecture.

This chapter introduces the Oracle9i Application Server and related components. A step-by-step installation of Oracle9i Application Server (Standard Edition), along with the Oracle Portal component, is performed. Advanced components such as Internet File System, Database Cache, and Web Cache are covered in Chapter 10.

The installation of Oracle9i Application Server (versions 1.0.2.x) on the Windows NT/2000 platform has pending issues with Oracle. The standard installation process does not work against Oracle9i databases. This chapter also discusses the workarounds necessary to use Oracle9i Application Server against Oracle9i databases.

Introduction to Oracle9i Application Server

Oracle9i Application Server (9iAS) is a scalable, reliable, and secure middleware that is designed specially for e-business. It is an integral part of Oracle's Internet product

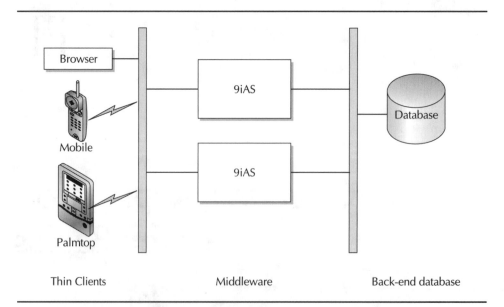

FIGURE 9-1. *Three-tier architecture*

suite. All the application logic resides in the middleware, and data storage services are provided by Oracle databases. Some of the important features of 9iAS are

- **Content delivery for the Web** The Oracle HTTP Server component of 9iAS delivers static as well as dynamic content to a web browser. The Oracle HTTP Server is a variant of the popular Apache HTTP Server from the Apache Software Foundation.[1] Earlier versions of Oracle Application Servers bundled a web server from Oracle, but starting with Oracle9i, Oracle has chosen to license Apache's HTTP Server and has discontinued its own web server. Oracle has added extensions to the standard Apache HTTP Server (version 1.3.x) to support SSL, PL/SQL, Perl, and servlets. Table 9-1 provides information on these extensions.

- **Transaction support** Content can be manipulated with applications written in Java, PL/SQL, or Oracle Forms. Full transactional support for applications written with these technologies is available, meaning that failed transactions from web applications are automatically rolled back.

- **Integrated database support** 9iAS is tightly coupled with Oracle8i/9i databases. Applications can access Oracle databases over Oracle Call Interface (OCI), SQLJ, or Java database connectivity (JDBC). The early releases of 9iAS were certified only against Oracle8i (version 8.1.7), but the latest releases (1.0.2.1.0 and 1.0.2.2.2) are certified against Oracle9i.[2]

- **Integrated portal** 9iAS includes the Oracle Portal component that can be used to consolidate content into customized portals with *portlets*. A portlet is a piece of information that is registered with Oracle Portal and can be placed within a region on a web page. Oracle Portal-to-Go can deliver content to mobile devices. Oracle Portal was called Oracle WebDB in earlier versions of Oracle Application Server.

- **Simple management** Oracle Enterprise Manager can be used to manage end-to-end services in a three-tier architecture. OEM Console can be used to manage Oracle HTTP Server as well as the origin database. The origin database holds the objects for 9iAS components, such as Oracle Portal and Oracle Internet File System, and acts as the primary storage for data.

- **Integrated file-system services** Oracle Internet File System can be used to store files of any type. The files are presented in a single hierarchy and can be accessed from Windows Explorer, FTP, web browsers, and email. Installation and configuration of Internet File System are covered in Chapter 10.

---

[1] The Apache HTTP Server is estimated to run on 56 percent of the web sites today (source: http://www.apache.org).

[2] Source: http://metalink.oracle.com

■ **Superior security**   Oracle Advanced Security guarantees network and data security. In addition to the security features provided by Oracle Advanced Security in the database tier, Database Cache, Oracle JVM, and PL/SQL in the middle tier can take advantage of Oracle Advanced Security features. More information on security features is included in Chapter 11. Both RSA and DES are supported.[3]

Oracle9i Application Server Services

Several services are installed with 9iAS depending on the features that you install. These services are responsible for functions such as communication, content management, presentation, caching, and developer support. The services are illustrated in the block diagram in Figure 9-2 and are introduced next.

Communication Services

The Oracle HTTP Server and its modules provide communication services. The HTTP Server *listens* for incoming requests from clients and either services them directly or hands them off to one of the modules. Oracle has extended the capabilities of Apache HTTP Server with the additional modules listed in Table 9-1.

In addition to the Oracle extensions, other standard modules such as PHP[4] can also be configured.

Oracle Plug-in for Microsoft Internet Information Server

This plug-in allows you to make PL/SQL and Java requests to Oracle databases through IIS 4.0 and higher. The functionality provided by this plug-in is identical to that provided by the mod_plsql and mod_ose modules against Oracle HTTP Server. More information on this configuration is provided in Chapter 10.

Content Management Services

Oracle Internet File System (iFS) allows you to store files and other data such as email inside an Oracle database. Files stored in iFS appear like any other file system to users. Content management is easy because all data appears to be in a single hierarchy and

---

[3]   DES is a standard developed by the National Institute of Standards and Technology for data encryption. A 56-bit key is used to encrypt the data. While this standard is still used by many financial institutions, it is not considered unbreakable simply because today's fast computers can break the key with a brute-force approach; however, compared with RSA, it is fast and is considered sufficient for many applications. RSA (the acronym was derived from the inventors, Ron Rivest, Adi Shamir, and Leonard Adleman) was invented in 1977. It is a public-key cryptosystem that can be used for encryption and authentication. RSA is more secure but is slower. It is sufficiently fast with small-sized messages; however, for large amounts of data, many companies use both DES and RSA together. DES is used for encryption and RSA for authentication.

[4]   Visit http://www.php.net for more information.

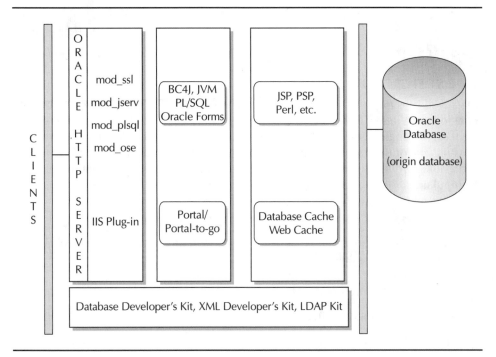

FIGURE 9-2.   *Services supported by Oracle9i Application Server*

Name of Module	Purpose/Description/Comments
mod_plsql	This module is responsible for PL/SQL subprograms.
mod_ssl	This module is required for secure HTTP requests over the Secure Sockets Layer (SSL). Port 443 is the default port for secure HTTP. Secure listener connections are possible with encryption via SSL. This is an extension to the standard SSL support provided by Apache HTTP Server.
mod_perl	A Perl interpreter is integrated into Oracle HTTP Server.
mod_jserv	Servlet requests are routed to the Apache JServ servlet engine by this module. Servlets across multiple zones can be shared.
mod_ose	This module manages session information and cookies.

TABLE 9-1.   *Extension modules for Oracle HTTP Server*

can be accessed from web browsers, Windows Network Neighborhood, FTP clients, or email clients. In addition to standard file operations, with iFS, version control and enhanced search are possible.

Presentation Services

Most web sites require dynamic content. PL/SQL Pages (PSP), JavaServer Pages (JSP), Oracle Forms, and CGI scripts can be used to create data-driven pages. The Apache JServ servlet engine handles servlet requests. JSP and PSP provide an extension to servlets. The only difference is that JSP uses Java and PSP uses PL/SQL. CGI scripts can also be written using the built-in Perl interpreter. Perl is convenient for text manipulation.

Application Development and Deployment

Data-driven applications can be developed with toolkits supplied with 9iAS. Three separate toolkits are available:

- Database Developer's Kit

- XML Developer's Kit

- LDAP Developer's Kit

Database Developer's Kit

Oracle's OCI and Java client libraries are part of the Database Developer's Kit. You can write native applications in C/C++, COBOL, FORTRAN, or Java and deploy them on the middle tier. Support for JDBC, SQLJ, and Java Message Service (JMS) is also provided.

Oracle Call Interface   Oracle Call Interface (OCI) is an application programming interface (API) that can be used to write native database applications in C/C++, COBOL, and FORTRAN. OCI libraries allow you to embed SQL statements within native code as well as manipulate Oracle data types. You can write callbacks in C from PL/SQL. These are called external procedures. Refer to *Oracle Call Interface Programmer's Guide* in Oracle documentation for additional information.

JDBC Support   JDBC API allows you access to Oracle databases from Java programs. Three kinds of JDBC drivers are available. You must choose a driver based on your application needs. Table 9-2 summarizes your JDBC choices.

   If you want to run your application against Oracle9i Server, the JDBC thin driver has some issues. You must obtain a patch from Oracle support to resolve these issues. For more information, refer to Note 146267.1 on http://metalink.oracle.com.

JDBC Driver	Comment/Description
Thin Driver	This driver is suitable for browser-based applications that need access to Oracle databases.
Server-Side Driver	Use this driver to execute Java applications within the Oracle Server using the internal JVM. Since the applications are running on the database server, no UI support (AWT and Swing components) is available.
OCI Driver	Use this driver to access Oracle OCI libraries on the client or in the middle tier. You can expect better performance, but since the OCI libraries are required, the applications will be larger.

TABLE 9-2. *JDBC Support in Oracle9i Application Server*

SQLJ   Oracle SQLJ is a preprocessor for SQL. It allows you to embed static SQL statements within Java programs. The preprocessor replaces any statements within your program containing a #SQL token with appropriate native Java calls. The program can then be executed via JDBC. SQLJ can be conveniently used to include static SQL in Java programs. In contrast, JDBC can be used for dynamic SQL, that is, you can prepare SQL statements and then execute them within your programs.

Oracle has been one of the primary supporters of SQLJ and is leading the initiative to make it an industry standard.

Java Message Service   Oracle's JMS extends Sun Microsystems' JMS by adding support for Advanced Queuing (AQ). AQ allows you to write workflow applications while taking advantage of Oracle's transaction support capabilities. *Oracle Application Developer's Guide – Advanced Queuing* in Oracle documentation provides complete information on the AQ feature.

XML Developer's Kit
Oracle XML Developer's Kit (XDK) is a set of libraries and utilities that allow you to enable your applications with XML. Four separate components are provided in the XDK:

- XML Parser for Java

- XML Class Generator for Java

- XSQL Servlet

- XML Transviewer JavaBeans

XML Parser for Java   This parser is used to parse XML documents and document type definitions (DTD) for use in Java applications.

XML Class Generator for Java   This component is used to generate Java source files from XML DTDs. This is a quick way to generate user interfaces for applications.

XSQL Servlet   SQL statements can be embedded within XML files and submitted to XSQL servlet. The servlet returns the data in XML so that it can directly be viewed in a web browser.

XML Transviewer JavaBeans   XML documents can be transformed and displayed through Java components to add a visual interface. For example, an XML document can be transformed to HTML by supplying an extensible stylesheet language (XSL) stylesheet.

LDAP Developer's Kit

This toolkit provides access to Oracle Internet Directory. Data stored within Oracle Internet Directory can be queried and modified with this API. Oracle Internet Directory (OID) is discussed in Chapter 10. A case study on enterprise security with OID is included in Chapter 12.

Portal Services

You can create a portal that consolidates all applications, business documents, and other URLs using Oracle Portal. In contrast to other portal development kits that require central administration, Oracle Portal allows you fine-grained access control. Users can manage their own areas on the portal.

Portal pages are composed of *portlets*. A portlet can be an application, a link, or any other stand-alone content. You can construct web pages by including portlets of your interest.

All content is stored inside an Oracle database and served by Oracle HTTP Server. Oracle Login Server manages authentication. Basic installation and configuration of Oracle Portal are discussed later in this chapter.

The Oracle Portal-to-Go component is used to deliver content to mobile devices. It isolates content acquisition from content delivery. An intermediate layer converts and delivers content in the target format of the mobile device. The supported target formats are

- Wireless Markup Language (WML)
- HTML
- Plain text

- Tiny HTML
- VoxML/Voice HTML

Caching Services

9iAS caching allows you to build scalable web sites. Two caches are available: Oracle Database Cache and Oracle Web Cache. These caches are available only with the Core and Enterprise editions. Database Cache is designed to cache frequently requested data from the database in the middle tier, thus improving performance. This reduces the load on the Oracle database and reduces roundtrips between the application server and database server.

Web Cache caches web pages that are served by Oracle HTTP Server. This improves performance for frequently used web pages. The size of the database and web caches is configurable.

Business Logic Services

These services support application logic in the middle tier. Both PL/SQL and Java are supported. PL/SQL packages are available to generate HTML pages using the PL/SQL engine. This is a convenient method of creating pages for PL/SQL savvy developers.

For Java developers, Oracle Business Components for Java is a portable environment for Java.[5] A JVM that supports Enterprise Java Beans, CORBA, and Java-stored procedures is included.

PL/SQL and Java modules can be moved from the middle tier to the database server or the client without need for further development.

Oracle Forms

Applications developed with Oracle Forms can be deployed using the Forms Services (previously called Forms Server). The forms applications are managed in the application layer while a Java applet in the client browser provides the UI. The applet is downloaded automatically from 9iAS to the client when a request is sent to Forms Services.

Content Creation

Static content in HTML pages can be served directly by Oracle HTTP Server. Dynamic content can be generated with a variety of technologies. You can pick one of these technologies to create data-driven pages:

- PL/SQL Server Pages
- JavaServer Pages

---

[5] 100 percent pure Java compliant

- CGI

- Perl

- Servlets

- XML

- Oracle Reports

Table 9-3 compares these technologies from the point of view of content creation.

Technology	Advantages	Typical Use	Comments/Additional Information
PL/SQL Pages (PSP)	*Separates application logic from presentation *Native to Oracle; easy integration with database *Manage code in PL/SQL packages *Security handled by database *PL/SQL is platform independent	Embed PL/SQL in HTML	*PL/SQL Web Toolkit makes formatting easy *Stored procedures once compiled are very fast in execution *Easy for experienced Oracle programmers *Deployed with mod_ plsql in middle tier.
Servlets	*Extensible with Java *Low resources requirements since JVM is shared *JDBC provides database access *Platform independent	For programmers who are savvy in Java	mod_jserv module is required to forward requests from HTTP Server to Apache JServ servlet engine.
JavaServer Pages (JSP)	*Combination of Java and HTML tags make presentation easy *XML and XSL support available *Java can be superior in situation manipulation	To reuse existing Java code	Requires mod_jserv module.

TABLE 9-3. *Comparing Technologies for Content Creation*

Technology	Advantages	Typical Use	Comments/Additional Information
CGI	*Combine data and presentation to return HTML pages *CGI can be written in a variety of languages including C/C++, Perl, etc.	For programmers who have experience with CGI	Requires mod_cgi module.
Perl	*Powerful text manipulation features *Perl interpreter is part of 9iAS	For programmers who have prior experience with Perl	Requires mod_perl module.
XML	*Emerging standard for formatted documents *Can merge data from multiple databases into one XML document	To create well-formed pages	Oracle XDK Kit provides extensive support for XML.
Oracle Reports	*Easy development with GUI *Output in Adobe Acrobat, XML, or HTML (CSS supported)	For programmers savvy with Oracle Reports	Reports servlet or web CGI required.

TABLE 9-3. *Comparing Technologies for Content Creation* (continued)

Oracle9i Application Server Editions

O9iAS is available in four different editions on the Windows NT/2000 platform:

- Core
- Minimal
- Standard
- Enterprise

The Core Edition is sufficient for sites that need to run Java applications. The Minimal Edition includes Oracle Portal and XML Developer's Kit. If you need transactional support, you must use either the Standard or Enterprise Edition. The database and web caches of Enterprise Edition are designed for sites with high traffic. The bundled components and features with these editions and the licensing requirements are summarized in Table 9-4.[6]

Component/Feature	Description/Comments	Availability
Database Cache	For caching frequently requested data from database	E
Web Cache	For caching frequently requested web pages	C, E
Forms Services	For Oracle Forms applications	E
Reports Services	For Oracle Reports applications	E
Oracle Portal	Portal component	M, S, E
Oracle Wireless Portal	For mobile devices	M, S, E
Discoverer	For analyzing data in a spreadsheet format	E
Containers for J2EE	Servlets, EJBs, and JSP	C
Advanced Security	Encryption, authentication, single signon, etc.	S, E
Enterprise Java Engine	100% pure Java for stored procedures, CORBA, etc.	S, E
Oracle HTTP Server	Apache HTTP Server extended with Oracle modules	C, S, M, E
Business Components for Java (BC4J)	Java compatible; XML applications	C, S, M, E
Management Server	Local and remote administration	E
Internet File System	For storing files in Oracle database	S, E
LDAP Kit	For directory services	M, S, E

TABLE 9-4.   *Oracle9i Application Server Components*

---

[6]   E: Enterprise Edition; S: Standard Edition; M: Minimal Edition; C: Core Edition.

Component/Feature	Description/Comments	Availability
Plug-in for Microsoft IIS	Access PL/SQL and Java components from IIS	S, E
Oracle XDK	XML-enabled applications	M, S, E
Database Client Developer's Kit	JDBC, JMS, and SQLJ	M, S, E

TABLE 9-4. *Oracle9i Application Server Components* (continued)

Additional components such as Oracle Workflow and Oracle9iAS Email are also available with version 1.0.2.2.2 of 9iAS. Refer to Oracle's web site for more information on these components.

NOTE
The plug-in for Microsoft IIS is not included with the Minimal Edition. This is an error in Oracle documentation.

Installation of Oracle9i Application Server

9iAS was released several months prior to Oracle9i Server; therefore, its early releases were certified against Oracle8i (8.1.7). Though 9iAS versions 1.0.2.1.0 and 1.0.2.2.0 have been certified against Oracle9i Server on the Windows NT/2000 platform, a few installation issues remain. A normal installation with Oracle Universal Installer against Oracle9i Server fails on the Windows NT/2000 platform. You must perform the installation with the workarounds described in this section.

Product Versions and Availability

The product versions that are available as this book goes to print are listed in Table 9-5. The installation procedures described in this chapter have been verified against these versions.

The product versions in Table 9-5 are available for download from http://technet.oracle.com.[7]

---

[7]   All Oracle software is available for evaluation purposes from this site upon free registration.

Product	Version
Oracle9i Server	9.0.1.1.1
Oracle9i Application Server	1.0.2.2.2

TABLE 9-5. *Available Product Versions*

Required Patches

The patches listed in Table 9-6 are required to complete an installation against an Oracle9i database. Be sure to download these patches for Windows NT/2000 from the Oracle support site (http://metalink.oracle.com) before commencing the installation.

System Requirements

O9iAS has the following hardware and software requirements:

- Intel 486, Pentium II or III (known Pentium 4 issues are described in the "Pentium 4 Installation" section later in this chapter), or equivalent CPU.

- Minimum RAM of 128MB.

- Disk space (NTFS)[8]

  - Minimal Edition: 600MB

  - Standard Edition: 2.25GB + 450MB for JVM database

  - Enterprise Edition: 3.1GB

- 500MB of free space in the SYSTEM tablespace of origin database.

- 200MB of free space in a user tablespace within the origin database.

NOTE
The database that holds all database objects for Oracle Portal and iFS is termed the origin database. *This is* not *the JVM database installed with the Standard Edition of 9iAS.*

---

[8] Assuming that Oracle database is installed on a separate machine

Product / Patch	Patch Number
Oracle8i Server 8.1.7.1.1 Patch	1711240
Oracle8i Server 8.1.7.1.5 Patch	1887405
Oracle Portal Patch 3.0.9.8.2	2104468

TABLE 9-6.   *Necessary Patches for Oracle9i Application Server*

- Internet Explorer or Netscape Navigator to test the installation.

- Microsoft Windows NT with SP5 or better or Windows 2000 with SP1. Oracle has not officially certified Windows XP on the certification matrix posted on http://metalink.oracle.com; however, 9iAS has been successfully installed on Windows XP Professional.

- Additional virtual memory of 360MB

- Microsoft patch for cmd.exe (Knowledge Base article Q268722) to fix an issue with the PATH environment variable.

- Patches described in Table 9-6.

Test Environment
9iAS was successfully installed in three separate configurations. These are described in Table 9-7.

Overview of the Installation
The installation of 9iAS must be performed after creating the origin database. The origin database holds the schema objects for the 9iAS components such as Oracle Portal and iFS. The origin database is typically created on a separate machine and must be accessible over Oracle Net Services. You can use Oracle8i or Oracle9i to hold the origin database. The Oracle Server patches are not required if you are using Oracle8i for an origin database.

You must also ensure that an Oracle HTTP Server is not installed on the machine on which you are installing 9iAS. Oracle 9iAS is installed with Oracle Universal Installer. At the end of the installation, Oracle Portal Configuration Assistant (OPCA) is automatically launched. OPCA is necessary to install the schema objects and PL/SQL packages in the origin database. Other components such as iFS can be configured post-installation.

Configuration	Description/Version	Comments
I	Pentium III, 256MB RAM, 10GB disk space, Windows NT 4.0 Server SP6a with Oracle9i Enterprise Edition (version 9.0.1.1.0) installed	Database Server.
	Pentium III, 256MB RAM, 8GB disk space, Windows NT 4.0 Server SP6a with Oracle9iAS Enterprise Edition (version 1.0.2.2.2)	Application Server.
II	Pentium III, 256MB RAM, 10GB disk space, Windows XP Professional with Oracle9i Standard Edition (version 9.0.1.1.0) and Oracle9i Application Server (version 1.0.2.2.2)	Database and Application Server on one machine; Standard Edition creates a separate database to hold the JVM.
III	Pentium III, 256MB RAM, 10GB disk space, Windows XP Professional with Oracle9i Application Server (version 1.0.2.2.2)	Application Server.
	Pentium III, 256MB RAM, 8GB disk space, Windows NT 4.0 Server SP6a with Oracle8i (version 8.1.7)	Database Server.

TABLE 9-7. *Test Environments for Oracle9i Application Server*

NOTE
*If you are using Oracle8i for your origin database, the installation procedure that is described in Oracle documentation is sufficient. The additional steps described here are required only if the origin database is on Oracle9i. The primary issue with Oracle9i is that the SYS user is required to use the **connect as SYSDBA** clause on Oracle9i. 9iAS installation attempts to connect to the origin database as the user SYS without this clause and therefore fails.*

Step-by-Step Installation of Oracle9i Application Server

A step-by-step installation of O9iAS using Configuration II of Table 9-7 is now performed.

Step 1: Complete System Requirements   The hardware and operating system requirements must be met prior to starting the installation. Log in to Windows with administrator privileges. To ensure that the system does not go into standby mode or hibernate during installation, disable the power settings as follows:

1. Right-click the Windows desktop and select Properties from the context menu.

2. Select the Screen Saver tab.

3. Click the Power button to change the power settings.

The complete installation requires more than five hours and will fail if the system goes into sleep mode during the installation.

Step 2: Set Operating System Environment   Ensure that the environment variables TMP and TEMP are pointing to a valid folder for temporary files. This folder must be located in a disk with sufficient free space. Also, set the following additional environment system variable:

```
NLS_LANG=.UTF8
```

To set an environment variable on Windows, perform the following steps:

1. From the Windows Control Panel, choose the System applet.

2. Select the Advanced tab and click Environment Settings.

3. In the System Variables section, set the options.

You can obtain a listing of the environment variables set on Windows by typing **set** in a command window.

Step 3: Verify Network Configuration   Ensure that your machine is configured properly for TCP/IP. You can use **ping** or **nslookup** to verify TCP/IP configuration.

```
C:\>nslookup aa.liqwidkrystal.com
Server:   calvin.liqwidkrystal.com
Address:  192.168.1.3
```

```
Name:    aa.liqwidkrystal.com
Address:  192.168.1.111
```

Step 4: Configure Browser   If you are using Internet Explorer as a client, you must perform these additional steps:

1. Launch Internet Explorer and choose Tools | Internet Options from the toolbar.

2. In the Temporary Internet Files section, click Settings.

3. Choose the setting Every Visit to the Page.

4. Click the Advanced tab. Check the selection Use HTTP 1.1 Through Proxy Connections.

Netscape Navigator does not require any changes. A sample screen for Internet Explorer configuration is shown here:

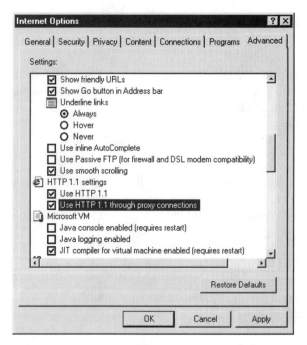

Step 5: Install Oracle9i Server   Perform a custom installation of Oracle9i Server from the distribution media using Oracle Universal Installer. Install the Oracle9i database and Oracle Net Services component. Do not install the Oracle Enterprise

Manager, Oracle9i Development Kit, or Oracle HTTP Server components. While OEM and Development Kit are not required, the Oracle HTTP Server component will conflict with the Oracle HTTP Server that is installed with 9iAS, so make sure that you have unchecked the Oracle HTTP Server component during installation.

In the test installation, Oracle9i Server is installed in the default Oracle Home named OraHome90 and the folder c:\oracle\ora90.

Step 6: Create Origin Database   Create an origin database and ensure that the following criteria are met:

- A user tablespace with 300MB free space is available. A tablespace named USERS has been created on the test installation.

- The SYSTEM tablespace has 500MB free space.

- A temporary tablespace with 20MB free space is available.

- At least one nonsystem rollback segment or undo tablespace exists. Query the DBA_ROLLBACK_SEGS view to verify the availability of rollback segments, as shown here:

```
SQL> select segment_name, status from dba_rollback_segs;
SYSTEM                          ONLINE
RBS0                            ONLINE
RBS1                            ONLINE
RBS2                            ONLINE
```

Additionally, set the following initialization parameters:

```
O7_DICTIONARY_ACCESSIBILITY = TRUE
PROCESSES = 200
DISPATCHERS = <null>
OPEN_CURSORS = 255
REMOTE_LOGIN_PASSWORDFILE = EXCLUSIVE
SHARED_POOL_SIZE = 125829120
JAVA_POOL_SIZE = 58720256
```

Be sure to set the sizes for the Shared Pool and the Java Pool in bytes. The installation will fail if you provide these settings in kilobytes or megabytes.

Database Cache component uses the REMOTE_LOGIN_PASSWORDFILE parameter. You can set it to either EXCLUSIVE or SHARED. If you set this parameter to SHARED, the password file can be shared by multiple databases; however, only the user SYS is allowed remote access.

The parameter has been set to EXCLUSIVE to ensure that other users with SYSDBA or SYSOPER privilege get remote access to the origin database. The origin database is named AA.

Step 7: Configure Oracle Net Services   Use Oracle Net Manager to configure the listener process and TNSNAMES for the origin database. The listener process must be configured to listen on a port other than 1521. You must also configure the listener and TNSNAMES for external procedures.

NOTE
If the database and 9iAS are installed on different machines, Net Listener can continue to use the default port of 1521; however, if you are using a single machine to house both 9iAS and the database, you must change the default port for Listener.

The name LISTENER_AA has been chosen for the listener process, and it has been configured to listen for connections on port 1526. The tnsnames.ora file has been configured with an appropriate connection identifier. The sample listener.ora is shown here for your reference.

```
SID_LIST_LISTENER_AA =
  (SID_LIST =
    (SID_DESC =
      (GLOBAL_DBNAME = aa)
      (ORACLE_HOME = C:\Oracle\ora90)
      (SID_NAME = aa)
    )
  )
SID_LIST_LISTENER =
  (SID_LIST =
    (SID_DESC =
      (SID_NAME = PLSExtProc)
      (ORACLE_HOME = C:\Oracle\ora90)
      (PROGRAM = extproc)
    )
    (SID_DESC =
      (GLOBAL_DBNAME = aa)
      (ORACLE_HOME = C:\Oracle\ora90)
      (SID_NAME = aa)
    )
  )
LISTENER_AA =
  (DESCRIPTION_LIST =
    (DESCRIPTION =
      (ADDRESS_LIST =
        (ADDRESS = (PROTOCOL = IPC)(KEY = EXTPROC1))
      )
      (ADDRESS_LIST =
```

```
        (ADDRESS = (PROTOCOL = TCP)(HOST = aa)(PORT = 1526))
    )
  )
)
```

Step 8: Verify Loopback Connection   Perform a loopback test to verify that the database and Net Services are configured properly. You must use the connect string to make the connection.

```
SQL> connect sys/change_on_install@aa as sysdba
Connected.
```

Step 9: Verify EXTPROC Configuration   Use the TNSPING utility to verify that Net Services are configured for external procedures.

```
C:\oracle\ora90\network\ADMIN> tnsping extproc_connection_data
TNS Ping Utility for 32-bit Windows: Version 9.0.1.1.1 -
Production on 27-JAN-20
02 14:07:13
Copyright (c) 1997 Oracle Corporation.  All rights reserved.
Used parameter files:
C:\Oracle\ora90\network\admin\sqlnet.ora
C:\oracle\ora90\network\ADMIN\tnsnames.ora
Used TNSNAMES adapter to resolve the alias
Attempting to contact (DESCRIPTION = (ADDRESS_LIST = (ADDRESS =
PROTOCOL = IPC)
(KEY = EXTPROC1))) (CONNECT_DATA = (SID = PLSExtProc)
(PRESENTATION = RO)))
OK (1080 msec)
```

Step 10: Shut Down Oracle Services   Shut down the origin database using SQLPlus. Use the Services Applet to shut down all the Oracle services running on your machine. Be sure to shut down the services for Oracle Intelligent Agent, Listener, and the database services. You can skip this step if the origin database is installed on another machine.

Step 11: Install Oracle9i Application Server   Install O9iAS by executing isetup.exe[9] from the distribution media. You must install 9iAS in a separate Oracle Home from the database.

During the installation, you are prompted to provide a variety of information. Table 9-8 summarizes this information for the sample installation.

---

[9]   If you are using a version of Oracle9i Application Server that is lower than 1.0.2.2.2, isetup.exe will fail. You must use the Oracle Universal Installer provided with Oracle9i Server and point the installer to the products.jar file in the stage folder of disk 1 to install earlier versions of 9iAS.

Screen	Field/Setting	Description	Sample Setting
Apache Listener Configuration for Oracle Portal	Portal DAD name	Database access descriptor is used to access the database.	portal30
	Portal schema name	Schema that owns Oracle Portal.	portal30
	TNS connect string	To access origin database.	aa
Wireless Edition Repository	Hostname	Name of database server.	aa
	Port	Port used by Net Listener.	1526
	SID	Origin database.	aa
Wireless Schema	Username	Owner of wireless schema; this user is created during the installation.	wireless
	Password	Password for wireless schema owner.	wireless
System Password for Wireless Schema	Password	Password for the DBA user named SYSTEM.	manager

TABLE 9-8. *Configuration Settings for Oracle9i Application Server*

9iAS Standard Edition was installed in a new Oracle Home named isuites in the folder c:\oracle\isuites. This is the default installation folder suggested by 9iAS.

CAUTION
Do not install 9iAS in the same Oracle Home as the origin database as it will overwrite binary files belonging to the origin database.

The installation process launches OPCA in the final stage of the installation. Abort the installation at this stage by clicking the Done button. A sample screen is shown here:

OPCA does not install properly at this point since it attempts to connect to the database as the user SYS (the user SYS can connect only as SYSDBA to Oracle9i databases). This is performed in step 16.

Step 12: Install Oracle Server Patch Version 8.1.7.1.1   Download Patch 1711240 from the Oracle support web site. Extract the file into an empty folder (you should obtain 259 files). Execute setup.exe from the folder named stage. Install this patch in the same Oracle Home as 9iAS (isuites in this example).

Step 13: Install Oracle Server Patch Version 8.1.7.1.5   Download Patch 1887405 from the Oracle support web site. Extract the files into an empty folder (you should obtain 532 files). Navigate to the folder named 81715, and copy the files classes111.zip and classes12.zip into the folder c:\oracle\isuites\jdbc\lib. These files exist from the previous installation, and you must overwrite them.

Step 14: Configure TNSNAMES Configuration for Application Server   The tnsnames.ora file for 9iAS must be configured to connect to the origin database. Use Net Configuration Assistant to configure this file. Alternatively, you can copy the database server's configuration file, as shown here:

```
C:\oracle\ora90\network\ADMIN> copy tnsnames.ora
c:\oracle\iSuites\network\admin
Overwrite c:\oracle\iSuites\network\admin\tnsnames.ora? (Yes/No/All): y
1 file(s) copied.
```

Step 15: Start Oracle Services and Database   Start up the Oracle services for Listener and Oracle9i Server. Open the origin database.

Step 16: Install Oracle Portal   In step 11, the configuration of Oracle Portal was aborted. This step can be completed now.

NOTE
If you are installing Oracle Portal against an Oracle8i database (version 8.1.7), you must use an additional workaround described in the "Known Issues with Oracle9i Application Server" section later in this chapter.

Launch OPCA from the Start menu (or execute c:\oracle\isuites\assistants\opca\ launch.bat) to see the Welcome screen. Choose the option to install Portal and Login Server, as shown in Figure 9-3.

In the following screens, you need to provide information to help create the Oracle Portal schema and Login Server. Table 9-8 summarizes the information that you must provide OPCA.

After screen 5, OPCA shows a warning dialog box, as shown in Figure 9-4. Choose Yes to overwrite the portal schema.

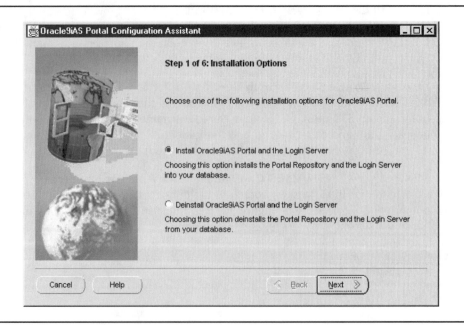

FIGURE 9-3. *Installation of Oracle Portal*

Step	Field	Setting for Test Installation
1 of 6	Install Oracle9iAS Portal and the Login Server	Choose this radio button.
2 of 6	SYS password	change_on_install
	Connect Information	aa:1526:aa
3 of 6	Portal Repository Schema	portal30
	Portal Repository DAD	portal30
4 of 6	Login Server Repository Schema	portal30_sso
	Login Server Repository DAD	portal30_sso
5 of 6	Default, Temporary, Document, and Logging Tablespace	Set the temporary tablespace to TEMP and the other tablespaces to USERS.
6 of 6	Complete Installation	Click the Finish button.

TABLE 9-9.   *Configuration Settings for Oracle Portal*

The installation of Oracle Portal takes more than 90 minutes. At times, it might appear that the installation has hung, but resist the temptation to abort.

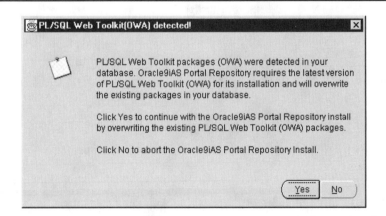

FIGURE 9-4.   *Overwriting Oracle Portal schema*

NOTE
You can query the V$SESSION view to keep track of the installation. Your installation process is running a SQLPlus session that is executing a batch of PL/SQL scripts with the .plb extension.

The installation log is written to a file named install.log in the folder c:\oracle\ isuites\assistants\opca. View this file in a text editor and ensure that there were no errors during the installation.

Step 17: Shut Down Oracle Services for Application Server   You must now install the O9iAS patch. To do so, you must shut down the Oracle services for 9iAS. Shut down the TNS Listener, HTTP Server, and any other services from the 9iAS installation. Leave the origin database and listener running.

Step 18: Install Oracle9iAS Patch   Extract the 3.0.9.8.2 patch for 9iAS into an empty folder. Execute setup.exe from the folder named stage and install the patch in the Oracle Home for 9iAS (isuites). You should see a warning dialog box, as shown here:

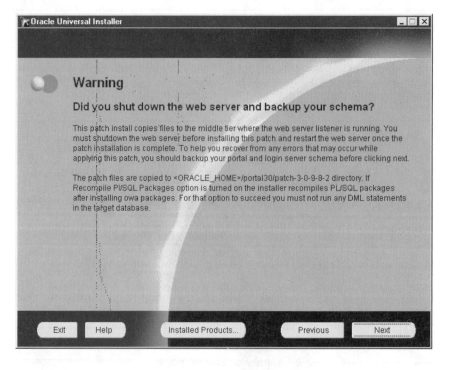

Click Next to select the components to be installed. Select all the listed components. Ensure that the check box for recompiling PL/SQL packages is checked. The upgrade should take 20–30 minutes.

Step 19: Verify the Installation   Launch your web browser and point it to a URL of the format *<machine>:<port>/pls/portal DAD*.[10] A portion of the page from the test installation at the URL http://aa/pls/portal30 is shown in Figure 9-5.

Known Issues with Oracle9i Application Server

There are some known issues with 9iAS. Some of these are documented in the product's README file, and some others are documented on the Oracle Support site and Oracle Bug Database. The main issues are documented here, along with the available patches and workarounds.

Pentium 4 Installation

Oracle9iAS versions 1.0.2.2.1 and lower cannot be installed on machines running Pentium 4. You must use version 1.0.2.2.2. The issue is documented in Note 136038.1 on the Oracle support web site.

Oracle Universal Installer

If you are using 9iAS 1.0.2.2.1 or lower, the Oracle Universal Installer included with 9iAS fails due to an incompatible JRE version. The workaround is to use OUI

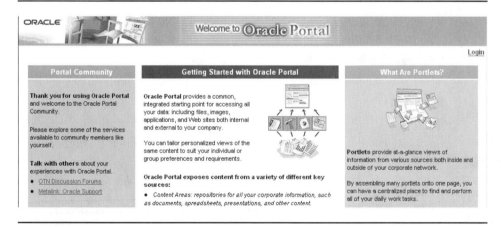

FIGURE 9-5.   *Oracle Portal home page*

---

[10]   database access descriptor

(version 2) that is included with Oracle9i Server to install 9iAS. Launch OUI from the Start menu and point the installer to the products.jar file in the folder named *stage* on disk1.

Patch for JDBC Thin Driver

If you are using JDBC thin driver, download Patch 1725012 from the Oracle support web site. On Windows, this patch is also included in RDBMS Patch Release 8.1.7.2.

OEM Console

Patch 2113802 is required for using the OEM Console bundled with 9iAS version 1.0.2.2.2 against Oracle8i/9i databases. Like other patches, this patch can be downloaded from the Oracle support site.

Oracle HTTP Server Port Conflict

You can configure the UDP port that Oracle HTTP Server listens on. Ideally, you should configure Oracle HTTP Server to listen on port 80, which is the default port for HTTP requests. If this port is already used (for example, by another web server), Oracle Universal Installer searches for the first free port, starting at 7777, and uses this port for Oracle HTTP Server. You can modify these settings later by editing the httpd.conf file. This file is located in the c:\oracle\isuites\Apache\Apache\conf folder of the test installation.

Oracle Portal Installation Against an Oracle8i Database

If you are planning to install Oracle Portal against an Oracle8i database (only version 8.1.7 or higher is supported), you must modify the launch.bat before running Oracle Portal Configuration Assistant. Edit the file from the c:\oracle\isuites\assistants\opca folder, changing the string from

```
USERS TEMP USERS USERS TRUE FALSE TRUE TRUE > install.log
```

to

```
USERS TEMP USERS USERS TRUE TRUE TRUE TRUE > install.log
```

The installation process is identical to that described earlier in this chapter for Oracle9i databases.

Patches for Oracle Enterprise Manager

The Oracle Enterprise Manager bundled with 9iAS requires additional patches. Install Patch 2113802 to use OEM against an Oracle8i/9i database on Windows NT/2000.

This chapter discussed the basic features and installation of Oracle9i Application Server. Chapter 10 looks at additional components such as iFS, Database and Web Cache, and administration.

CHAPTER
10

Oracle9i Application Server Additional Topics

n Chapter 9 you learned how to install Oracle9i Application Server (9iAS) on Windows NT/2000. Oracle9i Application Server has additional key features that meet a range of application and performance needs in production sites. For example, Oracle patented caching technology allows 9iAS to handle large amounts of traffic. The Oracle Internet File System (iFS) can be used to manage external files from multiple sources within a single hierarchy. This chapter shows you how to configure and use these components but does not delve into topics related to application development as these are beyond the scope of this book.

This chapter begins with caching technologies available with 9iAS. If you are planning to deploy large web sites on 9iAS, you must use the caching techniques described in this chapter. Without these, the performance of your site will be inadequate.

NOTE
Throughout this chapter, assume that Oracle9i Server is installed in the folder c:\oracle\ora90 and Oracle 9iAS is installed in c:\oracle\iSuites.

Oracle Database Cache

One of the main benefits of 9iAS over other application servers is that it is tightly integrated with Oracle databases. (Cold Fusion Application Server is a good example of an application server that provides database support.) Oracle Database Cache makes 9iAS more powerful and scalable for data retrieval functions. Database Cache, a component of 9iAS (Enterprise Edition), sits in the middle tier and caches frequently requested data from Oracle databases. Applications that predominantly need read-only data from an Oracle database can benefit greatly from Database Cache. Specifically, you should use Database Cache in the following situations:

- Your applications retrieve data from Oracle databases.

- The database and 9iAS are on separate machines.

- Your applications use the SQL or OCI layer. Applications that make OCI calls through ODBC/JDBC can also take advantage of Database Cache.

- Your applications predominantly require read-only views of data, and very few DML operations are conducted on tables.

Database Cache is installed in the middle tier with Oracle9i Application Server. If you have a three-tier architecture with multiple Oracle9i Application Servers, you can install multiple caches. If you are using a four-tier architecture in which the web servers are running separately from the application servers, Database Cache is installed on the application servers.

Huge performance benefits can be attained if your database or the network is heavily loaded. Database Cache is completely transparent to applications. Applications have no knowledge whether the data is being returned from Database Cache or the database itself.

From the application developer's perspective, it is useful to think of a database cache as a read-only database. In fact, Database Cache is implemented using Oracle database technology. The related database files, control files, and redo log files are stored in the c:\oracle\isuites\dbs folder.

How Database Cache Works

Database Cache is conceptually similar to other caching mechanisms except that it is designed specifically for caching data from Oracle databases. Frequently accessed data from the database can be found in the cache (termed a *hit*). Data that has never been requested (or is not used frequently) will not be available in the cache and must be retrieved from the database. This is considered a *miss.* As an administrator, your goal must be to maximize the ratio of hits to misses. Figure 10-1 provides a simple illustration of the architecture used by Database Cache.

As seen in Figure 10-1, Database Cache provides storage for data in the middle tier. When an application makes a request for the same data again, the SQL Analyzer retrieves the data from the cache instead of the database. If the data is not found in

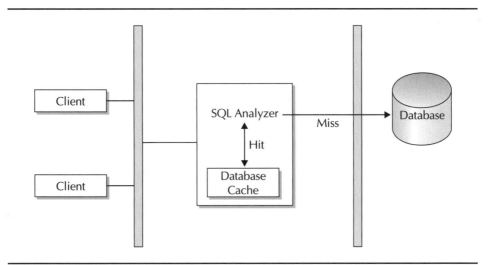

FIGURE 10-1. *Architecture using Database Cache*

the cache, the query is forwarded to the database server. Of course, there will be a performance hit when a query is issued for the very first time because of the overhead of copying data to the cache.

> **NOTE**
> *In the current release of Database Cache, you can cache only entire tables. Future releases are expected to permit caching of smaller data sets.*

An administrator can define the caching policies to improve the effectiveness of Database Cache (to increase hits). A caching policy provides a set of guidelines that Database Cache uses to cache tables. A typical set of policies would include the following steps.

Step 1: Define Synchronization Guidelines   A table can be refreshed on demand or at specified intervals. On-demand synchronization is useful when you know that a large number of changes have been made on a table (for example, after a load). If, on the other hand, data in a table changes infrequently or at specific times (say, at the end of the day), you can configure the cache to synchronize after a set time interval. Tables that grow quickly or change frequently are bad candidates for caching.

You can also choose to perform complete or incremental synchronization. Use the former in a situation where a large amount of changes have occurred on a table and you want to refresh the whole table in the cache. Incremental synchronization works best when small changes are made on the table.

Step 2: Define the Set of Tables That Are Cached   As a DBA, you can compile a list of tables that are good candidates for caching and cache them. You can monitor how well the cache is being used with OEM. Tables that are not being accessed frequently must be removed from Database Cache and replaced with frequently queried tables. Based on your needs you can monitor and set the size of the cache.

Synchronization can be managed using Oracle Enterprise Manager or with the DBMS_ICACHE package in PL/SQL as described later in this section.

Installation of Database Cache

In a three-tier architecture, Database Cache is created on the machine running 9iAS. Database Cache feature is installed with the Enterprise Edition of 9iAS. It is not available on other editions of 9iAS. During installation of 9iAS, you must choose the option to install Database Cache, as shown in this sample screen:

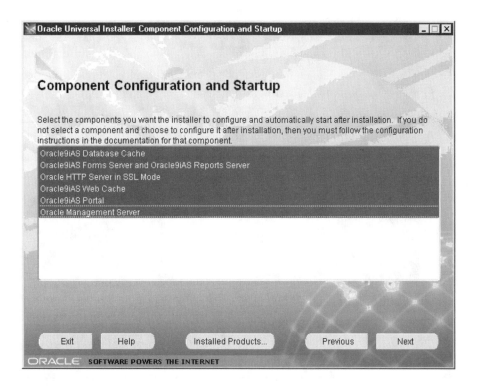

At the end of 9iAS installation, Oracle Universal Installer launches Database Cache Configuration Assistant. You must provide SYSDBA credentials on the origin database and the password for a Windows NT/2000 user that has the Log On As a Service privilege on Windows, as shown in Figure 10-2.

On Windows 2000 and XP, launch Administrative Tools and choose Local Security Policy | Local Policies | User Rights Assignment. Double-click the Log On As a Service policy and add the appropriate user to the list that is granted this right.

Database Cache Configuration Assistant creates a cache on disk. The default size of the cache in memory is 25MB on Windows NT/2000. Additionally, two services named OracleServiceiCache and OracleWTCiCache are created on Windows NT/2000 for Database Cache. You should set these services to start up automatically if you plan to use database caching permanently on your site.

Isolated Installation of Database Cache

Database Cache can also be installed after completing 9iAS installation. Execute wtacca.bat to launch Database Cache Configuration Assistant, and the wizard will guide you through the installation. You need to provide SYSDBA and Windows NT

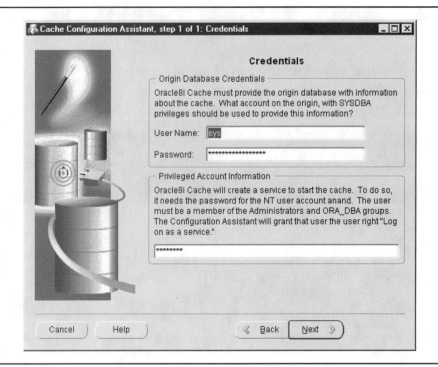

FIGURE 10-2. *Credentials for Database Cache*

credentials for the creation of the cache. You should see a progress dialog box similar to the one shown here:

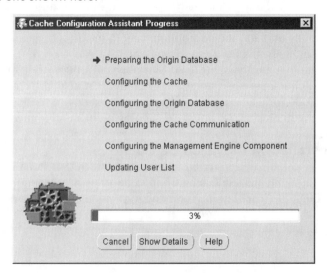

Database Cache uses a connection identifier named ORA_CACHE_ORIGIN to connect to the origin database. You must ensure that this identifier is configured in the tnsnames.ora before attempting to create a cache. A sample entry from the test installation is shown here:

```
ORA_ICACHE_ORIGIN =
  (DESCRIPTION =
    (ADDRESS_LIST =
      (ADDRESS = (PROTOCOL = TCP)(HOST = aa.liqwidkrystal.com)
(PORT =
1521))
    )
    (CONNECT_DATA =
      (SERVICE_NAME = aa.liqwidkrystal.com)
    )
  )
```

You can use the **tnsping** command to verify that this identifier is available.

```
C:\ > tnsping ora_icache_origin
TNS Ping Utility for 32-bit Windows: Version 8.1.7.0.0 - Production
on 04-FEB-2002 22:39:45
(c) Copyright 1997 Oracle Corporation.  All rights reserved.
Attempting to contact (ADDRESS=(PROTOCOL=TCP)(HOST=aa.liqwidkrystal.com)(PORT=1521))
OK (400 msec)
```

CAUTION
If your origin database is on Oracle8i, the SERVICE_NAME must be fully qualified with the database SID and DB_DOMAIN; otherwise, you will get a TNS-12514 error.

Configuration of Database Cache

Database Cache can be configured with Cache Manager or the DBMS_ICACHE package in PL/SQL. Cache Manager is included as part of OEM's DBA Studio. Choose Tools | Database Applications | DBA Studio from the OEM Console menu to launch DBA Studio. Expand the Caches folder to view the cache properties, as shown in Figure 10-3.

All cache settings are specified in the cache property sheet. Choose the General tab to start up and shut down caching. Use the Cached Tables tab to manage tables in cache and Cached PL/SQL to manage anonymous PL/SQL units in the cache.

You can also launch DBA Studio from the Start menu or by executing **oemapp.bat dbastudio** from the command line.

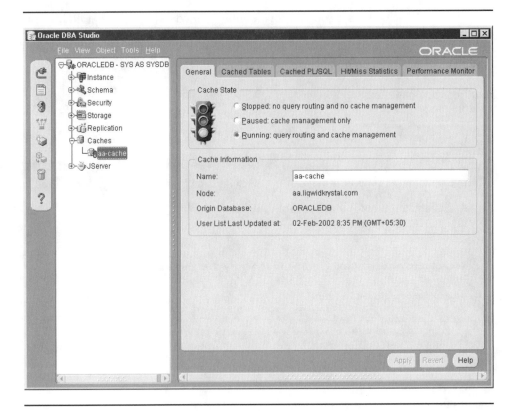

FIGURE 10-3. *Configuring Database Cache with Cache Manager*

NOTE
Oracle9i Application Server is bundled with
OEM Version 2.2.0 on Windows NT/2000.

Managing Tables in Database Cache

Select the Cached Tables tab in Cache Manager to view a list of tables currently in the cache. Click the + icon to add tables to the cache and the Wastebasket icon to remove a table from the cache. A sample screen is shown in Figure 10-4. Similarly, choose the Cached PL/SQL tab to manage PL/SQL blocks in the database cache.

Cache Manager shows you a progress dialog box as objects are being added to the cache. Click the Show Details button to view a report of the caching operation. A sample screen is shown in Figure 10-5.

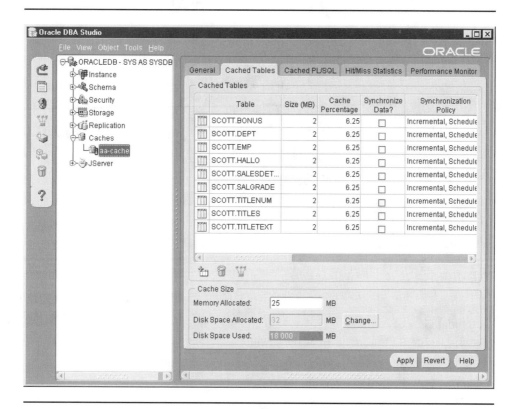

FIGURE 10-4. *Adding and removing tables from Database Cache*

Sizing Database Cache

As seen in Figure 10-4, you can view the amount of space allocated to Database Cache and the amount of memory in use from Cache Manager. Click the Change button to modify the cache settings.

Since the database cache uses Oracle database technology, you can expand the cache by increasing the size of an existing data file or by adding new data files.

Monitoring Database Cache

Your primary goal is to maximize the number of hits in Database Cache. You must ensure that the tables in the cache are chosen carefully. Cache Manager can be used to view statistics on the use of database cache. Choose the Hit/Miss Statistics tab to obtain information on hits and misses in the cache. You can also obtain a

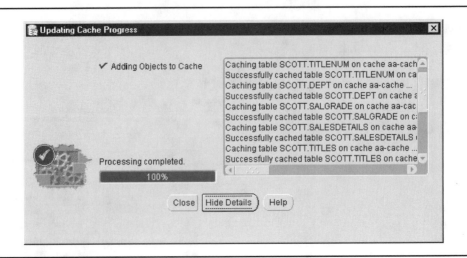

FIGURE 10-5. *Cache Manager report*

graphical view of cache performance by choosing the Performance Monitor tab. A variety of views on hits and misses are available as seen here:

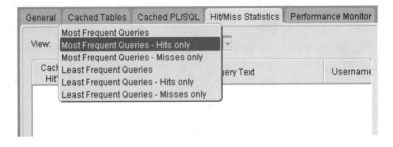

Setting Synchronization Policies

Selecting proper synchronization policies is critical to the effectiveness of the database cache. You must monitor the cached tables closely and ensure that the cache is synchronized frequently enough while avoiding unnecessary synchronization. Use the Cache Manager property sheet to specify a synchronization policy for a table. The sample screen here shows how objects are synchronized once every 24 hours.

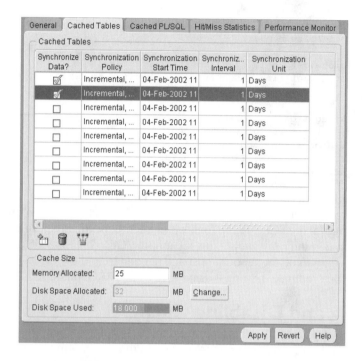

Managing Database Cache Using PL/SQL Package

When you install Database Cache, a package named DBMS_ICACHE is created in the cache. You can use this package to add and remove tables in the cache. Procedures for monitoring the cache and obtaining reports on the cache are also available.

To use the package, you must connect as a user with SYSDBA privilege to the cache. Once connected, you must first provide credentials to access the cache before performing an operation. The following sample session illustrates the use of this package.

```
SQL> connect sys/change_on_install@ora_icache as sysdba
Connected.
SQL> execute dbms_icache.set_origin_credentials('system','manager');
PL/SQL procedure successfully completed.
SQL> execute dbms_icache.sync_table('scott','dept');
PL/SQL procedure successfully completed.
SQL> execute dbms_icache.remove_table('scott','dept');
PL/SQL procedure successfully completed.
```

```
SQL> set serveroutput on
SQL> declare tabsize number;
  2  begin
  3  dbms_icache.get_table_size('scott','emp',tabsize);
  4  dbms_output.put_line ('Number of MB required in cache :'||tabsize);
  5  end;
  6  /
Number of MB required in cache :2
PL/SQL procedure successfully completed.
SQL> execute dbms_icache.add_table('scott', 'emp',
DBMS_ICACHE.SYNC_COMPLETE, TRUE, SYSDATE, 8 * 60 * 60);
PL/SQL procedure successfully completed.
```

In this sample session, the SET_ORIGIN_CREDENTIALS procedure has been used to provide the credentials necessary to connect to the cache. Then an on-demand synchronization of the SCOTT.DEPT table has been performed before removing it from the cache. In the latter part of the session, the GET_TABLE_SIZE procedure has been used to determine the amount of space needed to add the SCOTT.EMP table to the cache before finally adding it using the ADD_TABLE procedure.

Enabling and Disabling Cache

You can control whether queries are routed to the Database Cache or not. If the Database Cache is running, queries are routed to the cache else they are sent directly to the database. Choose the General tab and select the appropriate radio button from the Cache Manager dialog box in Figure 10-3. Note that you can route queries to the database temporarily while performing cache management functions.

Configuring Application Environment

Applications deployed in the middle tier can take advantage of Database Cache. In order for this to work, you must set the ORA_OCI_CACHE environment variable to 1. On Windows NT/2000, use the System applet in Control Panel to create a system variable named ORA_OCI_CACHE and set it to 1. To disable the use of cache, set this variable to 0.

Troubleshooting Database Cache

The performance of Database Cache can be monitored with Cache Manager. In addition, Database Cache writes to the Event Log. Use Windows Event Viewer to view the Application Log and find events for the source oracle.icache.

Like Oracle databases, Database Cache writes alerts to an ALERT.LOG file. Background trace files are also maintained. These files are maintained in a directory structure under the c:\oracle\isuites\admin\icache folder.

You have seen how Database Cache can be used to cache frequently used tables in the middle tier. Additionally, if your site has web pages that are frequently accessed, you can use Oracle Web Cache technology to improve performance.

Oracle Web Cache

Web Cache is a component that provides caching function for web pages. Unlike other web servers that can cache only static web pages, Oracle Web Cache is also capable of caching dynamic pages (JSP, PL/SQL Pages, servlets, and CGI) in the middle tier.

Oracle Web Cache sits in between the client and the Oracle HTTP Server. When an HTTP or HTTPS request arrives to Web Cache, it responds to the request if the data is available in its cache. If not, it forwards the request to the Oracle HTTP Server. Like Database Cache, a hit is recorded if the page is found in the cache; otherwise, it is deemed a miss. Oracle Web Cache provides the following benefits:

- **Scalability**   Web Cache allows Oracle HTTP Server to scale to several thousands of simultaneous requests. Network traffic is also reduced between application servers and database servers.

- **Better performance**   Performance benefits can be obtained since documents are stored in memory. Web Cache supports GZIP encoding. (Set the HTTP request header field to ACCEPT-ENCODING: GZIP.) Web browsers that support this compression format can benefit from this.

- **Reliability**   In a large site, you can configure several web servers. Web Cache can be configured for automatic fail-over and load-balancing. In the case that a web server goes down, Web Cache automatically directs requests to other available web servers. Additionally, Web Cache is also capable of distributing requests between available web servers.

- **Caching of static and dynamic content**   Oracle Web Cache can cache static content such as HTML and image files. In addition, it uses a set of rules to cache dynamic content generated with JSP, PL/SQL Server Pages, Java servlets, and the like. Content from the same URL with slight differences is automatically made available from the Web Cache. For example, the same URL might have a different version of a document that has small changes from the earlier version. Session information such as a personalized greeting is also cached. So, if your page has a welcome field such as *Welcome <user>*, Web Cache does not reload the whole page.

- **Invalidation feature**   A document in Oracle Web Cache can be invalidated. Invalidating a document forces Oracle Web Cache to refresh the document on the next request for that document. Oracle Web Cache Manager can be used to send an invalidate request to the Web Cache or to set an expiration time limit on a document. A web page containing stock market information or weather information would be a good candidate for this feature.

How Oracle Web Cache Works

Oracle Web Cache sits in front of the Oracle HTTP Server. When an HTTP request is sent to a web site, the request is sent to Web Cache. If the document is in a valid state in the cache, a hit is recorded and Web Cache sends a response to the client. If not, the request is sent to the Oracle HTTP Server and the response is routed through the cache back to the client. In this manner, the page is added to the cache.

Like Database Cache, you have complete control on what is cached and what is not in Web Cache. You must define cacheability rules for URLs that you want cached. Once these rules are configured, documents from these URLs are automatically cached. Cacheability rules are defined using Oracle Web Cache Manager.

Installation and Configuration of Oracle Web Cache

Oracle Web Cache is installed along with the Enterprise Edition of 9iAS. Three services related to Web Cache are created on Windows NT/2000 during the installation. You can control these services from the Services applet or by using the Web Cache Control utility.

Web Cache Control utility can be used to start up and shut down Web Cache services from the command line. The executable is named webcachectl.exe on Windows NT/2000. The following example obtains the status of the Web Cache services.

```
C:\>webcachectl status
OracleiSuitesWebCacheAdmin is not running.
OracleiSuitesWebCache is not running.
OracleiSuitesWebCacheMon is not running.
```

Use the START and STOP commands to start up and shut down services.

Oracle Web Cache Manager

Oracle Web Cache Manager is the primary tool to manage Oracle Web Caches. You can use this tool from a browser by pointing to a URL of the form *<host>:4000/ webcacheadmin*. The Web Cache Manager is configured to listen on port 4000. A sample screen from the test installation is shown in Figure 10-6.

On the main page, you can obtain a status of the Web Cache. You can also start up and shut down the cache from the main page.

The default administrator account for Web Cache Manager is named *administrator* with the password *administrator*. You must change these passwords as soon as possible.

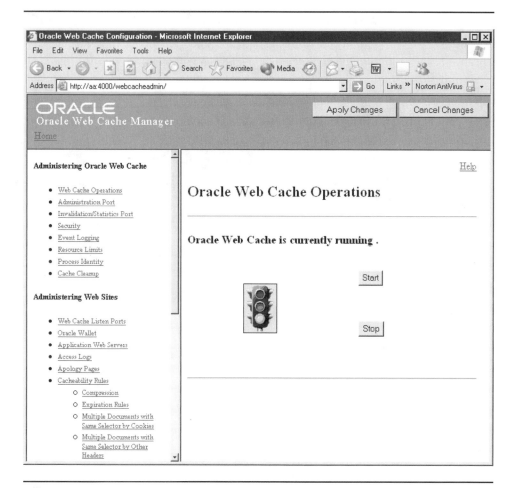

FIGURE 10-6. *Oracle Web Cache Manager screen*

Security settings for Web Cache can be specified from Web Cache Manager. Click the Security link on the main page to modify the security settings. Web Cache Manager can also be used to control access to web servers. You can specify specific subnets or IP addresses that are given or denied access to the Web Cache and, therefore, the web server. A sample screen that permits connection from a single machine named aa.liqwidkrystal.com is shown here:

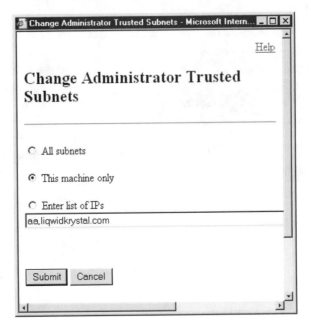

At the very minimum, you should complete the following tasks before using Web Cache in production:

1. Set the port numbers on which Web Cache listens for HTTP and HTTPS requests (port 80 and 443, by default).

2. Change the passwords for the special Web Cache users—administrator and invalidator.

3. Add web servers that will service requests. You must provide hostname and port information for each web server. You can also set capacity limits for a web server. Capacity limits are set as a percentage of the total capacity of all web servers configured for the Web Cache.

4. Specify cacheability rules (rules are specified using regular expressions).

5. Set thresholds for fail-over.

Additionally, you can enable logging and monitor performance from Web Cache Manager. Web Cache services must be restarted before changed settings can take effect. Refer to *Oracle9iAS Web Cache Administration and Deployment Guide* in Oracle documentation for more information on configuring Web Cache.

Troubleshooting Oracle Web Cache

In addition to the information provided by Web Cache Manager, additional log files are written to the c:\oracle\isuites\webcache\logs folder. On Windows NT/2000 additional warnings and alerts are written to the Application Log. Use Windows Event Viewer to view messages from the source named Oracle9iAS Web Cache.

Additional documentation and examples on Web Cache are available in the folder c:\oracle\isuites\webcache of your installation.

Oracle Internet File System

iFS provides a single repository for files within an Oracle database. Any type of file can be stored in the repository and made available to clients via common protocols such as File Transfer Protocol (FTP), Simple Mail Transfer Protocol (SMTP), IMAP, HTTP, Network File System (NFS), and Server Message Block (SMB). SMB is a file-sharing system that allows you to access files and other resources such as printers in Windows networks. SMB Protocol allows you to access iFS from Windows Explorer. Additionally, you can write custom Java applications that derive subclasses from the folder and file classes.

Internet File System Architecture

Internet File System has the notion of a domain for administrative purposes. A domain in iFS consists of a domain controller, a repository, and nodes. The domain controller allows you to start up and monitor nodes. Nodes are host machines that run iFS services and allow clients access to files in the repository. The iFS repository resides in an Oracle8i/9i database (Oracle Server Versions 8.1.7.2 and higher support iFS). Server applications running on nodes service requests from services. There are two kinds of server applications:

- Protocol servers

- Agents

Protocol servers provide support for the file transfer and network protocols while agents perform background functions such as garbage collection. Figure 10-7 illustrates the iFS architecture.

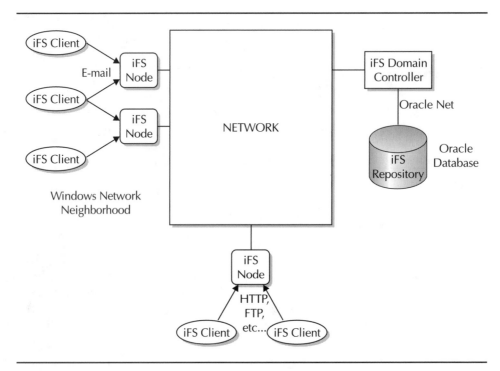

FIGURE 10-7. *Internet File System architecture*

Installation of Oracle Internet File System

Oracle iFS is available as a stand-alone product or as part of 9iAS Standard and Enterprise Editions. You can install iFS in an Oracle8i or Oracle9i database. If you are installing iFS against Oracle9i, you must install it in the same ORACLE_HOME as the database. If you install it against Oracle8i, you must install iFS in a separate ORACLE_HOME from the database.

Oracle Universal Installer launches iFS Configuration Assistant automatically at the end of the installation if you have chosen to install iFS. A wizard interface will guide you through the installation. Prior to iFS installation, you must complete the following tasks on Windows NT/2000:

   1. Ensure that you are logged in to Windows as a user with administrative privileges.

2. Oracle iFS is resource intensive. Ensure that you have at least 512MB of RAM and 500MB of free disk space on the machine running iFS. Additionally, you must have another 600MB of swap space. If the database for the iFS repository is on the same machine, you will need an additional 512MB of RAM and 1.5GB of additional disk space.

3. Ensure that the database has the JServer option installed. The banner displayed when you connect from SQL*Plus should display the JServer information. You can also execute the following query to verify that JServer is installed on the database:

```
'DBMS_JAVA';
OBJECT_TYPE
------------------

PACKAGE
PACKAGE BODY
SYNONYM
```

The preceding query must return exactly three records. Additionally, you must ensure that the following minimum values for initialization parameters are set:

```
java_pool_size = 30MB
open_cursors = 300
processes = 100
shared_pool_size = 50MB
```

4. Ensure that TNSNAMES is configured to connect from the machine on which iFS is being installed to the database holding the repository.

NOTE
You can install iFS on any machine on your network. Use Oracle Universal Installer to install Oracle Client for Windows (Administrator option) before installing iFS. In this chapter, discussion is restricted to iFS installation with 9iAS on the same machine.

5. Oracle Universal Installer launches iFS Configuration Assistant at the end of 9iAS installation. Figure 10-8 shows the Welcome screen of iFS Configuration Assistant. Follow the wizard to complete the installation.

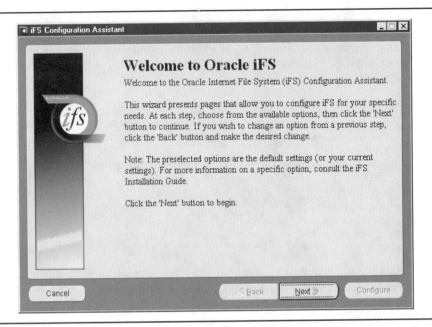

FIGURE 10-8. *Welcome screen of iFS Configuration Assistant*

6. Before commencing the installation, iFS Configuration Assistant verifies that the database is configured properly for iFS. A sample screen is shown here:

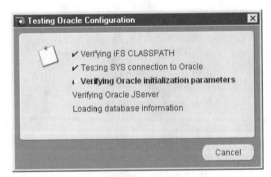

7. Next, you must provide the schema name and password for the iFS repository. The user IFSSYS is the default schema for the repository. On the next screen, you must choose iFS options from the Options screen, as shown in Figure 10-9.

8. In the next two screens, you set the iFS Server Manager options and the language options. Following this, you can choose the protocol servers that you wish to configure. A sample screen is shown in Figure 10-10.

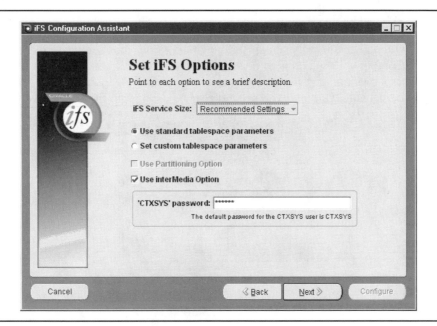

FIGURE 10-9. *Choosing iFS options*

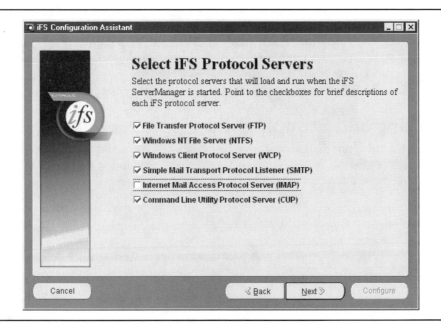

FIGURE 10-10. *Choosing iFS protocol servers*

9. You can then configure the ports the protocol servers listen on and iFS email options (if you have chosen SMTP or IMAP protocols). The assistant provides you with a summary screen showing the options that you have selected. Confirm your selection to begin the installation. The test installation of iFS took over an hour. At many points it appears as if the installation has stalled. Be patient! Wait until you see a dialog box similar to the one shown here:

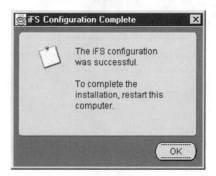

10. Reboot the computer to complete the installation.

Isolated Installation of Internet File System

Oracle iFS is a stand-alone component and can be installed separately at any time. You can install iFS on any machine on your network. Since iFS is resource intensive, we recommend that you install iFS on a separate machine from that running 9iAS and the database. Table 10-1 summarizes the isolated installation of iFS.

Ensure that the Listener and database are configured properly for iFS (see Chapter 6). Execute ifsconfig.bat from the c:\oracle\isuites\ifs1.1\bin folder to launch the iFS Configuration Assistant. Follow the wizard to complete the installation.

Starting and Stopping iFS

You must start iFS protocol servers and agents before clients can use iFS. Execute ifsstart.bat from the c:\oracle\isuites\ifs1.1\bin folder to launch iFS Server Manager. A login dialog box, as shown here, is displayed.

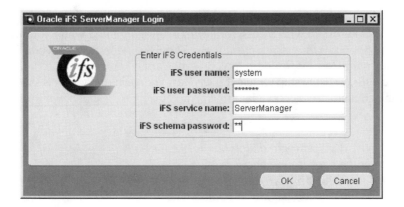

Scenario	Task(s)
Oracle iFS installed on a separate machine from that running 9iAS and Oracle9i database	*Perform Oracle client (administrator option) installation from Oracle9i media *Configure Oracle Net Services (Listener and TNSNAMES) *Install iFS in the same Oracle home as Oracle client
Oracle iFS installed on the same machine as 9iAS against a local Oracle9i database	*Install and configure database *Configure Oracle Net Services (Listener and TNSNAMES) *Install Oracle iFS in the same Oracle home as database
Oracle iFS installed on the same machine as 9iAS against a local Oracle8i database	*Install and configure database *Configure Oracle Net Services (Listener and TNSNAMES) *Install Oracle iFS in a separate Oracle home from the database
Oracle iFS on the same machine as 9iAS against a remote Oracle8i or Oracle9i database	*Install and configure remote database *Configure Oracle Net Services *Install 9iAS and iFS in the same Oracle home

TABLE 10-1. *Isolated Installation of Oracle Internet File System*

Supply the iFS login information to launch Server Manager. An administrator account named *system* with a password of *manager* is created when you install iFS. The default service name is *ServerManager*. The iFS services takes several minutes to start. On some test machines, it took 3–4 minutes.

Execute ifsstop.bat to stop Oracle iFS services. The login dialog box is shown again. Supply the administrator account information and click OK to shut down iFS services.

TIP

The Server Manager login dialog box is occasionally hidden in the background and is behind other windows on your desktop. It might appear as if the ifsstart.bat and ifsstop.bat files are hung. Use ALT-TAB *to switch to the Server Manager login screen. We believe that this behavior is specific to running Java on the Windows platform since we have observed this with other Java applications.*

Managing Services

You can use iFS Monitor to obtain a status of the protocol servers and agents. Specific services can be started and shut down using this utility. Choose File | Monitor from the Server Manager menu to launch the monitor. As seen in Figure 10-11, a list of protocol servers and agents is provided. Select a specific protocol server or agent and perform an operation on it.

Using iFS

You can access iFS using any of the protocols that you picked during installation (refer to Figure 10-10). As an administrator, you must create a folder hierarchy for iFS. Once the folder structure is created, you can create users and groups and set permissions using access control lists. A user can use FTP, Windows Explorer, HTTP, and other configured protocols to access iFS.

Managing iFS Users

You can use iFS Manager to manage users, groups, and permissions to iFS. Launch iFS Manager by executing ifsmgr.bat from the c:\oracle\isuites\ifs1.1\bin folder. Log in as a user with administrator privileges (the default user is *system* with password *manager*). The interface is similar to Oracle Enterprise Manager.

To create or modify a user, expand the Users folder in the Navigator and use the property sheet to define the user. A sample screen is shown in Figure 10-12.

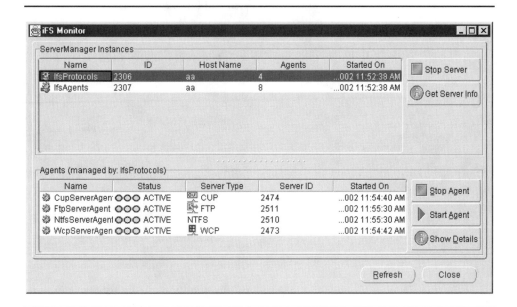

FIGURE 10-11.   *Monitoring iFS services*

You can set user passwords from the user property sheet. Similarly, to create or modify a group, expand the Group folder in the Navigator and use the property sheet.

NOTE
iFS users are different from database users.

Permissions are controlled with access control lists (ACLs). Use iFS Manager to define an ACL and assign users and groups to an ACL.

Managing iFS Structure

Much like other file systems, you can create a hierarchy of folders and place files in these folders. Once the folder hierarchy is defined, you must create mount points using iFS Manager. Mount points are named folders that appear like a top-level folder to a remote user. For example, if you have a folder named \home\public\download, you can define a mount point named "stage" that maps to this folder. Remote users access the \home\public\download folder by using this mount point. You can use ACLs to define permissions for iFS folders.

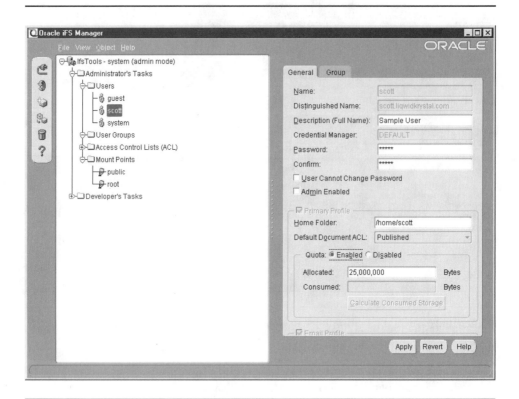

FIGURE 10-12. *Managing users with iFS Manager*

NOTE
*A mount point is similar to a share on Windows NT/2000 Network Neighborhood. If you have shared the folder named c:\home\public\download (using the shared name **stage**), users will access the folder using the shared name, not the physical folder name.*

Accessing iFS

Once authenticated, users can access iFS over any of the configured protocols. A few examples are included here.

Access with Windows Explorer You can access iFS from Windows Explorer after being authenticated on the iFS domain.

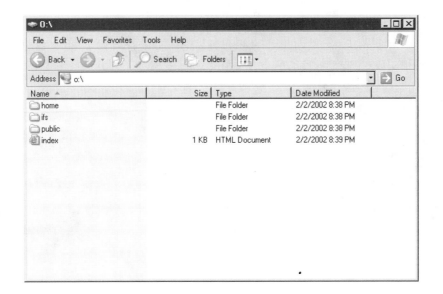

You can also access iFS from the command prompt, as shown here:

```
O:\>dir
 Volume in drive O is Oracle iFS v1.1.10.0.0
 Volume Serial Number is 0000-0001
 Directory of O:\
02/02/2002  08:38 PM    <DIR>          home
02/02/2002  08:38 PM    <DIR>          ifs
02/02/2002  08:39 PM              123  index.html
02/02/2002  08:38 PM    <DIR>          public
               1 File(s)            123 bytes
               3 Dir(s)   1,024,000,000 bytes free
```

The logical drive O:\ is automatically mapped to iFS.

FTP Access to iFS   You can FTP to the node on which iFS is installed using any FTP client. On Windows NT/2000, you can use **ftp.exe** or a utility such as CuteFTP (http://www.cuteftp.com/) to access iFS. The following sample session uploads a file to iFS.

```
C:\>ftp aa.liqwidkrystal.com
Connected to aa.liqwidkrystal.com
220 aa.liqwidkrystal.com/192.168.1.111 Oracle Internet File System
FTP Server 1.1.10.0.0 Production ready
User (aa:(none)): system
331 Password required for system.
Password:
```

```
230 User system logged in.
ftp> ls
200 PORT Command successful.
150 ASCII data connection for /bin/ls (192.168.1.111,2,049) (0 bytes).
mail
226 ASCII transfer complete.
ftp: 8 bytes received in 0.51Seconds 0.02Kbytes/sec.
ftp> put aa.bat
200 PORT Command successful.
150 ASCII data connection for aa.bat (192.168.1.111,2,057) (0 bytes).
226 ASCII transfer complete.
ftp: 239 bytes sent in 0.00Seconds 239000.00Kbytes/sec.
ftp> ls -l
200 PORT Command successful.
150 ASCII data connection for /bin/ls (192.168.1.111,2,063) (0 bytes).
total 2
-rwxr-xr-x   1 system iFS              239 Feb 03 11:16 aa.bat
drwxrwxr-x   2 system iFS             1024 Feb 02 20:38 mail
226 ASCII transfer complete.
ftp: 138 bytes received in 0.09Seconds 1.53Kbytes/sec.
```

Accessing iFS from a Web Browser   You can access iFS from a web browser if you have installed the HTTP Protocol. Ensure that Oracle HTTP Server is running. Point your browser at a URL of the form *http://<ifs node>:<port>/ifs/files*. You will be provided with a login screen. Once authenticated, you can access iFS with a web interface similar to that shown in Figure 10-13. You can upload or download files from this interface. Version control features such as check-in/check-out are also available.

For example, the URL on the test installation is http://aa.liqwidkrystal.com/ifs/files.

Windows Client for iFS   A Windows client for iFS is also available. The client is especially useful if you need to use the version control feature of iFS. Files can be checked in/checked out using this client.

To install the Windows client, execute setup.exe from the c:\oracle\iSuites\ifs1.1\ admin\client\winui folder. Follow the steps suggested by the Installshield Wizard to install the client. A program group named Oracle iFS Utilities 1.1.9.07 (the name of the program group varies with the iFS version) is created. Shortcuts are available for iFS operations, as shown in this sample screen:

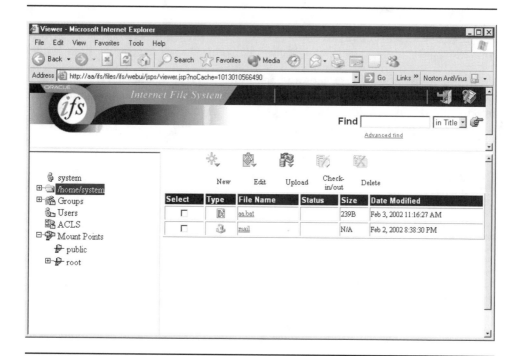

FIGURE 10-13. *Web interface to iFS*

To check in a file, use the shortcut named iFS Checkin. You can choose a file from the file dialog box and check in the file. Use the iFS Checkout shortcut to check out a file.

Command-Line Access to iFS   Administrative and normal user functions can be performed from the command line. Batch files and executables in the c:\oracle\ isuites\ifs1.1\bin folder can be used to perform these functions.

Execute ifssvrmgr.bat to launch iFS Server Manager in command-line mode. You must supply administrator account information.

```
C:\Oracle\iSuites\ifs1.1\bin>ifssvrmgr
Enter iFS user name       > system
Enter iFS user password   > manager
Enter iFS service name    > ServerManager
Enter iFS schema password > aa
Server STARTED: DefaultManager(10826) not managed
```

```
Internet File System 1.1.10.0.0
Server Manager 1.1.10.0.0
Copyright (c) 2000 Oracle Corporation.  All rights reserved.
DefaultManager>
```

You can stop and start services and agents from Server Manager. Type HELP at the prompt to obtain help on available commands. Use the LIST command to obtain information on servers, as shown here:

```
DefaultManager> list servers
Server Name            Managing Server   Hostname         ServerType
---------------------- ----------------- ---------------- --------
IfsProtocols                             aa               Manager
IfsAgents                                aa               Manager
IfsProtocols                             aa               Manager
IfsAgents                                aa               Manager
DefaultManager                           aa               Manager
WcpServer              IfsProtocols      aa               WCP
FtpServer              IfsProtocols      aa               FTP
CupServer              IfsProtocols      aa               CUP
SmtpServer             IfsProtocols      aa               SMTP
NtfsServer             IfsProtocols      aa               NTFS
WcpServer              IfsProtocols      aa               WCP
```

Commands are also available for typical user operations such as loading, copying, and moving files. The following sample session illustrates some of these commands.

```
C:\Oracle\iSuites\ifs1.1\bin>ifslogin anand/aa
 Login successful
C:\Oracle\iSuites\ifs1.1\bin>ifsput c:\tmp\aa.bat /home/anand/aaa.bat
ASCII transfer complete. (239 bytes transferred)
C:\Oracle\iSuites\ifs1.1\bin>ifsls
aaa.bat
mail
total 2
C:\Oracle\iSuites\ifs1.1\bin>ifsrename aaa.bat abc.bat
C:\Oracle\iSuites\ifs1.1\bin>ifsls
abc.bat
mail
total 2
C:\Oracle\iSuites\ifs1.1\bin>ifsrm abc.bat
C:\Oracle\iSuites\ifs1.1\bin>ifsls
mail
total 1
```

There is also a shell included with iFS. Execute ifsshell.bat to launch the shell. You can type iFS commands at the prompt directly. A few examples are shown here:

```
CMDLINE> login anand/aa
Login successful
CMDLINE> ls
mail
```

```
total 1
CMDLINE> put c:\tmp\aa.bat aaa.bat
ASCII transfer complete. (239 bytes transferred)
CMDLINE> rm aaa.bat
CMDLINE> exit
Logout successful; good bye
```

Use the HELP command to get help on iFS commands in the iFS shell.

Oracle Plug-In for Microsoft Internet Information Server

Oracle 9iAS Version 1.0.2.2.2 is packaged with the Oracle HTTP Server (Win32 Apache Web Server Version 1.3.19) on Windows NT/2000. If your site predominantly runs Windows-based servers, you can use an Oracle Plug-in for Microsoft IIS to make Microsoft IIS (4.0 and above) PL/SQL- and Java-aware. PL/SQL and Java components stored inside Oracle databases can be accessed via the plug-in.

NOTE
Oracle Plug-in for Microsoft IIS provides the functionality of the mod_plsql and mod_ose modules of Oracle HTTP Server.

PL/SQL stored procedures including PL/SQL Pages (PSP) can be accessed by using a predefined prefix (pls) in the URL. The plug-in supports only JSP and servlets.

Configuring Oracle Plug-In for Microsoft IIS

Oracle Plug-in for Microsoft IIS is installed with the Standard or Enterprise Edition of 9iAS. You must configure IIS to use the plug-in. Before doing that you must verify that you have met the requirements listed here:

- Windows NT (SP3), Windows 2000, or Windows XP Professional

- Internet Explorer 4.x and 5.x or Netscape Navigator 4.0.8 and higher (Internet Explorer 6.x is not supported)

- Microsoft IIS 4.0 and above

Ensure that IIS is running on a different port from Oracle HTTP Server. On the test installation, Oracle HTTP Server is running on port 80. IIS has been configured for port 8000.

To set the port, follow these steps:

1. Launch MMC from the shortcut Internet Information Services in the Start menu.

2. Choose your web site and right-click to view site properties.

3. Select the Web Site tab and set the port, as shown here:

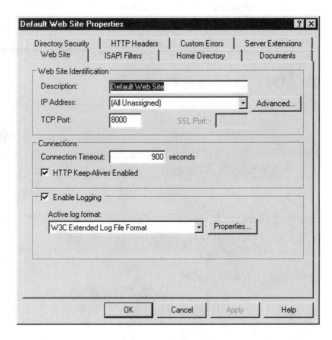

4. Configure the database access descriptor (DAD).

5. Create a new DAD or modify an existing DAD that will be used for Oracle Plug-in. You must disable Single Sign-on for this DAD and use basic authentication. You can do this as follows:

   ■ Start Oracle HTTP Server if it is not running.

   ■ Point your browser at the Gateway Configuration menu (http://<node>:<port>/pls/admin_/).

   ■ Click Gateway Database Access Descriptor Settings. Find the DAD settings on the resulting page. A sample from the test installation is shown in Figure 10-14.

6. Edit an existing DAD or create a new DAD.

Edit	Delete	Database Access Descriptor Name
📝	X	PORTAL30
📝	X	PORTAL30_SSO
📝	X	SAMPLE

FIGURE 10-14. *Modifying database access descriptor settings*

7. Set the authentication mode to Basic, as shown here:

> Authentication Mode
> Select the authentication mode to be used for validating access through
> this DAD. For Oracle Portal 3.0, the use of Single Sign-on authentication
> is required. For WebDB 2.x, the use of Basic authentication is required.
> Please consult the documentation for information of the remaining three
> authentication modes: Global Owa, Custom Owa, and Per Package.
>
> Authentication Mode [Basic ▾]

If you attempt to use a DAD that is configured for Single Sign-on, you will get an error message similar to the one shown here:

```
Call to WPG_SESSION API Failed.
Error-Code:6550
Error TimeStamp:Thu, 07 Feb 2002 16:45:17 GMT
Database Log In Failed
```

You can also configure the DAD from a text editor. Edit the wdbsvr.app file from the c:\oracle\isuites\Apache\modplsql\cfg folder and set Single Sign-On (SSO) for your DAD to **no**, as shown here:

```
enablesso   = No
```

You must now configure Microsoft IIS to use the plug-in. Launch Microsoft Management Console (MMC) by using the shortcut Internet Information Services from the Start menu, and then follow these steps:

1. Select your web site, right-click, and choose Properties.

2. Select the ISAPI Filters tab.

3. Click Add and add the Oracle plug-in (oraiisp8.dll), as shown in Figure 10-15.

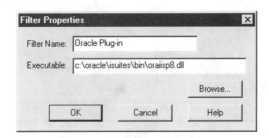

FIGURE 10-15. *Adding Oracle plug-in to Microsoft IIS*

4. Create a new virtual directory. To do so, select your web site, right-click, and choose New | Virtual Directory from the context menu.

5. Follow the instructions provided by the wizard to create a virtual directory named OraclePlugin, as shown here:

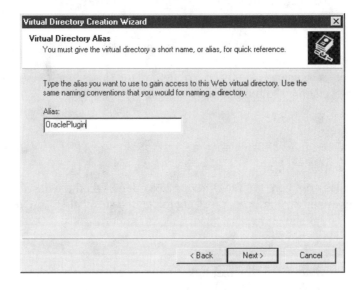

6. Provide additional settings for the virtual directory as listed in Table 10-2.

Screen	Setting/Description	Setting on Test Installation
Web Site Content Directory	Directory	c:\oracle\isuites\bin
Access Permissions	Permissions to read and execute scripts	Read, Run Scripts, and Execute check boxes selected
Anonymous Access	Allow anonymous access and basic authentication	Allow Anonymous Access and Basic Authentication (Password is sent in Clear Text) check boxes are selected

TABLE 10-2. *Virtual Directory Settings for Oracle Plug-in for Microsoft IIS*

7. Reboot the machine.

8. Test the configuration by accessing a PL/SQL or Java package available to you. For example, you can access Oracle Portal by using the URL http://aa.liqwidkrystal.com:8000/pls/portal30.

Chapters 9 and 10 covered the installation of Oracle 9iAS along with some key components. Several issues were encountered during the test installation of Oracle 9iAS (Version 1.0.2.2.2). Other issues on earlier versions are documented on the Oracle support site. We suggest that you obtain the latest version of the software and install it using the information provided in these chapters. A few case studies with sample applications are also included with 9iAS. These will help you get a jumpstart on deploying applications on 9iAS.

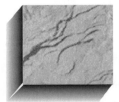

CHAPTER
11

Oracle9i Security
Features

ecurity is an issue of prime concern to many businesses today. Many companies have invested millions of dollars in securing their data and networks from competitors and other malicious users. More often than not, Oracle software manages sensitive data. This makes security doubly important. Oracle-based applications and data must be secured with local networks and the Internet. Features in Oracle9i Server, Oracle Net Services, and Oracle9i Application Server can address many fundamental security issues. Additional licensable software such as Oracle Advanced Security (ASO) and Oracle Internet Directory (OID) can help you enhance your security solutions. ASO allows you to use industry-standard solutions for encryption, data integrity, and authentication with Oracle software. OID provides standard directory services that can help you manage user information across your enterprise. This chapter includes an overview of security features available across Oracle software. The goal is to familiarize you with the security options available in each layer of software without delving into the nitty-gritty implementation details. These are well beyond the scope of this book; however, case studies in Chapter 12 reinforce topics covered in this chapter.

Before looking at the security features provided by Oracle software, the next section discusses what security entails.

Security Basics

In typical e-business environment clients, application servers and databases are spread across a combination of private and public networks. Security breaches are possible in application servers, in database servers, and at network level. Consider a network similar to the one shown in Figure 11-1.

First, data has to be secured at the database level by controlling user access to databases and the servers that house them. Second, the middle tier, consisting of HTTP Servers and application servers, has to be protected against unauthorized use. Finally, data has to be protected against eavesdroppers on the many networks involved with data transfer. Public networks and gateways are often used to transmit data across large distances. Security is more important in these situations.

Security Issues

There can be many security concerns; however, this section focuses on the following salient issues:

- Confidentiality

- Data integrity

- Large user communities

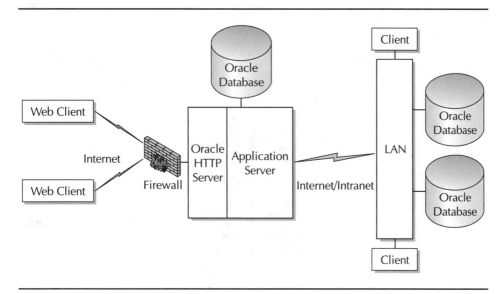

FIGURE 11-1. *A typical business network*

Confidentiality

Confidentiality is possibly the most fundamental of security needs. You must ensure that an individual is allowed to see only authorized data and nothing else. Confidentiality involves proper authentication, authorization, and access control. Proper authentication requires that a user be positively identified. The system must protect against imposters. Having authenticated a user, the system must check if the user is authorized to access what he or she is attempting to access. This is done through access control. Finally, physical identification was less of an issue in traditional business environments; however, the Internet has changed all that. It is much more difficult to positively identify an individual whose physical location is mostly unknown.

On top of all this, an important side issue is that confidentiality checks must not become a burden on authorized users.

Data Integrity

The integrity of data can be maintained by enforcing business rules and controlling access. While constraints enforce business rules, access is controlled with system and object privileges. Data must also be protected while the data is being transmitted on the network. You must ensure that data packets must not be modified or dropped while traveling on the network.

Large User Communities

In traditional business systems, the user base is well understood. It might be possible to create users on databases as and when required; however, it is likely that your company maintains several systems and that users are spread across geographical regions. Additionally, you might need to provide access to customers and vendors. What if an employee leaves the organization? How can you ensure that this employee is denied access to all systems in one shot across multiple locations?

What Can Go Wrong with Security?

There can be many points of failure as far as security is concerned. You have to constantly worry about what imposters, eavesdroppers, and other malicious users can do to your data. Data tampering is probably the most fundamental of security issues. A malicious individual can change a data value or a transaction without being detected. For example, a user could change a bank transaction such that an extra zero is added on a credit. A specific transaction suitable to the individual might also be repeated. For example, a credit applied to a credit card might be repeated several times. This type of malicious activity is called *data replay*.

Eavesdropping is another likely crime. An eavesdropper can store sensitive information such as passwords and credit card numbers by listening to traffic on the network for later use.

Since users are spread across large distances, positive user identification is difficult. At the simplest level, every system can be protected by a password. The problem is that there are so many systems and, therefore, so many passwords to remember that many individuals choose a simple password, or worse still, the same password across all systems! Password-based authentication can be self-defeating if used in this manner.

Oracle Software and Security

Now that some common security risks and points of failure have been identified, see how Oracle software allows you to mitigate security risks at various levels.

User authentication is mandatory before a session is allowed on the database. Users can also be authenticated on the database by the operating system. In contrast to Windows NT, which uses NT LAN Manager for login, both Windows 2000 and Windows XP Professional support Kerberos authentication. Once a session is established, system and object privileges control what the user is allowed to do on the database. Oracle databases promote least-privilege access to data. Users and applications are given the lowest privileges necessary to perform their jobs. Additional features are also available for data encryption and granular control of data. These features are discussed later in this chapter.

In the middle tier, Oracle HTTP Server and Oracle9*i* Application Server support strong authentication and encryption. The single sign-on feature allows users to access multiple applications and databases with a single password. Proxies allow an application to share a schema on the back-end database. This also stops a user from accessing the back-end database directly.

Additional software such as Oracle Advanced Security and Oracle Internet Directory can be licensed to extend the capabilities of Oracle databases and application servers. A variety of tools such as Oracle Wallet Manager, Login Assistant, and Oracle Policy Manager allow you to administer security easily. Further information on security features provided in each layer of Oracle software is presented in the remainder of this chapter.

Oracle9i Server Security Features

Oracle databases have many built-in security features for DBAs and application developers. The important features are listed here:

- Authentication

- Roles

- Profiles

- Auditing

- Database views

- Stored program units

- Data encryption

- Fine-grained access control

A combination of the previous features can allow you to design appropriate security for your site. While most of the features listed here are available with Oracle9i Standard Edition, a few are available only with the Enterprise Edition. A special mention is made in such cases in the following discussion.

Authentication

An Oracle session on the database is created only after the user is authenticated. You can authenticate the user with a username and password stored in the database or externally from the operating system. Passwords can be managed using password complexity function.

Additionally, the Enterprise Edition is capable of proxy authentication in the middle tier. This allows an application in the middle tier to perform a database transaction on behalf of the user. The Enterprise Edition also supports Secure Sockets Layer (SSL) protocol and other authentication methods available with Oracle Advanced Security.

Roles

Roles allow you to manage access and privileges for several users quickly. There are four kinds of roles available:

- Database
- Global
- Enterprise
- Application

Enterprise and application roles are available only with Oracle9i Enterprise Edition.

The traditional database role can be used to manage a set of system and object privileges across many users on a single database. When a user assumes a database role, they automatically obtain the privileges assigned to that role.

Global roles are similar to database roles in that they contain a set of privileges on a single database; however, global roles are meant for enterprise security and are stored in a directory. Global roles are assigned to a user by a directory service. A user cannot connect to a database and use the SET ROLE statement to assume a global role. In the following example, a global role named HRACCESS has been defined. A user can be authorized to use this role only by the enterprise directory service. Oracle Internet Directory or Microsoft Active Directory must be used as a directory service to support this feature.

```
SQL> create role hraccess identified globally;
Role created.
```

The Enterprise role feature also allows you to define a role in a directory service. In contrast to a global role, an enterprise role can also be used across multiple databases.

Finally, consider a situation in which you want to force a user to access the database from a specific application, or in which you want to grant an application on the middle tier proxy access to the database. Application roles are handy in these situations. The USING clause of the CREATE ROLE statement is used to create a secure application role, as shown in the example here:

```
SQL> create role hraccess identified using hr.hraccess;
Role created.
```

You can validate the application and take necessary actions within the package assigned to the role.

Profiles

Profiles allow you to control resources used by a session. For example, you can define the amount of CPU taken by a user session, thus preventing runaway queries. Or you can define a password policy to enforce password guidelines. Chapter 8 provides more information on profiles.

Auditing

You can audit the use of an Oracle database. Audit trails can be directed to the database or the operating system. An audit action can track a specific user or a specific action on the database. For example, you can audit modifications to any HR-related tables. Auditing is also discussed in Chapter 8.

The Enterprise Edition also has a fine-grained auditing feature. This is useful in a situation in which you want to audit a database operation only if it meets certain criteria. For example, you want to create an audit trail only when a specific user accesses a specific set of records in a table. Refer to the *Application Developer's Guide* in Oracle documentation for more information on fine-grained auditing.

Views

Views have traditionally been used to control access to specific rows and columns of a table. A view is constructed from a query, and only the data set returned from the query is available to the user. Consider the following example:

```
SQL> create view dept10 as select * from emp where deptno=10;
View created.
```

In this example, the view named DEPT10 shows a subset of the EMP table containing records for Department 10. An application using the DEPT10 view can abstract the DEPT table entirely. The next example creates a view that exposes only the employee name, ID, and job information in Department 10.

```
SQL> create view dept10_nosal as select empno, ename, job,mgr
from emp where deptno=10;
View created.
```

Views are not objects in a strict sense since they do not take up space in the database. The Oracle database stores the query on which the view is constructed in the data dictionary. The query is executed at run-time to determine the data set on which an operation has to be performed. You can query the data dictionary to obtain more information on the views created. The following query returns information on all the views created by a user.

```
SQL> select view_name, text from user_views;
DEPT10
select "EMPNO","ENAME","JOB","MGR","HIREDATE","SAL","COMM","DEPTNO"
from emp where deptno=10
DEPT10_NOSAL
select empno, ename, job,mgr from emp where deptno=10
```

Stored Program Units

Stored procedures and triggers can be used to perform secondary tasks securely in the background. For example, you can write a database trigger that runs a piece of PL/SQL code every time a DML operation is performed on the EMP table.

```
SQL> create trigger emp_check
  2   before
  3   delete or insert or update
  4   on emp
  5   begin
  6       <your code here>
  7   end;
  8   /
Trigger created.
```

In the PL/SQL block you could perform some extra validation or task. For example, you can write a copy of the record being modified to a backup table. A special trigger (ON LOGON) can be used to set application contexts. An example is included in the "Fine-Grained Access Control" section later in this chapter.

Stored procedures can be used to abstract operations from a database user. Consider the following example.

```
SQL> create or replace procedure mod_scott_emp (deptnum in number)
  2   authid definer
  3   as
  4   begin
  5      update emp
  6          set sal = sal * 1.10 where deptno = deptnum;
  7   end;
  8   /
Procedure created.
SQL> grant execute on mod_scott_emp to anand;
Grant succeeded.
```

In the previous example, the owner of the EMP table has created a procedure that performs an update of the EMP table. Observe that the procedure runs under the privileges of the owner of the procedure (authid definer) and not the invoker of the procedure. This means other users can update the EMP table using this procedure rather than with ad hoc DML operations.

Encrypting Data

You can encrypt sensitive data in an Oracle database using the DBMS_OBFUSCATION_TOOLKIT package. This eliminates the risk of data being viewed at the data-file level with binary utilities. The package supports both DES and 3DES encryption.

Typically, sites choose to encrypt only sensitive columns or specific tables. Of course, you have to figure out a way to maintain the key securely. The key can be stored in the database itself or on the file system. To illustrate this feature, a simple example of obfuscation is shown here:

```
SQL> declare
  2        string_to_be_obfuscated  varchar2(8) := 'a string';
  3        encryption_key varchar2(24) := 'the encryption key';
  4        obfuscated_string varchar2(2048);
  5        decrypted_orig_string varchar2(8);
  6  begin
  7     dbms_obfuscation_toolkit.des3encrypt (
  8       input_string => string_to_be_obfuscated,
  9       key_string   => encryption_key,
 10       encrypted_string => obfuscated_string);
 11     dbms_output.put_line (obfuscated_string);
 12     dbms_obfuscation_toolkit.des3decrypt (
 13       input_string => obfuscated_string,
 14       key_string => encryption_key,
 15       decrypted_string => decrypted_orig_string);
 16     dbms_output.put_line (decrypted_orig_string);
 17  end;
 18  /

+++K?+~W

a string
PL/SQL procedure successfully completed.
```

Note that the DES3ENCRYPT and DES3DECRYPT procedures are used for encryption and decryption, respectively. You can also encrypt raw data using the obfuscation toolkit.

Additionally, you can use the PL/SQL Wrapper utility to protect PL/SQL source code. If you do not do this, it is possible for a user to view PL/SQL sources by querying views such as USER_SOURCE. Execute **wrap.exe** from the command line to create a PLB (PL/SQL binary) file, as shown in the following example:

```
C:\>wrap iname=obfuscate_sample.sql
PL/SQL Wrapper: Release 9.0.1.1.1- Production on Fri Feb 15 20:06:22 2002
Copyright (c) Oracle Corporation 1993, 2001.  All Rights Reserved.
Processing obfuscate_sample.sql to obfuscate_sample.plb
```

The default extension for the resulting binary file (.plb) is a convention. You can choose any name for your file. A portion of the resulting binary file is shown here:

```
create or replace package scott.emp_ctx wrapped
0
abcd
3
9
9000000
2 :e:
PACKAGE:
1EMP_CTX:
```

Execute the PL/SQL script from the PLB file just as you would from a SQL script to create your PL/SQL program units. The data dictionary views display only the binary form of the source code, thus protecting your source. In fact, many of the system packages installed by Oracle are themselves in binary (PLB) form.

Fine-Grained Access Control

Oracle9i Server permits fine-grained control on rows in a table. This mechanism allows you to create policies for row-level security. This feature, called Virtual Private Database, is implemented by defining a predicate (a WHERE clause) that is tacked onto DML operations on a given table. An administrator can use the DBMS_RLS package to define related policies. The feature is available only on Oracle9i Enterprise Edition.

NOTE
Fine-grained access control was also available with Oracle8i. The Oracle Label Security product is built on top of fine-grained security and can be licensed separately.

Row-level security is even more useful for web-based applications. For example, if you are creating an online banking application, you want to ensure that a user gets access only to his or her account! The following examples illustrate this feature.

Assume that you want to provide a restricted view of the EMP table for an individual such that he/she is able to view their own personal information. You can set up row-level security by creating a context. A context stores session-level information. In the example, the following steps are performed:

1. Create a function named EMPSEC that sets the context.

2. Use the DBMS_RLS package to create the policy.

A sample session is shown here.

```
SQL> connect scott/tiger
Connected.
SQL> select empno, ename, sal from emp;
      7369 SMITH            800
      7499 ALLEN           1600
      7521 WARD            1250
      7566 JONES           2975
      7654 MARTIN          1250
      7698 BLAKE           2850
      7782 CLARK           2450
      7788 SCOTT           3000
      7839 KING            5000
      7844 TURNER          1500
      7876 ADAMS           1100
      7900 JAMES            950
      7902 FORD            3000
      7934 MILLER          1300
14 rows selected.
```

Notice that a query on the EMP table returns all records belonging to the table. Now set up row-level security. First, create the policy function.

```
SQL> create or replace function empsec
  2     (schemaname varchar2, objectname varchar2)
  3     return varchar2 is where_clause varchar2(1000);
  4  begin
  5    where_clause :=
  6    'ename = sys_context(''userenv'',''session_user'')';
  7    return where_clause;
  8  end;
  9  /
```

```
Function created.
SQL> execute dbms_rls.add_policy ('SCOTT','EMP','EMP_POL','SCOTT',
'EMPSEC');
PL/SQL procedure successfully completed.
```

The policy function EMPSEC adds a predicate (a WHERE clause) that restricts the query to records belonging to the user who has created the session. The USERENV context is built in and can be used to retrieve many attributes including terminal information and the IP address of client. In the example, a policy named EMP_POL was created in the SCOTT schema on the SCOTT.EMP table. The policy uses the EMPSEC procedure to retrieve the context. The effect of the policy is shown in the query here:

```
SQL> select empno, ename, sal from emp;
     7788 SCOTT          3000
```

Observe that the same query now returns one record, the record belonging to the connected user.

NOTE
The built-in SQL function USERENV is replaced by the USERENV context.

The next part of this session illustrates the effect of the policy on another user named KING (assume that this user exists in your database).

```
SQL> grant select on emp to king;
Grant succeeded.
SQL> connect king/king
Connected.
SQL> select empno, ename, sal from scott.emp;
     7839 KING           5000
```

In this example, you can see how it is possible to restrict the output from a query; however, it is unlikely that your application can conform to a tailor-made situation such as this, in which your policy is dependent on a built-in context. It is possible for an application to create its own context (called an *application context*). In the next example, an application context has been created to restrict a user's view on the DEPT table to records belonging to the user's department.

```
SQL> connect sys/change_on_install as sysdba
Connected.

SQL> -- Grant privileges to create and drop application contexts
SQL> grant create any context to scott;
```

```
Grant succeeded.
SQL> grant drop any context to scott;
SQL> connect scott/tiger
Connected.
SQL> -- user can view all records
SQL> select * from dept;
        10 ACCOUNTING     NEW YORK
        20 RESEARCH       DALLAS
        30 SALES          CHICAGO
        40 OPERATIONS     BOSTON

SQL> -- set application context; the context will be created later
SQL> -- Oracle Server does not validate that the context exists
SQL> create or replace procedure set_dept_context is
  2      deptnum number;
  3  begin
  4      select deptno into deptnum from emp
  5        where ename = sys_context('userenv','session_user');
  6      dbms_session.set_context('dept_context','dept',deptnum);
  7  end;
  8  /
Procedure created.
SQL> -- create a function that adds the WHERE clause
SQL> create or replace function predicate_context
  2      (app_schema varchar2, obj_name varchar2)
  3      return varchar2 is where_clause varchar2(1000);
  4  begin
  5      where_clause := 'deptno = sys_context(''dept_context'',
         ''dept'')';
  6      return where_clause;
  7  end;
  8  /
Function created.
SQL> -- create the context and the policy
SQL> create context dept_context using set_dept_context;
Context created.
SQL> execute dbms_rls.add_policy(
'SCOTT','DEPT','DEPT_POL','SCOTT','PREDICATE_CONTEXT');
PL/SQL procedure successfully completed.
SQL> -- set the context and test
SQL> execute set_dept_context;
PL/SQL procedure successfully completed.
SQL> select * from dept;
        20 RESEARCH       DALLAS
```

In this example, the application context is set explicitly by executing the SET_DEPT_CONTEXT procedure. This is not very practical since you cannot depend on the user to set the context in an ad hoc query. It is better to set the application context with an ON LOGON trigger to ensure that the context is set as soon as the user logs on to the database. The following example illustrates an ON LOGON trigger.

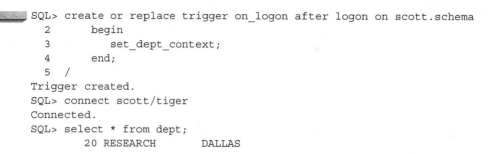

```
SQL> create or replace trigger on_logon after logon on scott.schema
  2      begin
  3          set_dept_context;
  4      end;
  5  /
Trigger created.
SQL> connect scott/tiger
Connected.
SQL> select * from dept;
        20 RESEARCH        DALLAS
```

Similarly, you must create an ON LOGON trigger for every user who will be using the DEPT table to ensure that the application context is set properly. Once row-level security is set, it applies to all applications that use the table. Users cannot bypass the security from any application, including ad hoc queries from SQL*Plus.

NOTE
You can also define triggers that fire upon logoff and database startup and shutdown.

Oracle Policy Manager

Oracle Policy Manager (OPM) is a GUI utility that is bundled with Oracle Enterprise Manager and can be used to manage policies. You can launch OPM by executing **oemapp.bat opm** from the command line or from the Start menu. The policy DEPT_POL created with the DBMS_RLS package in the example could have been created with OPM. A sample OPM screen is shown here:

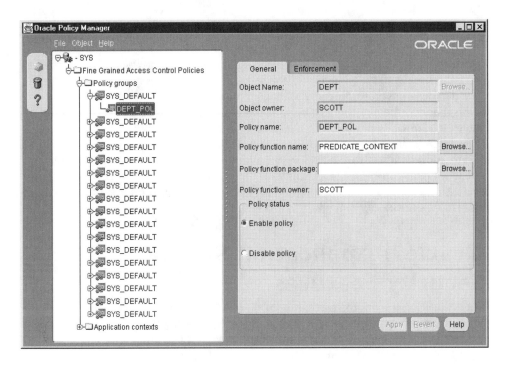

This section looked at a few important security features available with Oracle Server. Several other features, such as those available for Java security and proxy authentication, are not mentioned here. The following additional references in Oracle documentation provide excellent information on these security topics:

- *Oracle9i Database Administrator's Guide*
- *Oracle9i Security Overview*
- *Oracle9i Application Developer's Guide*

Oracle Net Services Security Features

Oracle Net Services provide a few security features that can be used to control access to a database. Oracle Connection Manager can be used to proxy requests targeted for a database server. Connection Manager can also be used to control client access. In this manner, specific clients can be allowed or denied access based on their IP addresses. Firewalls can be created within the intranet (typically, at department level) or for the Internet. Chapter 6 provides examples on Oracle Connection Manager.

An additional software component called Oracle Net Firewall Proxy allows you to integrate third-party firewalls with Oracle Net. This allows you to distribute databases securely across the Internet. A discussion on this component is beyond the scope of this book.

Oracle9i Application Server Security Features

Applications in the middle tier can in turn connect to the database using proxy connections. This allows several user sessions to share lightweight connections to the database as well as providing an additional layer of security. You can use the IP_ADDRESS or PROXY_USER attribute instead of giving each user a connection on the database. The USERENV context can be used to extract these attributes. For example, use

```
sys_context('userenv','proxy_user')
```

instead of the following in your applications.

```
sys_context('userenv','session_user')
```

Oracle HTTP Server included with Oracle 9iAS supports SSL encryption and X.509 certificates for authentication. Oracle Login Server provides Single Sign-on (SSO) capabilities for web-based clients. Oracle Portal is integrated with Single Sign-on. Oracle Portal is covered in Chapter 9. You can use the preconfigured database access descriptor PORTAL30_SSO to access the Single Sign-on login page (http://<node>:<port>/pls/portal30_sso). Login names can be verified using Oracle Internet Directory. The following two references provide excellent information on middle-tier security:

- Best Practices in HTTP Security, Bruce Lowenthal, http://technet.oracle.com

- Oracle9i Application Server Best Practices (Part No. A95201-01), http://technet.oracle.com

Oracle Advanced Security

In many cases, data travels large distances over a combination of private and public networks. Many things can go wrong. It is possible that a third party can snoop on the data transmission and tamper with data as it moves from point A to point B. Malicious users can eavesdrop on network traffic as data passes through a combination of land lines, microwave, and satellite links. Network sniffers can be used to pry into network packets. Identification is also more difficult in an environment where physical distances separate users and servers. A user can hijack a password and pretend to be someone else. A server could intercept data meant for another server and pretend to be the right target. How do you protect your system from all these threats? Oracle Advanced Security has some answers.

Oracle Advanced Security (ASO) is software that sits on top of Oracle Net Services and enhances security across the network for Oracle-based applications. This software is bundled only with Oracle9i Enterprise Edition and requires special licensing. Some Oracle applications such as Human Resources, Oracle Financial, and Oracle Manufacturing cannot use ASO on Windows NT/2000.

NOTE
ASO was called Advanced Networking Option in Net8 and was available in a U.S. Domestic Edition and an Export Edition. The U.S. government has since removed export restrictions, which has allowed Oracle to merge the two editions. There is now only one edition of ASO available, and it is available with Oracle9i Enterprise Edition.

Oracle Advanced Security Architecture

ASO adds a security layer on top of Oracle Net. ASO adapters allow applications to connect to authentication systems such as Kerberos and CyberSafe transparently, as shown in Figure 11-2.

Note that applications that do not use Oracle Net cannot use Oracle Advanced Security.

Oracle Advanced Security Solutions

You can use ASO to solve a variety of security issues. These include solutions for encryption, data integrity, and authentication.

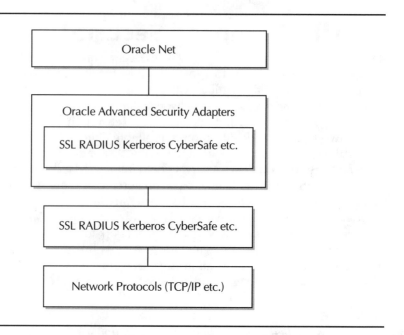

FIGURE 11-2. *Oracle Advanced Security Architecture*

Data Encryption

For network-based applications data encryption is required to maintain the confidentiality of data that is being sent across the network. A secure cryptosystem is used for data encryption. A secure cryptosystem converts data in plain text to cipher text using an encryption key before transmitting the data across the network. A cryptosystem on the receiving end has to decrypt the data from cipher text to plain text using a decryption key. This makes it almost impossible for an intruder on the network to decipher the data on the network.

Two kinds of cryptosystems are available: symmetric and asymmetric. A symmetric cryptosystem uses the same key for both encryption and decryption, while asymmetric cryptosystems use different keys for encryption and decryption.

ASO supports three symmetric encryption methods: data encryption standard (DES), 3DES, and RC4. Each of these encryption methods provides varying levels of security and performance for data being transmitted across a network. The encryption method that should be used on the client and the server is defined in the sqlnet.ora file. This file resides in the c:\oracle\ora90\network\admin folder. You can use Oracle Net Manager to configure all security settings, as illustrated in the "Configuring Encryption on Server and Client" section later in this chapter.

DES Encryption   DES algorithm has been used as a standard encryption algorithm in the U.S. government for several years. ASO supports 56-bit DES key (the older 40-bit DES key is also supported for backward compatibility). To use DES encryption on the server, the following setting must be used in sqlnet.ora:

```
SQLNET.ENCRYPTION_TYPES_SERVER= (DES)
```

3DES Encryption   3DES ensures a higher level of confidentiality since the DES encryption is performed three times; however, it takes a longer time for encryption and decryption. ASO supports 3DES in the two-key and three-key versions, with effective key lengths for encryption of 112 bits and 168 bits, respectively. Both the versions operate in outer cipher block chaining (CBC) mode. CBC is an encryption method that protects against block replay attacks by making the encryption of a cipher block dependent on all blocks that precede it, thus making unauthorized decryption incrementally more difficult. The following sample setting in sqlnet.ora uses 168-bit 3DES encryption on the server.

```
SQLNET.ENCRYPTION_TYPES_SERVER= (3DES168)
```

RC4 Encryption   The RC4 algorithm has been developed by RSA Data Security, Inc., and has become an international standard for high-speed encryption. RC4 uses a variable key-length stream cipher that is several times faster than DES, making it possible to encrypt large, bulk data transfers with minimal performance consequences. ASO supports 40-bit, 56-bit, 128-bit, and 256-bit keys. A sample entry in the client-side sqlnet.ora configuration file is shown here:

```
SQLNET.ENCRYPTION_TYPES_CLIENT= (RC4_256)
```

Diffie-Hellman-Based Key Management

The secrecy of encrypted data depends upon the existence of a secret key shared between the communicating parties. A key is a secret exclusively shared by parties on both ends of a connection. Without the key, it is computationally infeasible to decrypt an encrypted message without detection. Providing and maintaining such secret keys is referred to as key management.

Secure key distribution is complex in a multi-user environment. ASO uses the well-known Diffie-Hellman key negotiation algorithm to perform secure key distribution for both encryption and data integrity. The ASO key management function changes the session key with every session.

The authentication key fold-in technique is used to defeat a possible third-party attack on the key. It strengthens the session key significantly by combining a shared secret, known only to the client and the server. The client and the server begin communicating using the session key generated by Diffie-Hellman. When the client authenticates to the server, they establish a shared secret that is known only to both parties. ASO combines the shared secret and the Diffie-Hellman session key to generate a stronger session key designed to defeat a monkey-in-the-middle attack. The authentication key fold-in function is an embedded feature of ASO. No additional configuration is necessary.

Integrity of Data

Data being transmitted across a network can be modified or deleted by a malicious user. Data integrity algorithms use checksums to protect data traveling across the network and ensure that data has not been tampered with or corrupted during transmission. For example, some database blocks might have been modified during the transmission. The sender uses a hashing algorithm to generate the checksum. The receiver of the data uses the checksum to verify that the data has not been modified since the sender transmitted it. If the checksum does not match, a request is made to retransmit the data.

Oracle Advanced security offers you an implementation of the message digest 5 (MD5) algorithm or the secure hash algorithm (SHA-1) to protect against data modification and data reply attacks. Both these hash algorithms create a checksum that changes if the data is altered in any way. This protection operates independently from the encryption process. You can enable data integrity with or without enabling encryption. A sample setting in the server-side sqlnet.ora is shown here:

```
SQLNET.CRYPTO_CHECKSUM_TYPES_SERVER= (MD5)
```

Activating Encryption and Integrity

For any Oracle network connection, it is possible for both server and client to support more than one encryption algorithm and integrity algorithm. If encryption or integrity is enabled, the server and client negotiate the algorithm to be used when the connection is initialized. Only one encryption algorithm and one integrity algorithm are used in one connection. The available algorithms are defined in the sqlnet.ora configuration file on both the server and the client. If there are multiple algorithms specified in a setting, ASO uses the first algorithm that matches on the client and the server. You can use Oracle Net Manager to configure the sqlnet.ora.

NOTE
You can modify the SQLNET.ORA in a text editor directly; however, this is not a recommended practice.

Negotiating Encryption and Integrity

You can use one of four settings, specified in the sqlnet.ora configuration file on the server and the client to negotiate encryption and integrity. The combination of the settings determines if a connection is possible with security. In some combinations of these settings, a connection is still provided without security.

The four settings are ACCEPTED, REJECTED, REQUIRED, and REQUESTED. As mentioned earlier, you must use one of these settings on client and the server. The combination of the settings specified on the client and the server determines the resulting behavior. The settings along with associated behavior in various combinations are summarized in Table 11-1.

Setting on Server	Setting on Client	Comment/Description
REJECTED	ACCEPTED, REJECTED, or REQUESTED	Connection succeeds without security.
	REQUIRED	Connection fails with an error message.
ACCEPTED	REQUIRED	Connection is successful if a matching algorithm is found. Security is also enabled. If no matching algorithm is found, connection fails.
	REJECTED or ACCEPTED	Connection is made without security.
	REQUESTED	Connection is made without security if matching algorithm is not found, or with security if matching algorithm is found.
REQUESTED	REQUIRED	Connection succeeds only if matching algorithm is found with security enabled.
	ACCEPTED or REQUESTED	Connection succeeds with security if matching algorithm is found. If not, connection succeeds without security.
REQUIRED	REJECTED	Connection fails with error.
	ACCEPTED, REQUESTED, or REQUIRED	Connection succeeds with security if matching algorithm is found.

TABLE 11-1. *Negotiation of Security*

To better understand this process of negotiation, consider the following examples. Assume that the server has been configured with the REQUIRED method and the client has been configured with the REJECTED method. When a client attempts to connect to the server, an error is displayed, as shown here:

```
C:\ sqlplus
SQL*Plus: Release 9.0.1.0.0 - on Wed Jan 16 14:42:58 2002
(c) Copyright 2001 Oracle Corporation.  All rights reserved.
Enter user-name: scott@aa
Enter password:
ERROR:
ORA-12660: Encryption or crypto-checksumming parameters incompatible
```

In the next example, both the client and server are configured to require security; however, no matching algorithm is found.

```
C:\ sqlplus
SQL*Plus: Release 9.0.1.0.0 - on Wed Jan 16 14:51:43 2002
(c) Copyright 2001 Oracle Corporation.  All rights reserved.
Enter user-name: scott@aa
Enter password:
ERROR:
ORA-12650: No common encryption or data integrity algorithm
```

Configuring Encryption on Server and Client

Data encryption can be enabled on the server and client using Oracle Net Manager. Use the following steps to configure encryption.

1. Launch Net Manager. Choose Start | Programs | Oracle - OraHome90 | Configuration and Migration Tools | Net Manager.

2. Modify the profile. In the Navigator, expand the folder Oracle Net Configuration | Local and select Profile. Choose Oracle Advanced Security from the drop-down list and choose the Encryption tab, as shown in Figure 11-3.

Add the encryption algorithms of your choice. Choose Client to set the encryption setting on the client and Server for server-side setting. Type an encryption seed (a string

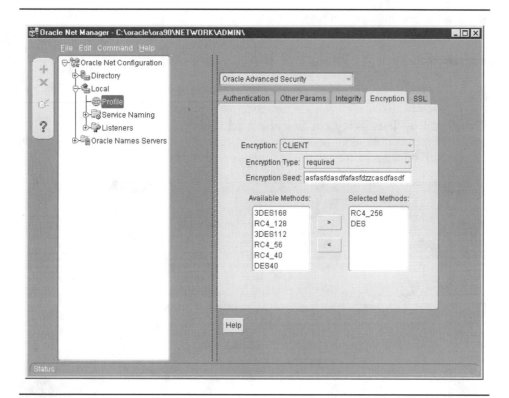

FIGURE 11-3. *Configuring encryption*

of 10–70 characters) and set the encryption type. Save the settings from the File menu. The sqlnet.ora is updated, as shown in the example here:

```
SQLNET.ENCRYPTION_TYPES_CLIENT= (RC4_256, DES)
SQLNET.ENCRYPTION_CLIENT = required
SQLNET.CRYPTO_SEED = asfasfdasdfafasfdzzcasdfasdf
```

Use a similar procedure to enable encryption on the server. You must ensure that at least one encryption algorithm matches. The encryption seed can be any string value and must match on the client and server. Sample settings on the test server are shown here:

```
SQLNET.ENCRYPTION_TYPES_SERVER= (DES, RC4_256)
SQLNET.ENCRYPTION_SERVER = required
SQLNET.CRYPTO_SEED = asfasfdasdfafasfdzzcasdfasdf
```

Configuring Integrity on Server and Client

Integrity is configured in the same manner as encryption. Choose the Integrity tab in Oracle Net Manager to specify the settings, as shown here:

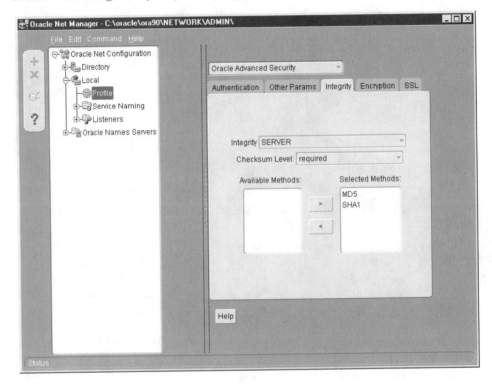

You can select one or both of the integrity algorithms available; however, the first algorithm will be given higher precedence during negotiation. Again, at least one algorithm must match on the client and server. Sample server settings in sqlnet.ora are shown here:

```
#Server settings
SQLNET.CRYPTO_CHECKSUM_SERVER = required
SQLNET.CRYPTO_CHECKSUM_TYPES_SERVER= (MD5)
SQLNET.CRYPTO_SEED = abcdefghijklmnopqrstuvwxyzabc
```

Matching settings on the client are shown here:

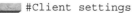

```
#Client settings
SQLNET.CRYPTO_CHECKSUM_CLIENT = required
SQLNET.CRYPTO_CHECKSUM_TYPES_CLIENT= (MD5, SHA1)
SQLNET.CRYPTO_SEED = abcdefghijklmnopqrstuvwxyzabc
```

Authentication

In local area networks, authentication is a smaller issue simply because an individual who has gained access to the network is physically identifiable (unless of course, they have accessed your network without authorization); however, if the user is at a remote location in a physically separate location, it is very difficult to confirm that the remote user is really who he or she claims to be. If the user information (login and password) has been compromised, there is no way to determine this ahead of time.

ASO supports a variety of third-party methods for authentication such as Kerberos, CyberSafe, RADIUS, smart cards, token cards, and certificate-based authentication. SSL is supported through wallets created by Oracle Wallet Manager. A case study in Chapter 12 illustrates the use of wallets for authentication.

NOTE
A discussion on authentication methods is beyond the scope of the book. Many excellent resources are available on the Web.

Additionally, ASO also has the ability to authenticate users centrally with single sign-on, thus limiting the threat of break-ins from multiple systems. Of course, the single sign-on then becomes the single point of failure!

Configuring Authentication Methods

Oracle Advanced Security supports dynamic loading of authentication methods. This means that the security options do not have to be enabled at instance startup. Additionally, external authentication can be configured on-the-fly. The supported authentication methods on Windows NT/2000 are summarized in Table 11-2.

Authentication Method	Description
Remote Authentication Dial-in User Service (RADIUS) authentication	Standard RADIUS authentication servers.
Kerberos5 authentication	Standard MIT Kerberos5.

TABLE 11-2. *Authentication Support in Oracle Advanced Security*

Authentication Method	Description
CyberSafe authentication	CyberSafe TrustBroker, a Kerberos-based authentication server is supported.
Secure Sockets Layer (SSL) authentication	Public key authentication based on the SSL standard.
Entrust-Enabled SSL authentication	Entrust/PKI from Entrust Technologies, Inc., provides certification generation, revocation, key, and certificate management.

TABLE 11-2. *Authentication Support in Oracle Advanced Security* (continued)

Authentication is again configured in the sqlnet.ora file using the SQLNET.AUTHENTICATION_SERVICES parameter. Oracle Net Manager can be used to configure authentication. Choose the authentication settings, as shown in the sample screen here:

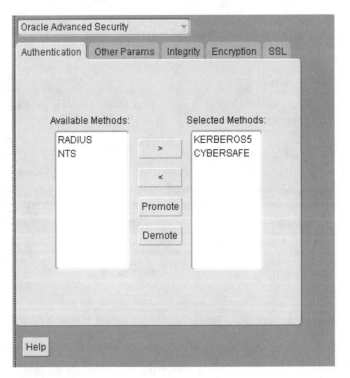

You can pick as many external authentication mechanisms as you wish. A sample setting for authentication is shown here:

```
SQLNET.AUTHENTICATION_SERVICES= (BEQ, TCPS, KERBEROS5, CYBERSAFE)
```

There are some dependencies if you choose to use this feature. You must first disable external authentication from the operating system using the REMOTE_OS_AUTHENT parameter, as shown here:

```
REMOTE_OS_AUTHENT=FALSE
```

You must have a Windows 2000 Primary Domain Controller (PDC) configured with Active Directory Server and Internet Authentication Service to use RADIUS and Kerberos authentication. Other authentication methods need UNIX or Linux servers.

Enabling and Disabling Authentication Methods

You must disable external authentication methods to use Oracle's default username and password authentication to connect to a database. The following setting in the server sqlnet.ora disables external authentication.

```
SQLNET.AUTHENTICATION_SERVICES = (none)
```

Single Sign-On

The Oracle single sign-on component is also available with ASO. Users can access multiple accounts and applications with a single password. Strong authentication with digital certificates is possible. Refer to *Oracle Single Sign-On Administrator's Guide* in Oracle documentation for more information.

Support for Public Key Infrastructure

Public key infrastructure (PKI) has emerged a leading standard for security and single sign-on. ASO supports SSL-based encryption and a variety of authentication methods including smart cards and X.509 certificates. Trusted certificates from Verisign, RSA, Entrust, and GTE CyberTrust are supported by ASO.

Oracle Wallet Manager can be used to manage containers called Oracle wallets to manage certificates. Oracle wallets store private keys, user certificates, and root certificates. Oracle Enterprise Login Assistant can be used to provide single sign-on capability in a client/server environment. A case study on PKI is included in Chapter 12.

Oracle Internet Directory

A directory is a special type of database that stores large amounts of corporate information in a central location. Directories are especially useful for large companies since information on resources such as employees, conference rooms, printers, and the books available in the corporate library can be maintained in one location. If you have databases and applications spread across several systems, it is also useful to rely on a central directory to maintain user and role information. This alleviates the need to replicate user and role information across several systems.

The Lightweight Directory Access Protocol (LDAP) is an implementation of a directory service that has gained wide acceptance in the industry. LDAP is considered ideal for web-based applications since it does not require any special networking software on the client. The Internet Engineering Task Force (IETF) has approved the current implementation of LDAP (Version 3).

Oracle Internet Directory (OID) is Oracle's own implementation of an LDAP Version 3–compliant directory. Since the directory is stored inside an Oracle database, OID is highly scalable and robust. Oracle recommends that you create a separate database to hold a directory. OID is really an application that is built on top of the directory and can use Oracle Net Services to access a directory on a remote database. Additional tools such as OID Control Utility and Oracle Directory Manager are used to manage directory services and directory information. Refer to Chapter 12 for a case study that illustrates Oracle Internet Directory.

This chapter touched on several aspects of security related to Oracle software. The goal was to whet your appetite for security and provide pointers to help you design robust solutions for your site. Chapter 12 has sample implementations covering the topics introduced in this chapter.

CHAPTER
12

Case Studies

his book provides great breadth and depth on a variety of Oracle9i topics for the Windows platform. Depending on your current level of expertise and your needs, you might have a few queries left unanswered. This chapter gives some practical examples in the form of case studies that cut across the entire range of Oracle technologies. A step-by-step approach has been adopted to succinctly show you how to perform a specific task without touching on the theory behind the technology.

The Test Installation

Unless mentioned otherwise, the configuration shown in Table 12-1 was used in all the case studies.

Machine	Description/Configuration
aa.liqwidkrystal.com	Pentium III, 1GHz CPU, 10GB hard disk space, Ethernet adapter
	Windows XP Professional, with TCP/IP configured
	Oracle9i Enterprise Edition with Oracle HTTP Server and Oracle Net configured
	Oracle Home, c:\oracle\ora90\
	Microsoft Internet Explorer 6.0.26 (standard with Windows XP Professional) Netscape Navigator 4.72
aa2.liqwidkrystal.com	Pentium III, 733MHz CPU, 8GB hard disk space, Ethernet adapter
	Windows NT Workstation 4.0 with SP6, with TCP/IP configured
	Oracle9i Application Server Enterprise Edition with Oracle HTTP Server
	Oracle Home, c:\oracle\isuites\
	Microsoft Internet Explorer 5.0
Web Client	Microsoft Internet Explorer 6.0.26

TABLE 12-1. *Configuration of Test Installation Used in Case Studies*

The machine aa2.liqwidkrystal.com was used as the Oracle client in all case studies. The following case studies are presented in this chapter:

1. Browser-based SQL queries

2. Migration from MS SQL Server 7.0 to Oracle9i

3. PHP-based applications against Oracle9i

4. Use of Oracle Internet Directory for enterprise user security

5. Backup strategy for small- to medium-sized sites

6. Tablespace point-in-time recovery

Case Study 1: Browser-Based SQL Queries

A summary of the case study requirements and the scenario is provided in Table 12-2.

Scenario	You want to execute ad hoc SQL queries from remote clients from a web browser. You do not have Oracle clients nor SQL*Plus installed on the remote clients.
Solution	Use iSQL*Plus for Windows to access remote database in a two- or three-tier architecture.
Software Required	Oracle HTTP Server, iSQL*Plus, Oracle Net, and Oracle9i database.
Prerequisites	Oracle iSQL*Plus installed—available on Oracle9i media and installed automatically with Enterprise Edition. You can perform a custom installation and install this on any machine running Oracle HTTP Server. Oracle HTTP Server in middle or database tier. Oracle Net configured on database server and the machine running Oracle HTTP Server. Any Java-enabled browser can act as a web client (no additional Oracle software is required on the web client).
Additional References	iSQL*Plus User's Guide and Reference—click the Help icon in iSQL*Plus screens.

TABLE 12-2. *Case Study on iSQL*Plus*

Step-by-Step Instructions

1. Verify that the Oracle HTTP Server configuration file (c:\oracle\ora90\ Apache\Apache\conf\httpd.conf) has the following entry:

   ```
   include "C:\oracle\ora90\Apache\Apache\conf\
   oracle_apache.conf"
   ```

2. Verify that Oracle HTTP configuration (**oracle_apache.conf**) has the following entry:

   ```
   include "C:\oracle\ora90\sqlplus\admin\isqlplus.conf"
   ```

3. Verify that the iSQL*Plus configuration file isqlplus.conf exists in the folder c:\oracle\ora90\sqlplus\admin\.

4. Verify the path and other entries in the isqlplus.conf file.

5. Launch your web browser and point to the URL of the form *http://<node>:<port>/isqlplus* to view the login screen. A sample screen from the test installation at http://aa.liqwidkrystal.com/isqlplus is shown here:

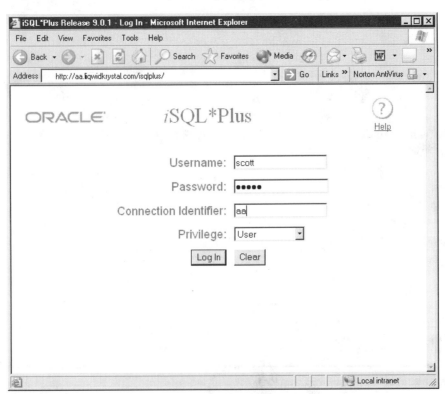

6. Log in to the database. You can type your query in the available text field and click Execute to view the results. A sample screen is shown here:

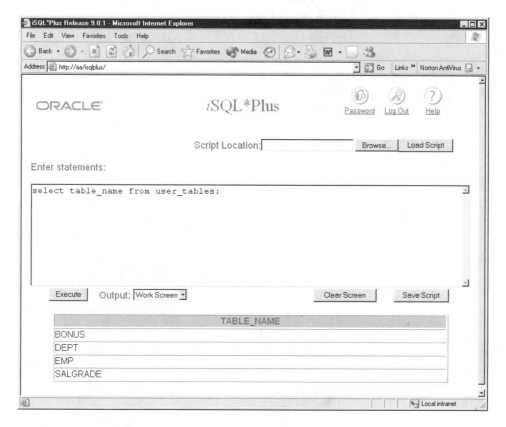

Additional Remarks

Additional configuration is required to connect as SYSDBA or SYSOPER. Click Security Link in the online Help screen to get additional information. You might need to configure an additional mime type in your browser, as shown here:

```
File extension: .sql
Mime type: text/plain
Application to use: notepad.exe
```

To configure mime types for Windows, launch Windows Explorer and choose Tools | Folder Options from the toolbar. To add a mime type, click File Types, then New. To modify an existing mime type, click Change.

Case Study 2: Migration from MS SQL Server 7.0 to Oracle9i

A summary of the case study requirements and the scenario is provided in Table 12-3.

Step-by-Step Instructions

1. Perform a custom installation of Oracle9i using Oracle Universal Installer and install Oracle Migration Workbench (OMW) if it is not already installed on your machine.

2. If you have not installed Oracle Enterprise Manager (OEM), perform a custom installation of this component. Create an OEM repository, as described in Chapter 7.

3. Ensure that you have sufficient space in the SYSTEM and TEMP tablespaces to hold the MS SQL Server database. The space that you will need depends on the size of your database.

4. Launch OMW. Choose Start | Programs | Oracle-OraHome90 | Configuration and Migration Tools | Migration Workbench. At the login screen, enter the user information for the OEM repository owner.

5. Choose Action | Capture Source Database to launch the Capture Wizard. Follow the instructions provided by the wizard. Select the database that you want to migrate from MS SQL 7.0 (Service Pack 2, Version 7.00.842 was used in the test migration). Here the PUBS database has been selected.

Scenario	You want to migrate a database from MS SQL Server 7.0 to Oracle9i on Windows.
Solution	Use Oracle Migration Workbench 2.0 to perform the migration.
Software Required	Oracle9i, Oracle Net (optional), Oracle Migration Workbench.
Prerequisites	Suitable database backups of MS SQL Server and Oracle9i database have been taken.
Additional References	OMW online help.

TABLE 12-3. *Case Study on Oracle Migration Workbench*

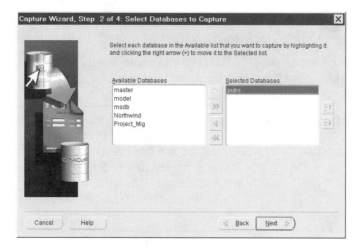

6. You need to provide the password for the SA user in one of the screens. You can map SQL Server data types to Oracle data types during the migration process.

7. Verify the SQL Server objects that were captured in the source model. A sample screen from the test installation is shown in Figure 12-1.

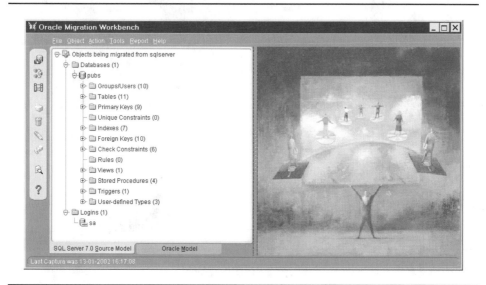

FIGURE 12-1. *Source model of pubs database in Migration Workbench*

8. Complete the migration by choosing to create the Oracle model. Select Action | Create Oracle Model to start the wizard.

9. View the report provided by OMW to verify that there are no errors. The report is created in HTML format in the c:\oracle\ora90\omwb\log folder. A portion of the report is shown in Figure 12-2.

10. OMW creates a new tablespace that has the name of the MS SQL Server database. In the example, a tablespace named PUBS was created to hold the migrated database. By default, the objects are created in a new schema created by OMW. The name of the schema is derived from the owner of the MS SQL database (SA in the example).

3. Error and Warnings Report

Summary for pubs database

Object Type	Total number of objects to migrate	Number of Objects Failed	
		Create Oracle Model	Migrate to Oracle
Tablespaces	1	0	0
Users	3	0	0
Tables	11	0	0
Roles	10	0	0
Indexes	7	0	0
Views	1	0	0
Triggers	1	0	0
Stored Procedures	4	4	0
Packages	4	0	0
Check Constraints	6	0	0
Primary Keys and Unique Constraints	9	0	0
Foreign Keys	10	0	0

FIGURE 12-2. *Oracle Migration Workbench report*

11. Verify that the objects were migrated properly by querying the data dictionary. A sample query on the DBA_OBJECTS view from the test migration is shown here. The output shown is truncated to conserve space.

```
SQL> select object_name, object_type, created from dba_objects
where owner='SA';
OBJECT_NAME        OBJECT_TYPE          CREATED
-----------        -----------          ----------------

AUIDIND            INDEX                13-JAN-02
AUTHORS            TABLE                13-JAN-02
```

Additional Remarks

OMW is unable to migrate some T-SQL procedures and system variables properly. These have to be manually migrated later.

A database in SQL Server is approximately the equivalent of a tablespace in Oracle; therefore, a new tablespace is created for every SQL Server database that you migrate.

Other databases that can be migrated to Oracle9i using this utility are

- Informix Dynamic Server 7.3

- Microsoft Access

- MySQL

- Sybase Adaptive Server 11

During the installation of OMW, you can choose to install plug-ins for specific databases that you wish to migrate to Oracle9i. A list of available plug-ins is displayed during installation.

Case Study 3: PHP-Based Applications Against Oracle9i

In this case study, you will see how you can access Oracle databases from PHP applications running on Oracle HTTP Server. Table 12-4 provides a summary.

Step-by-Step Instructions

1. Download PHP binaries for Win32 from www.php.net or any other mirror site. PHP version 4.0.4 (php-4.0.4pl1-Win32.exe) was downloaded in the test installation.

Scenario	You want to write web applications with PHP that use Oracle9i as the back-end database.
Solution	Add PHP module to Oracle HTTP Server.
Software Required	PHP for Win32, Oracle HTTP Server, Oracle9i database.
Prerequisites	Oracle HTTP Server, Oracle9i database, and Oracle Net installed configured.
Additional References	www.php.net and www.phpbuilder.com.

TABLE 12-4. *PHP Applications Against Oracle9i*

2. Execute php-4.0.4pl1-Win32 and install PHP in the folder c:\php.

3. Copy the file php4ts.dll into the \windows\system32 folder.

```
C:\php>copy php4ts.dll \windows\system32
        1 file(s) copied.
```

4. Make a copy of the file php.ini-dist and create a file named php.ini in the \windows folder.

```
C:\WINDOWS>copy \php\php.ini-dist php.ini
        1 file(s) copied.
```

5. Edit php.ini and set the folder for extensions and a temporary directory. These parameters already exist in the file. Find them and provide the folder settings, as shown here:

```
extension_dir  =    C:\php\extensions
session.save_path        = c:\tmp
```

6. Add Oracle modules to PHP. To do so, uncomment or add the following lines in the php.ini file:

```
extension=php_oci8.dll
extension=php_oracle.dll
```

7. Add PHP module to Oracle HTTP Server configuration. Modify httpd.conf in the c:\oracle\ora90\Apache\Apache\conf folder and add the following lines to the file:

```
LoadModule php4_module c:/php/sapi/php4apache.dll
AddType application/x-httpd-php .php .php3 .php4 .phtml
AddType application/x-httpd-php-source .phps
```

CAUTION
You must use forward slashes in the preceding entries. Backward slashes will not work.

8. Restart Oracle HTTP Server. Choose Start | Programs | Oracle -OraHome90 | Oracle HTTP Server | Start HTTP Server powered by Apache.

9. Verify that the Oracle module has been added properly. Create a file named test.php with the following contents and save it to the c:\oracle\ora90\ Apache\Apache\htdocs folder:

```php
<?php
phpinfo();
?>
```

10. Start your browser and point it to the test.php file. You should see a page that shows information about your configuration. Scroll down the page and find the Oracle section. Ensure that Oracle modules are enabled. A portion of the screen is shown here:

oci8

OCI8 Support	enabled
Revision	$Revision: 1.104.2.1 $

oracle

Oracle Support	enabled

11. Write sample PHP scripts to test SQL calls to Oracle9i Server. The following PHP script was used to create a table in the database.

```php
<?php
PutEnv("ORACLE_SID=AA");
$connection = Ora_Logon ("scott", "tiger");
if ($connection == false){
  echo Ora_ErrorCode($connection).": ".Ora_Error($connection).
  "<BR>";
  exit;
}
$cursor = Ora_Open ($connection);
if ($cursor == false){
  echo Ora_ErrorCode($connection).": ".Ora_Error($connection).
```

```
     "<BR>";
     exit;
   }
   $query = "create table email_info " .
          "(fullname varchar(255), email_address varchar(255))";
   $result = Ora_Parse ($cursor, $query);
   if ($result == false){
     echo Ora_ErrorCode($cursor).": ".Ora_Error($cursor)."<BR>";
     exit;
   }
   $result = Ora_Exec ($cursor);
   if ($result == false){
     echo Ora_ErrorCode($cursor).": ".Ora_Error($cursor)."<BR>";
     exit;
   }
   Ora_Commit ($connection);
   Ora_Close ($cursor);
   Ora_Logoff ($connection);
   ?>
```

The argument AA in the PUTENV call is the Oracle Net connection identifier.

12. Write sample PHP scripts to test OCI calls. A sample is given here:

```
<?php
if ($submit == "click"){
  // The submit button was clicked!
  // Get the input for fullname and email then store it in
     the database.
PutEnv("ORACLE_SID=AA");
  $connection = OCILogon ("scott","tiger");
  if ($connection == false){
    echo OCIError($connection)."<BR>";
    exit;
  }
  $query = "insert into email_info values ('$fullname', '$email')";
  $cursor = OCIParse ($connection, $query);
  if ($cursor == false){
    echo OCIError($cursor)."<BR>";
    exit;
  }
  $result = OCIExecute ($cursor);
  if ($result == false){
    echo OCIError($cursor)."<BR>";
    exit;
  }
  OCICommit ($connection);
  OCILogoff ($connection);
```

```
    }
    else{
      echo '
        <html><body>
        <form method="post" action="ora3.php">
        Enter your full name
        <input type="text" name="fullname"></input><br>
        Enter your email address
        <input type="text" name="email"></input><br>
        <input type="submit" name="submit" value="click"></input>
    </form>
        </body></html>
      ';
    }
    ?>
```

A sample screen from the preceding PHP script is shown in Figure 12-3. The
script inserts records into the EMAIL_INFO table.

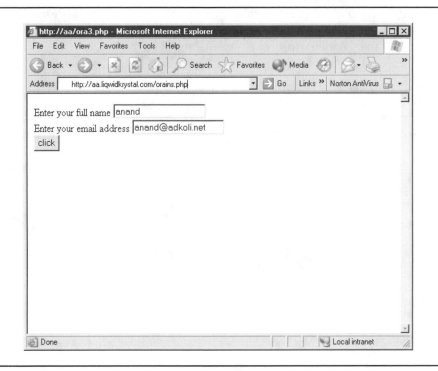

FIGURE 12-3.   *PHP script with embedded OCI calls*

Additional Remarks

You can use the CGI executable instead of the Oracle module for Apache. To do so, configure your httpd.conf with the following lines:

```
ScriptAlias /php4/ "C:/php/"
Action application/x-httpd-php4 "/php4/php.exe"
AddType application/x-httpd-php4 .php
```

PHP still supports OCI8. As this books goes to print, we are not aware of any development activity to support OCI Version 9.

Case Study 4: Use of Oracle Internet Directory for Enterprise User Security

In this case study, a preexisting database named AA holds the tables containing employee-related information. The standard demo table EMP, owned by the SCOTT/TIGER user, is used in the example. Oracle Internet Directory (OID) and its related objects are created in a separate database named OID. The case study is performed on the machine aa.liqwidkrystal.com that has Oracle9i Enterprise Edition installed.

The case study requirements are listed in Table 12-5.

Scenario	You have a database that holds employee information for your company. Employees from around the world access this database. You do not want to maintain user IDs on the database for this application. Instead, you want to use a central directory that will authenticate users and give them access to the tables in this database.
Solution	Use Oracle Internet Directory to manage users centrally; create a shared schema for the database and map enterprise users to this schema using Enterprise Security.
Software Required	Oracle9i database, Oracle Net, Oracle Internet Directory.
Prerequisites	Oracle9i database is configured with Oracle Net.
Additional References	*Oracle Internet Directory Installation Guide for Windows NT, Oracle Internet Directory Administration Guide.*

TABLE 12-5. *Case Study on Oracle Internet Directory*

A Windows user named ANAND is mapped to an enterprise user (cn=anand) in OID and granted access to the SCOTT.EMP table via a schema named GUEST. The schema GUEST has no privileges on the SCOTT.EMP table.

Step-by-Step Instructions

1. Launch OUI and choose the Oracle9i Management and Integration 9.0.1.0.1 installation option. Click Next to view the Installation Types screen.

2. Choose Oracle Internet Directory from the available products and complete the installation of OID. You will require about 1.2GB of free disk space. During the installation you will be asked whether you want to create a new database instance for OID or use an existing instance. Choose to create a new database named OID. An Oracle Schema and an Oracle Context (cn=OracleContext) are automatically created during the installation of OID. A Windows service named OracleDirectoryService_oid is also created. A default administrator user named (CN=ORCLADMIN) with the password WELCOME is automatically created.

3. Start the OID service named OracleDirectoryService_oid if it is not running. You can also perform this task using the OIDMON utility, as shown here:

```
c:\>oidmon connect=oid start
OracleDirectoryService Already Running
```

4. Use the OIDCTL utility to start an instance using the default configuration set (Set 0).

```
c:\>oidctl connect=oid server=oidldapd instance=2 start
```

5. Choose Start | Programs | Oracle - OraHome90 | Integrated Management Tools | Oracle Directory Manager (ODM) to launch ODM. Use the (cn=orcladmin) user to connect to OID using ODM on the non-SSL port.

6. Select Entry Management in the Navigator. Right-click, choose Create, and make a new Country entry (c=us). Similarly, create an organization entry (o=liqwidkrystal). A sample screen from ODM with the entry (o=liqwidkrystal,c=us) is shown in Figure 12-4.

7. Select Start | Programs | Oracle - OraHome90 | Integrated Management Tools | Enterprise Security Manager to launch ESM. Again, use (cn=orcladmin) to connect to OID on the non-SSL port. Choose Operations | Create Enterprise User from menu and create a new user named ANAND with the DN (cn=anand, o = liqwidkrystal, c=us).

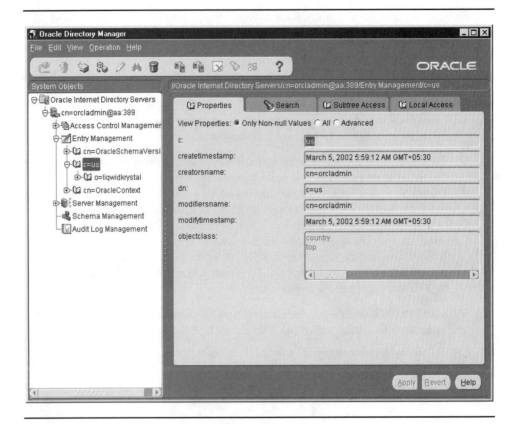

FIGURE 12-4. *Organization entry in ODM*

8. Next, create a new Oracle Context using Net Configuration Assistant (NETCA). Launch NETCA and choose the option Directory Usage Configuration from the Welcome screen. Click Next.

9. Choose the option Create Additional or Upgrade Existing Oracle Context and create a new Oracle Context named (cn=OracleContext, o=liqwidkrystal, c=us). Specify (o=liqwidkrystal, c=us) as the root for this Oracle Context. This process takes a few minutes.

10. Launch ODM or refresh the (c=us) entry if ODM is already running to confirm that the enterprise user ANAND and the new Oracle Context (cn=OracleContext, o=liqwidkrystal, c=us) have been created properly. A sample screen is shown next:

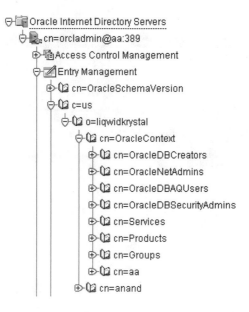

11. Verify that a file named ldap.ora was created in the c:\oracle\ora90\
network\admin folder. The file should have entries as shown here:

```
# LDAP.ORA Network Configuration File:
C:\oracle\ora90\network\admin\ldap.ora
# Generated by Oracle configuration tools.
DEFAULT_ADMIN_CONTEXT = "o=liqwidkrystal,c=us"
DIRECTORY_SERVERS= (aa:389:636)
DIRECTORY_SERVER_TYPE = OID
```

12. Register the AA database in OID using Database Configuration Assistant
(DBCA). Launch DBCA and choose the option to Configure Database
Options. Choose AA from the list of available databases and click Next.
Select the option to register the database in OID and provide authentication
information for (cn=orcladmin), as shown in Figure 12-5. You will be
prompted for the location of the initialization parameter file.

13. Verify that the following initialization parameter has been set in the AA
database.

```
SQL> show parameter rdbms_server_dn
NAME                TYPE         VALUE
---------------- ----------- --------------
rdbms_server_dn  string       cn=aa,cn=OracleContext,
                              o=liqwidkrystal,c=us
```

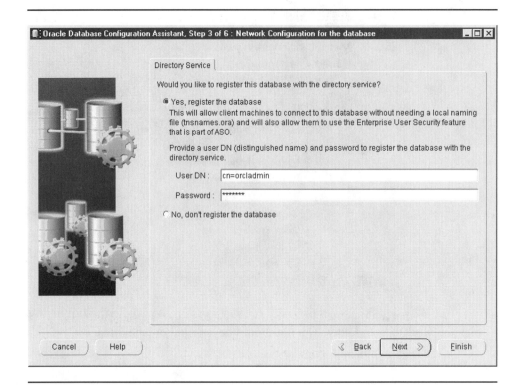

FIGURE 12-5. *Registering a database in OID*

   14. Next, configure Net Listener and the database for SSL. Launch Oracle Net
        Manager (NETMGR) and choose Local | Profile in the Navigator. Select
        Oracle Advanced Security from the drop-down list and remove the NTS
        authentication by clicking the left arrow.

15. Choose the SSL tab and configure the database wallet. Provide the location of the wallet as c:\tmp\pki\databases\aa. Uncheck the Require Client Authentication check box, as shown here:

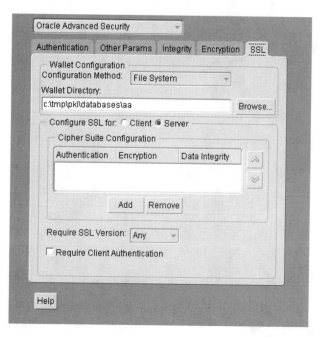

16. Create a new connection identifier for SSL. Choose Service Naming in the Navigator and click the + icon to create a new entry named AASSL. Select the protocol TCP/IP with SSL and configure SSL for Port 5000.

17. Configure the Listener to listen for SSL requests on Port 5000. Choose Listener in the Navigator and select Listening Locations. Add a new address, as shown here:

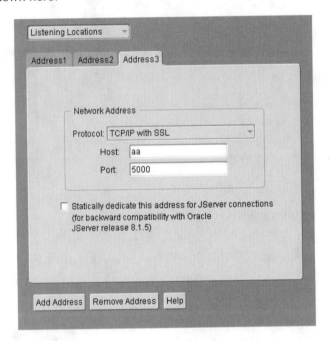

18. Check sqlnet.ora, listener.ora, and tnsnames.ora in the c:\oracle\ ora90\network\admin folder to ensure that you have configured SSL properly. Sample entries are shown here for your reference.

```
# SQLNET.ORA Network Configuration File:
C:\oracle\ora90\NETWORK\ADMIN\sqlnet.ora
# Generated by Oracle configuration tools.
WALLET_LOCATION =
  (SOURCE =
    (METHOD = FILE)
    (METHOD_DATA =
      (DIRECTORY = c:\tmp\pki\databases\aa)
    )
  )
SSL_CLIENT_AUTHENTICATION = FALSE
SQLNET.AUTHENTICATION_SERVICES=(TCPS)
SSL_VERSION = 0

# TNSNAMES.ORA Network Configuration File:
```

```
c:\oracle\ora90\NETWORK\ADMIN\tnsnames.ora
# Generated by Oracle configuration tools.
AASSL =
  (DESCRIPTION =
    (ADDRESS_LIST =
      (ADDRESS = (PROTOCOL = TCPS)(HOST = aa)(PORT = 5000))
    )
    (CONNECT_DATA =
      (SERVICE_NAME = aa)
    )
  )

# LISTENER.ORA Network Configuration File:
C:\oracle\ora90\NETWORK\ADMIN\listener.ora
# Generated by Oracle configuration tools.
WALLET_LOCATION =
  (SOURCE =
    (METHOD = FILE)
    (METHOD_DATA =
      (DIRECTORY = c:\tmp\pki\databases\aa)
    )
  )
LISTENER =
  (DESCRIPTION_LIST =
    (DESCRIPTION =
      (ADDRESS = (PROTOCOL = IPC)(KEY = EXTPROC0))
    )
    (DESCRIPTION =
      (ADDRESS = (PROTOCOL = TCP)(HOST = aa)(PORT = 1521))
    )
    (DESCRIPTION =
      (ADDRESS = (PROTOCOL = TCPS)(HOST = aa)(PORT = 5000))
    )
  )
SID_LIST_LISTENER =
  (SID_LIST =
    (SID_DESC =
      (SID_NAME = PLSExtProc)
      (ORACLE_HOME = C:\oracle\ora90)
      (PROGRAM = extproc)
    )
    (SID_DESC =
      (GLOBAL_DBNAME = aa)
      (ORACLE_HOME = C:\oracle\ora90)
      (SID_NAME = aa)
```

```
      )
    (SID_DESC =
      (GLOBAL_DBNAME = oid)
      (ORACLE_HOME = C:\oracle\ora90)
      (SID_NAME = oid)
    )
  )
SSL_CLIENT_AUTHENTICATION = FALSE
```

19. Create the database wallet using Oracle Wallet Manager (OWM). Choose
    Start | Programs | Oracle - OraHome90 | Integrated Management Tools |
    Wallet Manager to launch OWM. Choose Wallet | New from the menu.
    You will be prompted for a password. Provide a password that is longer
    than eight characters. An empty wallet is created. You will be prompted for
    a certificate request. Click Yes to request for a certificate for the database.
    Click Advanced and request a database wallet, as shown here:

20. Select the certificate request from the Certificates folder. Launch your
    web browser and point it to a URL for a certificate authority (CA) such as
    www.thawte.com. Select the link to create a test certificate and complete
    the registration form to obtain a test certificate.

21. Select Operations | Import User Certificate and choose the option to paste
    a certificate. You might be asked for a root certificate. You can obtain this
    from the CA site, too. Paste the root certificate, if required, and then the
    user certificate. Save the wallet in c:\tmp\pki\databases\aa, the target
    location for the database wallet. Enable Auto Login from the Wallet menu.
    Save the certificate. You should see two files named ewallet.p12 and
    cwallet.sso in the folder.

22. Restart Listener using the LSNRCTL utility.

```
C:\>lsnrctl start
<output is truncated>
Listening on: (DESCRIPTION=(ADDRESS=(PROTOCOL=tcps)(HOST=aa)
    (PORT=5000)))
The command completed successfully
```

Ensure that the SSL port (TCPS) is listed in the output of the command. If the listener starts up, the database wallet is created properly.

23. Create a shared schema named GUEST that will be used to provide access to the SCOTT.EMP table. You must give CREATE SESSION privileges.

```
SQL> connect system/manager@aa
Connected.
SQL> create user guest identified globally as '';
User created.
SQL> grant create session to guest;
Grant succeeded.
```

24. Create global roles in the database. These roles will be mapped to enterprise roles that you will create in OID later. A database role named EMPROLE is created for this purpose.

```
SQL> create role emprole identified globally;
Role created
```

25. Next, grant the EMPROLE permissions to query the SCOTT.EMP table.

```
SQL> connect scott/tiger@aa
Connected.
SQL> grant select on emp to emprole;
Grant succeeded.
```

26. Create Oracle Net Configuration for clients. For convenience, you can create this in the oracle\wallets folder in the user's profile. For example, use \winnt\profiles\anand\oracle\wallets on Windows NT and \documents and settings\anand\oracle\wallets on Windows XP. Create a sqlnet.ora and tnsnames.ora file and place them in the oracle\wallets folder in your user profile. Sample files are shown here:

```
# SQLNET.ORA Network Configuration File:
# C:\oracle\ora90\NETWORK\ADMIN\sqlnet.ora
# Generated by Oracle configuration tools.
WALLET_LOCATION =
  (SOURCE =
    (METHOD = FILE)
    (METHOD_DATA =
      (DIRECTORY = C:\Documents and Settings\anand\ORACLE\WALLETS)
    )
  )
SSL_CLIENT_AUTHENTICATION = FALSE
SQLNET.AUTHENTICATION_SERVICES=(TCPS)
SSL_VERSION = 0

# TNSNAMES.ORA Network Configuration File:
# C:\oracle\ora90\NETWORK\ADMIN\tnsnames.ora
# Generated by Oracle configuration tools.
```

```
AASSL =
  (DESCRIPTION =
    (ADDRESS_LIST =
      (ADDRESS = (PROTOCOL = TCPS)(HOST = aa)(PORT = 5000))
    )
    (CONNECT_DATA =
      (SERVICE_NAME = aa)
    )
  )
```

Note that the wallet location for the user ANAND has been set to the c:\documents and settings\anand\oracle\wallets folder.

27. Create a user wallet following a procedure similar to that described earlier for creating a database wallet. Save the wallet for (cn=anand) in the c:\documents and settings\anandoracle\wallets folder.

28. Map the enterprise user to the database GUEST schema using ESM. Launch ESM and select LiqwidKrystal | Enterprise Domains | Oracle Default Domain. Select the Database Schema Mapping tab and map the enterprise user ANAND to the GUEST schema. A sample screen is shown in Figure 12-6.

29. Launch ESM and choose Operations | Create Enterprise Role, and create an enterprise role named EMPLOYEE. A sample screen is shown here:

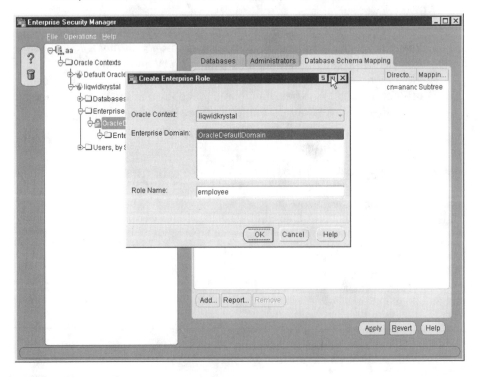

FIGURE 12-6.   *Mapping an enterprise user to database schema*

30. Expand LiqwidKrystal | Enterprise Domains | Oracle DefaultDomain |
Enterprise Roles, and select the role EMPLOYEE created in the previous
step. Add the enterprise user ANAND to this role.

31. Select the Database Global Roles tab and map the enterprise role
EMPLOYEE to the database global role EMPROLE. A sample screen is
shown in Figure 12-7.

32. Enable SSL connections to directory. To do so, launch ODM, select Server
Management | Directory Server | Default Configuration Set and choose the
SSL settings tab. Select the SSL Enable check box and provide SSL settings.
Port 636 was enabled for SSL on the test installation.

33. Restart OIDMON.

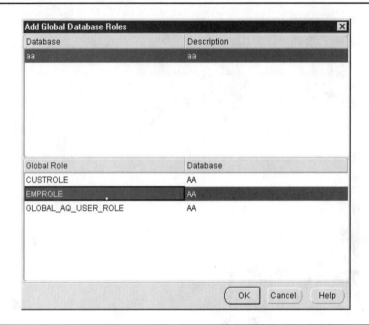

FIGURE 12-7. *Mapping an enterprise roles to global roles*

34. Use LDAPBIND to ensure that the database can query the directory.

```
C:\>ldapbind -p 636 -U 3 -W "file:c:\tmp\pki\databases\aa"
-P sfg1antsaa
bind successful
```

If you are unable to bind to the directory, check your database wallet location.

35. Launch the Services applet from Control Panel. Select the Oracle Listener service from the list of services and double-click. Select the Log On tab and select This Account in the Log On As area. Enter the Windows account that enabled Autologin for the database wallet (AA\anand in the test installation). Repeat the process for the Oracle database service. Restart the Listener and database service for the new permissions to take effect.

36. Launch Enterprise Login Assistant (ELA) by selecting Start | Programs | Oracle - OraHome90 | Integrated Management Tools | Enterprise Login Assistant. Provide the password for the user wallet to authenticate yourself. Upon successful login, you will see a screen similar to the one shown here:

37. Launch SQL*Plus and connect to the database using a forward slash, as shown here:

```
C:\Documents and Settings\anand\ORACLE\WALLETS>sqlplus /@aassl
SQL*Plus: Release 9.0.1.0.1 - Production on Tue Mar 5 23:25:40 2002
(c) Copyright 2001 Oracle Corporation.  All rights reserved.
Connected to:
Oracle9i Enterprise Edition Release 9.0.1.1.1 - Production
With the Partitioning option
JServer Release 9.0.1.1.1 - Production
SQL>
```

38. Query the SESSION_ROLES view to ensure that you have been granted the EMPROLE global role.

```
SQL> select * from session_roles;
ROLE
------------------------------

EMPROLE
```

Additional Remarks

You can also configure password security on clients if you do not want to use SSL. A wallet is still required for the database. Refer to *Oracle Advanced Security Administrator's Guide* in Oracle documentation for more information.

Oracle recommends that you create a new Configuration Set in ODM for SSL. Use the default Configuration Set (0) for non-SSL connections. To create a new configuration set, select Server Management | Directory Server in ODM, right-click, and select Create.

Case Study 5: Backup Strategy for Small- to Medium-Sized Sites

Many small- to medium-sized sites can use this as a minimum strategy for a backup. The case study requirements are listed in Table 12-6.

In the case study, assume that the database with SID of AA holds the recovery catalog and the database to be backed up is named HR. Other databases can also be included in the backup.

Scenario	You have a few databases on your site, and you want to create a standardized backup strategy that allows you to optimize the space required for backup and the time needed to recover.
Solution	Use Oracle Recovery Manager with a recovery catalog and create a backup strategy with incremental backups.
Software Required	Oracle9i database, Oracle Net, Oracle Recovery Manager (RMAN).
Prerequisites	Oracle9i and Oracle Net configured.
Additional References	*Recovery Manager User's Guide.*

TABLE 12-6. *Backup Strategy for Small- to Medium-Sized Sites*

NOTE
The C:\ drive is being used for creating the backup set in RMAN. This is purely for illustrative purposes. On the job, you should create your backups on another physical disk or a tape device.

Step-by-Step Instructions

1. Create a tablespace in the AA database to hold the recovery catalog.

   ```
   SQL> create tablespace rcat datafile 'c:\oracle\oradata\aa\
   rcat.ora' size 5m;
   Tablespace created.
   ```

2. Create the recovery catalog owner.

   ```
   SQL> create user rman identified by rman default tablespace rcat
     2  temporary tablespace temp;
   User created.
   SQL> grant connect,resource, recovery_catalog_owner to rman;
   Grant succeeded.
   ```

3. Create recovery catalog using RMAN.

   ```
   C:\>rman catalog rman/rman@aa
   Recovery Manager: Release 9.0.1.1.1 - Production
   (c) Copyright 2001 Oracle Corporation.  All rights reserved.
   ```

```
connected to recovery catalog database
recovery catalog is not installed
RMAN> create catalog
recovery catalog created
```

4. Register the target database (HR) in the catalog.

```
C:\>rman target sys/change_on_install@hr catalog rman/rman@aa
Recovery Manager: Release 9.0.1.1.1 - Production
(c) Copyright 2001 Oracle Corporation.  All rights reserved.
connected to target database: HR (DBID=3120069798)
connected to recovery catalog database
RMAN> register database;
database registered in recovery catalog
starting full resync of recovery catalog
full resync complete
```

5. Take a full database backup. This step is optional but recommended.

```
RMAN> backup database;
Starting backup at 21-FEB-02
allocated channel: ORA_DISK_1
<lines truncated>
input datafile fno=00001 name=C:\ORACLE\ORADATA\HR\SYSTEM01.DBF
input datafile fno=00002 name=C:\ORACLE\ORADATA\HR\UNDOTBS01.DBF
<lines truncated>
channel ORA_DISK_1: starting piece 1 at 21-FEB-02
channel ORA_DISK_1: finished piece 1 at 21-FEB-02
channel ORA_DISK_1: backup set complete, elapsed time: 00:04:07
Finished backup at 21-FEB-02
```

6. Take a level 0 backup. Run this script every Sunday, so you have a weekly backup.

```
RMAN> backup incremental level 0 database;
Starting backup at 21-FEB-02
using channel ORA_DISK_1
channel ORA_DISK_1: starting incremental level 0 datafile backupset
channel ORA_DISK_1: specifying datafile(s) in backupset
including current controlfile in backupset
input datafile fno=00001 name=C:\ORACLE\ORADATA\HR\SYSTEM01.DBF
<lines truncated>
channel ORA_DISK_1: starting piece 1 at 21-FEB-02
channel ORA_DISK_1: finished piece 1 at 21-FEB-02
piece handle=C:\ORACLE\ORA90\DATABASE\03DHCLLB_1_1 comment=NONE
channel ORA_DISK_1: backup set complete, elapsed time: 00:03:58
Finished backup at 21-FEB-02
```

7. Take a level 2 backup on Monday and Tuesday. These backups will include only the changed blocks on the database.

```
RMAN> backup incremental level 2 database;
<output truncated>
```

8. Take a level 1 backup on Wednesday. This will include all the blocks that have been modified since the last backup at the same or lower level. In this case, that would be Sunday (level 0).

```
RMAN> backup incremental level 1 database;
<output truncated>
```

9. Repeat a level 2 backup on Thursday and Friday.

10. Repeat a level 1 backup on Saturday.

11. Start the cycle again from a level 0 on Sunday.

Additional Remarks

Ensure that all databases are running in ARCHIVELOG mode and that automatic archiving is enabled. You should take your backups to a secondary device such as tape.

Case Study 6: Tablespace Point-in-Time Recovery

Tablespace point-in-time recovery (TSPITR) is useful in a situation in which a table has gotten dropped erroneously or a schema has become corrupted (logically). This feature allows you to recover a tablespace containing those objects up to a specific point in time at which the unwanted operation or transaction was performed. The feature is demonstrated here with RMAN, using a setup similar to that used in the previous case study. Table 12-7 summarizes the case-study requirements.

NOTE
Assume that the target database (HR) is registered in the recovery catalog and valid backup sets are available.

Scenario	You have dropped the EMPLOYEES table by mistake at 20:20 hours, and you want to recover it.
Solution	Perform TSPITR recovery using RMAN.
Software Required	Oracle Database, Oracle Net, and RMAN.
Prerequisites	RMAN installed, recovery catalog available, and valid backups available.
Additional References	*Recovery Manager User's Guide.*

TABLE 12-7. *Performing Tablespace Point-in-Time Recovery*

Step-by-Step Instructions

1. Assume that you have dropped the HR.EMPLOYEES table by mistake at 20:20 hours.

```
SQL> select count(*) from employees;
  COUNT(*)
----------
       107
SQL> drop table employees cascade constraints;
Table dropped.
```

2. Create a parameter file for the auxiliary instance. You can copy the parameter file belonging to the HR database and add the following entries:

```
lock_name_space = auxdb
control_files=/oracle/auxdb/cf/auxdb.f
log_file_name_convert=('C:\ORACLE\ORADATA\HR','C:\TMP\HR')
db_file_name_convert=('C:\ORACLE\ORADATA\HR','C:\TMP\HR')
```

An auxiliary instance is a temporary read-only copy of the database that will be created by RMAN during the recovery process. The preceding settings provide patterns to convert filenames from those used by the HR database to those created for the auxiliary database. The parameter file has been saved in the folder c:\tmp\tspitr.

3. Create an auxiliary instance, and call it AUXDB.

```
C:\>oradim -NEW -sid auxdb -intpwd aa -pfile c:\tmp\tspitr\
init.ora
```

4. Create entries for the auxiliary instance in the Listener configuration file and a connection identifier, if necessary. A portion of the LISTENER.ORA is listed here:

```
SID_LIST_LISTENER =
  (SID_LIST =
    (SID_DESC =
      (SID_NAME = PLSExtProc)
      (ORACLE_HOME = C:\oracle\ora90)
      (PROGRAM = extproc)
    )
    (SID_DESC =
      (GLOBAL_DBNAME = aa)
      (ORACLE_HOME = C:\oracle\ora90)
      (SID_NAME = aa)
    )
    (SID_DESC =
      (GLOBAL_DBNAME = hr)
      (ORACLE_HOME = C:\oracle\ora90)
      (SID_NAME = hr)
    )
    (SID_DESC =
      (GLOBAL_DBNAME = auxdb)
      (ORACLE_HOME = C:\oracle\ora90)
      (SID_NAME = auxdb)
    )
  )
```

In this case, all three databases are on the same machine; therefore, there is a service entry for each of the three databases: AA, HR, and AUXDB.

5. Start the auxiliary instance.

```
C:\>sqlplus
SQL*Plus: Release 9.0.1.0.1 - Production on Fri Feb 22 00:47:06 2002
(c) Copyright 2001 Oracle Corporation.  All rights reserved.
Enter user-name:
Enter user-name: sys/aa@auxdb as sysdba
Connected to an idle instance.
SQL> startup nomount pfile=c:\tmp\tspitr\init.ora
ORACLE instance started.
Total System Global Area  118255568 bytes
Fixed Size                   282576 bytes
Variable Size              83886080 bytes
Database Buffers           33554432 bytes
Redo Buffers                 532480 bytes
```

6. Start RMAN. Specify the target database, the database holding the recovery catalog, and the auxiliary instance.

```
C:\>rman target sys/change_on_install@hr catalog rman/rman@aa
auxiliary sys/aa@auxdb
Recovery Manager: Release 9.0.1.1.1 - Production
(c) Copyright 2001 Oracle Corporation.  All rights reserved.
connected to target database: HR (DBID=3120069798)
connected to recovery catalog database
connected to auxiliary database: hr (not mounted)
```

7. Set an NLS_LANG variable to match the character set of the database.
This is a required workaround for RMAN. First, find the character set of the
database being recovered and set an environment variable at the command
prompt, as shown here:

```
SQL> select value from v$nls_parameters
  2  where parameter = 'NLS_CHARACTERSET';
VALUE
--------------------------------------------------------
WE8MSWIN1252
C:\>set NLS_LANG=american_america.WE8MSWIN1252
```

8. Perform point-in-time recovery using RMAN. Several lines of output from
RMAN have been deleted to conserve space.

```
RMAN> recover tablespace example until time "to_date('2002
FEB 21 20:02','yyyy mon dd hh24:mi')";
Starting recover at 22-FEB-02
 printing stored script: Memory Script
{
# set the until clause
set until  time "to_date('2002 FEB 21 20:02',
'yyyy mon dd hh24:mi')";
# restore the controlfile
restore clone controlfile to clone_cf;
# replicate the controlfile
replicate clone controlfile from clone_cf;
# mount the controlfile
sql clone 'alter database mount clone database';
Starting restore at 22-FEB-02
allocated channel: ORA_AUX_DISK_1
sql statement: alter database mount clone database
sql statement: alter system archive log current
starting full resync of recovery catalog
full resync complete
executing command: SET NEWNAME
executing command: SET NEWNAME
….
Starting restore at 22-FEB-02
using channel ORA_AUX_DISK_1
….
channel ORA_AUX_DISK_1: restore complete
```

```
Finished restore at 22-FEB-02
sql statement: alter database datafile  1 online
sql statement: alter database datafile  2 online
sql statement: alter database datafile  3 online
channel ORA_AUX_DISK_1: restore complete
....
starting media recovery
archive log thread 1 sequence 5 is already on disk as file
C:\ORACLE\ORA90\RDBMS
\ARC00005.001
archive log filename=C:\ORACLE\ORA90\RDBMS\ARC00005.001
thread=1 sequence=5
media recovery complete
Finished recover at 22-FEB-02
database opened
# export the tablespaces in the recovery set
host 'exp userid =\"sys/aa@auxdb as sysdba\" point_in_time_
recover=y tablespaces
= EXAMPLE file=tspitr_a.dmp';
# import the tablespaces in the recovery set
host 'imp userid =\"sys/change_on_install@hr as sysdba\"
point_in_time_recover=y
 file=tspitr_a.dmp';
sql "alter tablespace  EXAMPLE online";
host command complete
database closed
database dismounted
Oracle instance shut down
RMAN>
```

9. Connect to the HR database and verify that the lost tables have been recovered properly.

```
SQL> select count(*) from employees;
COUNT(*)
----------
       107
```

10. Schedule a full backup of the database as soon as possible. Existing backup sets will not be useful since the database has been opened with the RESETLOGS option.

This chapter provided six case studies designed to give you a taste of administration tasks required in real Oracle sites. As a DBA, your primary goal is to ensure that your databases are managed so that you can recover from any situation. After all, that is the reason you are using an Oracle9i database!

APPENDIX
A

Additional Resources on the Web

he World Wide Web is an excellent resource for information. We have listed some top resources that we use regularly in Table A-1.

Web Site/Owner	URL	Description/Comments
Oracle Corporation	www.oracle.com	Obtain the latest product information, links to other Oracle resources, white papers, comparative studies, etc.
Oracle Technology Network	technet.oracle.com	Requires free registration. Excellent resource for technical white papers, product specifications, code samples, product downloads, documentation, forums, etc.
Oracle Documentation Site	docs.oracle.com	Online documentation for Oracle Server and Applications.
Oracle OTN Documentation	technet.oracle.com/docs	Complete documentation in HTML and PDF format.
Oracle Support	metalink.oracle.com or support.oracle.com	Technical bulletins, Oracle bug database, forums, alerts, patches, product certification information, etc.
Oracle Portal Studio	portalstudio.oracle.com	Resource for Oracle Portal and Oracle9i Application Server.
Osborne/McGraw-Hill	www.osborne.com	Information on Oracle Press series, code samples, etc.

TABLE A-I.   *Additional Resources on the Web*

Web Site/Owner	URL	Description/Comments
Oracle-related links	links.oracle-home.com	Free training resources, code samples, and other technical information.
Oracle-related training	www.intelinfo.com/ free_oracle_training.html	Free Oracle training resources.
Oracle Virtual Information Store	www.dba-village.com	Forum, news, events, and technical resources.
Internet.com network	www.dbasupport.com	Articles, tips and tricks, and links to other resources.
Versign Corporation	www.verisign.com	Verisign digital certificates.
Thawte Consulting	www.thawte.com	Background and technical information on digital certificates.
Microsoft Corporation	www.microsoft.com	Product information, knowledge base, MSDN, and other utilities.
MS Download Site	download.microsoft.com	Product updates and latest service packs.
Microsoft Corporation	www.microsoft.com/ windowsxp/pro/evaluation/ whyupgrade/featurecomp.asp	Comparison of Windows-based operating systems.
Anand Adkoli Home	www.adkoli.net	Code samples, book information, and forum.
Oracle Masters	www.oramasters.com	Oracle technical support.
Executive Software	www.execsoft.com	Information and comparison of FAT16, FAT32, and NTFS; Diskeeper product information.
Raxco Software	www.raxco.com	PerfectDisk2000.

TABLE A-I.   *Additional Resources on the Web* (Continued)

APPENDIX

B

Oracle9i New Features for Windows

any new features have been introduced in Oracle9i. Table B-1 provides a summary of new features added in Oracle9i on the Windows platform.

For additional information, refer to the following in Oracle documentation:

- *Oracle9i Network, Directory and Security Guide for Windows*
- *Oracle Provider for OLE DB Developer's Guide*
- *Oracle COM Automation Feature Developer's Guide*
- *Oracle Plug-in for Microsoft IIS Configuration and User's Guide*
- *Oracle9i Database New Features*

Feature	Description/Comments
Integration with Microsoft Internet Information Services	The Oracle plug-in for IIS allows you to use PL/SQL and Java within applications.
Oracle Internet Directory and Microsoft Active Directory	Access to a central Oracle Internet directory is possible from Windows desktop if you have Active Directory services installed already.
Oracle Wallets and Windows Security	Oracle wallets are stored in Windows Registry or Active Directory and can be used by Microsoft Certificate Store.
Java Stored Procedures and COM	COM automation supports Java stored procedures.
Oracle9i OLE DB Provider	Supports XML and database events.
Microsoft Transaction Server	An Oracle9i database can be a resource manager for Microsoft Transaction Server.

TABLE B-1.　*New Oracle9i Features on Windows*

Index

X–Z

INTERNATIONAL CONTACT INFORMATION

AUSTRALIA
McGraw-Hill Book Company Australia Pty. Ltd.
TEL +61-2-9417-9899
FAX +61-2-9417-5687
http://www.mcgraw-hill.com.au
books-it_sydney@mcgraw-hill.com

CANADA
McGraw-Hill Ryerson Ltd.
TEL +905-430-5000
FAX +905-430-5020
http://www.mcgrawhill.ca

GREECE, MIDDLE EAST,
NORTHERN AFRICA
McGraw-Hill Hellas
TEL +30-1-656-0990-3-4
FAX +30-1-654-5525

MEXICO (Also serving Latin America)
McGraw-Hill Interamericana Editores S.A. de C.V.
TEL +525-117-1583
FAX +525-117-1589
http://www.mcgraw-hill.com.mx
fernando_castellanos@mcgraw-hill.com

SINGAPORE (Serving Asia)
McGraw-Hill Book Company
TEL +65-863-1580
FAX +65-862-3354
http://www.mcgraw-hill.com.sg
mghasia@mcgraw-hill.com

SOUTH AFRICA
McGraw-Hill South Africa
TEL +27-11-622-7512
FAX +27-11-622-9045
robyn_swanepoel@mcgraw-hill.com

UNITED KINGDOM & EUROPE
(Excluding Southern Europe)
McGraw-Hill Education Europe
TEL +44-1-628-502500
FAX +44-1-628-770224
http://www.mcgraw-hill.co.uk
computing_neurope@mcgraw-hill.com

ALL OTHER INQUIRIES Contact:
Osborne/McGraw-Hill
TEL +1-510-549-6600
FAX +1-510-883-7600
http://www.osborne.com
omg_international@mcgraw-hill.com

GET YOUR **FREE SUBSCRIPTION**
TO ORACLE MAGAZINE

Oracle Magazine is essential gear for today's information technology professionals. Stay informed and increase your productivity with every issue of *Oracle Magazine*. Inside each free bimonthly issue you'll get:

- Up-to-date information on Oracle Database, E-Business Suite applications, Web development, and database technology and business trends
- Third-party news and announcements
- Technical articles on Oracle Products and operating environments
- Development and administration tips
- Real-world customer stories

IF THERE ARE OTHER ORACLE USERS AT YOUR LOCATION WHO WOULD LIKE TO RECEIVE THEIR OWN SUBSCRIPTION TO ORACLE MAGAZINE, PLEASE PHOTOCOPY THIS FORM AND PASS IT ALONG.

Three easy ways to subscribe:

① Web
Visit our Web site at www.oracle.com/oraclemagazine. You'll find a subscription form there, plus much more!

② Fax
Complete the questionnaire on the back of this card and fax the questionnaire side only to +1.847.647.9735.

③ Mail
Complete the questionnaire on the back of this card and mail it to P.O. Box 1263, Skokie, IL 60076-8263

Oracle Publishing

FREE SUBSCRIPTION

○ Yes, please send me a FREE subscription to *Oracle Magazine*   ○ **NO**

To receive a free subscription to *Oracle Magazine*, you must fill out the entire card, sign it, and date it (incomplete cards cannot be processed or acknowledged). You can also fax your application to +1.847.647.9735.
Or subscribe at our Web site at www.oracle.com/oraclemagazine/

○ From time to time, Oracle Publishing allows our partners exclusive access to our e-mail addresses for special promotions and announcements. To be included in this program, please check this box.

○ Oracle Publishing allows sharing of our mailing list with selected third parties. If you prefer your mailing address not to be included in this program, please check here. If at any time you would like to be removed from this mailing list, please contact Customer Service at +1.847.647.9630 or send an e-mail to oracle@halldata.com.

signature (required)   date

X

name   title

company   e-mail address

street/p.o. box

city/state/zip or postal code   telephone

country   fax

YOU MUST ANSWER ALL NINE QUESTIONS BELOW.

① WHAT IS THE PRIMARY BUSINESS ACTIVITY OF YOUR FIRM AT THIS LOCATION? (check one only)

- ☐ 01 Application Service Provider
- ☐ 02 Communications
- ☐ 03 Consulting, Training
- ☐ 04 Data Processing
- ☐ 05 Education
- ☐ 06 Engineering
- ☐ 07 Financial Services
- ☐ 08 Government (federal, local, state, other)
- ☐ 09 Government (military)
- ☐ 10 Health Care
- ☐ 11 Manufacturing (aerospace, defense)
- ☐ 12 Manufacturing (computer hardware)
- ☐ 13 Manufacturing (noncomputer)
- ☐ 14 Research & Development
- ☐ 15 Retailing, Wholesaling, Distribution
- ☐ 16 Software Development
- ☐ 17 Systems Integration, VAR, VAD, OEM
- ☐ 18 Transportation
- ☐ 19 Utilities (electric, gas, sanitation)
- ☐ 98 Other Business and Services

② WHICH OF THE FOLLOWING BEST DESCRIBES YOUR PRIMARY JOB FUNCTION? (check one only)

Corporate Management/Staff
- ☐ 01 Executive Management (President, Chair, CEO, CFO, Owner, Partner, Principal)
- ☐ 02 Finance/Administrative Management (VP/Director/ Manager/Controller, Purchasing, Administration)
- ☐ 03 Sales/Marketing Management (VP/Director/Manager)
- ☐ 04 Computer Systems/Operations Management (CIO/VP/Director/ Manager MIS, Operations)

IS/IT Staff
- ☐ 05 Systems Development/ Programming Management
- ☐ 06 Systems Development/ Programming Staff
- ☐ 07 Consulting
- ☐ 08 DBA/Systems Administrator
- ☐ 09 Education/Training
- ☐ 10 Technical Support Director/Manager
- ☐ 11 Other Technical Management/Staff
- ☐ 98 Other

③ WHAT IS YOUR CURRENT PRIMARY OPERATING PLATFORM? (select all that apply)

- ☐ 01 Digital Equipment UNIX
- ☐ 02 Digital Equipment VAX VMS
- ☐ 03 HP UNIX
- ☐ 04 IBM AIX

- ☐ 05 IBM UNIX
- ☐ 06 Java
- ☐ 07 Linux
- ☐ 08 Macintosh
- ☐ 09 MS-DOS
- ☐ 10 MVS
- ☐ 11 NetWare
- ☐ 12 Network Computing
- ☐ 13 OpenVMS
- ☐ 14 SCO UNIX
- ☐ 15 Sequent DYNIX/ptx
- ☐ 16 Sun Solaris/SunOS
- ☐ 17 SVR4
- ☐ 18 UnixWare
- ☐ 19 Windows
- ☐ 20 Windows NT
- ☐ 21 Other UNIX
- ☐ 98 Other
- ☐ 99 None of the above

④ DO YOU EVALUATE, SPECIFY, RECOMMEND, OR AUTHORIZE THE PURCHASE OF ANY OF THE FOLLOWING? (check all that apply)

- ☐ 01 Hardware
- ☐ 02 Software
- ☐ 03 Application Development Tools
- ☐ 04 Database Products
- ☐ 05 Internet or Intranet Products
- ☐ 99 None of the above

⑤ IN YOUR JOB, DO YOU USE OR PLAN TO PURCHASE ANY OF THE FOLLOWING PRODUCTS? (check all that apply)

Software
- ☐ 01 Business Graphics
- ☐ 02 CAD/CAE/CAM
- ☐ 03 CASE
- ☐ 04 Communications
- ☐ 05 Database Management
- ☐ 06 File Management
- ☐ 07 Finance
- ☐ 08 Java
- ☐ 09 Materials Resource Planning
- ☐ 10 Multimedia Authoring
- ☐ 11 Networking
- ☐ 12 Office Automation
- ☐ 13 Order Entry/Inventory Control
- ☐ 14 Programming
- ☐ 15 Project Management
- ☐ 16 Scientific and Engineering
- ☐ 17 Spreadsheets
- ☐ 18 Systems Management
- ☐ 19 Workflow

Hardware
- ☐ 20 Macintosh
- ☐ 21 Mainframe
- ☐ 22 Massively Parallel Processing

- ☐ 23 Minicomputer
- ☐ 24 PC
- ☐ 25 Network Computer
- ☐ 26 Symmetric Multiprocessing
- ☐ 27 Workstation

Peripherals
- ☐ 28 Bridges/Routers/Hubs/Gateways
- ☐ 29 CD-ROM Drives
- ☐ 30 Disk Drives/Subsystems
- ☐ 31 Modems
- ☐ 32 Tape Drives/Subsystems
- ☐ 33 Video Boards/Multimedia

Services
- ☐ 34 Application Service Provider
- ☐ 35 Consulting
- ☐ 36 Education/Training
- ☐ 37 Maintenance
- ☐ 38 Online Database Services
- ☐ 39 Support
- ☐ 40 Technology-Based Training
- ☐ 98 Other
- ☐ 99 None of the above

⑥ WHAT ORACLE PRODUCTS ARE IN USE AT YOUR SITE? (check all that apply)

Software
- ☐ 01 Oracle9i
- ☐ 02 Oracle9i Lite
- ☐ 03 Oracle8
- ☐ 04 Oracle8i
- ☐ 05 Oracle8i Lite
- ☐ 06 Oracle7
- ☐ 07 Oracle9i Application Server
- ☐ 08 Oracle9i Application Server Wireless
- ☐ 09 Oracle Data Mart Suites
- ☐ 10 Oracle Internet Commerce Server
- ☐ 11 Oracle interMedia
- ☐ 12 Oracle Lite
- ☐ 13 Oracle Payment Server
- ☐ 14 Oracle Video Server
- ☐ 15 Oracle Rdb

Tools
- ☐ 16 Oracle Darwin
- ☐ 17 Oracle Designer
- ☐ 18 Oracle Developer
- ☐ 19 Oracle Discoverer
- ☐ 20 Oracle Express
- ☐ 21 Oracle JDeveloper
- ☐ 22 Oracle Reports
- ☐ 23 Oracle Portal
- ☐ 24 Oracle Warehouse Builder
- ☐ 25 Oracle Workflow

Oracle E-Business Suite
- ☐ 26 Oracle Advanced Planning/Scheduling
- ☐ 27 Oracle Business Intelligence
- ☐ 28 Oracle E-Commerce
- ☐ 29 Oracle Exchange
- ☐ 30 Oracle Financials

- ☐ 31 Oracle Human Resources
- ☐ 32 Oracle Interaction Center
- ☐ 33 Oracle Internet Procurement
- ☐ 34 Oracle Manufacturing
- ☐ 35 Oracle Marketing
- ☐ 36 Oracle Order Management
- ☐ 37 Oracle Professional Services Automation
- ☐ 38 Oracle Projects
- ☐ 39 Oracle Sales
- ☐ 40 Oracle Service
- ☐ 41 Oracle Small Business Suite
- ☐ 42 Oracle Supply Chain Management
- ☐ 43 Oracle Travel Management
- ☐ 44 Oracle Treasury

Oracle Services
- ☐ 45 Oracle.com Online Services
- ☐ 46 Oracle Consulting
- ☐ 47 Oracle Education
- ☐ 48 Oracle Support
- ☐ 98 ther
- ☐ 99 None of the above

⑦ WHAT OTHER DATABASE PRODUCTS ARE IN USE AT YOUR SITE? (check all that apply)

- ☐ 01 Access   ☐ 08 Microsoft Access
- ☐ 02 Baan   ☐ 09 Microsoft SQL Server
- ☐ 03 dbase   ☐ 10 PeopleSoft
- ☐ 04 Gupta   ☐ 11 Progress
- ☐ 05 BM DB2   ☐ 12 SAP
- ☐ 06 Informix   ☐ 13 Sybase
- ☐ 07 Ingres   ☐ 14 VSAM
- ☐ 98 Other
- ☐ 99 None of the above

⑧ DURING THE NEXT 12 MONTHS, HOW MUCH DO YOU ANTICIPATE YOUR ORGANIZATION WILL SPEND ON COMPUTER HARDWARE, SOFTWARE, PERIPHERALS, AND SERVICES FOR YOUR LOCATION? (check only one)

- ☐ 01 Less than $10,000
- ☐ 02 $10,000 to $49,999
- ☐ 03 $50,000 to $99,999
- ☐ 04 $100,000 to $499,999
- ☐ 05 $500,000 to $999,999
- ☐ 06 $1,000,000 and over

⑨ WHAT IS YOUR COMPANY'S YEARLY SALES REVENUE? (please choose one)

- ☐ 01 $500, 000, 000 and above
- ☐ 02 $100, 000, 000 to $500, 000, 000
- ☐ 03 $50, 000, 000 to $100, 000, 000
- ☐ 04 $5, 000, 000 to $50, 000, 000
- ☐ 05 $1, 000, 000 to $5, 000, 000

123101